THE ENDURING LEGACY OF *Rodriguez*

THE ENDURING LEGACY OF *Rodriguez*

Creating New Pathways to
Equal Educational Opportunity

CHARLES J. OGLETREE, JR.
KIMBERLY JENKINS ROBINSON
Editors

Harvard Education Press
Cambridge, Massachusetts

Library of Congress Control Number 2015937066

Paperback ISBN 978-1-61250-831-3
Library Edition ISBN 978-1-61250-832-0

Published by Harvard Education Press,
an imprint of the Harvard Education Publishing Group

Harvard Education Press
8 Story Street
Cambridge, MA 02138

Cover Design: Ciano Design
Cover Image: Donovan Reese/Getty Images

The typefaces used in this book are Adobe Garamond Pro and ITC Legacy Sans

*For my grandparents, Willie and Essie Reed,
and my parents, Charles Ogletree, Sr., and Willie Mae
Ogletree, who saw something in me going forward.*
—Charles J. Ogletree, Jr.

*For my parents, Wilbur H. Jenkins, Jr., and the late
Doris Sroufe Jenkins, who instilled in me at a young age
the importance of education and the fight for equality.*
—Kimberly Jenkins Robinson

CONTENTS

Foreword   ix
   James E. Ryan

ONE   **Introduction**   1
   The Enduring Legacy of *San Antonio Independent*
   School District v. Rodriguez
     Charles J. Ogletree, Jr. and Kimberly Jenkins Robinson

PART I   UNDERSTANDING *RODRIGUEZ* AND EDUCATIONAL
   OPPORTUNITY IN THE UNITED STATES

TWO   *Rodriguez v. San Antonio Independent School District*   23
   Forty Years and Counting
     David G. Hinojosa

THREE   *Rodriguez* **in the Court**   45
   Contingency and Context
     Camille Walsh

FOUR   *Rodriguez* **Past, Present, and Future**   65
     Michael A. Rebell

FIVE   **Still Separate, Still Unequal in a Post-*Milliken* Era**   87
   Why *Rodriguez* Would Have Been Good but Not Enough
     Amy Stuart Wells, Lauren Fox, and Alana Miles

PART II   EXPLORING NOVEL STATE REFORMS THAT SUPPORT
   EQUAL EDUCATIONAL OPPORTUNITY

SIX   **From *Rodriguez* to *Abbott***   119
   New Jersey's Standards-Linked School Funding Reform
     David G. Sciarra and Danielle Farrie

SEVEN   **Bridging the Teacher Quality Gap**   143
        Notes from California on the Potential
        and Pitfalls of Litigating Teacher Quality
        William S. Koski

EIGHT   **It Takes a Federalist Village**   167
        A Revitalized Property Tax as a Linchpin for Stable,
        Effective K–12 Public Education Funding
        Mildred Wigfall Robinson

NINE   **Tearing Down Fences**   183
        School Boundary Lines and Equal Educational
        Opportunity in the Twenty-First Century
        Genevieve Siegel-Hawley

PART III   CREATING INNOVATIVE FEDERAL AVENUES FOR
           PROMOTING EQUAL ACCESS TO AN EXCELLENT EDUCATION

TEN   **How Reconstructing Education Federalism Could
        Fulfill the Aims of *Rodriguez***   203
        Kimberly Jenkins Robinson

ELEVEN **Leveraging Federal Funding for Equity and Integration**   227
        Derek W. Black

TWELVE **Remedying Separate and Unequal**   249
        Is It Possible to Create Equal Educational Opportunity?
        Erwin Chemerinsky

CONCLUSION   **Creating New Pathways to Equal Educational Opportunity** 263
             Charles J. Ogletree, Jr. and Kimberly Jenkins Robinson

Appendix: School Finance Litigation Cases   275
Notes   281
Acknowledgments   329
About the Editors   331
About the Contributors   333
Index   339

FOREWORD

THE SUPREME COURT'S 1973 decision in *San Antonio Independent School District v. Rodriguez* preserved local control of school finances by rejecting a challenge to the unequal distribution of property tax dollars among public school districts in Texas. But in order to reach this ruling, the Court broke a promise it had made nearly twenty years before.

In 1954, Chief Justice Earl Warren, delivering a unanimous opinion in *Brown v. Board of Education,* wrote, "It is doubtful that any child may reasonably be expected to succeed in life if he is denied the opportunity of an education. Such an opportunity, where the state has undertaken to provide it, is a right which must be made available to all on equal terms." To those who had seen their opportunities denied by the inherent inequalities of segregation, Warren's proclamation offered a flicker of hope. The *Brown* decision seemed to put forth a radical new vision for the future—one in which the educational fortunes of all children, regardless of race, were bound together by the promise of equal opportunity.

But the promise was not kept. In 1973, Justice Powell, writing for the majority in *Rodriguez,* contended that "[though] education is one of the most important services performed by the State, it is not within the limited category of rights recognized by this Court as guaranteed by the Constitution." By denying an implicit right to education, and rejecting the idea that a system of unequal distribution invidiously discriminated against the poor, the Supreme Court effectively washed its hands of the issue.

Now, more than forty years after *Rodriguez,* equal educational opportunity remains elusive. More than sixteen million children in this country live in poverty. Twenty-one percent of black and Hispanic students attend high-poverty schools—schools that, according to an abundance of research, consistently fail to attract and retain skilled teachers. Despite improved performance, minority students remain more than twenty points behind their white peers on the National Assessment of Educational Progress math and reading exams, a difference of about two grade levels. Students from the lowest-income families are five times more likely to drop out of high school than are children from the wealthiest families. Over the last two decades, the rate of college completion for affluent children has risen by more than 20 percent, compared with only 4 percent for children from low-income backgrounds. The college completion rate for low-income males has actually fallen over that same time period. A good education—the key to achieving the American Dream—remains out of reach for many who need it the most.

In 1966, standing before students at the University of Cape Town and against the kindred evils of apartheid in South Africa and institutional racism in the United States, Robert Kennedy declared, "We must recognize the full human equality of all of our people . . . we must do this, not because it is economically advantageous—although it is; not because the laws of God command it—although they do; not because people in other lands wish it so. We must do it for the single and fundamental reason that it is the right thing to do." Whether or not it is enshrined in the United States Constitution, access to a meaningful education is a fundamental *human* right. We have an obligation to provide every child with a high-quality education—not because some court has commanded it, but because we know without hesitation that it is right.

The Supreme Court has told us what, in its opinion, the Constitution does *not* guarantee—saying no to a claim for equal funding in *Rodriguez* and, in 1974, no to desegregating across district lines in *Milliken v. Bradley.* But this need not be the end of the story, either within courtrooms or outside of them. What is needed is not resignation but a path forward.

In this volume, some of the country's leading scholars in the field of education law begin to chart that path. They push back against the claim that holding education to be a fundamental right would invariably lead to the birth of a suite of other welfare rights; they discuss how district boundaries continue to encourage racial and socioeconomic isolation in public schools; and they explore challenges to school funding disparities in the state courts. They present much-needed fresh thinking on taxation, teacher evaluation, and integration and ask what a grand solution might entail, from creating a truly unitary system of education to addressing a moral exclusion of children that has taken root in our society.

This book, marking *Rodriguez's* fortieth anniversary, offers us a chance to reflect on what we have done in service of the next generation and calls on us to do better. It heralds a new chapter in our continuing struggle to expand opportunity and improve outcomes.

—James E. Ryan
Dean, Harvard Graduate School of Education
Charles William Eliot Professor of Education

ONE

Introduction

The Enduring Legacy of *San Antonio
Independent School District v. Rodriguez*

CHARLES J. OGLETREE, JR.
AND KIMBERLY JENKINS ROBINSON

IN 1973, THE UNITED STATES Supreme Court held in *San Antonio Independent School District v. Rodriguez* that the federal Constitution does not protect children in school districts with a low property tax base from receiving
substantially less funding for their education than peers in districts with
a high property tax base. The Court rejected the application of the most
searching level of constitutional inquiry—strict scrutiny—to the plaintiffs'
challenge of the Texas school finance system because the wealth discrimination within the system did not infringe on the rights of a suspect class
and because education was not a fundamental right protected by the Constitution. The Court ruled the system constitutional on the grounds that
the system responded to the legitimate interest of Texas in fostering local
control of education.[1]

The *Rodriguez* decision dealt a considerable blow to the advocates for civil
rights and school finance who viewed the case as an important vehicle for
fulfilling the Court's promise in *Brown v. Board of Education* in 1954 that
education "is a right which must be made available to all on equal terms."
Federal courthouses had served as one of the primary vehicles for civil rights

reformers to advance equal educational opportunity through school desegregation litigation. In addition, enforcement actions by the Department of
Justice and by the Department of Health, Education, and Welfare under Title VI of the Civil Rights Act of 1964 also provided important support for
school desegregation through lawsuits in federal court and administrative
enforcement actions.[2]

Yet, the aim of the plaintiffs in *Rodriguez*—equal educational opportunity—remains a central goal for many policy makers, education reform organizations, school finance advocates, and civil rights groups. Many parents
also embrace this aim as essential for the U.S. education system given the
country's historical reliance on public schools to mitigate the adverse effects
of disadvantage and to provide access to the American Dream.[3] Although
Rodriguez essentially closed the courthouse door to federal constitutional
challenges to school finance disparities, many litigants and reformers have
continued the battle cry of *Rodriguez* through state court school finance litigation, state legislative reform, local equity efforts, and federal legislative and
executive action. These efforts reveal how the legacy of *Rodriguez* endures today. It endures as policy makers, advocates, and reformers strive to break the
link between a child's zip code and her destiny, between parents' wealth and
the wealth of educational opportunity their child receives.

We undertook this volume to advance two primary goals: to encourage
analysis of the enduring legacy of the *Rodriguez* decision and to promote
the development of new ideas on how to realize the unfinished work of the
Rodriguez plaintiffs. In pursuing these goals, we sought to move beyond the
debates over whether the *Rodriguez* majority reached the right decision and
whether money influences educational outcomes to generate innovative proposals for the legal and policy reforms needed to make equal access to an excellent education a reality for the nation's schoolchildren.

As we planned this volume, we invited some of the nation's leading school
finance attorneys and education law and policy scholars to contribute. With
the support of the University of Richmond School of Law and the Charles
Hamilton Houston Institute for Race and Justice at Harvard Law School, we
hosted a conference at the University of Richmond School of Law on March
8, 2013, to debate these important issues.[4] Most of the speakers in the conference have contributed to this volume.

In our brief introduction we describe the *Rodriguez* lower court decision,
the Supreme Court's majority decision by Justice Lewis F. Powell, Jr., and the

dissenting decisions by Supreme Court Justices Thurgood Marshall, Byron White, and William J. Brennan, Jr. The 5-4 vote for the majority opinion reveals that the Court was deeply divided over the case. Therefore, we concisely summarize the dissenting opinions as a window into the path toward equal educational opportunity that would have been created if the four dissenting justices had prevailed. We then consider some of the developments that have occurred in the wake of *Rodriguez,* highlighting both the federal and state avenues that advocates have used for school finance reform. Finally, we conclude with a brief summary of each of the chapters in the book.

SAN ANTONIO INDEPENDENT SCHOOL DISTRICT V. RODRIGUEZ

Demetrio Rodriguez was a Mexican American military veteran of World War II and the Korean War. As a parent who resided in the Edgewood School District in 1968, Rodriguez helped form the Edgewood District Concerned Parents Association after approximately four hundred students at Edgewood High School walked out of school in the spring of 1968 to protest, among other issues, the substandard educational facilities at the school. Although the parents in the association did not have substantial knowledge about school finance, they understood that they had voted in favor of spending for their schools and that despite this support their schools were inferior to schools in other districts in San Antonio. The Mexican American parents contacted a local attorney, Arthur Gochman, to see whether the law provided a legal remedy for these disparities. Gochman ultimately decided to file the litigation in federal court and selected Rodriguez to serve as the named plaintiff due to the fact that his name sounded Mexican American.[5] In chapter 2, David Hinojosa provides additional details on the school finance litigation in Edgewood, Texas.

A Federal District Court Strikes Down the Texas School Finance System

The Mexican American parents who initiated the action that led to *Rodriguez* brought a class action on behalf of themselves and their children as well as on behalf of all other children throughout Texas who reside "in school districts with low property valuations." They challenged the funding disparities in the Texas school finance system under the Fourteenth Amendment to the Constitution. At the time of the litigation, as well as today, Texas funded the

public schools with state, local, and federal funds. With the federal government providing approximately 10 percent of the funds, the state and local
contributions represented the lion's share of funding. Districts raised all local funds by taxing property within the district. State funding was provided
partly on a per capita basis and partly based on each district's relative ability
to tax. Despite some state efforts at equalization, significant funding disparities between school districts persisted.[6]

The U.S. District Court for the Western District of Texas struck down the
Texas school funding system as a violation of the plaintiffs' equal protection
rights under the Fourteenth Amendment. The court noted that in Edgewood
the per-pupil value of taxable property was $5,429, and in Alamo Heights it
was $45,095. Although Edgewood taxed at a high rate, Edgewood yielded
$21 per pupil. In contrast, Alamo Heights taxed at a lower rate and yielded
$307 per pupil. State funding failed to equalize the substantial disparities in
the local yield.[7]

The district court relied on prior Fifth Circuit and Supreme Court decisions to determine that the funding system must satisfy strict scrutiny on
the grounds that the system was based on wealth and adversely affected a
"fundamental interest." The district court noted that the plaintiffs had not
requested equal funding for each child but, rather, had requested the application of "fiscal neutrality," which "requires that the quality of public education may not be a function of wealth, other than the wealth of the state as a
whole." The court found the state's response to this request "insubstantial"
and explained that "not only are defendants unable to demonstrate compelling state interests for their classification based upon wealth, they fail even
to establish a reasonable basis for these classifications." The court concluded
that the Texas system failed to advance local control given that some districts
were able to raise high amounts for their schools while using a low tax rate
while others were left to raise significantly smaller amounts even though they
imposed a higher tax rate.[8] The state appealed to the U.S. Supreme Court,
which agreed to hear the case.

Justice Powell's Majority Opinion

The Supreme Court reversed the lower court's decision. Writing for the
Court, Justice Lewis Powell began his analysis by summarizing how the
Texas school finance system functioned and how it had changed over time.

By the 1970–1971 school year, three years after the litigation had begun, the state contributed 48 percent of education funds, the local governments 41.1 percent, and the federal government 10.9 percent. Powell acknowledged the disparate abilities of Edgewood and Alamo Heights to raise funds for education through the property tax as well as the racial composition of each district, with Edgewood educating 90 percent Mexican American and 6 percent African American students and Alamo Heights educating predominantly "Anglo" students and only 18 percent Mexican American students and less than 1 percent African American students. Despite increases in state funding for education and state efforts to reduce funding disparities, significant interdistrict disparities in per-pupil spending remained.[9]

The Court held that the Texas system did not discriminate on the basis of wealth. Justice Powell noted the ambiguity in the class of individuals subject to discrimination and then considered whether Texas had engaged in discrimination against three possible classes of individuals: "(1) against 'poor' persons whose incomes fall below some identifiable level of poverty or who might be characterized as functionally 'indigent,' or (2) against those who are relatively poorer than others, or (3) against all those who, irrespective of their personal incomes, happen to reside in relatively poorer school districts." He concluded that Texas had not discriminated against any of these classes, noting that prior cases that had found wealth discrimination held two common characteristics: the individuals were wholly unable to pay for a benefit, and they suffered a complete deprivation of the possibility to obtain this benefit. He found these characteristics missing because the plaintiffs had failed to show that the "system discriminates against any definable category of 'poor' people or that it results in the absolute deprivation of education."

Justice Powell then rejected plaintiffs' arguments that education was a fundamental right. After acknowledging the importance of education, he concluded that the Constitution neither explicitly nor implicitly protected education as a constitutional right. He dismissed the plaintiffs' arguments that the close relationship between education and other constitutionally protected rights should render education a constitutional right by stating that although the Court vigorously protects the right to vote and speak, it had "never presumed to possess either the ability or the authority to guarantee to the citizenry the most effective speech or the most informed electoral choice." Powell further noted that even if the Court acknowledged that the

Constitution afforded protection to a minimum education as a protection for the ability to exercise an individual's right to speak or vote, he had no indication that the education provided in Texas fell below that level. He also contended that the potential reach of the plaintiffs' argument seemed limitless and would appear to grant rights to food, clothing, and housing.

Offering several additional reasons for the Court's conclusions, Powell noted that the request to condemn the Texas system would require the Court to intervene in an area that had traditionally been delegated to state lawmakers. He contended that the justices did not possess the familiarity or expertise on school finance that they needed to reach a wise decision. Instead, state and local officials possessed superior knowledge of the complex education policy decisions that underlie the case, including whether a correlation exists between the quality of education and expenditures. He similarly highlighted the ongoing debates regarding the proper aims of an education system and the optimal relationship between state and local education boards and explained that he wished to avoid imposing "inflexible constitutional restraints that could circumscribe or handicap the continued research and experimentation so vital to finding even partial solutions to educational problems and to keeping abreast of ever-changing conditions." Furthermore, he maintained, a ruling for the plaintiffs effectively would invalidate the school finance systems in every state, and, as a result, he could not fathom a case with a greater ability to upset the existing balance of power between the national and state governments. For these reasons, rational basis review was the appropriate level of scrutiny.

The Court held that the Texas school funding system "abundantly satisfies" the rational basis standard. Justice Powell explained that the system encourages local control of education while providing a basic education for every child, highlighting recent Supreme Court decisions that had reaffirmed the importance of local control for education. He affirmed the ability of Texas to conclude that alternative approaches to school finance which increased state responsibility also might decrease local control. He ended his rational basis analysis by stating that "to the extent that the Texas system of school financing results in unequal expenditures between children who happen to reside in different districts, we cannot say that such disparities are the product of a system that is so irrational as to be invidiously discriminatory."

Justice Powell cautioned that the Court's opinion should not be cited as an endorsement of the Texas funding system. Indeed, he acknowledged that funding systems "may well have relied too long and too heavily on the local property tax." However, he opined that this concern did not influence the constitutional decisions before the Court. Instead, scholars and legislators must be left to reach the final decisions on these issues.[10]

Justice Marshall's Dissent

Justice Thurgood Marshall penned an eloquent dissent that criticized the majority opinion for retreating from its prior commitment to ensuring that educational opportunity is distributed on equal terms. As one of the winning lawyers in *Brown,* he reminded the Court of the unfinished work of *Brown* when he quoted that decision for his contention that the Court should not settle for a "'political' solution sometime in the indefinite future while, in the meantime, countless children unjustifiably receive inferior educations that 'may affect their hearts and minds in a way unlikely ever to be undone.'" He also criticized the majority's analysis of the Texas finance system, because "what the Court fails to emphasize is the cruel irony of how much more state aid is being given to property-rich Texas school districts on top of their already substantial local property tax revenues." After acknowledging that some question the relationship between school funding and school quality, Marshall responded to this debate by noting that the Court had already recognized that disparities in educational facilities violated the Equal Protection Clause even before it had invalidated school segregation by drawing on desegregation litigation victories in higher education that he helped to secure in 1950—*Sweatt v. Painter* and *McLaurin v. Oklahoma State Regents of Higher Education.*[11]

Justice Marshall then disagreed with the majority's rejection of wealth as a suspect class and its refusal to render education a constitutional right. He challenged the majority's contention that past cases recognizing wealth discrimination required an absolute inability to pay for a benefit or a complete denial of an opportunity to acquire a benefit by citing cases that recognized wealth discrimination without requiring such prerequisites. He recognized that past cases had only invalidated wealth discrimination based on an individual's wealth but argued that discrimination on the basis of the taxable property where an individual lives represents a more egregious form of discrimination because the individual cannot control it and because it does not reflect the characteristics or abilities of an individual. Marshall similarly disputed the majority's conclusion that fundamental interests are only found "explicitly or implicitly" in the constitutional text by noting that the Court had provided protection against state interference with the right to appeal when one is convicted of a crime, the right to procreate, and the right to cast a vote in state electoral contests, even though these interests cannot be found within the Constitution. Given the Court's protection of these interests against state discrimination "because they are, to some extent, interrelated with constitutional guarantees," Marshall insisted that education also should be treated as a fundamental right in light of numerous Court decisions that had recognized the essential importance of education as well as the close relationship between education and the ability to exercise the right to free speech, the right of association, and the right to vote.

Justice Marshall concluded that the Texas system violated the Equal Protection Clause because Texas had not provided a legitimate state interest for the system. After noting a state interest in local control of education, he found that "local control is a myth for many of the local school districts in Texas" given that the state's reliance on property taxes resulted in some districts having very little to spend on education even though they taxed at a high rate while other districts could tax at a low rate and spend at a high rate. Given the state's selection of a financing scheme that did not advance its interests, and the many possible alternatives for advancing local control for all districts, the Texas system denied the plaintiffs equal protection of the laws.

Justice White's Dissent

Justice Byron White's dissent also vigorously challenged the majority's conclusion that the Texas school finance system rationally advanced the interest of local control of schools. He critiqued this argument by examining the practical and legal ability of districts such as Edgewood to raise funds for education. He noted that the per-pupil value of taxable property in Alamo Heights was $49,078, while it was $5,960 in Edgewood. Given the disparities in the tax base, Edgewood was unable to yield the same revenues as Alamo Heights at the same tax rate. The record revealed that when Alamo Heights applied a tax rate of $.85 per $100 of assessed property value, Alamo Heights yielded $330 per pupil, while Edgewood applied a $1.05 tax rate and yielded only $26 despite applying a higher rate. Furthermore, if Edgewood attempted to raise the same amount as the highest yield in the district and was willing to raise its tax rate to the $5.76 per $100 needed to do this, state law capped the tax rate at $1.50 per $100. Therefore, Edgewood was precluded by law and in fact from yielding the tax revenues that even came close to the revenues raised in other districts within the same county.[12]

In light of this factual and legal landscape, Justice White found the state had failed to advance local control and initiative for districts with such low property tax bases that the parents within the district have little to no opportunity to increase their funding for schools. In fact, White criticized the majority's analysis by stating that "requiring the State to establish only that unequal treatment is in furtherance of a permissible goal, without also requiring the State to show that the means chosen to effectuate that goal are rationally related to its achievement, makes equal protection analysis no more than an empty gesture." Therefore, he argued, the Texas system violated the Equal Protection Clause because it invidiously discriminated against the parents and schoolchildren in Edgewood, Texas, particularly given the state's numerous alternatives for advancing local control of education.

Justice Brennan's Dissent

Justice William Brennan's dissent noted his agreement with Justice White that the Texas school funding scheme lacked a rational basis. He also endorsed the analysis of Justice Marshall that a right need not be "explicitly or implicitly guaranteed by the Constitution" to be deemed a fundamental right; rather, the analysis turns on "a function of the right's importance in terms of the effectuation of those rights which are in fact constitutionally guaranteed." Brennan maintained that given the indisputable nexus between education and the rights to vote and free speech, the Court should have subjected the Texas funding system to strict scrutiny and found it lacking.[13]

The *Rodriguez* Litigants Today

Demetrio Rodriguez continued to live in the same poor neighborhood where he lived when the case was first litigated, according to Paul Sracic, the author of a 2006 book dedicated to the case. After the case, he continued to fight for well-financed schools and was recognized for his contributions to the fight for access to quality education. On April 22, 2013, Rodriguez passed away from complications of Parkinson's disease. His daughter Patricia, one of the catalysts for Rodriguez's decision to take part in the suit, is a third-grade bilingual teacher in the Edgewood School District.[14]

IN THE WAKE OF *RODRIGUEZ*

After *Rodriguez,* advocates have remained committed to litigation as an important tool for school finance reform. Numerous lawsuits have been filed that sought to advance the aims of *Rodriguez.* The analysis below examines the trends in federal and state court litigation that followed the decision and acknowledges that, despite ongoing litigation and reform, additional legal and policy reforms are needed to close the educational opportunity gap.

Federal Litigation Regarding School Finance Reform After *Rodriguez*

Rodriguez appears to leave open the possibility of a federal constitutional claim for an inadequate education. In rejecting the plaintiffs' argument that education must be guaranteed as a fundamental right to protect the rights to speak and to vote, the Court opined that "even if it were conceded that some identifiable quantum of education is a constitutionally protected prerequisite to the meaningful exercise of either right, we have no indication that the present levels of educational expenditures in Texas provide an education that falls short." This was because the plaintiffs only alleged relative spending differences.[15] Although some scholars have interpreted this language to indicate that a federal adequacy claim might prove more successful, what would be required to prove such an extreme deprivation in federal court remains unanswered.[16]

However, the Court in *Plyler v. Doe* in 1982 did prohibit the complete denial of an education to schoolchildren. The Supreme Court established in *Plyler* that schoolchildren whose parents illegally entered the United States are "persons" under the Fourteenth Amendment and are entitled to the equal protection of the laws. Even though the Court noted that public education is not a fundamental right and cited *Rodriguez* to support this proposition, it also stated that the denial of education to some groups of children conflicted with one of the goals of the Equal Protection Clause: "the abolition of governmental barriers presenting unreasonable obstacles to advancement on the basis of individual merit." The Court then explained that denying undocumented children an education would force them to remain illiterate for the rest of their lives, prevent them from functioning in civic society, and foreclose even modest contributions to the nation's progress. Taking these factors into account, the Court held that a state could not deny undocumented children a primary or secondary education unless it furthered a substantial goal of the state, which Texas had failed to provide.[17]

The only federal court litigation to gain any success in challenging an entire state school finance system due to disparities in funding occurred in *Powell v. Ridge* in 1999. In that case, parents of schoolchildren who lived in Philadelphia sued Pennsylvania governor Thomas Ridge and other state education officials under Title VI of the Civil Rights Act of 1964. Plaintiffs alleged that the Pennsylvania school finance system had a racially discriminatory disparate impact on the schoolchildren in Philadelphia. For instance, the plaintiffs alleged that the system provided on average greater state funding to districts with high proportions of white students than to districts with high proportions of nonwhite students and that these disparities harmed the students in underfunded districts by relegating them to larger classes, providing fewer curricular offerings, and resulting in other educational disadvantages. The United States Court of Appeals for the Third Circuit held that the plaintiffs had stated a claim under the disparate impact regulations for Title VI of the Civil Rights Act and under Section 1983, which provides a remedy for violation of federal law. The court further held that a private right of action existed to enforce the Title VI disparate impact regulations and that these regulations also could be enforced through 42 U.S.C. § 1983.[18]

However, this new avenue for federal school finance litigation proved short-lived. Just two years later, in *Alexander v. Sandoval* in 2001, the Supreme Court held that plaintiffs could not enforce the disparate impact regulations under Title VI through a private right of action in court. Currently, the U.S. Department of Education's Office for Civil Rights (OCR) alone possesses the authority to bring an action against a state or district whose funding system has a racially discriminatory disparate impact. In the fall of 2014, the OCR released a "Dear Colleague" letter to states and school districts that provided clear guidance on the nature of their obligation to ensure that the distribution of educational resources does not have an adverse impact on the basis of race, color, or national origin in violation of the Title VI regulations.[19] This new guidance and possible enforcement action may bring renewed attention to resource disparities from states and school districts.

State School Finance Litigation and Reform

When it closed the federal courthouse door to federal constitutional challenges to school funding disparities, the *Rodriguez* majority noted that the solutions to these disparities were best left to state and local officials and the public. However, Justice Powell was careful to note the importance of school finance reform: "The need is apparent for reform in tax systems which may well have relied too long and too heavily on the local property tax. And certainly innovative thinking as to public education, its methods, and its funding is necessary to assure both a higher level of quality and greater uniformity of opportunity." Therefore, Powell's majority opinion invited state-level reforms that promoted greater equality of educational opportunity.[20]

Substantial state litigation and state reform of school finance litigation followed the *Rodriguez* decision. For this reason, some credit *Rodriguez* as indirectly leading to school funding reform. During the time of *Rodriguez* and in the years since, most state legislatures have passed wealth-equalization formulas for funding their public schools, and every state has enacted some type of school financing equalization scheme. School funding litigation has proliferated since 1973 and has focused on ensuring greater equity in school funding, adequacy of school funding, or both.[21]

Equity litigation claims focus on equal per-pupil funding or an equal opportunity to offer equal funding, while adequacy claims seek to ensure that students have the funding that they need to receive an adequate education as defined by specific objectives often included in state standards. In reality, these two theories often coalesce around what James Ryan has labeled "rough comparability," because equity cases typically focus on ensuring "substantial equality" rather than perfect equity, while adequacy cases also seek to reduce disparities in educational resources as they aim to ensure students receive an adequate education.[22]

The states' highest courts have ruled on the constitutionality of school funding systems in forty-two of the fifty states. The appendix captures this litigation by identifying plaintiff victories and losses with an emphasis on litigation at the highest court in the state. In twenty-three states, plaintiffs have prevailed in the state's highest court at least once. Plaintiffs have lost and never prevailed at the state's highest court in nineteen states.

When plaintiffs' claims have failed, these decisions sometimes echo the concerns of Justice Powell in *Rodriguez*. For example, in 2009 the Indiana Supreme Court rejected a challenge to its school finance system because the judiciary was not the appropriate branch to assess the constitutionality of the education system given the state constitution's delegation of education to the discretion of the legislature.[23] The highest courts in Oklahoma and Illinois rejected school finance claims for similar reasons.[24] Other courts expressed doubts about the connection between funding disparities and disparities in educational opportunity.[25]

However, plaintiffs also have secured some important victories. For instance, in chapter 6, David Sciarra and Danielle Farrie provide a comprehensive assessment of the long-running *Abbott v. Burke* education litigation in New Jersey, which Sciarra and others have led. As their chapter details, over the course of more than thirty-five years the New Jersey Supreme Court has handed down decisions that have supported continued decreases in funding disparities between rich districts and poor districts.[26]

In addition, Michael Rebell led the New York City Public Schools to an important victory in *Campaign for Fiscal Equity v. State* (*CFE*) in 1995 when he and others convinced the highest court in the state of New York to define the "sound basic education" that the state's constitution guarantees as one that equips all students to perform their civic duties, including voting and serving on a jury in a knowledgeable and capable fashion, as well as to secure employment in an economy increasingly dominated by "service sector jobs" that demand greater skills than manufacturing jobs.[27] In chapter 4, Rebell highlights how courts have demonstrated a ready capacity to address complex school funding issues despite the contention of the *Rodriguez* majority that the Court lacked the capacity to do so. More importantly, he notes that at least twenty-nine courts have reviewed the social science evidence and found that money spent well matters for education, a debate that Justice Powell cited as one that discouraged the Court from invalidating the Texas system in *Rodriguez*.

Most recently, in 2014, in *Vergara v. State,* a superior court in California ruled that teacher tenure laws violated the state constitutional requirements for education. The court noted that all of the parties agreed that competent teachers provide a critical element for an effective education and that incompetent teachers significantly undermine successful educational outcomes. The court held that the California teacher employment statute, the last-in first-out requirement, and the teacher dismissal statutes had disproportionate adverse effects on poor and minority students in the state.[28] As William Koski, who serves as plaintiffs' counsel in other school finance litigation in California, discusses in chapter 7, litigation aimed at ensuring that all students receive equal access to effective teachers represents one of the new and innovative ways that lawyers are challenging disparities in educational resources.

While recognizing these important victories, it is worthwhile to acknowledge that school finance victories often encounter significant setbacks. A school finance victory typically requires multiple trips to court. For instance, the important wins in New Jersey required no fewer than fifteen decisions from the state's highest court.[29] Furthermore, legislatures do not consistently follow through with promised funding increases. After the *CFE* victory, for example, the New York legislature passed legislation that would increase the state appropriation over four years by $5.5 billion in additional operating aid to schools throughout the state. However, after two years, increases in foundation aid statewide were halted once 37.5 percent of the four-year goal was met. By 2014, the state had failed to pay close to $4 billion of its past obligations to schools. Unfortunately, disappointments such as these are not unusual.[30]

Despite these frequent setbacks, much, but not all, of the research indicates that school funding litigation has resulted in some increased funding for schools, particularly for poor districts, and has reduced funding disparities.[31] Debate remains over the size of the reduction in spending disparities or the influence of school finance litigation.[32] One positive trend in school funding has been increased funding for students with unique needs, including students from low-income homes and those with special educational needs.[33]

Although we acknowledge that some progress on school finance reform has occurred since *Rodriguez*, we undertook this volume because we agree with the many scholars who have contended that reforms to school funding systems to date have been inadequate, given evidence that several decades of school funding litigation and state-level reforms have proven that school funding systems are quite resistant to comprehensive and long-term reform and that substantial additional reform is needed to close the educational opportunity gap.[34] A 2013 report from President Obama's Commission on Equity and Excellence confirmed the inadequacy of past reforms: "These initiatives have not addressed the fundamental sources of inequities and so have not generated the educational gains desired. Despite these efforts and proclamations, large achievement gaps remain, and local finance and governance systems continue to allow for, *and in many ways encourage*, inequitable and inadequate funding systems and inefficient and ineffective resource utilization."[35]

Similarly, James Ryan commented that "not a single suit has done much to alter the basic structure of school finance schemes" and that "school finance litigation has done as much to entrench the current structure of educational opportunity as it has to challenge it. District lines remain as important as ever, and segregation remains widespread and increasing."[36] Evidence of the resistance of school finance systems to reform may be found in part by recalling that the *Rodriguez* majority noted the need for reform of state reliance on property taxes, yet in the 2010–2011 school year, 81 percent of local revenues came from local property taxes and local funding provided approximately 35 percent of school funding.[37] We believe that further reform in the distribution of educational opportunity is necessary to ensure equal access to an excellent education.

The persistence of deeply entrenched disparities in educational opportunity demands the development of novel reforms to federal, state, and local law and policy that determine the landscape of educational opportunity.

CHAPTER SUMMARIES

The chapters in Part I explore past and ongoing school finance litigation with an emphasis on the Rodriguez litigation as well as the potential for future reform. In chapter 2, "*Rodriguez v. San Antonio Independent School District*, Forty Years and Counting," David Hinojosa examines the march to fair and equal funding in Texas public schools, from the Edgewood High School student walkout in San Antonio and the filing of *Rodriguez* in 1968 to the most recent Texas school finance decision in 2014. Hinojosa also surveys the impact of *Rodriguez* on school funding across the country and concludes with a brief discussion of the controversy surrounding the role of the courts in school funding cases.

In chapter 3, "*Rodriguez* in the Court: Contingency and Context," Camille Walsh analyzes the legal and historical contexts of *Rodriguez* in order to understand the explicit and implicit factors that contributed to the Court's ruling. She analyzes the way in which race and poverty were discussed in the lower court opinions, amicus briefs, and oral arguments, arguing that the multiple identity positions claimed by the students and families at every stage of the case were largely rendered invisible by the formal processes of the courts. In addition, she traces the context of the anticommunist impulse running through many of the briefs and the internal memos, drafts, and notes leading up to the majority opinion and identifies *Rodriguez* within a Cold War discourse of anxiety around expansion of educational access and resources. Finally, she locates *Rodriguez* as a key moment of contingency in the development of equal protection analysis in the early 1970s, pointing to its importance in foreclosing alternative visions for the application of equal protection and the judicial scrutiny of inequality.

In chapter 4, "*Rodriguez* Past, Present, and Future," Michael Rebell analyzes the decision and argues that the Court incorrectly concluded that holding education to be a fundamental interest under the federal constitution would require similar rulings regarding other social services. He further notes the overwhelming evidence of the failure of large numbers of schools throughout the country to provide the basic level of educational opportunity that students need to become capable voters and to exercise their First Amendment rights. Rebell then contends that *Rodriguez* does not need to be reversed at this point; instead, the Supreme Court needs to reconsider the core issue that was left open in the 1973 decision: whether there is a federal right to a basic level of education that will prepare students to function effectively as civic participants. He argues that a positive outcome of such a hypothetical case is plausible even with today's conservatively oriented court and concludes by positing that a failure by the Court to uphold a federal right to education might well galvanize a national movement to enact a constitutional amendment that would do so.

In chapter 5, "Still Separate, Still Unequal in a Post-*Milliken* Era: Why *Rodriguez* Would Have Been Good but Not Enough," Amy Stuart Wells, Lauren Fox, and Alana Miles argue that even if the Supreme Court had upheld the challenge in *Rodriguez,* the intersection of migration patterns and school district boundaries would continue to encourage racial and class isolation and inequality within public schools. They conducted a five-year study of migration patterns within a hypersegregated suburban county in the New York City metro area, Nassau County. The chapter identifies how a school's or district's reputation or prestige deteriorates as it changes from an almost all white to a more diverse student body, which influences peoples' choices about where to live, where to send their children to school, and with whom they will associate. Given these findings, they conclude that although a different ruling in *Rodriguez* would have helped low-income communities, it also would have required a different ruling in the 1974 U.S. Supreme Court decision *Milliken v. Bradley,* a case that typically prevented courts from requiring interdistrict school district desegregation, in order to overcome the racial isolation and separation accomplished through school district boundaries and migration patterns.[38]

Part II offers new ideas for state-level reforms that advance equal educational opportunity. In chapter 6, "From *Rodriguez* to *Abbott*: New Jersey's Standards-Linked School Funding Reform," David G. Sciarra and Danielle Farrie argue that the legacy of the landmark *Rodriquez* case was to solidify the centrality of the state's role and responsibility for public education. In a handful of states, litigation and legislative efforts to improve state school finance equity have yielded much-needed improvements. However, Sciarra and Farrie's research demonstrates that few states have progressive funding systems designed to provide the extra resources required to deliver an equal educational opportunity for all students, regardless of their background, their family income, or where they live. Most states also fail to take the critical step of linking their finance systems to their curricular standards to ensure that all students have the resources needed to be successful. The chapter offers a thorough analysis of the recent successful transition from regressive to progressive school funding in New Jersey, highlighting the role of the legislature in linking content, performance, and accountability standards to school finance reform, which provides the resources needed by students to achieve those standards, particularly English language learners, low-income students, and students in concentrated school poverty. Sciarra and Farrie argue that this standards-linked funding reform—wherein states determine the actual costs of meeting state educational standards for all students, with a particular focus on the needs of students in high-poverty, low-wealth communities—is a necessity for the successful implementation of a fair school funding system. They also explore the potential for an increased role for the federal government in encouraging and sustaining school finance reform.

In chapter 7, "Bridging the Teacher Quality Gap: Notes from California on the Potential and Pitfalls of Litigating Teacher Quality," William S. Koski contends that it is nearly beyond dispute that the quality of a child's classroom teacher affects her performance and that it is becoming increasingly apparent that good teachers matter more for economically disadvantaged children. Despite this widespread consensus, it is also common knowledge that schools with concentrations of economically disadvantaged children and African American and Latino children tend to be staffed by the least experienced teachers, the lowest paid teachers, and those who are most likely to be laid off for budgetary reasons. To begin to address this issue, recent state and federal policy has been designed to enable school districts to attract and retain high-quality teachers, fairly distribute those teachers among all schools, and, most recently, remove barriers that prevent administrators from dismissing poor teachers or eliminate obstacles to assigning teachers to the classroom in which they are needed most. In addition, some advocates have begun to turn to the courts in an attempt to ensure that all children have access to high-quality teachers. In this chapter, Koski considers several recent lawsuits and litigation strategies designed, at least in part, to close the "teacher quality gap" in California; identifies the potential pitfalls of each of the strategies; and discusses the potential of a comprehensive, yet modest, "all of the above" litigation approach to ensuring equality of educational opportunity by providing economically disadvantaged children high-quality teachers.

In chapter 8, "It Takes a Federalist Village: A Revitalized Property Tax as a Linchpin for Stable, Effective K–12 Public Education Funding," Mildred Wigfall Robinson explains that after *Rodriguez,* state supreme courts became the fora for litigating challenges to school finance systems, with both notable successes and equally notable failures. She examines the extent to which sources of revenue other than property taxes, retail sales taxes, and income taxes are being tapped as funding sources and analyzes the financial viability and economic implications of the described shifts. She also reexamines the direct role of the federal government (demonstrably quite minor compared with that of state and local governments) in supporting public education and concludes by arguing that a reconceived federal deduction for property taxes paid to support public education might prove a useful way of indirectly providing increased federal support.

In chapter 9, "Tearing Down Fences: School Boundary Lines and Equal Educational Opportunity in the Twenty-First Century," Genevieve Siegel-Hawley acknowledges that our public schools, charged with advancing opportunity, are today more balkanized than ever and that racially isolated schools serving high proportions of students in poverty still do not systematically set students on a path toward upward social mobility. This largely holds true regardless of the system of school funding. Thus, she asserts, school integration deserves a renewed and determined focus alongside important efforts to equalize funding. Such attention must recognize that patterns of segregation in schools are heavily driven by jurisdictional boundaries which separate multiple school districts in the same metro area, just as they are also influenced by attendance zone boundaries within a single district. Siegel-Hawley revisits and analyzes policies designed to integrate students across broad metropolitan communities in the South and presents new research to indicate that comprehensive city-suburban school desegregation plans continue to be linked to lower levels of both school *and* housing segregation. She closes with innovative and specific policy options for a more regional pursuit of educational equity and integration.

The chapters in Part III provide novel ideas for creating innovative federal avenues for promoting equal access to an excellent education. In chapter 10, "How Reconstructing Education Federalism Could Fulfill the Aims of *Rodriguez*," Kimberly Jenkins Robinson recognizes that education federalism—the balance of power among federal, state, and local governments over education—recently has undergone substantial revisions through such legislation as the No Child Left Behind Act of 2001 (NCLB), the U.S. Department of Education's Race to the Top competitions, and the Department of Education's decision to grant states waivers from NCLB compliance. These recent reforms provide the nation an opportune time to examine how education federalism should be structured to ensure that all students have an equal opportunity to receive an excellent education. After offering several reasons why the United States should reexamine its approach to education federalism, Robinson proposes an alternative framework for reconstructing education federalism so that it can support—rather than impede—reforms that seek to ensure that all students obtain equal access to an excellent education. Her approach requires the federal government to build on the strengths of federal policy making as it engages in education reform, including setting equal access to an excellent education as a national priority, establishing a floor of educational opportunity, investing in research on how states could best provide an excellent education to all schoolchildren, and reallocating resources to states and localities that lack the capacity to offer such an education.

In chapter 11, "Leveraging Federal Funding for Equity and Integration," Derek Black contends that following the Supreme Court's holding in *Rodriguez*, the federal government has largely been ignored as a catalyst for funding equity. In fact, the federal initiative originally designed to ensure equity for poor students, the Elementary and Secondary Education Act (ESEA), has morphed into a general education and entitlement program that routinely ignores obvious inequalities and sometimes makes them worse. The ESEA, however, remains a huge leveraging tool that Congress could use to address the pressing problems of poverty and segregation. Black contends that ESEA funds should be targeted at schools and districts with high levels of poverty, that the exact amounts of the grants should be based on how much fiscal effort a state is exerting on behalf of its schools and the extent to which a state progressively funds high-need districts, and that Congress should attach strict conditions to those funds, mandating funding and resource equity both within and between districts for high-need schools. He maintains that these measures could drastically increase the ability of schools to meet students' needs, though targeting funds at high-poverty districts could create perverse incentives to further segregate some schools and districts. Thus, he contends that the ESEA must also monitor changes in student enrollment and incentivize integrative changes while penalizing segregative changes.

In chapter 12, "Remedying Separate and Unequal: Is It Possible to Create Equal Educational Opportunity?," Erwin Chemerinsky recognizes that just after the sixtieth anniversary of *Brown* American public schools are increasingly separate and unequal. He notes how American education is characterized by suburban schools that are predominately white and spend far more on education than city schools, which are almost entirely students of color (with private schools, overwhelmingly white). He highlights how Supreme Court decisions over the last several decades have contributed enormously to this problem. Chemerinsky contends that the key to a solution is to make sure that all children in each metropolitan area are attending the same school system so that there is truly a unitary and equal system of education. He then considers whether this would be possible or constitutional.

The Enduring Legacy of Rodriguez offers a collection of insights regarding one of the most important and enduring challenges confronting our nation: the educational opportunity gap. Although our nation proclaims itself the land of opportunity, in truth each year the educational opportunity of millions of schoolchildren is hindered by their socioeconomic status, race, immigration status, and zip code. The long-standing disparities in educational opportunity betray our national identity, shackle our economic future, and mock the nation's professed commitment to justice and fairness.

This volume also advances the ongoing reform efforts aimed at ensuring equal educational opportunity. It proposes an array of pioneering ways to move the United States toward a more excellent and equitable education system and, in so doing, offers not only powerful tools for reformers but also hope and encouragement that the elusive goal of equal educational opportunity remains within the nation's grasp.

PART I

Understanding *Rodriguez* and Educational Opportunity in the United States

TWO

Rodriguez v. San Antonio Independent School District

Forty Years and Counting

DAVID G. HINOJOSA

IN 1968, APPROXIMATELY four hundred high school students living in the impoverished west side of San Antonio, Texas, walked out of their classes at Edgewood High School, protesting the condition of their schooling.[1] The students realized that the quality of education they received at Edgewood, and the classrooms in which they were instructed, did not measure up well to wealthier neighboring school districts, leading to high dropout rates and, for those who did graduate, poor college preparation. In fact, the inadequacies and inequities hit even closer to home as their new sister school in the district, Kennedy High School, located in a "more affluent" part of the district, had not only a more expansive course selection but also air conditioning and better science labs.[2] At the rally, civil rights activist Willie Velasquez warned the students about the quality of education they were receiving, stating that "with the education you get at Edgewood, most of you are going to wind up in Vietnam or as a ditchdigger."[3]

Their peaceful yet powerful civil protest helped propel the filing of a federal civil rights action by parents and students of the Edgewood community a few months later, *San Antonio Independent School District v. Rodriguez*, which took on the state of Texas and its grossly unfair school funding system all the way to the United States Supreme Court. It was a monumental effort to change the landscape of school funding and to provide equal educational opportunities not only in Texas but across the United States. Forty years later, following the Supreme Court decision in 1973, an important question remains: was it worth it?

Some say that those efforts failed, in large part, because the U.S. Supreme Court ultimately rejected the challenge and held that there was no fundamental right to an equitable funding system. Others argue that the courts have failed in trying to adjudicate a largely political issue, taking away precious time, energy, and resources that could be used to improve education policy.

Still others maintain that the *Rodriguez* efforts succeeded by shining a light on the utterly disparate inequities in Texas's schools and by empowering advocates across the country to challenge their unfair funding systems. In Texas, parents, children, and school districts have challenged the state's school finance system five times since *Rodriguez*, with the most recent trial concluding in 2014. As a result, funding gaps between property-rich and property-poor districts in Texas and other states have largely decreased since 1968, though broken legislative promises continue to plague the system, forcing the parties to return to the courts.[4]

Completely successful or not, *Rodriguez* and its progeny helped expose unequal educational opportunities to the public, in turn forcing state legislatures and state courts to address them . . . at least to some degree. And without such pressure, many high-need students and students in property-poor districts would likely be worse off today.

SETTING THE STAGE FOR *RODRIGUEZ*

When, in 1968, the Edgewood High students reached the superintendent's office, they presented a list of nine grievances to the district. Seven days after the walkout, the Edgewood Independent School District (ISD) board of trustees agreed to resolve all nine grievances.[5] But after realizing that the grievance process would not remedy the root causes of the unequal educational opportunities, Edgewood parents, including Demetrio Rodriguez and Alberta Snid, filed suit in federal court two months later, alleging that the Texas school funding system discriminated against them on the basis of their lack of wealth and that education was a fundamental right under the U.S. Constitution.[6] If the courts found that either education was a fundamental right or the lack of wealth was a suspect class, Texas would have to demonstrate a compelling reason to treat classes of people differently and that its methods of achieving its compelling interest were narrowly tailored—a tremendous hurdle for the state to overcome. The U.S. Supreme Court had not settled any of these questions, but with the progressive court led by Chief Justice Earl Warren still intact, there was no better time for the Court to resolve such matters.

The plaintiffs were armed with largely irrefutable facts describing the gross inequities in the system between the haves in the wealthy districts and the have-nots in the poor districts. On December 23, 1971, the three-judge panel declared the school finance system unconstitutional under the Equal Protection Clause of the U.S. Constitution.[7]

Texas appealed to the U.S. Supreme Court, which had since flipped by three conservative justices appointed by Republican President Richard Nixon. On March 21, 1973, in a 5-4 decision, the Supreme Court reversed the lower court opinion, delivering a knockout blow to the plaintiffs and millions of children attending schools in property-poor districts. It was no longer the same court that had decided *Brown v. Board of Education*. Greatly disappointed, plaintiff parent Demetrio Rodriguez summed up the tragic Supreme Court ruling, saying, "The poor people have lost again."[8]

In a stinging dissent, Justice Thurgood Marshall berated the majority opinion for its "retreat from our historic commitment to equality of educational opportunity."[9] Justice White, likewise, contended that the Texas system failed to pass even the rational basis test, stating that the Texas system "provides a meaningful option to Alamo Heights and like school districts but almost none to Edgewood and those other districts with a low per-pupil real estate tax base."[10]

Despite having not persuaded a majority of the court to rule otherwise, Justice Marshall did have the last word. In the final footnote of the opinion, he suggested that Rodriguez and the other plaintiffs turn to state courts for relief on the same claims.[11] Eleven years later, Rodriguez, Edgewood ISD, and others did just that.

EDGEWOOD I—RODRIGUEZ RESURRECTED

In the immediate years following the *Rodriguez* decision, efforts to equalize funding in Texas fell short. In 1984, Edgewood ISD and other low-wealth districts, parents (including Rodriguez), and children heeded Justice Marshall's advice and sued Texas with the help of the Mexican American Legal Defense and Educational Fund (MALDEF), claiming that the school finance system was inequitable and unconstitutional under the state's education and equal protection clauses.[12] A separate low- and mid-wealth plaintiff group known as the Alvarado ISD plaintiffs intervened as well, also alleging state constitutional equity claims. And property-rich districts intervened, though as defendants, to preserve their financial and educational advantages.

Following a nearly three-month trial in 1987, Travis County District Judge Harley Clark held that the school finance system was unconstitutional under the education clause and that education was a fundamental right. The court found stark disparities among low- and high-wealth school districts and noted that the heavy concentration of high-need children in property-poor districts further exacerbated the problem of unequal opportunity.[13]

Once again, however, the celebration was short-lived. Texas appealed, and in a 2-1 decision by the Austin Third Court of Appeals, the ruling was reversed on grounds similar to *Rodriguez*.[14] Although the decision was a major setback, both parties knew that the Texas Supreme Court would have the last word.

On October 2, 1989, Rodriguez, Edgewood ISD, and all parents, children, and educators of property-poor districts in Texas finally received the news from a final reviewing court they had been searching for over the past twenty-one years: the Texas public school finance system was unconstitutional. In a unanimous decision, the Texas Supreme Court declared that the state's education clause requires that "children who live in poor districts and children who live in rich districts . . . be afforded a substantially equal opportunity to have access to educational funds."[15] Edgewood superintendent James "Jimmy" Vasquez pronounced, "This is vindication of 20 years of struggle."[16] The court refused to reach the issues of whether education was a fundamental right and whether lack of wealth was a suspect class under the Texas Constitution because the court ruled the system violated the education clause.[17]

In reviewing the history of the education clause, the court rejected the notion that "efficient" meant "an 'economical,' 'inexpensive,' or 'cheap' system."[18] The court went on to hold that under the efficiency provision of the education clause, "there must be a direct and close correlation between a district's tax effort and the educational resources available to it; in other words, districts must have substantially equal access to similar revenues per pupil at similar levels of tax effort."[19]

In examining the efficiency of the system, the court observed large inequities in funding between property-poor and property-rich districts. The evidence showed that the hundred poorest districts taxed their residents nearly $.28 more than the hundred richest districts but spent less than half on their students' education compared with the richest districts' expenditures, at an average of $2,978 per student.[20] The court noted that the distinct advantages built into the school finance system in favor of high-wealth districts allowed them "to provide their students broader educational experiences including more extensive curricula, more up-to-date technological equipment, better libraries and library personnel, teacher aides, counseling services, lower student-teacher ratios, better facilities, parental involvement programs, and drop-out prevention programs. They are also better able to attract and retain experienced teachers and administrators."[21]

The court ultimately concluded that the system was neither "financially efficient nor efficient" in the sense of providing the resources necessary for a "general diffusion of knowledge."[22] It gave the legislature until May 1, 1990, to remedy the constitutional deficiencies, or else it would order the schools closed.

EDGEWOOD II–V—THE TEXAS TWO-STEP

Following *Edgewood I*, the Texas Legislature finally reached an agreement in the sixth special session, passing Senate Bill (SB) 1. After full implementation, SB 1 was expected to place 95 percent of Texas schoolchildren within an equalized school finance system.[23] However, SB 1 wholly excluded 132 superwealthy school districts, and, thus, the Edgewood and Alvarado groups sued yet again.

The district court made quick work of the case, holding the system unconstitutional, and the Texas Supreme Court affirmed.[24] Like the *Edgewood I* court, the *Edgewood II* court examined tax advantages among individual school districts across Texas.[25] The court noted that if the wealthy districts taxed their residents at the mandatory tax rate of $.91 required of other districts under SB 1, those districts would reap millions more for their students.[26]

Unfortunately, the Alvarado plaintiffs filed what has been coined by one attorney representing the Edgewood plaintiffs as "an ill-conceived motion for rehearing."[27] Alvarado, in essence, sought an advisory opinion on an immaterial matter, which should have been rejected outright. Yet, a majority of the court used it as an opportunity to create new law, going beyond the advisory opinion sought and holding that the legislature need only establish an equitable system between property-rich and property-poor school districts up to the cost of providing an adequate education in order to discharge its duty of providing an efficient school funding system.[28] After providing all school districts with access to the revenue needed to provide a basic, adequate education at similar tax effort, the legislature could then allow school districts to enrich inequitably their educational offerings, though such enrichment could not become so great that it made the system inefficient. The court cited no real authority for retreating from the powerful *Edgewood I* decision.[29] Justices who concurred with the denial of the rehearing voiced their displeasure with the majority decision, exclaiming that it "expounds on social policy preferences rather than resolving a motion."[30] Nevertheless, this short, unsubstantiated opinion opened the door for future Texas courts to water down the strong *Edgewood I* holding.

Saddled with an unconstitutional system, in 1991 the Texas legislature passed SB 351, which created 188 taxing districts, whereby districts in the same county—wealthy and poor alike—would access funding from the same pool of tax dollars.[31] SB 351 significantly advanced equity in school funding, but the wealthy districts were not so fond of sharing their excessive property wealth and sued the state, charging that SB 351 violated the Texas Constitution by requiring local districts to levy a statutorily mandated tax without an election and by creating what the court deemed an unconstitutional state property tax, or an ad valorem tax.[32] This time around though, property-poor school districts like Edgewood ISD intervened as defendants on the side of the state. The Texas Supreme Court agreed with the wealthy districts, ruling the system unconstitutional under both claims and giving the legislature until June 1, 1993, to devise a constitutional system.[33]

Because the key failings of SB 351 hinged on the lack of a constitutional amendment authorizing the creation of the county education taxing districts, the legislature proposed such to Texas voters. However, the politically powerful wealthy school districts defeated the amendment. In late spring of 1993, the legislature passed SB 7, its latest attempt to resolve the unconstitutionality of the Texas school finance system. To bring property-poor districts closer to property-rich districts, the legislature added "equalization" provisions to the system. For example, school districts could not tax above $1.50. The equalized wealth levels created under SB 7 prevented wealthy school districts from accessing substantially greater revenue for each penny of tax effort. For revenues generated in excess of the wealth levels, districts had to exercise one of five options to reduce their wealth level, including sharing with the state revenues above the levels (also known as recapture).[34]

These equalized wealth levels operated, in theory, to bring all school districts and most local revenue into one system. However, the legislature built into the system a $600-per-pupil advantage for property-wealthy districts. Superwealthy districts accessed significantly greater funds under "temporary" hold-harmless provisions, which were intended to keep the wealthy districts from absorbing too much of a hit from the reduced access to enrichment dollars.

This time around no one was satisfied. Nine separate parties challenged various aspects of the system. The Edgewood and Alvarado districts filed equity claims. The wealthy districts attacked the wealth-sharing recapture provisions, arguing that such "options" were an unconstitutional statewide property tax. A separate group of wealthy districts challenged the potential consolidation of districts as a violation of rights secured under the Voting Rights Act of 1965. Still another group argued that an efficient public school system required that the state provide private school vouchers.

On January 30, 1995, eleven years after the filing of *Edgewood I*, the Texas Supreme Court denied all challenges and finally held the system constitutional. The court, however, warned the legislature of the system's imperfections, stating that "the challenge to the school finance law based on inadequate provision for facilities fails only because of an evidentiary void. Our judgment in this case should not be interpreted as a signal that the school finance crisis in Texas has ended."[35]

On the issue of equity, the court continued to subscribe to the requirement that, under the efficiency clause, "districts must have substantially equal access to similar revenues per pupil at similar levels of tax effort."[36] However, the majority jumped on the *Edgewood II* opinion denying the motion for rehearing and a concurrence in *Edgewood III* to further strip away the rights to an equitable education for students in property-poor districts.[37] In evaluating the financial efficiency of the system, the court held that this standard "applies *only* to the provision of funding necessary for a general diffusion of knowledge."[38]

In this case, the court tied the bow linking equity and adequacy. It criticized the equity plaintiffs for merely examining the differences in revenue generated at existing tax rates and at maximum tax rates under SB 7. Thus, the court dismissed the relevance of the undisputed $600 gap built into the formulas in favor of property-wealthy districts because it had no direct tie to the cost of an adequate education.[39] Instead, it examined the property tax and yield differences between wealthy and poor districts needed to generate the revenue necessary for an adequate education. This analysis was based on the formulas projected under SB 7 and assumed that the hold-harmless provisions would be phased out.[40] Although no party had litigated the cost of an adequate education, the court pulled a figure from the record—$3,500—and asserted that that was the cost of a basic, adequate education. It found that the wealthy districts held a $.09 tax advantage over the poor districts ($1.22 versus $1.31, respectively) to generate $3,500, concluding that such a difference was not "so great that it renders Senate Bill 7 unconstitutional."[41]

Despite rendering the system constitutional, the court did not do so with great confidence, pronouncing, "We conclude that the system becomes minimally acceptable only when viewed through the prism of history. Surely Texas can and must do better."[42] Eight years later that premonition came to light as school districts filed another challenge.

In 2001, four property-wealthy school districts filed suit challenging the $1.50 cap on property taxes as an unconstitutional state tax. The districts complained that they were forced to tax at or near the cap simply to provide an adequate education and that they had no meaningful discretion to set their own property tax rate.[43] Edgewood ISD and other property-poor districts intervened to protect the system's equalization provisions. Although the property-poor districts also believed that the funding under the cap was insufficient and inequitable, they also understood that the cap helped keep all the districts tied together and that the wealthy districts were targeting recapture of their tax dollars and the redistribution of that tax revenue to other districts in the state as authorized under SB 7.[44]

The district court initially dismissed the case, in part, on grounds that the claim was not ready to be filed because only 19 percent of school districts taxed at the cap and that a majority of districts would need to be taxing at the cap before the claim would be allowed to proceed in the courts.[45] The Texas Supreme Court reversed, returning the case to the district court. It held that only one district needed to prove that it was forced to tax at or near the cap to prevail on an Article VIII claim and that districts could prove they were forced to tax at the cap to provide an accredited education or to provide a general diffusion of knowledge.[46]

On remand, several school districts joined the lawsuit in one of three groups, each arguing that the funding was inadequate to provide a general diffusion of knowledge.[47] The Edgewood ISD group included twenty-two property-poor, majority Latino school districts.[48] The Alvarado ISD group included 260 property-poor and mid-wealth school districts.[49] Together, these districts educated one-fourth of the state's public school students. Both groups challenged the system as inadequate and inequitable for both facilities funding and instruction. The Edgewood plaintiffs also maintained their position as defendant-intervenors to defend the equalization provisions, a position they could not entrust to the state. The West Orange–Cove CISD plaintiffs (WOC) added another forty-three districts, including property-poor and mid-wealth districts, educating in total another quarter of the state's schoolchildren.[50]

In this first adequacy case tried in Texas, not only were there funding and taxing issues, but the quality of Texas public schooling was also now on trial. Over the previous ten years, 97 percent of the growth in Texas public schools came from Latino and African American students.[51] Low-income students constituted more than 50 percent of Texas public schoolchildren, and English language learner (ELL) students constituted 15 percent.[52] School districts lined up, testifying about the challenges they faced with changing student demographics and higher academic standards, including the transition to a more rigorous curriculum and a standardized testing system known as the Texas Assessment of Knowledge and Skills (TAKS).

Following a six-week trial in 2004, the district court ruled in favor of all of the school districts' claims, except for the property-poor districts' equity claim concerning instructional costs. While the court found facilities funding both inequitable and inadequate for low-wealth school districts, it summarily denied their equity claim relating to the gaps in taxes and revenue for maintenance and operation of instructional programs.[53]

Included among the district court's findings were some that seemingly supported the equity claim, stating that property-poor districts did not have funds necessary for a broader competitive curriculum; for recruiting, hiring, and retaining highly qualified teachers; for providing dropout prevention programs to at-risk students; and for providing bilingual and compensatory education, which disproportionately affected property-poor districts.[54] The

Edgewood and Alvarado plaintiffs and the state appealed the equity ruling, and Texas appealed the remaining judgment.

On direct appeal, the Texas Supreme Court first disposed of a series of challenges made by the state to extinguish the case altogether, including defenses alleging that the questions of adequacy and equity were political questions. On the merits of the claims, however, the court seemingly struggled with the rule of law established in prior cases, the deference owed to trial courts in fact-finding, and consistency in applying the facts to the law.

The court's treatment of the property-poor districts' equity claims shined a light on the court's haphazard analysis. In *Edgewood IV* the court held that it would not include hold-harmless districts as part of its equity analysis because the state intended to phase out the hold-harmless provisions over three years. Because the legislature eventually made those provisions permanent and even increased their funding over the years, it would stand to reason that the courts should include those districts in an equity analysis. And when those districts were included, the evidence showed large gaps. Comparing the districts at the ninety-fifth and fifth percentiles of property value per student, the wealthy districts had $1,678 more (or 40 percent) per student.[55]

Nevertheless, the court *excluded* the hold-harmless districts from its analysis, stating that in order to compare the size of the gap in *Edgewood IV* with the gap today, it would now have to exclude those districts as it did in 1995. After leaving the hold-harmless districts out of its analysis, the court concluded that the school finance system did not violate the financial efficiency mandate of the Texas Constitution.[56]

The court also struck down the property-poor districts' facilities claims. In *Edgewood IV*, the court made clear that "an efficient system of public education requires not only classroom instruction, but also the classrooms where that instruction is to take place."[57] MALDEF, as counsel for the Edgewood ISD plaintiff districts, built an incredible record detailing the deficiencies in the Edgewood districts' facilities and describing the state's failure to establish a consistent, well-funded, and permanent facilities program. The evidence included photos of decaying buildings with unstable foundations, leaky roofs with whole sections of ceiling tiles missing, science labs with no science equipment, several thirty-year-old "temporary" portable buildings, and old migrant farm worker camps converted to classrooms, with costs for repairs estimated in the tens of millions of dollars. The districts further demonstrated the link between student achievement and the condition of facilities—all unrebutted testimony.

The Texas Supreme Court acknowledged that there was "much evidence that many districts' facilities [were] inadequate" but then turned to new legal standards proffered by the state defendants in their briefing to the court.[58] First, the court stated that Edgewood failed to present evidence of districts' similar facility needs, agreeing with the defendants "that facilities needs vary widely depending on the size and location of schools, construction expenses, and other variables."[59] The court also stated that the plaintiff districts "must offer evidence of an inability to provide for a general diffusion of knowledge without additional facilities, and that they have failed to do so."[60] Edgewood quickly filed a motion asking the court to reconsider evidence in the record on these two new standards or to remand the case to the trial court for further consideration, but the court summarily denied the motion.

Turning to the adequacy claim, the supreme court modified the district court's definition in part, holding that "the public education system need not operate perfectly; it is adequate if districts are *reasonably* able to provide their students the access and opportunity the district court described."[61] It acknowledged the significant change in rigor in the state testing system and its related impact on school districts, including "summer school, remedial class, curriculum specialists, [and] reduced class-size."[62] Additionally, the influx of ELL and low-income students compounded the challenge, especially in light of the fact that the compensatory and bilingual education weights had not increased since being arbitrarily set in 1985.[63]

The court, however, dismissed these critical facts, stating that the lower court focused too much on inputs rather than outputs. It is hard to envision educational outputs not being affected by inputs. The court obviously struggled ideologically with the debate, stating: "The large number of districts, with their redundant staffing, facilities, and administration, make it impossible to reduce costs through economies of scale."[64]

Setting aside depressing dropout and graduation rates, the court handpicked two outputs to hold that the system was adequate: improved Texas scores on the National Assessment for Educational Progress (NAEP) and on the TAKS tests in the first two years of testing.[65] Ultimately, on the adequacy claim, it held that "we cannot conclude that the Legislature has acted arbitrarily in structuring and funding the public education system so that school districts are not reasonably able to afford all students the access to education and the educational opportunity to accomplish a general diffusion of knowledge."[66]

The court did affirm the trial court's ruling on the ad valorem claim, holding that the $1.50 cap on property taxes had, in effect, become both a floor and a ceiling.[67] Oddly enough, in weighing the merits of the ad valorem tax claim, the court assigned much weight to the very evidence it dismissed under the adequacy claim, including evidence of districts struggling to maintain accreditation ratings in light of the increasing standards and accompanying costs, changing student demographics, and unavailability of qualified teachers.[68] It concluded that the current state of the school finance system was akin to "the State simply set[ting] an ad valorem tax rate of $1.50 and redistribut[ing] the revenue to the districts."[69]

In ordering the remedy, the Texas Supreme Court acknowledged the importance of the equalization provisions, stating that although the tax cap made the system unconstitutional under Article VIII, it also operated to maintain the efficiency in the system.[70] The court granted a stay of the injunction until June 2006.

Although the court denied the adequacy claim, it did note that a constitutional violation was on the horizon. Quoting former lieutenant governor Bill Ratliff, the court stated, "I am convinced that, just by my knowledge of the overall situation in Texas, school districts are virtually at the end of their resources, and to continue to raise the standards . . . is reaching a situation where we're asking people to make bricks without straw."[71] That time, too, arrived sooner than expected.

EDGEWOOD VI—RESPONDING TO THE STATE'S SLASH AND BURN

In response to *Edgewood V,* the legislature cut a deal in May of 2006.[72] Once again, political wagering took precedence over student need as the Texas legislature reduced taxes and created a three-tier system. To address the tax cap issue, it compressed tax rates over a couple of years by one-third and capped property tax rates at $1.17.[73] The legislature also created a new hold-harmless provision, referred to as "target revenue," which ensured that school districts received as much funding as they did in the 2005–2006 and 2006–2007 school years, thus freezing in the inequities. The wealthy districts also successfully pushed for unrecaptured pennies, getting $.06 above the compressed rate when they recouped all tax money generated from those pennies.

Apart from facilities funding generated from interest and sinking fund taxes (which are not subject to recapture provisions), this was the first time since 1993 that legislation allowed wealthy districts to keep all of their revenue generated from taxes. The legislature added another twist by requiring school districts to hold elections to raise taxes above $1.04, taking that role away from local school boards.

Five years later, though, the legislature reacted to fiscal conservatives' demands and slashed public education funding by $5.4 billion for the 2011–2012 and 2012–2013 school years. While it is true that the economic downturn hit Texas, like most of the nation, hard and, in turn, impacted state resources, Governor Rick Perry himself touted Texas's resilience, asserting that "companies across the country are looking to Texas as the place to grow their business."[74] In fact, Texas's rainy day fund had reached a historic high of $8 billion in 2013.[75] The legislature left districts with many tough choices to make, and across Texas thousands of teachers lost their jobs, districts were forced to cut special programs, and the Texas Education Agency (TEA) granted close to 8,600 class size waivers.[76]

Included in the cut was $1.3 to $1.4 billion for special programs, such as before-school and afterschool tutoring, most of which helped struggling students disproportionately served in property-poor districts.[77] In response to concerns over whether the state should restore funds to the Foundation School Program or to special programs, Commissioner of Education Robert Scott testified that it was "akin to asking the guy on the operating table whether he wants his heart or his lungs back."[78]

The substantial funding cuts came at a time when Texas yet again ratcheted up student performance standards and integrated college-ready components into the more rigorous default curriculum, which required high school students to take four years of coursework in math (including Algebra II), science, social studies, and English language arts. Most welcomed the increased rigor, but the legislature also gave in to testing companies and significantly expanded its high-stakes tests from four exit-level subject TAKS tests to fifteen separate end-of-course (EOC) exams, known as the State of Texas Assessment for Academic Readiness (STAAR).[79]

Many schools were not prepared for the expansion and the significant jump in rigor. After eight years of teaching to the TAKS tests, many Latino, African American, low-income, and ELL students still struggled with those tests. In 2011, 86 percent of white students met the minimum TAKS standard on all tests in all grade levels, compared with only 71 percent of Latino students, 65 percent of African American students, 68 percent of low-income students, and 58 percent of ELL students.[80]

This left parents and school districts with little recourse but to turn to the courts once again. In 2011 four separate plaintiff groups filed suit against the state of Texas. The Equity Center filed first on behalf of the Texas Taxpayer and Student Fairness Coalition (TTSFC)—a group consisting of 443 low- and mid-wealth school districts—and five individual taxpayers, asserting equity, adequacy, and ad valorem tax claims as well as claims brought under the Texas equal protection and the equal and uniform tax clauses.[81] The Texas School Coalition, a group of high-wealth school districts, next sued through six of its members, including lead Calhoun County ISD, alleging adequacy and ad valorem claims. They also contended that the system *was* financially efficient, thus pitting themselves against the property-poor districts on that issue. Five property-poor school districts—Edgewood, McAllen, Harlingen, La Feria, and San Benito—and four parents and their schoolchildren from Amarillo ISD and Pasadena ISD next filed suit. They brought equity and ad valorem tax claims, and a more narrow adequacy claim focused on the funding for low-income and ELL students—the first of its kind in Texas. Fort Bend ISD and eighty-two other low-, mid-, and high-wealth school districts, including Houston, Dallas, and Austin, filed suit bringing adequacy, equity, and ad valorem tax claims. In total, more than half of the state's 1,029 school districts enrolling approximately 75 percent of all public school students sued the state.

About three months later a newly created association known as TREEE (Texans for Real Efficiency and Equity in Education), a few parents, and, later, the Texas Association of Business, intervened in the case. Self-describing their intervention as the Waiting for Superman lawsuit, they alleged that the system was "qualitatively inefficient" because it was not producing results with little waste. TREEE cited a number of policy reasons unrelated to funding, including the lack of choice in public schools, the statutory cap on charter schools, teacher certification requirements, statutory due process rights for teachers, class size limits, and the lack of a private financial auditing agency. Edgewood filed a motion to dismiss the intervention, arguing that the intervenors lacked standing and that their complaints involved political questions. The district court denied the plea but carried the challenge to standing to the trial on the merits.

On June 26, 2012, the Charter School Association and a group of charter school parents filed suit challenging the irrationality of the statutory cap on charters, the lack of facilities funding for charter schools, and the inadequacy of funding for charter schools based on statewide "averages."

Travis County District Court Judge John K. Dietz, who also presided over the *Edgewood V* trial, set the case for trial beginning October 22, 2012. The court admitted more than five thousand exhibits and heard live testimony from more than eighty witnesses during the three-month trial.[82]

The Edgewood and TTSFC plaintiffs made sure this time around that the equity issue would not sit second fiddle to any of the other claims, hiring two equity experts and positioning Calhoun County's equity expert between the Alvarado and Edgewood equity experts. The Equity Center's "simple average" analyses of school finance data showed substantial revenue and tax advantages for the wealthy districts, including one analysis showing the bottom 10 percent of districts having to tax $.66 higher in order to generate the same revenue ($7,998) that the top 10 percent of districts generated at their existing tax rates.[83]

Edgewood expert Albert Cortez conducted a series of "weighted average" analyses, each also showing substantial gaps in revenue and taxes (see table 2.1). In replicating the *Edgewood IV* analysis, he examined tax rates needed to generate the funds necessary for a general diffusion of knowledge between the 15 percent of students in the wealthiest and poorest districts. At each estimated level of funding, the wealthy districts had tax advantages far

TABLE 2.1 Taxpayer cost of providing an adequate education in 2012

Adequacy level	15% Property-poor tax	15% Property-rich tax
$5,000	$ .98	$ .74
$5,500	$1.08	$ .81
$6,000	$1.18	$ .88
$6,500	$1.28	$ .96
$7,000	$1.38	$1.03

Source: Texas Taxpayer and Student Fairness Coalition v. Williams, No. D-1-GN-11-003130, Ex. 4251, Cortez 2nd Supp. Report at 12; *Texas Taxpayer and Student Fairness Coalition v. Williams*, No. D-1-GN-11-003130, 2014 WL 4254969, *202 (D. Tex. 2014).

exceeding the $.09 difference in *Edgewood IV*.[84] As with *Rodriguez* and *Edgewood I,* the facts revealed inequities in neighboring districts. Edgewood ISD, with a property value of only $60,631 per student, was taxed at the maximum rate of $1.17 but generated only $5,825 per student; Alamo Heights ISD had a property value of $980,903 per student, which taxed $.13 less at $1.04 but generated $6,348 per student.[85]

The lack of equity resulted in unequal educational opportunities, with low-wealth district superintendents testifying to losing newly trained teachers to wealthier districts, to having to increase class sizes, and to being forced to cut intervention specialists and compensatory programs.[86] La Feria superintendent Nabor Cortez perhaps best summed up the arbitrariness in the inequality of the system testifying that the property-poor districts in the Rio Grande Valley all wished they had an island in their district like the property-wealthy Point Isabel ISD, which includes South Padre Island—"We all would love to have an island in our district, but we don't. We don't. We are poor and we are without our island."[87] Commissioner of Education Robert Scott conceded that Texas should not value certain students more than others because of where they live and go to school, stating that such was "offensive to the very nature of what we expect our schools to do."[88]

Edgewood plaintiff parent Yolanda Canales testified about her children's experiences in a property-poor district, Pasadena ISD, compared with the schools they attended in property-wealthy Clear Creek ISD, where her family moved when its financial situation improved. In Clear Creek ISD, she immediately noticed such differences as higher quality teachers, additional educational resources and extracurricular programs, smaller class sizes, and more tutoring.[89] But personal circumstances, including the real estate market crash, forced Canales to return to Pasadena, where she once again witnessed the difference in educational opportunities: she had to pay for night school for her daughter; the credit-recovery program was not monitored by a full-time teacher; science experiments were nonexistent; insufficient number of textbooks; a limited three-hour pre-K program for her youngest child was understaffed, underresourced, and overcrowded.[90] When asked what she wanted out of this lawsuit, she testified that she "just want[s] fairness; equal opportunities for my children as well, regardless of the neighborhood we live in."[91]

Regarding the adequacy claim, the plaintiff districts essentially presented a joint case, though Edgewood offered experts on bilingual and compensatory education in support of its narrower adequacy claim. The districts presented experts who highlighted the special challenges property-poor districts had in recruiting and retaining high-quality teachers, in providing high-quality pre-K programs for ELL and low-income students, and in keeping class sizes at tolerable levels for their high-need populations.

There was much testimony on the rising standards and the performance of Texas students. The state asserted that achievement gaps shrank on the TAKS tests, though the data also showed that the gaps remained sizable and the performance had leveled off.[92] The state also proffered testimony showing increases in SAT and ACT participation rates of tests for minority students, although performance remained flat.

The plaintiff groups countered with evidence showing a much different picture. With the increased college-readiness standards adopted by the state, performance rates showed that Texas had a ways to go in preparing its students for college. Statewide, for example, only one-fourth of all students met the SAT/ACT's college-ready criterion (26.9 percent), and incredible gaps existed among the races: 52 percent for Asian students, 41.4 percent for whites, 12.7 percent for Latinos, and 8.1 percent for African Americans.[93]

Scores on the more rigorous STAAR EOC exams showed students struggling across the state. After three administrations, 47 percent of low-income ninth graders failed to meet the minimum standard.[94] The reduced funding was compounded by the fact that many communities were unable to raise taxes either because they were already taxing at the maximum (such as Edgewood ISD) or their communities could not afford a tax increase. And unlike with *Edgewood V,* this time the evidence showed that Texas student performance on the NAEP remained flat or worsened with nearly every test since 2005.[95]

Immediately following closing arguments in February 2013, Judge Dietz announced his oral ruling from the bench, declaring that the system was inequitable, inadequate, and unsuitable in violation of Article VII and that school districts lacked meaningful discretion in setting their local property tax rates under Article VIII. More specifically for the Edgewood plaintiffs, the court declared that the funding for low-income and ELL students was arbitrary, inadequate, and unsuitable. It was a resounding victory for families in property-poor districts who convinced the trial court that the system was financially inefficient, unlike in 2004.

The court rejected the Charter School Association's facilities and charter cap claim, finding that the legislature retained final policy decision-making authority over charter schools. And the court rejected the intervenors' claims.[96]

TO BE CONTINUED . . .

Early in the 2013 regular session, Republican leadership announced that they did not intend to address any ruling by the courts until the Texas Supreme Court rendered its final decision, but a strong, organized effort of education advocates pushed for additional funding. Bills were filed to restore, in part, education funding cuts made in 2010–2011 and aimed to put most of the money in the basic allotment, which would help raise the funding for the lowest-property-wealth school districts. Fearing that the release of findings on the equity issue might harm their efforts to access greater revenue advantages in the legislature, the Calhoun County plaintiffs sent the court a letter in late April 2013, encouraging it to wait for the legislature to consider the school finance bills. The three other plaintiffs groups sent a letter to the court asking that it not delay its final judgment, but the court took no action.

At the end of the session, the state finally passed legislation adding $3.4 billion back into education; reducing the number of high-stakes EOC exams to graduate from fifteen to five; and modifying high school curriculum requirements. This marked the first time in the history of Texas school finance litigation (known to the author) that the legislature passed legislation attempting to remedy the deficiencies noted by a trial court before a final state supreme court ruling.

The court reopened the trial to consider the legislative changes, over the objection of the Edgewood plaintiffs who argued that the changes were insubstantial, and a three-week hearing commenced on January 21, 2014.[97] Six months later, Judge Dietz again held the system unconstitutional on all counts.[98] In a scathing rebuke of the Texas school finance system, the court determined that rather than attempting to solve the problems, the state "buried its head in the sand making no effort to determine the cost of providing all students with a meaningful opportunity to acquire the essential knowledge and skills reflected in the state curriculum and to graduate at a college- and career-ready level."[99] Expectedly, the state and the intervenors filed appeals of the judgment, as did the wealthy Calhoun County districts on the equity issue and the charter plaintiffs on their facility and charter-cap claims.

Thus, the pursuit of equal opportunity through the courts initiated by Demetrio Rodriguez and others forty years ago remains unfinished.

THE IMPACT OF *RODRIGUEZ* BEYOND THE TEXAS BORDER

The *Rodriguez* case undoubtedly influenced the early Texas Supreme Court cases, which have been described as "the hammer that forced the Texas legislature to create a significantly more equitable Texas school finance system."[100] But the impact of *Rodriguez* goes beyond Texas. Although *Rodriguez* was not the first school finance case filed alleging inequities in a state school funding system, the dissenting opinion by Justice Marshall unquestionably empowered education advocates in other states.[101] One well-known scholar and practitioner describes *Rodriguez* as leading "to an unprecedented era of constitutional activity by the state courts in rectifying inequities in state education finance systems," and I contend that not only did it spur litigation but also legislation.[102]

By the mid-1970s, eighteen state legislatures had taken action to improve their equalization formulas, albeit in varying degrees of success.[103] Most increased minimum foundational funds for low-wealth districts, but only up to a certain level.[104] Consequently, low-wealth school districts, parents, and students turned to the courts.

State courts responded by upholding a number of school finance challenges in the early years following *Rodriguez*.[105] The courts soon reversed course with fifteen *denying* challenges in the 1980s, many relying on similar grounds authored in *Rodriguez*.[106] But by the late 1980s, the pendulum swung back in favor of the plaintiffs in *Edgewood I, Rose v. Council for Better Education*, and *Helena Elementary School District No. 1 v. State*.[107] As the appendix shows, in twenty-three states plaintiffs have secured victories in the highest court at least once and nineteen times for state defendants. Only four states have never entertained litigation.[108]

CAN THE COURTS GET THE JOB DONE?

Critics who lament court action in school finance often point to the ineffectiveness or overreaching power of the courts, using California and New Jersey as poster states for their cause.[109]

In *Serrano v. Priest,* the California Supreme Court held in 1976 that funding distinctions based on wealth of a school district were a suspect classification and that education was a fundamental right under the California Constitution; and it held its system unconstitutional.[110] It was a tremendous court pronouncement, but in response California leveled down the spending of the wealthy districts to the level of the poor districts, and voters compounded the problem by passing a proposition that capped increases on local property taxes.[111]

New Jersey has also been the subject of considerable litigation, dating back to the *Robinson v. Cahill* case in 1973.[112] In *Robinson*, the New Jersey Supreme Court held the system unconstitutional after determining that the funding inequities proved the state's failure to fulfill "its obligation to afford all pupils that level of instructional opportunity which is comprehended by a thorough and efficient system of education for students" as required under its state constitution.[113] In separate litigation filed in 1981 in *Abbott v. Burke*, plaintiffs challenged the constitutionality of the New Jersey school funding system because of the significant disparities in expenditures between poor urban school districts and wealthy suburban districts and the lack of adequate funds.[114] Twenty-one opinions followed, although most involve only specific funding elements in the remedial phase.

While both California and New Jersey seem to merit criticism aimed at court intervention, such criticism must be tempered with an understanding of the proper role of the courts in these cases. Since 1803 in *Marbury v. Madison*, courts have been called on to interpret constitutional provisions and the actions of legislatures. Faced with highly inequitable systems that harmed children solely because of the side of the tracks they lived on and where they went to school, the courts were called on to determine whether such systems pass constitutional muster. The fact that the California legislature and, in turn, California voters decided to level-down the system in response to the California Supreme Court's decision in *Serrano* was the fault of the people and its elected officials—not the courts. And the fact that the New Jersey legislature has repeatedly disobeyed court orders to enact a constitutional system may speak volumes about the legislature's unfortunate decision to pander to political interests rather than fulfill its constitutional duty.

Lobato/Ortega v. Colorado is one of the latest state supreme court rulings in school finance, issued in May 2013, and it demonstrates how a court can allow a challenge to go forward but then stray from dutifully interpreting the state constitution.[115] *Lobato* plaintiffs and plaintiff-intervenors included numerous parents, students, and school districts challenging the adequacy of the Colorado school funding system. The Colorado Supreme Court had earlier overturned the lower courts' decisions finding adequacy claims non-justiciable.[116] Following a five-week trial in 2011, the district court held the system unconstitutional, highlighting the gross deficiencies in the system—especially for ELL, low-income, and special education students in lower-wealth districts.[117]

Similar to the change in the composition of the U.S. Supreme Court justices in *Rodriguez,* though, the Colorado Supreme Court had flipped when two justices were appointed by the conservative democratic governor. In May 2013, only about two months following oral argument in this complex case, the majority held the system constitutional. Ignoring the history surrounding the education clause, and instead using selective definitions to interpret the words "thorough" and "uniform," the court held that the current system met the constitutional mandate because it was "of a quality marked by completeness, is comprehensive, and is consistent across the state."[118]

In a stinging dissent reminiscent of Justice Marshall's in *Rodriguez,* Chief Justice Michael Bender noted that "the record . . . reveals an education system that is fundamentally broken" with more challenging student demographics, decreased education funding, and dismal achievement.[119] He cited substantial evidence demonstrating the inadequacy of the system, including minimal funding for ELL programs that was arbitrarily cut off after two years and "classrooms where children 'had worn a dent in the floorboards around a heater they had to huddle around during the cold of winter.'"[120] The majority's retreat from its constitutional duty owed to Colorado's at-risk children essentially leaves their education to the whims of an unresponsive legislature, because, unlike *Rodriguez,* the children may have nowhere else to turn for educational opportunity.[121]

As these cases suggest, advocates were essentially forced to file actions in state court because civic action had failed. Similar actions in Massachusetts, Kansas, North Carolina, Kentucky, Arizona, Montana, and Washington, among other states, have helped spearhead school finance reform efforts through the courts aimed at helping those students and communities most in need. But as the *Lobato* case in Colorado suggests, a court's decision to water down the constitutional duties of state legislatures can have little effect on educational policy, and, ultimately, voters and elected officials will need to weigh the evidence and decide whether or not to make equal educational opportunity a reality for all.

CONCLUSION

After more than forty years following the Supreme Court's decision, state legislatures and state courts continue to grapple with claims of inequitable and inadequate funding systems. But does this mean that Demetrio Rodriguez's and other advocates' pursuits of equal educational opportunities through the courts have had no positive or lasting effect? Of course not.

Whether you look at school funding systems in Texas, New Jersey, Kansas, or Massachusetts, the inequities of today are a far cry from the inequities of yesteryear. As a former clerk for Justice Powell noted, "Right or wrong, *Rodriguez* unleashed school-funding innovation throughout the country that continues to this day."[122] Equity claims remain particularly important because what constitutes a "minimum" program "is [still] in large part shaped by what the richer districts judge to be 'sufficient' for the poorer."[123]

And while school finance litigation should not be mistaken as the be-all, end-all solution for the many problems plaguing our schools, it is a feasible solution to resolving inherent, man-made deficiencies in school funding. The courts often remain the only path for proud, resilient communities like Edgewood, which often do not have a persuasive voice in the state legislature.

Thus, until the United States can adopt a constitutional amendment, or the Supreme Court can revisit its decision in *Rodriguez,* state courts will continue to be called on to rule on these very important issues when legislatures fail to uphold their duties owed to public school children.[124] It is especially important today in light of state legislatures' continued ramping up of academic, testing, and accountability standards for all students and school districts while seldom paying any attention to the resources needed to achieve those standards. María "Cuca" Robledo Montecel commented on the crossroads that we face when she said that "equal educational opportunity can remain a well-intended but unfulfilled promise or move to becoming the engine of shared prosperity for generations of Americans."[125]

As Demetrio Rodriguez once said—and the same still rings true today—"We are doing the harm to this country by not having equal education. That's the only thing you can give a poor people. Give them an education and they'll be better citizens; they will help this country more."[126] But until that day comes, the courts must remain open to valid challenges by disadvantaged communities and schoolchildren.

THREE

Rodriguez in the Court

Contingency and Context

CAMILLE WALSH

THIS CHAPTER EXAMINES the historical context and the political roots of the *Rodriguez* case inside and outside the Court. By delving into the records, notes, memos, and archival material produced around the case, I navigate the arguments and historical circumstances in *Rodriguez* in order to better understand the factors that contributed to the Court's ruling and the legacy left by the *Rodriguez* rationale. The three sections of this chapter all ultimately address how implicit or explicit connections were articulated in the case, whether connections between race and class or between economic inequality and anticommunism, and how those connections contributed to a changing framework of modern equal protection jurisprudence. Most previous scholarship on the case has not addressed either the claim of race discrimination as central to the understanding of the Court's ruling (even if by omission) or the historical context of the Cold War at the moment when the Court shut the door on protecting the poor from systemic inequalities.

First, I analyze the way in which race and poverty were discussed in the lower court opinions, amicus briefs, and oral arguments, arguing that the multiple identity positions claimed by the students and families in the case were largely rendered invisible by courts. Next, I trace the consistent anticommunist impulse running through many of the briefs and the internal memos, drafts, and notes leading up to Justice Lewis Powell's majority opinion. I argue that we can identify *Rodriguez* within a Cold War discourse of what Lani Guinier calls "racial liberalism" in the post-*Brown* era that focused on treating the symptoms rather than the disease of racism. This Cold War racial liberalism coexisted simultaneously with a judicial anxiety around expansion of educational access and resources based on economic class. Finally, I locate *Rodriguez* within the shifting and contingent moment of historical development of equal protection analysis in the 1970s, pointing to its importance in foreclosing alternative visions for the application of equal protection and the judicial scrutiny of inequality.[1]

RACE AND CLASS IN COURT

The *Rodriguez* case began with a father seeking a meaningful education for his sons. Demetrio Rodriguez, a forty-two-year-old veteran, sent three of his four sons to Edgewood Elementary School in San Antonio in 1968, where the "building was crumbling, classrooms lacked basic supplies, and almost half the teachers were not certified and worked on emergency permits." Rodriguez had been involved in a number of campaigns for Mexican American rights in Texas during the 1960s, including LULAC and the Mexican American Betterment Association. He recognized that his sons were receiving a dramatically unequal education in comparison with other neighborhoods in the city, and he and a group of other Mexican American parents approached Arthur Gochman, a local attorney well known for his work defending civil rights and participating in sit-ins to desegregate various facilities in San Antonio. Gochman later stated that he had hoped Rodriguez's Latino surname would help emphasize the racial aspects of the case, marking it as distinct from school finance litigation based solely on wealth disparities.[2]

Indeed, it is important to understand that, from the very beginning of the case, the *Rodriguez* claimants demanded equal protection on the basis of racial discrimination as well as discrimination based on economic class. The claims for the plaintiffs in *Rodriguez* were always connected to race and class and education, all at once. Gochman articulated three claims for relief in his class action lawsuit against local and state officials on behalf of all low-income or racial minority children similarly situated in Texas. First, he argued that poverty was a suspect class that was detrimentally impacted by the school finance laws. Second, he argued that education was a fundamental constitutional right that was similarly harmed by the law. And, finally, and most frequently left out of later discussions and analysis of the case, he argued that the plaintiffs were experiencing unconstitutional discrimination on the basis of race as a result of the racially disparate impact of the laws in the provision of unequal education.[3]

The three-judge Texas district court panel that heard Gochman's complaint needed to find only one of his three arguments valid in order to demand "compelling justification" from the state for its school financing system. The panel held, however, that the state had failed to "even establish a reasonable basis" for its financing system, without entering the debate on poverty as a suspect class, education as a fundamental right, or race as an equal protection trigger. The district court failed Texas on rational basis, the most deferential judicial standard of review, and the state appealed the case. The very brief decision, in fact, mentioned "minority status" when discussing evidence that the richest school districts had 8 percent minority pupils while the poorest had 79 percent. The judges prefaced this reference with "as might be expected," an offhand indication that the linkage of race and class and the problem of a huge racial wealth gap with a direct effect on education was not a surprise to the judges. This is the only mention the district court judges made of race in their opinion, but, as amici later argued, it could serve as a finding of fact that race and class discrimination were intimately, and not surprisingly, tied in the case "as might be expected." Many sympathetic parties also presented evidence on all three fronts of the litigation—race, class, and the right to education—as the case moved through the certiorari process, pointing out that the Edgewood schools' student body was 90 percent Hispanic and 6 percent African American while the student body at nearby Alamo Heights was nearly entirely white. Edgewood schools were 50 percent more crowded than Alamo Heights schools, however, and had only one-third the library books and one-fourth the guidance counselors, among many other inequalities.[4]

That de facto racially segregated schools were also often receiving vastly unequal funding was not news to many parents, school officials, and even politicians at the time. The U.S. Senate held hearings in 1970 and 1971 on the problem of equal educational opportunity, and resource and funding disparities related to race and poverty were included in the focus. Jose A. Cardenas, the superintendent of the Edgewood Independent School District at the time of the case, testified at these hearings to say that state funding in Texas had done little to equalize resources. He pointed out that Alamo

Heights schools were so racially homogeneous that they had to combine students with another school district in order to reach the Texas state minimum of twenty-six Spanish-speaking children in order to receive a $150,000 grant for a bilingual education program. Edgewood schools, in contrast, had to share that same amount among twenty-two thousand Spanish-speaking students. In his affidavit during the *Rodriguez* case, Cardenas stated that despite their higher tax rate, Edgewood schools were only able to raise $26 per child in property tax funds, while Alamo Heights was able to raise $333. Sarah Carey from the Lawyers' Committee for Civil Rights Under Law also testified before Senator Walter Mondale's committee about the *Rodriguez* case and school finance litigation in the 1970s. Carey testified that the goal of *Rodriguez* was in part to go further than the 1971 *Serrano v. Priest* case in California and merge wealthy white districts with poor minority districts in order to desegregate racially segregated districts. She pointed out that San Antonio's school district lines were "drawn with great care so that Chicanos are in one area and the whites are in another." Mondale responded that the San Antonio city fathers had also put all the public housing in one district, Edgewood. Carey acknowledged that school finance cases like *Serrano* only got at the "fiscal problem," while the metropolitan desegregation cases, such as *Rodriguez*, "got at the racial issues" and that both would be necessary to address to fulfill the principles of the Constitution.[5]

Segregation in Texas was geographically complex and historically contingent and had always incorporated economic, linguistic, and racial elements. In 1971 the U.S. Commission on Civil Rights examined Texas school systems with at least 10 percent Mexican American enrollment and found that school expenditures declined as the proportion of Mexican Americans increased. But Texas had a long legacy of school segregation, including a 1905 state law that required public school teachers to use only English and that instituted separate schools for students with Spanish-sounding surnames. Due to contingent ideas of legal "whiteness" in the southeastern part of the state, many school boards in Texas in the wake of *Brown* had actually avoided desegregating all-white schools by integrating African American schools and Mexican American schools and then claiming the schools were desegregated because Mexican Americans were "other whites." As a NAACP amicus brief later said, "*Plaintiffs are all Mexican Americans. They* claimed relief as and for Mexican Americans."[6]

But for the Supreme Court, the claim of race discrimination and the evidence of its historical basis in Texas would be treated simply as a red herring, as one of Justice Powell's clerks later described it in an internal memo. Several amicus curiae opposing the *Rodriguez* claimants as well as the appellants themselves only discussed race as a sort of trade-off with class, implying that any attempt to encourage more equal fiscal resources in schools would actually be to the detriment of students of color, either because of white flight or because of exceptional cases in which urban districts actually had higher revenues than their suburban counterparts. In response, one brief by several state governors argued that "it is singularly unattractive to propose that this Court trade off discrimination against the poor in exchange for eliminating racial discrimination." Gochman, however, in his motion to affirm the decision of the district court, pointed to evidence that as the percentage of minority residents in a district increased, the tax rate also increased up to the statewide cap while the revenues available for education decreased. He also emphasized the tradition of educational discrimination against Mexican Americans in Texas, citing the example of a 1950 injunction against the state school system preventing it from continuing to segregate Mexican American students. At oral argument, Gochman again argued that race was an important factor for the claimants, but only Justice William O. Douglas raised the question of race with Charles Alan Wright, the attorney for the state of Texas, toward the end of his oral argument. Wright admitted that "the racial issue is in this litigation" but argued that the correlation between racial composition and poverty in San Antonio was a "happenstance."[7]

Ultimately, the racial discrimination claim Gochman made would go unaddressed in the majority opinion. Justice Powell's notes during deliberations show that he also considered race and class as somehow mutually exclusive, and he referred routinely to his experience in rural counties in Virginia as examples of places where there was high poverty but a low percentage of African Americans. His argument seemed to be that the mere existence of large numbers of poor white people negated a possible connection between race and poverty in this case. If race was not 100 percent explicit, either in the legislation or in the practice of segregation, it was beyond legal redress for Powell. It was also presumably important to dismiss the racial discrimination claim out of hand given that Powell did not want to see comparisons of *Rodriguez* with *Brown*. Across the bottom of the conference notes he prepared for the case, he wrote in large letters that *"Brown* was based on *racial discrimination."*[8]

In an early internal memorandum indicating the justices' first impressions of the case, the initial votes hewed closely to the final 5-4 split. Chief Justice Warren Burger cast a straw vote for reversal, stating that he agreed with Wright's brief and felt that the "holding would result in restructuring our system of state and local gov[ernmen]t." Justice Potter Stewart also cast an early vote for reversal, arguing that "money is some index, but the [equal protection] clause does not require egalitarianism." Stewart went on to state that "unless there is a specific, identifiable class of people that is being discriminated against, the [equal protection] clause does not apply." Justice William Rehnquist also noted his agreement with Stewart's assessment of the case in his vote for reversal. Justice Harry Blackmun's vote for reversal, according to Powell's notes, was based simply on his assessment that the "Texas system provides adequate basic aid." Justice Byron White voted to affirm "with a narrower opinion," agreeing with the district court that in "a district which is 'locked-in,' and where [the] state provides no way to equalize there is a denial of [equal protection]." Justice Douglas also voted to affirm, stating that the case was a "problem of equality." In his initial vote to affirm, Justice Thurgood Marshall argued that the district "can equalize the money even if [*sic*] can't equalize education," and Justice Powell noted that Marshall agreed this could not be done. Justice William Brennan also voted to affirm the case and was quoted in conference notes as saying, "Few cases have troubled me more." Agreeing with the methodology of the district court decision, he stated that the claimants "don't have to show a compelling interest—there is no rational interest."[9]

The final opinion was issued on March 21, 1973, six months after oral arguments. Justice Powell authored the majority decision, which was joined by Justices Stewart, Blackmun, Rehnquist, and Burger. Stewart filed a concurring opinion, and Justices Brennan, Marshall, and White each wrote dissenting opinions, which Justice Douglas joined. Powell claimed that the financing plan was "certainly not the product of purposeful discrimination against any group or class" and instead was "rooted in decades of experience in Texas and elsewhere, and in major part is the product of responsible studies by qualified people." His majority opinion reflected his understanding that, under constitutional jurisprudence, if education were declared a fundamental right or interest, it would be virtually impossible to sustain the funding structure in Texas, since the state would not be able to meet the compelling interest standard required for infringement on a fundamental right. His solution was to conclude that education was not a fundamental right recognized by the Constitution. In response to the wealth discrimination argument, the majority held that wealth was not a protected category for the purposes of equal protection scrutiny, thereby categorically reversing constitutional direction.

But what of the third argument posed by the plaintiffs? The majority opinion mentioned the racial identification of the plaintiffs early on, in the context of a description of the nature of the lawsuit and the description of its place of origin. Other than a brief mention of race in listing the statistical identifications of the two school districts under comparison, the opinion continued for another fifty-three pages without any comment on race. In the last two pages, however, Powell's opinion again mentioned that these children were not just poor but also nonwhite, an issue he shrugged off by stating that there was no consensus whether "the poor, the racial minorities, or the children in overburdened core-city school districts would be benefited by abrogation of traditional modes of financing education." He then cited one example of a school district with a majority of Mexican American students whose per-pupil taxable wealth level was above the local average and used this to argue that it was no more than "a random chance that racial minorities are concentrated in property-poor districts." He followed with the statement that "these practical considerations, of course, play no role in the adjudication of the constitutional issues presented here." Indeed, in a page of handwritten notes on an early draft of the opinion, Powell wrote, "Don't admit or refer to 'discriminatory treatment of children'—it is not 'discriminatory'; there are inequalities resulting from [the] system."[10]

Justice Marshall, in a powerful sixty-four page dissent joined by Justice Douglas, addressed each of the arguments raised by the majority, mentioning race twice—perhaps in proportion to the degree the majority considered it in its ruling. First, when discussing the majority's refusal to accept the finding of fact by the district court that poor and minority group members tended to live in property-poor districts, he responded that such a finding suggested "discrimination on the basis of both personal wealth and race." When arguing that wealth classifications should (and had in previous decisions) constituted a suspect class, he mentioned that there were reasons to consider wealth discrimination differently than discrimination based on race or ethnicity. He acknowledged that while poverty may entail a social stigma similar to that historically attached to racial and ethnic groups, "personal poverty is not a permanent disability; its shackles may be escaped." Yet given that the actual victims of the law at issue in this case were children, it is questionable how much they could do to escape their class status. And given that those children were still almost entirely racial minorities, it is unclear why it was crucial to mark the division between the two categories in this dissent, except that Marshall was himself bound by the strictures of a legal system that recognized only one category of identity at a time. In order to write a dissent defending the need for equal protection against wealth discrimination as a constitutionally protected category, Marshall had to treat race as inconsequential to the case, because intersections of identity and discrimination were constitutionally incomprehensible.

The Court's treatment of the case, particularly the claim of racial discrimination, served to render the claimants racial identity invisible by ignoring the race discrimination claim in order to focus only on the issue of wealth discrimination. This approach only makes sense within the "colorblind constitutionalism" framework that Neil Gotanda has described and critiqued in twentieth-century Supreme Court jurisprudence. Gotanda describes this fetishization of formal race categories by the Court as the primary means by which justices can find a legal logic that rolls back affirmative action legislation even as it purports to abide by the antidiscrimination rhetoric of *Brown*. If race, as both Gotanda and Guinier argue for the late twentieth-century Court, means literally nothing other than skin color, then historical context is unnecessary, economic disparities are moot, and constitutional remedies for otherwise troubling inequalities can be dramatically curtailed. By starting from the premise that race was a constitutional irrelevance unless stated explicitly and formally in the school finance law at issue, therefore, the *Rodriguez* Court was able to ignore the dramatically racially disparate impact of the property tax–based financing law even when it was presented as an explicit part of the case by the claimants.[11]

During the Supreme Court appellate process, the advocacy and civil rights organization La Raza filed a joint amicus curiae brief with the American Civil Liberties Union (ACLU), arguing that "racial discrimination . . . is not an afterthought to the litigants here" but, rather, was "the very core of this case." Far from the core of the Court's opinion, however, the intersecting identities of the claimants in *Rodriguez* seemed invisible to the majority.

There were, perhaps, other issues the justices found more pressing than the connection between race discrimination and unequal educational funding, other underlying anxieties that may have contributed to the majority's belief that school finance equalization presented a dangerous slippery slope in that historical moment.[12]

ANTICOMMUNISM AND ADJUDICATION

One historically specific undercurrent in the *Rodriguez* case was the anti-communist politics that permeated the prior two decades. Since the rise of McCarthyism in the 1950s, there had been a widespread fear among political figures as well as everyday activists that any acknowledgment that inequalities on the basis of disparate wealth were unjust would lead to communism and cause the United States to lose the Cold War. While racial inequality was beginning to be identified in certain circles—sometimes grudgingly—as unjustifiable and even economically inefficient under capitalism by the 1970s, income inequality and resource inequalities were still widely accepted as the sine qua non of the free market. *Rodriguez* is located within a broader Cold War context in which certain kinds of formal racial equality—"racial liberalism"—were acceptable and even helpful in battling Soviet propaganda, while claims of discrimination or unequal treatment on the basis of poverty were more likely to be defended as a logical byproduct of capitalism and protected against lurking socialist impulses. As Guinier wrote on the fiftieth anniversary of the *Brown* decision, "While anticommunist fervor helped fuel the willingness of national elites to take on segregation, it also channeled dissent from the status quo into status-based legal challenges that focused on formal equality through the elimination of de jure segregation." The coalition of intersecting race and class identities that the *Rodriguez* case put forward was thus precisely the antithesis of what Cold War–era judicial politics encouraged.[13]

The Supreme Court's relationship with anticommunist politics was complex. Anticommunist concerns about justices potentially too sympathetic to the poor or too amenable to the New Deal, specifically, had regularly emerged in various confirmation hearings since the 1930s. These sentiments, combined with a belief in judicial restraint in the post-*Lochner* era, after that 1905 decision fell out of favor in 1937, meant that at the height of McCarthyism a few decades later, according to one legal historian, "the Court simply rubber-stamped congressional and state laws that interfered with freedom of speech and expression." Morton Horwitz has called the decision in *Dennis v. U.S.* in 1951 the "most notorious example of the Court's capitulation to the forces of repression." *Dennis* only makes sense in a historically specific context in which Senator Eugene McCarthy and his anticommunist crusade were at their highest point and more robust civil liberties frameworks had yet to be firmly ensconced by the Court. In *Dennis,* the Court ruled that the Smith Act, which created criminal penalties for advocacy of the overthrow of the U.S. government, was constitutional and that the trial and conviction of eleven Communist Party leaders in 1949 did not violate their First Amendment rights to free speech, press, and assembly.[14]

But with the confirmation of Justice Brennan in 1956 came a dramatic shift. That year, on a day known as Red Monday, several cases rolled back a series of decisions that had permitted major erosions in civil liberties in the name of anticommunism. By the following summer, in 1957, the Jenner-Butler bill was introduced into Congress by a group of McCarthyite politicians and opponents of the *Brown* decision. The bill would have dramatically reduced the Court's appellate jurisdiction to hear cases in areas like civil rights and civil liberties and prevented the Court from hearing lawsuits challenging federal loyalty and the power of states to regulate "subversive" activities, as well as any judicial review of the regulations and bylaws of school boards and educational agencies to address "subversive" activities among teachers. Though it was narrowly defeated in Congress in 1958, the Jenner-Butler bill gave segregationists who believed the Court had overreached in *Brown* and anticommunists who believed the Court was permitting communistic ideas to run rampant under the guise of civil liberties common cause to attempt to limit the Court's judicial review power.[15]

The coalition between anticommunist and antidesegregation ideologies was only one side of the coin, however. Anticommunism in the mid-twentieth century was a strong enough ideology to cover nearly all the players in the debate over school segregation, and desegregation advocates were able to deploy anticommunist rhetoric to their advantage in many contexts. The U.S. Department of Justice amicus brief in *Brown* in 1952 argued that it was "in the context of the present world struggle between freedom and tyranny that the problem of racial discrimination must be viewed," because "racial discrimination furnishes grist for the Communist propaganda mills."[16] Mary Dudziak has argued compellingly that the pressures of Soviet propaganda about

U.S. racism helped propel national political figures toward support for desegregation and civil rights, even if only on the surface. Gerald Rosenberg has more bluntly stated that the rhetoric of the Cold War was ultimately beneficial for the civil rights movement. And the NAACP praised the *Brown* decision on the day it was issued for, among other things, "being very effective in combating propaganda of Communists." Ultimately, as historian Martha Biondi has claimed, while anticommunism helped motivate desegregation in some instances, it also often pushed aside coalition-building movements that linked race and class. Since these were the very intersectional, coalitional claims presented in *Rodriguez,* the case confronted political as well as constitutional challenges.[17]

Less than twenty years after *Brown,* for the justice tasked with drafting the opinion of the Court in *Rodriguez,* the case was not about a coalition of intersecting identities and the right of a child to an equal education but about the dangers of encroaching communism. Justice Powell, just prior to his nomination for the Supreme Court, had in fact written a memo entitled "Attack on American Free Enterprise System" (known as the Powell Memo) that was not leaked until long after his confirmation, but that usefully highlights his political views regarding corporate interests and the role of the judiciary within a culturally specific era of capitalist anxiety. On the fortieth anniversary of this memo in 2011, the *Richmond Times-Dispatch* celebrated it as having "achieved a near-iconic cachet in many conservative circles." The memo was addressed to Eugene B. Sydnor, Jr., the chairman of the education committee at the U.S. Chamber of Commerce, and the opening line states bluntly: "No thoughtful person can question that the American economic system is under broad attack." In identifying the "Sources of the Attack," Powell listed "the Communists, New Leftists and other revolutionaries who would destroy the entire system" as obvious dangers, but even more troubling to him were those from "perfectly respectable elements of society," such as college campuses, religious organizations, media, arts and literature, and politicians.[18]

Like many prominent members of his era, Powell's anticommunism was deeply ingrained. When Powell served on the Richmond Board of Education earlier in his career, he suggested that a course teaching that "communism requires totalitarian dictatorship" be added to the high school curriculum. Political scientist Paul Sracic has characterized Powell's understanding of democracy as "filtered through the prism of anticommunism," a belief system made visible in the memo. The Powell Memo reflects his fears of left-wing attacks on the economic structure of the United States and specifically his fears that groups would attempt to institutionalize "socialism or some sort of statism (communism or fascism)" in its place.[19] Of particular interest to Powell, as the future self-identified "education justice" on the Court, was the way in which the battle between the free market system and "socialist" ideas would manifest in the realm of education.

Most bewildering to Powell was what he saw as the free enterprise system's toleration, "if not participat[ion] in, its own destruction"—specifically, the way in which campuses generating criticism of the economic system were supported by either tax funds "generated largely from American business" or "contributions from capital funds controlled or generated by American business." His memo reflected the life-or-death mentality of the Cold War in response to the perceived critique of capitalism, arguing that the first need was for businessmen to recognize that the ultimate issue was the "survival" of the free market system. Permeating the memo was the fear of losing power—or of not having it at all. The anticommunist anxieties and free market protectionist sympathies he later brought to bear on his deliberations in *Rodriguez* can be seen in evidence in this earlier political work.

In his deliberations on *Rodriguez*, Powell's ongoing anticommunist worries were made explicit. In his notes preparing for the initial conference on the case with his fellow justices, he immediately began to try to draw a line differentiating *Rodriguez* from *Brown* precisely because he viewed discrimination based on wealth as different from discrimination based on race, and, he wrote, "in a free enterprise society we could hardly hold that wealth is suspect. This is a communist doctrine but is not even accepted (except in a limited sense) in Soviet countries." Race discrimination, therefore, was at least superficially embarrassing for the United States during the Cold War, whereas wealth discrimination and inequality were bedrock Americanism.

In many of his memos and notes on the case, Powell returned to the idea that the ultimate effect of overturning the property tax–based school financing law in Texas would be "national control of education." He stated that he "would abhor such control for all the obvious reasons . . . the irresistible impulse of politicians to manipulate public education for their own power and ideology—e.g. Hitler, Mussolini, and all Communist dictators." The slippery slope Powell saw as inevitable was deeply colored by his assumption that more equal funding sources or federal support for education was tantamount to virtual socialist redistribution and national control.[20]

Powell was not the only one to see the connection between equalizing school funds and anticommunist rhetoric. One amicus brief filed in support of the school district by attorneys general from thirty-one states claimed that "there is little stopping place in plaintiff's logic short of compulsory state-run boarding schools on the early Soviet model." Powell was particularly taken with a brief filed by a group of state government representatives from thirty states (known as the Maryland brief) that had effectively deployed the anticommunist rhetoric of conservative sociologist James Coleman. Indeed, the Maryland brief was cited more than anything else in his voluminous notes and instructions to his clerks on the case, and always with deference and approval.[21]

Coleman was well known for his foreword to the book *Private Wealth and Public Education*, by John E. Coons, William H. Chine II, and Stephen D. Sugarman. This book was the blueprint for many of the school finance lawsuits filed in the 1970s, from *Serrano* in California to *Rodriguez*, but Coleman had done a rapid about-face in his views on school financing and unequal education in the few years since its publication, and his rhetoric against both school finance reform and busing for desegregation proved useful to the opposition to the *Rodriguez* case. The Maryland brief cited heavily Coleman's statements that school finance reform based on *Rodriguez* would be an equivalent exploitation of public schools, as in "Hitler's Germany . . . Stalin's Russia . . . Mao's China and . . . Castro's Cuba." In the representatives' argument, it would lead inexorably toward nationalization, centralization, and statist dictatorship, if not directly to communism or fascism. The brief quoted Coleman's argument that democratic regimes were similar to totalitarian regimes in that they were "more likely to see the schools as instruments of social change than . . . the local government." Coleman argued that the conflicts over school integration in the post-*Brown* era were the perfect illustration of this, "because the national government, pressed by organizations at the national level, attempt[ed] to use the schools to create racial integration which is absent in other aspects of life and thus to bring about a major transformation of the social structure."[22]

But the Maryland brief also reflected the way in which the anticommunist discourse deployed in the case could wrap itself in the language of color blindness and concern for racial minorities, even when they were otherwise signaling to opponents of *Brown* that they sympathized. The authors of the brief studiously avoided mention of race or the race discrimination claim for almost all of the 119 pages, but in their one mention of race they claimed that the ruling was "actually destructive of the interests of urban areas and the interests of minority children." Predicting that school finance reform would lead to higher taxes in urban areas and lower school expenditures for inner-city school districts, they claimed that the *Rodriguez* model would in fact "harm" the high percentage of racial minorities in those districts by limiting their educational opportunities even further. This claim, made by several other opposing parties, as well as Justice Powell in his majority opinion, was largely derived from the Maryland brief and its purported concern for inner-city schools.[23]

Other justices did not appear immune to this argument either, though the documents and notes on the case were preserved only by Powell. A memo by one of Justice Blackmun's clerks during deliberations illustrated the concern that tax-based inequalities in a capitalist country had to be fundamentally consistent with the free market and highlighted the corresponding fear that "equalization of incomes would be a direct outcome of equalization of school property tax bases." Even Gochman, perhaps sensing the importance of the free enterprise logic in the arguments of his opponents, tried to link his clients' claim to the right to education to that idea in his oral argument, stating that "it's important to the free enterprise system, to the individual not to be poor." And Justice White particularly pressed him on the question of alternative kinds of reforms or financing systems that would answer the objections of the claimants "other than simply state control."[24]

A handwritten letter from a member of the public sent to the justices a few days after the opinion in *Rodriguez* was announced argued vehemently against the decision, referring explicitly to the "white upper class" as the winner in the case and reinforcing the Cold War imperative that seemingly unjust judicial decisions might ultimately be used by communists as propaganda tools. At one point the author of the letter stated, "I am just now beginning to understand what the Communist meant when they said that the U.S. has a bourgeois government (a government for the rich). In this case, you certainly have proved it."[25]

While anticommunist sentiments explain some of the motivation in *Rodriguez* to avoid anything that smelled like "equalizing" in education, in recent years we have seen movements, like the Tea Party, that have focused on the Department of Education and tax-based public education funding in particular as "blatantly unconstitutional" and argued for the abolition of "national control" in education with some of the same rhetoric.[26] The idea that inequality is an ultimately necessary—if occasionally sorrowful—by-product of a capitalist economic system has remained prevalent, as has a concern that sharing resources more widely across school district or town lines would be a communistic process of subtraction and mediocrity. But as loud as such voices are now, the pervasiveness of anticommunist politics has often been taken for granted in the mid-twentieth-century United States, so widespread was the sentiment. This contextual analysis offers insight into the insistence of the *Rodriguez* majority to deny the right to education, to clearly separate racial and class identities (and ignore the racial claim as the one with an actual anticommunist subtext), and to shut the door firmly on the idea that wealth or poverty could be treated as a suspect classification for the purposes of equal protection analysis.

RODRIGUEZ AND THE CONTINGENCY OF EQUAL PROTECTION

Rodriguez is a case that comes at a pivotal moment in the broader constitutional development of equal protection analysis in the 1970s. The case had significant impact in each of the three arguments on which it was based. The Court's ruling put an end to the idea that wealth classifications would continue to be treated as constitutionally suspect under certain conditions by firmly rebutting that possibility. It also pulled back on the era of expanding fundamental rights, as the opinion denied fundamental right status to education. And the decision discouraged intersectional claims in favor of formal category arguments rather than arguing that discrimination or inequality might be occurring as a result of both race and class (or race and gender or class and gender, etc.), and made clear that categories would only be considered in isolation from one another. As Kimberlé Crenshaw has said about such intersectional claims, their position "could not be told."[27]

Michael Klarman has argued that modern equal protection analysis has gone through different stages depending on the historical context of the Court. *Rodriguez*, he argues, was the case in which "the door to discovery of new fundamental rights was firmly shut." In the 1973 *Keyes v. School District No. 1* case, the Court's first modern school desegregation case from the North, four Warren Court–era justices (Douglas, Brennan, Stewart, and Marshall) circulated a memorandum suggesting that constitutional violations could be found because of the infringement of the fundamental right to education, sidestepping the de facto/de jure segregation debate entirely. This memo was written in what Klarman describes as the "heady pre-*Rodriguez* days, when it generally was assumed that education, like voting and access to the criminal process, was a fundamental right for equal protection purposes." Indeed, as Klarman argues, the idea that the Burger Court was a "counterrevolution that wasn't" might apply when considering the extension of equal protection to (formal) gender, but the true "counterrevolutionary" accomplishment of the 1970s Court was in foreclosing the chance to address the disparate and intersecting effects of wealth and poverty. By focusing narrowly on formal legislative processes for equal protection claims, as opposed to the Warren Court's interest in egalitarian results as a central concern for protecting equality, the Burger Court "put a halt to [the] redistributive tendencies" of the 1960s decisions.[28]

The suspect classification status for wealth had been encountered in various contexts in previous cases, from poll taxes limiting access to the vote to fees for appellate transcripts for criminal defendants. When courts encountered other suspect classes, for example race or national origin, they literally approached them with suspicion. Unless the government could provide compelling justification, such as national security, for using these suspect categories, legislation containing them was invariably struck down. The alternative and more commonly used standard was the "rational basis" test, in which the government simply had to give a "rational" reason for a court to uphold a law. The two-tiered framework that was in effect tenuously in the middle decades of the twentieth century would give way to a three-tiered framework by the mid-1970s, incorporating an intermediate tier of scrutiny for "semi-suspect classifications" such as gender.

Unfortunately for the *Rodriguez* claimants, their case reached the Supreme Court at a moment when it was unclear whether the binary construction of equal protection analysis would be permanent or the levels of scrutiny would continue to expand. In 1969, the Court stated in *McDonald v. Board of Election Commissioners* that "a careful examination" would occur "where lines are drawn on the basis of wealth or race, two factors which would independently render a classification highly suspect."[29] After *McDonald*, many lower courts simply assumed that the Supreme Court had in fact made wealth a suspect class, particularly where education was involved, given the interpretation of Warren's *Brown* language as a virtual declaration of education as a fundamental right. School funding schemes were the perfect test arena for this assumption. In the years before *Rodriguez,* several state and lower federal courts agreed with claims that local property tax–based school financing violated the Equal Protection Clause by discriminating on the basis of wealth.[30] Ultimately, the majority decision in *Rodriguez* denying suspect class protections to the poor forced litigation efforts to refocus on state constitutions and state equal protection guarantees.

One way to understand the deep and complicated connections between racial segregation and economic inequality in a case like *Rodriguez* is through the critique of "formal race" equal protection analysis Gotanda offers. Gotanda argues that the stumbling block in applying substantive equal protection is the Court's treatment of the range of contexts in which racial subordination can occur—employment, housing, education, and the like—as "isolated phenomena" rather than "aspects of the broader, more complex phenomenon called race." This method of analysis both limits the ability of the government to address correlations and connections between purportedly separate problems as well as ignores what Gotanda calls "historical-race and the cumulative disadvantages that are the starting point for so many Black citizens." Indeed, Gotanda points to the "spectrum" approach suggested by Justice Marshall's dissent in *Rodriguez* as an illustration of the problem of the strict-scrutiny-or-nothing equal protection analysis applied by the *Rodriguez* majority.

The argument that education was a fundamental interest implicated in the school financing system, and implicitly guaranteed by the Constitution, was clearly the most difficult decision for the Court majority, and for Powell himself. If a law impinged on a fundamental right, it could be overturned even if no suspect class was involved. The Court had repeatedly held that such actions as forced sterilization, refusal to allow citizens to travel between states, or even prohibitively high filing fees for marriage or divorce imposed intolerable burdens on these fundamental rights, even if there was no relationship to a suspect category such as race or national origin.[31] In *Brown,* there seemed to be strong dicta supporting the assumption that education was a fundamental right, especially given its importance for the exercise of other explicit constitutional rights such as freedom of speech or implied rights such as the right to vote. But in *Rodriguez,* the majority and dissent were in deep disagreement over whether education was a fundamental right.

Part of the dilemma may be that the narrative of the Rodriguez family and their fellow claimants was always bigger than isolating any one of the three claims. They were experiencing unequal resources because of their low-income neighborhood, because of their race, and the indignity was heightened because it was occurring in the realm of public education. Put together, these three arguments seem to strongly suggest that they were not receiving the "equal protection of the laws." Kenneth Karst argues that one explanation for the divergent ideas of equal protection analysis in the majority and dissent in *Rodriguez* is the difference between a "redundant" fundamental interest framework from the majority and the broader principle of equal citizenship that seems to underlie the dissent. This ideal of equal citizenship would potentially address substantive inequalities that result from race and poverty by acknowledging their corresponding stigmas, particularly with regard to the "close connection between education and the political participation that is at the heart of citizenship." Just four years after *Rodriguez*, Karst summed up the decision's impact on the jurisprudential development of the Court, saying, "If *Rodriguez* was an attempt to impose order on equal protection doctrine, the attempt failed."[32]

The discussions between Powell and his clerks highlight the way in which equal protection "order" was still being imposed by the Court, one decision at a time. Larry Hammond, one of Powell's law clerks who worked most closely with him in formulating the final opinion in *Rodriguez,* and who also repeatedly expressed reservations about the direction of the opinion (he initially wanted to affirm the lower court ruling), wrote the justice a handwritten thank-you note dated the day the ruling was announced. In it was a foreboding note of warning about the legacy of the decision. Hammond said that if the Court continued to utilize the "two-level doctrine" of equal protection jurisprudence in the *Rodriguez* opinion, "our case can be defended fairly as respect for 'law.'" With foresight, he then wrote that otherwise, "if the C[our]t departs from this approach in the near future[,] this case will look like a result-oriented political judgment by [five] men." Hammond ended his letter by saying, "I have great confidence in the future course of *your* judgment in this area, but less in the course others may pursue." In fact, an intermediate tier of scrutiny was developed by the Court just a few years after *Rodriguez,* and in another decade something looking a little like the "sliding-scale" framework of equal protection jurisprudence put forward by Marshall seemed to have taken hold. Hammond's warning that the two-level doctrinal basis provided for the *Rodriguez* ruling would only be defensible if the two levels remained static and unchanging proved prescient.[33]

One of the other lingering questions in the case that was raised at oral argument and in the majority opinion as well was what would happen if children were actually denied an education. If they did not have a right to it, did that mean they could have it denied completely? Powell struggled with whether this would be different enough from a simply unequal education so as to warrant a different level of constitutional scrutiny, but by the time the Court confronted just such a case, in *Plyler v. Doe* in 1982, he had decided that he didn't want the *Rodriguez* principle he had authored to be used to justify complete exclusion from education. When the case reached the Court, Powell pushed for a heightened level of equal protection scrutiny based on the fact that the class at issue was composed of what he called "innocent children," though he never mentioned that the *Rodriguez* complainants were certainly indistinguishable in their innocence. Though his innocent children class was not the basis for the Court's ultimate overturning of the Texas law forbidding public education funds to the children of undocumented immigrants, it is telling that he tried to find a way to differentiate the case from his reasoning in *Rodriguez* while avoiding the question of race. In order to obtain a slim majority in *Plyler,* the majority had to backtrack from directly holding education as a fundamental right subject to equal protection analysis, though there is evidence in Brennan's draft opinion that four justices were ready to explicitly declare education a fundamental constitutional right. Powell, the holdout, refused to overrule his decision in *Rodriguez,* which he viewed as one of the most important in his time on the bench.[34]

CONCLUSION

In deliberations of *San Antonio Independent School District v. Rodriguez,* the *intersecting* claims of race and class discrimination within the right to education went largely unexamined by most of the amici and many of the justices. *Rodriguez* presented the Court with a dilemma of unequal and largely segregated education that asked for a different kind of response than some of the other education cases (i.e., the *Rodriguez* family was not asking to attend the Alamo Heights schools) but that targeted many of the same core concerns and dilemmas raised by *Brown* as well as other education and equal protection cases of the civil rights era. *Rodriguez* asked whether wealth could be claimed as an invalid basis for inequality in a Cold War–era capitalist nation, whether the intersection of race and class could be heard by a Court embedded in the formally isolated categories of its own equal protection jurisprudence, and whether education would be treated as a fundamental right if doing so would cause profound changes in the mechanisms of local school funding and control. Part of the legacy of *Rodriguez* is that a child's experience of injustice in education may not be able to be told if it spans multiple identities and intersecting forms of inequality. But as Mario Obledo, director of the Mexican American Legal Defense and Educational Fund for San Antonio, testified before the Senate prior to the case, "To a school child, segregation is segregation, irrespective of how it is labeled by the courts."[35]

FOUR

Rodriguez Past, Present, and Future

MICHAEL A. REBELL

THE FORTIETH ANNIVERSARY of the U.S. Supreme Court's ruling, by a close 5-4 vote, that education is not a "fundamental interest" under the U.S. Constitution in *San Antonio Independent School District v. Rodriguez* provides a fitting occasion to reconsider with the benefit of hindsight the decision's validity and its long-term significance.[1] It is now clear that *Rodriguez* was wrongly decided; that the decision nevertheless did not totally impede progress toward overcoming inequities in the funding of public education or preclude substantial judicial contributions toward this progress; that if American education is to meet its formidable future challenges, the decision must ultimately be reconsidered; and that a clear federal right to meaningful education must be articulated by the Supreme Court and enforced by the Congress.

RODRIGUEZ WAS WRONGLY DECIDED

In *Rodriguez,* the Supreme Court, despite acknowledging its gross inequities, upheld Texas's system for financing public education, deeming local control of education a sufficiently rational justification for its continuance. The majority refused to grant the more probing strict scrutiny status to the plaintiffs' claims for two reasons: low-income families and residents of property-poor school districts do not constitute a "suspect class," and education is not a "fundamental interest" under the federal constitution. The Court's reasoning on the latter point was especially unpersuasive. Justice Lewis Powell wrote, "Nothing this Court holds today in any way detracts from our historic dedication to public education. We are in complete agreement with the conclusion of the three-judge panel below that 'the grave significance of education both to the individual and to our society' cannot be doubted. But the importance of a service performed by the State does not determine whether it must be regarded as fundamental for purposes of examination under the Equal Protection Clause."[2]

This explanation for rejecting "the importance of a service performed by the State" as a major consideration in whether the matter should be considered a "fundamental interest" was not convincing, especially in light of the precedent on this point that had been established in 1969 in *Shapiro v. Thompson*. There, the Court held that interstate travel constituted a fundamental interest, despite the fact that the Constitution contains no explicit textual reference to interstate travel. Nevertheless, it discounted the lack of textual reference because "in moving from State to State . . . appellees were exercising a constitutional right, and any classification which serves to penalize the exercise of that right, unless shown to be necessary to promote a compelling governmental interest, is unconstitutional."[3]

Justice Thurgood Marshall, in his strong dissent, stressed the importance of education for exercising First Amendment rights "both as a source and as a receiver of information and ideas" and the importance of education for exercising the constitutional right to vote. He argued that if a right to travel can be considered fundamental because of its nexus to the constitutional concepts of "federalism" and "personal liberty," the critical role of education for the exercise of the constitutional rights to free speech, voting, and assembly would seem at least as compelling.

To bolster the feebleness of its primary holding that the importance of a right and its nexus to constitutional text are not determinative of fundamental interest status, the majority decision also expressed a concern that designating education as a fundamental interest might create a "slippery slope" that would require extending similar favored treatment to other important social policy areas like welfare or housing. But designating education a fundamental interest does not necessarily require granting similar status to all or any other social services. There are reasonable bases for distinguishing education from other services; indeed, the Court itself stated in 1954 in *Brown v. Board of Education* that "today, education is perhaps the most important function of state and local governments. . . . In these days, it is doubtful that any child may reasonably be expected to succeed in life if he is denied the opportunity for an education."[4] This is a powerful statement which does indicate that education holds a priority status among the various services government provides.[5]   *Brown precedent*

Ironically, almost a decade after *Rodriguez*, the Court did make such a distinction among social services when it applied "intermediate" scrutiny status, which previously had been used only in gender and illegitimacy cases, to education in *Plyler v. Doe* in 1982. In invalidating the denial of educational opportunity to undocumented immigrant children, the Court held that education is not "merely some governmental 'benefit' indistinguishable from other forms of social welfare legislation. Both the importance of education in maintaining our basic institutions, and the lasting impact of its deprivation on the life of the child, mark the distinction."[6]

In addition to its stated fear of creating a slippery slope precedent, the Court in *Rodriguez* was also affected by a concern that educational policy issues were not judicially manageable:

> This case also involves the most persistent and difficult questions of educational policy, another area in which this Court's lack of specialized knowledge and experience counsels against premature interference with the informed judgments made at the state and local levels. Education, perhaps even more than welfare assistance, presents a myriad of "intractable economic, social, and even philosophical problems." . . . On even the most basic questions in this area the scholars and educational experts are divided. Indeed, one of the major sources of controversy concerns the extent to which there is a demonstrable correlation between educational expenditures and the quality of education—an assumed correlation underlying virtually every legal conclusion drawn by the District Court in this case.

The Supreme Court's assumption that educational policy issues like inequities in funding are beyond the scope of judicial competence has, however, been belied by the actual experience of the state courts that have handled a myriad of fiscal equity and education adequacy cases over the last forty years. After the Supreme Court closed the gates to the federal courts for fiscal equity litigants, plaintiffs seeking to pursue these issues brought them to the state courts. Such litigations have now been pursued in forty-five states, and, contrary to the U.S. Supreme Court's assumptions, many of the state courts have deftly managed the policy issues in these cases.[7] On some issues, rather than "handicapping . . . continued research and experimentation," the state courts' involvement has actually enhanced the ability of educational scholars and policy makers to deal with the "intractable economic, social, and even philosophical problems" that fiscal equity and other educational policy issues sometimes raise.

PROGRESS TOWARD FISCAL EQUITY AND EDUCATION ADEQUACY IN THE STATE COURTS

Since most state courts lack a tradition of extensive constitutional litigation on public policy issues, the state forums are "long shots for plaintiffs challenging discrimination in school finance systems."[8] Surprisingly, however, most state courts have acted decisively to uphold constitutional claims in this area. Shortly after the Supreme Court issued its decision in *Rodriguez,* the California Supreme Court reconsidered in 1976 an earlier ruling that had invalidated the state's education finance system based on its interpretation of federal law, holding that even if education was not a fundamental right under the federal constitution, it had that status under California's constitution.[9] At about the same time, courts in New Jersey, Connecticut, and West Virginia also declared their state education finance systems unconstitutional.[10]

Difficulties in actually achieving equal educational opportunity at the remedy stage in these initial cases, however, seem to have made other state courts less inclined to uphold these claims.[11] Accordingly, at the end of the 1980s, civil rights lawyers changed their focus from equal protection claims based on disparities in the level of educational funding among school districts to claims based on opportunities for a basic level of education guaranteed by the specific provisions in the state constitutions. The education clauses of almost all of the state constitutions contain language that requires the state to provide students some substantive level of basic education. The specific language used to convey this concept includes calls for establishing an "adequate" education, a "sound basic education," a "thorough and efficient" education, or a "basic system of free quality public elementary and secondary schools."[12]

Most of these provisions were incorporated into the state constitutions as part of the common school movement of the mid–nineteenth century, which created statewide systems for public education and attempted to inculcate democratic values by bringing together under one roof students from all classes and all ethnic backgrounds. Some of them, especially in the New England states, date back to eighteenth-century revolutionary ideals of creating a new republican citizenry that would "cherish the interests of literature and science," an archaic phrase that the Massachusetts Supreme Judicial Court has interpreted to require the provision of "an adequate education."[13]

Although the state constitutions use different language to connote this concept of a substantive basic education, there is broad consensus among the courts that have applied these concepts as to its core meaning. Virtually all of the courts that have defined their constitutional language have agreed that a basic education which meets contemporary needs is one which ensures that a student is equipped to function capably as a citizen and to compete effectively in the global labor market. For example, the New Jersey Supreme Court defined the constitutional requirement as "that educational opportunity which is needed in the contemporary setting to equip a child for his role as a citizen and as a competitor in the labor market," and the New York Court of Appeals described a "sound basic education" in terms of preparing students to "function productively as civic participants capable of voting and serving on a jury . . . capably and knowledgeably" and as including "the ability to obtain competitive employment."[14]

In these cases, courts focused on the substance of the education students were actually receiving in the classroom rather than on the more abstract consideration of comparative levels of school district funding at issue in the equity cases. The evidence in the education clause cases graphically exposed the flagrant lack of opportunity that the educational systems in most of the states continued to impose on millions of poor and minority students decades after the Supreme Court's decision in *Brown*, and the judges responded accordingly. For example, in 2000 many high schools in California's low-income and minority communities did not offer the curriculum students needed just *to apply* to the state's public universities.[15] Similarly, passing an examination in a laboratory science course was required for high school graduation in New York State in 2003, but at the time thirty-one New York City high schools had no science labs.[16]

In addition to the persuasive power of the evidence of distressing educational inadequacy that has been revealed in the record of these cases, another major reason for plaintiffs' victories was the emergence of the standards-based education reform movement at about the same time. These reforms responded to a series of major commission reports in the 1980s that warned of a "rising tide of mediocrity" in American education.[17] These led to a major effort by the federal government to articulate specific national academic goals. Continued focus on the need for educational reforms geared to specific goals led in 2001 to enactment of the No Child Left Behind Act (NCLB).[18] NCLB and the applicable federal regulations call for the development of standards at the state rather than the national level, and the state standards-based reform movement has, in recent years, become the primary arena for these reform initiatives.

Standards-based reform put into focus the fundamental goals and purposes of our system of public education. It reinforced the courts' orientation to probe the intent of the eighteenth- and nineteenth-century drafters of the state constitutional clauses that established public education systems and to evaluate the contemporary significance of these provisions. In addition, the new state standards provided the courts practical tools for developing judicially manageable approaches for dealing with complex educational issues and implementing effective remedies and offered judges workable criteria for crafting practical remedies in these litigations.

In most of these litigations, the question of whether "money matters"—one of the "persistent and difficult" educational policy issues that, according to the Supreme Court in *Rodriguez*, courts were incapable of addressing properly—has been a central legal issue that the state courts have extensively considered. Economist Eric Hanushek argues that "key resources—ones that are the subject of much policy attention—are not consistently or systematically related to improved student performance."[19] His position initially centered on his analyses of thirty-eight primary studies of the relationship between teacher-student ratios, teacher education, teacher experience, salary, and other such inputs, with outcomes mostly based on standardized test scores but that also included some instances of drop-out rates, college continuation, student attitudes, and other factors.

Hanushek's approach has been widely challenged as being misleading because it does "not adequately address serious questions of causation" and because it does "not adequately [account] for across-district variations" in the costs of educational services such as teacher salaries and "in the proportion of students with special needs, who require additional, more costly services."[20] The production function approach Hanushek uses has also been criticized for being too dependent on standardized test scores.[21]

Hanushek's methodology was closely scrutinized by a group of University of Chicago researchers who used more precise decision rules for conducting a comprehensive meta-analysis. The group concluded that nine of his studies were inappropriate and that thirty-one other studies should have been included.[22] Analyzing this larger universe, they concluded that "a broad range of school inputs are positively related to student outcomes, and . . . that moderate increases in spending may be associated with significant increases in achievement."[23] More recent studies concur with the view that increased educational expenditures can lead to positive student outcomes.[24]

Contrary to the Supreme Court's expectation, the courts have proved quite adept in dealing with the "does money matter?" issue. They have received extensive evidence on the relationship between the availability of adequate resources and educational outcomes and have had little difficulty in assessing the core social science and policy issues involved. For example, in the 2005 *Montoy v. State of Kansas* litigation, more than half a dozen experts on both sides of the issue presented detailed testimony on whether money matters. After summarizing its findings regarding the detailed testimony, the Court concluded that it "was persuaded . . . by the evidence that there is a causal connection between the poor performance of the vulnerable and/or protected categories of Kansas students and the low funding provided their schools."[25]

Overall, the issue of whether money matters in education was directly considered as of 2007 by the state courts in thirty of these cases.[26] In twenty-nine of them, the courts determined that money does indeed matter.[27] At this point, the extensive debate in the academic literature and the slew of evidence submitted in numerous fiscal equity and educational adequacy cases seems to have resulted in a virtual consensus that, of course, money matters—if it is spent well. As Hanushek himself has now acknowledged, "Money spent wisely, logically, and with accountability would be very useful indeed."[28] The courts' rulings on this issue are very much aligned with the thinking of most experts in the field; and, in fact, some of the leading social scientists have indicated that the judicial process has clarified and advanced scholarly understanding of the issue.[29]

RECONSIDERING *RODRIGUEZ*

Despite *Rodriguez*'s closing of the federal courts to fiscal equity and educational adequacy litigations in 1973, progress has been made toward overcoming inequities in the funding of public education in the decades since because of the willingness of many state courts to pick up the mantle. There is much to be learned from the extensive experiment in state court constitutionalism.

The vitality and the range of doctrinal development and remedial experimentation involved in the scores of cases that have been litigated in forty-five states over this time period constitute a remarkable illustration of the workings of the "laboratory" of the states that Justice Louis Brandeis saw as a major asset of our federal system.[30] The experience of the state courts with fiscal equity and educational adequacy litigations over the past forty years demonstrates that judicial intervention can effectively promote equity and adequacy in education; that there are judicially manageable standards for courts to use in this regard; and that courts can appropriately and competently deal with the complex social science and educational policy issues involved in this enterprise.

It also is clear that there are limits to what can be accomplished through state-by-state litigation. In twenty-six states, courts have issued rulings that have attempted to promote meaningful educational opportunities, especially for low-income and minority students, while courts in nineteen other states have refused to accept jurisdiction or have otherwise found for the defendants, and in four other states no litigations have been initiated.[31] The courts' intervention in education finance matters has resulted in significant increases in both the adequacy of educational funding and the equity of resource distributions in many states.[32] In other instances, though, strong resistance from the governor and/or the legislature has delayed or impeded mandated reforms.[33]

Although the remedies issued by the states where the plaintiffs have prevailed have often resulted in increased equity and improvements in educational opportunities and educational achievement, the viability and the long-term sustainability of these reforms are sometimes tempered by the reality that rights declared by state courts do not have the power and the sustained impact of a federal constitutional right. As Jonathan Kozol has put it, "No matter what the state in which a case takes place, the most important disadvantage advocates for equal education or for adequate education have to face is that attorneys are unable to incorporate within their pleadings claims deriving from the U.S. Constitution—the only constitution that has truly elevated moral standing in the eyes of most Americans—and cannot, as a consequence, defend the rights of children in these cases *as Americans*."[34] Ultimately, then, *Rodriguez* does need to be reconsidered, because providing meaningful educational opportunities to all American children and realizing the national goal of preparing students to function productively as civic participants who can compete in the global economy in the twenty-first century simply cannot be accomplished on a state-by-state basis.

The fact is that despite forty years of state court litigation and twenty-five years of state standards-based reforms, there still is, in the words of the National Commission on Equity and Excellence in Education, "a broken system of education funding in America."[35] The commission, a twenty-five-member federal advisory committee chartered by Congress, described that "broken system":

> With few exceptions, states continue to finance public education through methods that have no demonstrable link to the cost of delivering rigorous academic standards and that can produce high achievement in all students, including but not limited to low-income students, English language learners, students with disabilities, students in high poverty and students who live in remote schools and districts. Few states have rationally determined the cost of enabling all students to achieve established content and performance standards . . . Most states do not properly ensure the efficient use of resources to attain high achievement for all students.[36]

America's failure to solve the school funding problems highlighted by *Rodriguez* and the inadequate levels of educational opportunity offered by many states and school districts have even greater negative consequences today than they did forty years ago. In the words of the commission,

> While some young Americans—most of them white and affluent—are getting a truly world-class education, those who attended schools in high poverty neighborhoods are getting an education that more closely approximates school in developing nations . . . With the highest poverty rate in the developed

world, and amplified by the inadequate education received by many children in low-income schools, the United States is threatening its own future . . . High levels of education are key to self-reliance and economic security in a world where education matters more than ever for the success of societies as well as individuals.

But American schools must do more than ensure our future economic prosperity; they must foster the nation's civic culture . . . So much depends on fulfilling this mission: the shared ideals that enable our governmental system to hold together even in the face of factious political disagreements; the strength of our diversity; the domestic tranquility that our Constitution promises; and the ability to maintain the influence—as example and power—that America has long projected to the world. We neglect these expectations at our peril.[37]

To deal with these consequential problems, the commission recommended "bold action by the states—and the federal government—to redesign and reform the funding of our nation's public schools."[38] The report presented a detailed set of proposals to accomplish this task. Among them was a call for all the states to

- Identify and publicly report the teaching staff, programs, and services needed to provide a meaningful educational opportunity to all students of every race and income level;
- Determine and report the actual cost of resources identified as needed to provide all students a meaningful educational opportunity based on the efficient and cost-effective use of resources;
- Adopt and implement a school finance system that will provide equitable and sufficient funding for all students to achieve state content and performance standards;
- Ensure that their respective finance systems are supported by stable and predictable sources of revenue; and
- Develop systems to ensure that districts and schools effectively and efficiently use all education funding to enable students to achieve content and performance standards.[39]

The blunt reality is that although states and local school districts can continue to play a useful, complementary role in implementing educational policy, in the twenty-first century the achievement of both equity and excellence can only be realized through significant and sustained initiatives like the ones that the commission has recommended. As the title of the commission's report, "For Each and Every Child," suggests, the "bold action" it recommends is based on an implied federal right of every American child to a "meaningful educational opportunity."[40] Therefore, the commission also called for strong action by the federal government to prod the states to adopt necessary reforms.[41]

STANDARDS-BASED REFORM AND other policy initiatives at the state level have already largely eviscerated the system of local school district control that the Supreme Court extolled in *Rodriguez*. The implementation of NCLB, the Individuals with Disabilities Education Act (IDEA), and Race to the Top (RTTT) statutes over the past decade has caused the federal government to become heavily involved in directing educational policy and overseeing its implementation at both the state and local levels. Congress and the courts now need to convert what is, in essence, an *implied*, federal right to meaningful educational opportunity into a clear declaration that the U.S. Constitution recognizes and requires enforcement of a right to a meaningful educational opportunity for all American children.

Acknowledgment by Congress and/or the courts that there is indeed a right to education under the U.S. Constitution will focus attention on the vast inequities and inadequacies in our national education system and galvanize action, at both the federal and state level, to overcome them, along the lines of the commission's recommendations. As Susan Bitensky put it,

> Were education to be recognized as an affirmative right under the Constitution . . . besides acting as an agent of moral suasion, the right would also have the singular effect of making the federal government the ultimate guarantor of education for school-age children holding the right . . . Reform efforts could be freed from the hobbling strictures of state and local governments' piecemeal and often resource poor responses, as the federal government would bring its uniquely national perspective, powers, and resources to bear upon what has become, in scope and consequence, a truly national problem. Recognition of the right would work the kind of systemic change without which progress in ameliorating the crisis may be needlessly retarded or altogether frustrated.[42]

Congress has not taken steps to seriously consider the Equity and Excellence Commission's recommendations; and given its current partisan impasses, it is unlikely to do so for the foreseeable future. Is it at all realistic to look to the courts? Although the last forty years of state litigation in this area have demonstrated the need for, and the feasibility of, such a right to education, the strong precedent of the 1973 *Rodriguez* decision would seem to present an insuperable obstacle to re-raising this issue at the national level. If the more liberally oriented justices on the Court in 1973 were unwilling to declare the existence of a federal right to education, is there any plausible possibility that the more conservative justices today would consider reversing the long-established *Rodriguez* precedent?

I argue that the *Rodriguez* decision does not preclude a reconsideration of the need for a national right to meaningful educational opportunity and that the current Supreme Court need not reverse the 1973 decision in order to declare the existence of such a right. The basis for articulating a federal right to meaningful education opportunity is actually already embedded in the majority decision in *Rodriguez*. While the Court found that funding inequities at issue in that case did not rise to fundamental interest status, it *did not* find that strict scrutiny was inappropriate for *all* education claims. It specifically left open the possibility that students who were deprived of an education sufficient to prepare them to be capable voters and to exercise their First Amendment rights might have a valid federal constitutional entitlement to strict scrutiny review.

The Court raised this issue while noting that the plaintiffs in *Rodriguez* had presented no evidence that indicated that any students were receiving an inadequate education: "The State repeatedly asserted in its briefs . . . that it now assures 'every child in every school district an adequate education.' No proof was offered at trial persuasively discrediting or refuting the State's assertion."[43] Furthermore, in 1986 in *Papasan v. Allain*, the Supreme Court specifically stated that it still had not "definitively settled the questions whether a minimally adequate education is a fundamental right and whether a statute alleged to infringe that right should be accorded heightened equal protection review."[44] In fact, Chief Justice Warren Burger, who had joined the majority in *Rodriguez*, years later, when he was off the bench, stated that he believed that there is a right to education suffusing the Constitution as a whole.[45]

The adequacy issue was not raised in *Rodriguez* because the plaintiffs there solely focused on the dollar disparities in funding between school districts.

As discussed in the previous section, over the past four decades since the *Rodriguez* decision was issued, the adequacy issue has been extensively litigated in the state courts, and the vast majority of these courts have found that large numbers of children throughout the country are being denied the opportunity for an adequate education. A hypothetical current case involving the denial of meaningful educational opportunity to students from low-income households could bring to the Court's attention the strong evidence of educational inadequacy that plaintiffs developed in many of the state adequacy cases, thereby presenting persuasive evidentiary justification for the adequacy claim that was lacking in *Rodriguez*. Virtually all state courts that have considered this kind of evidence have found that their respective educational systems are depriving poor and minority students of adequate educational opportunities.[46] The virtual unanimity of state court findings in this regard is itself a strong indication of a pervasive national problem of educational inadequacy of which the U.S. Supreme Court should take note.

In *Rodriguez* the justices engaged in a substantial colloquy that highlighted the kinds of essential knowledge and skills that the Court would likely consider to be most relevant in this regard. The Court's consideration of the relationship between fundamental interests protected by the federal constitution and an adequate education began with Justice Marshall's strong insistence in his dissent on the importance of education for the functioning of our constitutional democracy. In particular, Marshall emphasized the importance of education for exercising First Amendment rights, "both as a source and as a receiver of information and ideas," and the importance of education for exercising the constitutional right to vote.

Justice Powell, writing for the majority, accepted Justice Marshall's basic perspective. Summarizing the dissenters' arguments on this point, he stated, "Specifically, they insist that education is itself a fundamental personal right because it is essential to the effective exercise of First Amendment freedoms and to intelligent utilization of the right to vote. . . . A similar line of reasoning is pursued with respect to the right to vote. . . . The electoral process, if reality is to conform to the democratic ideal, depends on an informed electorate: a voter cannot cast his ballot intelligently unless his reading skills and thought processes have been adequately developed." He then indicated that he had no disagreement with this perspective, stating, "We need not dispute any of these propositions" because the plaintiffs, who had focused on the funding inequity issues, had not presented any evidence that any students were not receiving such an adequate education.

> Even if it were conceded that some identifiable quantum of education is a constitutionally protected prerequisite to the meaningful exercise of either right, we have no indication that the present levels of educational expenditures in Texas provide an education that falls short. Whatever merit appellees' argument might have if a State's financing system occasioned an absolute denial of educational opportunities to any of its children, that argument provides no basis for finding an interference with fundamental rights where only relative differences in spending levels are involved and where—as is true in the present case—no charge fairly could be made that the system fails to provide each child with an opportunity to acquire the basic minimal skills necessary for the enjoyment of the rights of speech and of full participation in the political process.[47]

In short, a minimally adequate education for federal constitutional purposes appears to be one that provides students with the essential skills that they will need for "full participation in the political process." Specifically, this means the "reading skills and thought processes" needed for political discourse and debate and to exercise intelligent use of the franchise and of the right to vote.[48] Given the strong emphasis on the importance of voting rights articulated by the *Rodriguez* Court (and in a host of major Supreme Court pronouncements before and since that decision[49]), evidence that states currently are not, in fact, providing many low income and minority students with the educational opportunities they need to exercise the franchise intelligently would be compelling.

Should the U.S. Supreme Court reconsider the adequate education issue left open by *Rodriguez*, it would need to review closely the particular skills that students need to function capably as citizens in a democratic society. The importance of developing such skills was at the heart of the constitutional requirements for an adequate education that many of the state courts articulated in the state adequacy cases. A probing examination of this issue was undertaken in New York in 2001 by the trial court in *Campaign for Fiscal Equity, Inc. v. State* (*CFE*), which considered in detail students' preparation to function as capable citizens, during the extensive seven-month trial that was held in that case.[50] In the *CFE* trial, Justice Leland DeGrasse first instructed the parties to have their expert witnesses analyze a charter referendum proposal that was then on the ballot in New York City. The specific question posed was whether graduates of New York high schools would have the skills needed to comprehend that document. The attorneys for the parties were also asked to have their witnesses undertake similar analyses of the judge's charges to the jury and of certain documents put into evidence in two complex civil cases that had recently been tried in state and federal courts.

Plaintiffs' witnesses closely reviewed the charter revision proposal and identified the specific reading and analytical skills that an individual would need in order to understand that document. They then related these skills to the standards for English language arts, social studies, mathematics, and sciences set forth in the Regents' learning standards recently adopted by New York State. They also described the types of skills a juror would need to comprehend and apply concepts like "the preponderance of the evidence" and to understand economic concepts like "opportunity costs" and scientific studies and showed how the skills needed to comprehend these ideas were also cultivated by the Regents' learning standards.

The defendants introduced polling data showing that the vast majority of American voters obtain their information from radio and television news and make up their minds on how to vote for candidates and propositions before they enter the voting booth. Their implicit argument was that since most voters do not actually read complex ballot propositions, they need not possess the level of skill necessary to comprehend such documents. They also claimed that dialogue among members of the jury could substitute for a lack of understanding of particular points by some of the individual jurors.

Overall, the implied premise of the defendants' position was that citizens do not actually need to function at a high skill level and do not need to be capable of comprehending complex written material as long as the subjects dealt with in the material are regularly discussed in the mass media or as long as they can obtain assistance from other citizens in carrying out their civic responsibilities. Justice DeGrasse's decision resoundingly rejected this position.

An engaged, capable voter needs the intellectual tools to evaluate complex issues, such as campaign finance reform, tax policy, and global warming, to name only a few. Ballot propositions in New York City, such as the charter reform proposal that was on the ballot in November 1999, can require a close reading and a familiarity with the structure of local government.

Similarly, a capable and productive citizen doesn't simply show up for jury service. Rather she is capable of serving impartially on trials that may require learning unfamiliar facts and concepts and new ways to communicate and reach decisions with her fellow jurors . . . jurors may be called on to decide complex matters that require the verbal, reasoning, math, science, and socialization skills that should be imparted in public schools. Jurors today must determine questions of fact concerning DNA evidence, statistical analyses, and convoluted financial fraud, to name only three topics.[51]

The analysis undertaken by state courts in New York and elsewhere regarding the level of skills citizens need to exercise their civic responsibilities and constitutional rights is important. Although society may have accepted unreflectively a wide gap between its democratic ideal and the actual functioning level of its citizens in the past, now that the issue has come to the fore, its implications cannot be avoided. Our society cannot knowingly perpetuate a state of affairs in which voters cannot comprehend the ballot materials about which they are voting and in which jurors cannot understand legal instructions or major evidentiary submissions in the cases they are deciding. In order to function productively in today's complex world, citizens need a broad range of cognitive skills that will allow them to function capably and knowledgeably, not only as voters and jurors but also in petitioning their representatives, asserting their rights as individuals, and otherwise taking part in the broad range of interchanges and relationships involved in the concept of civic engagement.

At the present time, large numbers of low-income and minority students in most states are either dropping out of school or leaving school without achieving minimal proficiency levels in reading, mathematics, and other areas necessary to function as capable citizens. Accordingly, should the U.S. Supreme Court agree to consider these issues, a strong case can be made that the actual skills that these students have acquired by the time they leave school are far short of the citizenship skills they need to be capable voters and civic participants.

ADVANCING A FEDERAL RIGHT TO EDUCATION

In the years since *Rodriguez* was decided, many scholars have put forward a variety of legal arguments for why the decision should be reconsidered and a federal right to education upheld.[52] Recent works by Goodwin Liu and Akhil

Reed Amar have set forth particularly cogent legal rationales for the contemporary declaration of such a right.[53] Their insights bolster the reading of *Rodriguez* set forth in the previous section.

Both Liu and Amar argue convincingly that the drafters of the Fourteenth Amendment did understand that they were creating new substantive national rights when they declared in the first two clauses of the amendment that "all persons born or naturalized in the United States are citizens of the United States" and that all of them are entitled to the "privileges and immunities" of the United States. Some, but far from all, of those legislators who voted for the amendment did think at the time that it encompassed a federal right to education. The evolution of the importance of education in the twentieth and twenty-first centuries, as reflected both in the apparent assumption of the general public that such a right already exists and by the Supreme Court's acknowledgment of the preeminent role of education in contemporary society in *Brown* and other cases, means that a federal right to education currently does implicitly exist as a part of the country's "unwritten constitution." What is needed at this point is for the Supreme Court and/or Congress to articulate that fact explicitly and act on it.

In an important article published in 2006, Liu closely examines the history of the enactment of the Fourteenth Amendment and concludes that, properly understood, the amendment "authorizes and obligates Congress to ensure a meaningful floor of educational opportunity." According to Liu, beyond granting legal status to newly freed blacks, the citizenship clause established a national political community and made allegiance to it the primary aspect of our political identity. Congress has an affirmative duty under Section 5 of the Fourteenth Amendment to enforce national citizenship rights. Although education was not widely regarded as among the fundamental rights of citizenship at the time, the "framers understood that citizenship was an evolving concept."[54]

Liu describes in detail the efforts of members of Congress from 1870 to 1890 "to effectuate the guarantee of national citizenship through ambitious efforts to provide funding, leadership and support for public education." These efforts included the establishment of the Freedmen's Bureau to promote education and other welfare measures for the newly freed black citizens and the federal Department of Education. Three members of Congress, George Hoar, LeGrand Perce, and Henry Blair, introduced major pieces of federal legislation to promote public education. The Hoar bill looked to establish a "thorough and efficient system of public education throughout the whole country," with each state required to provide all children ages six to eighteen with "suitable instruction" in reading, writing, arithmetic, American history, and other subjects and the president authorized to determine whether each state had established "a system of common schools which provides reasonably for all children therein."[55] The Perce and Blair bills, respectively, aimed to provide substantial federal funding for education and congressional oversight to ensure that all students had an education sufficient to prepare them to be effective citizens.

The major rationale for these bills was similar to Thurgood Marshall's justification for urging that education be considered a fundamental constitutional interest in *Rodriguez:* "If every man is to vote, government must ensure the capacity for the exercise of that share in the government."[56] Although they received substantial congressional support, none of these bills were enacted into law, primarily because of states' rights objections to the potential federal or federally funded schools. After the Civil War, the Department of Education was downgraded to a bureau housed in the Department of the Interior and given a greatly reduced budget. And after the Supreme Court issued rulings in the *Slaughterhouse Cases* in 1872 and the *Civil Rights Cases* in 1883, which substantially narrowed the scope of the national citizenship and privileges and immunity clauses, efforts to promote a significant role for the federal government in public education markedly declined.[57] Over the last 150 years, however, the Supreme Court's rulings in the *Slaughterhouse* and *Civil Rights Cases* have been substantially discredited, and the federal government has taken on a major role in funding schools and in influencing educational policy nationwide through the Elementary and Secondary Education Act, including NCLB, IDEA, RTTT, and other such statutes. Yet, federal efforts to date have not proved effective in ensuring equity and excellence, because in the absence of recognition of a federal right to education, federal forays into the educational policy arena have been incoherent, irregular, and incomplete.

Amar, in a recent analysis of America's "unwritten constitution," sets forth a strong argument that the privileges and immunities clause of the Fourteenth Amendment, together with the retention of the rights "by the people" in the Ninth Amendment, open the door for the assertion of new constitutional rights that reflect an important component of national citizenship.[58] His analysis of constitutional history demonstrates that although "unwritten" constitutional principles cannot contradict the text or specific intent of the framers, the implicit constitutional principles that accompany and complement the text have always been integral to the actual development of constitutional law.

Although responsibility for education was not vested in the federal government in the original text of the Constitution, the adoption of the Thirteenth, Fourteenth, and Fifteenth Amendments after the Civil War substantially transformed the scope of the Constitution and the manner in which many of its original provisions must now be read.[59] The establishment of national citizenship, and its privileges and immunities, has infused the Ninth Amendment's reservation of the rights of the people and the guarantee in Article 4 of a "republican form of government" with new, substantive meaning: "One of the core unenumerated rights of the people under the Ninth Amendment is the people's right to discover and embrace new rights and to have these new rights respected by government, so long as the people themselves do indeed claim and celebrate these rights in their words and/or actions."[60]

Consistent with the Supreme Court's strong statements regarding the critical importance of education for both individual and national success in the modern era, "most people in America think one has a 'right' to equal educational opportunity," and when they learn that education is not a fundamental right, they say, "It should be."[61] Many of the members of Congress apparently agree. At the time of the passage of NCLB, a number of them stated explicitly that all children have a right to education:

> Every child in this country has the right to a free public education. Every child. That is an awesome responsibility, and one that should not have to be shouldered by local communities alone. The States and the Federal Government are partners in this worthy goal.[62]

> The proposal before the Senate represents an important step in the right direction by recognizing the right of every child to receive a high quality education.[63]

> Almost 37 years ago, the Federal Government made a promise to the children of our Nation, a promise that all children, regardless of race, income, faith or disability, would have an equal chance to learn and to succeed. Thirty-seven years later, the Federal Government is still failing to meet that promise, and Republicans and Democrats have come together to say enough is enough.[64]

Congress as a whole, in enacting NCLB, implicitly acknowledged that all students in the United States have such a right. The stated purpose of the statute is to ensure that "all children have a fair, equal and significant opportunity to obtain a high quality education."[65] The act's very structure, which pressures schools to overcome achievement gaps and penalizes schools that are not making Adequate Yearly Progress toward ensuring that all of their students will be proficient in meeting challenging state standards, takes that right seriously and seeks to thoroughly enforce it.

The founding fathers recognized that schools would instill in the citizens "a new Republican character" that would be critical to the success of the new democratic regime they were creating.[66] Since their time, the Fifteenth, Nineteenth, Twenty-Fourth, and Twenty-Sixth Amendments have extended the right and the responsibility to vote and fully function as productive citizens beyond the initial pool of white male landholders to encompass people of all races, women, the indigent, and all citizens over eighteen years. Accordingly, the federal government now clearly has a responsibility to ensure that *all* of these citizens are properly prepared during their schooling years to carry out this role competently and responsibly.

Justice Marshall and the other *Rodriguez* dissenters recognized this fact. The failure of the states to meet this educational challenge over the past forty years, as well as the enhanced importance that education has assumed during this period for maintaining America's competitive standing in the global economy, should convince the majority of the current Supreme Court to reconsider *Rodriguez* and to declare that there is indeed a fundamental constitutional interest in educational equity and educational excellence.

Congress, utilizing its powers and duties under Section 5 of the Fourteenth Amendment, as well as its spending power, should foursquarely accept responsibility in its reauthorization of the Elementary and Secondary Education Act for ensuring that all children throughout the country are provided a meaningful educational opportunity. In doing so, Congress should adopt the recommendations of the Equity and Excellence Commission for promoting fiscal equity and educational adequacy. In addition, it should consider building on the current Common Core State Standards in English language arts and mathematics and establish national content standards in all core subjects. The legislators should also examine the significant differences in levels of funding among the various states and, where appropriate, provide additional federal aid to lessen those disparities.

But is this call for the Supreme Court and the Congress to acknowledge and enforce a federal right to meaningful educational opportunity credible in this time of intense partisanship and fiscal constraint? The fact that the potent recommendations of the Equity and Excellence Commission were unanimously endorsed by all of its members—liberals and conservatives alike, including leading national scholars, government officials, school leaders, and heads of major national educational advocacy organizations—indicates that the need to mend the current plight of the American educational system is not a Democratic issue or a Republican issue but a critical American issue. And the commission's pairing of strong steps to ensure equity and sufficiency of funding with forceful action to promote efficient and cost-effective means for providing educational services sets out an appropriate direction for accomplishing these ends, even in times of fiscal constraint.[67]

Some have warned that asking the current Supreme Court to reconsider *Rodriguez* at this time is not likely to prove successful and may further entrench the negative aspects of the 1973 decision. I used to hold that view myself. But the increased urgency of the issue, the experience of the state courts in revealing the national extent of these problems that ultimately they cannot fully solve on their own, and the potency of recent legal scholarship on the vibrancy of a federal right to education have convinced me that the Court may be able to come together on this matter.

In any event, it is time to bring the issue of the necessity of a federal right to education to the fore. If the Supreme Court and the Congress ultimately prove unwilling to articulate and enforce such a right, the effort involved in mounting a major new case to reconsider *Rodriguez* may well galvanize the American people to take action themselves to establish this basic right to which the vast majority of them clearly subscribe. They could do this by passing a constitutional amendment to ensure that all of American's schoolchildren are provided a meaningful educational opportunity.[68]

FIVE

Still Separate, Still
Unequal in a Post-*Milliken* Era

Why *Rodriguez* Would Have Been Good but Not Enough

AMY STUART WELLS, LAUREN FOX,
AND ALANA MILES

WHILE THE LEGAL scholars in this volume can explain the many constitutional reasons why *San Antonio Independent School District v. Rodriguez* undermined equal educational opportunities, we, as education researchers, examine why a ruling in favor of the *Rodriguez* plaintiffs would have taken the United States one step closer to a more just educational system but still not far enough. Thus, while we join with civil rights advocates in longing for a different *Rodriguez* decision, we focus here on what was needed, in conjunction with *Rodriguez,* to make the educational system far more equitable.

In fact, our chapter is dedicated to the long-term consequences of another Supreme Court ruling, the 1974 *Milliken v. Bradley* decision, which came sixteen months after *Rodriguez*. At stake in *Milliken* was whether the federal courts could order an urban-suburban school desegregation remedy to address racial segregation in the Detroit Public Schools. The legal question was whether federal judges could order fifty-three suburban school districts in the Detroit metropolitan area to be a part of an interdistrict school desegregation remedy. The federal district court and court of appeals had both ruled they could based on evidence of the public and private practices used to maintain racial segregation across suburban school district boundaries. Had the Supreme Court agreed, the remedy would have most likely consolidated the urban and suburban school districts into one metropolitan-wide district.

But when the *Milliken* case reached the Supreme Court, the majority reversed the lower court decisions, citing, as it had in *Rodriguez,* the preeminence of the local control of public schools. The Court ruled that without further evidence of the suburban districts' direct involvement in the segregation of the city's schools, federal courts could not violate the local control principle by ordering a metro-wide remedy: "No single tradition in public education is more deeply rooted than local control over the operation of schools; local autonomy has long been thought essential both to the maintenance of community concern and support for public schools."[1]

The Supreme Court, therefore, absolved the suburbs of any responsibility for using local control to create and maintain racially isolated communities, despite much evidence to the contrary. This ruling echoed the *Rodriguez* decision that the Texas system of school finance did not violate the Fourteenth Amendment's Equal Protection Clause in part because it is a legitimate state interest to permit and encourage "participation in and significant control of each district's schools at the local level."[2]

In 1973 and again in 1974, therefore, the U.S. Supreme Court emphasized local control of public schools as the primary reason to *not* order more equal distribution of resources of public funds or greater access to higher performing schools. In the forty years since, we have seen that this strong support of local control has had negative consequences for low-income students of color.

Still, the impact of these two significant rulings has differed across place and time. As other authors in this volume and elsewhere point out, there has been progress toward school finance reform in numerous individual state court cases since *Rodriguez.*[3] The implications of this are that it has happened in a piecemeal way, helping some students in some states more than others, resulting in much funding inequality within many states and across state boundaries.[4]

Similarly, the impact of *Milliken* and ongoing efforts to implement meaningful school desegregation plans have been uneven as well. For instance, *Milliken*-type *inter*district desegregation remedies were needed in the more fragmented Northeast and Midwest and less so in the South's larger, county-wide school districts, where substantial school-level desegregation could occur through *intra*district remedies despite the *Milliken* ruling.[5]

The result of these uneven efforts to circumvent both *Rodriguez* and *Milliken* across state and local contexts is that, by the twenty-first century, many of the contemporary educational "equity" needs of any given state or public school district are related to school funding issues that would have been addressed more unilaterally by a different *Rodriguez* ruling. Yet, in other contexts, such as the northeastern suburban county we studied, the *Rodriguez* decision would have been insufficient.

No doubt, both the *Rodriguez* and *Milliken* rulings, grounded in the importance of local control, were highly problematic in terms of funding and student access to better, more integrated schools. But based on our recent research in Nassau County, Long Island, one of the most separate and unequal counties in the United States, a pro-plaintiff ruling in *Milliken* would have made far more difference in the lives of disadvantaged students. In making this claim we venture beyond the sort of tangible factors, such as resources and facilities, *Rodriguez* would have addressed to examine the question at the heart of both *Brown v. Board of Education* and *Milliken*: can racially and socioeconomically separate schools ever be equal?

Our research examines this central issue across distinct school district boundary lines by documenting inequality in terms of both *tangible* (funding levels and material resources, public and private) and *intangible* (status, reputation, and prestige) factors and their relationship to each other. Building on pre-1954 higher education desegregation cases and their focus on both factors, we study the processes by which inequality is maintained within the education system, even when public school funding is fairly evenly distributed. In this chapter we describe several small, separate school districts that, despite having fairly equal public (federal, state, and local combined) funding, remain highly unequal. In this way, our research speaks directly to why a different ruling in *Rodriguez* would have helped low-income communities on Long Island but also how much more helpful a different outcome in *Milliken* would have been.

METRO MIGRATIONS: A STUDY OF SUBURBAN CHANGE, RACIAL SEGREGATION, AND UNEQUAL PUBLIC SCHOOLS

Our mixed-methods study of separate and unequal school districts was aimed at understanding the role of public education in the migration patterns of people across urban-suburban spaces and school district boundary lines. We knew from prior research that many communities in metropolitan areas across the United States are experiencing rapid demographic change as more African Americans, Latinos, Asians, and poor people in general are moving to the suburbs at the same time that many cities are attracting affluent, well-educated whites to "gentrifying" neighborhoods.[6] We refer to this pattern of metro migrations as "trading places"; others have called it the "great inversion."[7]

The most consistent variable amid this inversion of urban-suburban populations is racial and social class segregation.[8] Thus, even as the patterns of migration and settlement have become more complicated—more multidimensional and multidirectional—racial/ethnic and class segregation remains a defining feature across boundaries.[9] Furthermore, even though these metro migrations are occurring in a post–civil rights era, when white Americans say they are less prejudiced and embrace diversity, we see similar patterns of "white flight" from demographically changing suburbs and "white draw" into pockets of mostly white enclaves within diverse cities.[10]

The unanswered question was, what role do public schools—their boundary lines, their tangible resources, their intangible reputations, and their racial and social class makeup—play in these urban-suburban migration patterns? The overarching goal of our research, therefore, was to learn where home buyers/renters of different backgrounds end up living within a racially and socioeconomically segregated metropolitan area and how their migrations relate to both tangible (resources) and intangible (status) distinctions across boundaries, especially school district or school attendance boundaries. This framework required us to study a diverse, fragmented, and segregated suburban county in the Northeast and to employ a mixed-methods approach, which enabled us to combine elements of both quantitative and qualitative approaches to research the "broad purposes of breadth and depth of understanding and corroboration."[11]

The Context of Our Study of Suburban Change

Nassau County is on Long Island, bordering New York City to the East and sharing Queens' entire eastern border. The overall demographics of Nassau County are similar to those of the U.S. population as a whole, as the white, non-Hispanic population has shrunk from 97 percent of all county residents in 1950 to about 63 percent today. Meanwhile, the Hispanic and Asian populations have grown rapidly from almost zero to nearly 16 percent and 9 percent, respectively. The African American population, meanwhile, which grew rapidly in the latter part of the twentieth century, has stabilized at about 12 percent.[12]

Interacting with this growing diversity is Nassau County's dubious distinction of being one of the nation's most governmentally fragmented, segregated, and unequal counties in terms of race/ethnicity and income.[13] Lodged within the county's approximately 220 square miles are four towns, two cities, sixty-four villages, and hundreds of unincorporated hamlets. These different governments provide local control and several localized services, including garbage and snow removal, fire fighters, and, perhaps most importantly, zoning regulations affecting the cost of real estate and, thus, who can afford to live there.

The fifty-six separate and unequal school districts in Nassau County combined enroll fewer than 205,000 students, with an average district size of 3,660 students. Most of these small suburban districts have only one high school. The boundary lines for the school districts intersect with local municipal boundaries in inconsistent and unpredictable ways, only adding to the degree of fragmentation. For instance, there are school districts that encompass all or part of nine villages at the same time that there are villages that are divided by as many as nine school districts.

Kendra Bishoff reports that the national average of school district fragmentation is .72, or a 72 percent probability that any two randomly selected students will live in different school districts.[14] The two Long Island counties of Nassau and Suffolk have a fragmentation score of .986 combined, making it a nearly 100 percent probability that any two students will be divided by a district boundary. Related to this fragmentation, Long Island was ranked tenth in the country in terms of black/white residential segregation and nineteenth in Hispanic/white segregation. School segregation is even starker. Indeed, one national study found the Long Island school districts among the top three in terms of the degree of racial segregation across district boundaries.[15]

Thus, the issues *Milliken* plaintiffs were attempting to address are clearly salient in Nassau County. And while the public funding issues related to the *Rodriguez* case are also significant in the state of New York, they are less so in Nassau County. According to 2012 school finance data, New York State had the highest average per-pupil funding—$19,552 versus the national average of $10,608—of any state. Unfortunately, across its 680 school districts, New

York is consistently ranked in the top ten states for per-pupil fuding inequality, with a general pattern of poor students receiving less.[16]

Still, within-state funding inequities vary across regions, and counties and are highly susceptible to context-specific variables.[17] This context-dependent argument clearly relates to our findings in Nassau County, where, despite stark differences in student poverty rates across district boundaries, the distinctions in public funding levels are far less pronounced than they are in the rest of the state (see figures 5.1 and 5.2). In fact, there is a relatively weak relationship between student demographic characteristics of each district and funding levels.

Our document analysis and interview data reveal several possible explanations for this context-specific finding on Long Island, including the success of Nassau County state legislators in securing additional state funding for school districts on Long Island. Furthermore, given the many pockets of affluence in the county and the historically high property taxes in those wealthy communities, more of the additional state funding is channeled to poorer districts in the county, in part to keep them fiscally solvent in order to stave off periodic calls for consolidation of the many tiny school districts. We know of at least one instance in which a coalition of state legislators and school district leaders from Nassau went to Albany to seek extra funding for one of the poorest and virtually all-black school districts in the county, which was facing fiscal insolvency and a state takeover. Amid proposals that this poor black and Hispanic district merge with a neighboring district of mostly white and middle- to upper-middle-class students, this coalition was formed, bringing together state representatives and advocates from both the predominantly white and black school districts. The goal of this political alliance was to request additional state funds for the predominantly black district so that it could remain autonomous. When the state legislature granted the additional funding, including a large capital fund for facilities, the interests of the powers that be in both segregated contexts were served.

This sort of "segregation bribe," along with the political power often vested in affluent suburban constituents, has evolved into a context- and time-specific situation in which the differences in per-pupil funding (tangible factors) across separate and unequal Nassau County school districts are not always as large as the distinctions in perceptions of the quality of those districts (intangible factors), which we know from our research relate to the race of the students within them.[18] Hence, our research exploring the importance of boundaries is even more significant in this context of relatively equal funding amid stark demographic differences across highly segregated and fragmented school districts.

As illustrated in figures 5.1 and 5.2, in Nassau County there is no clear relationship between student demographics and district pupil expenditure.[19] In fact, several school districts with no poor students and no students of color have below-average per-pupil public funding. These data suggest that Nassau County is an excellent place to study the issues the Supreme Court underlined in the 1954 *Brown* decision, namely that even when "tangible" factors may be equal, separate schools defined by race are inherently unequal. These data do not make the *Rodriguez* issues of equal public funding irrelevant in places like Nassau County, but they do suggest that the story of inequality is much more complex.

Research Design

In light of this weak relationship between average district per-pupil funding and the race/ethnicity and socioeconomic status of students who live in these districts, we wanted to understand how and why residents ended up in

FIGURE 5.1 Relationship between school districts' average per-pupil expenditures and percentages of students qualifying for free or reduced-price lunch in Nassau County, Long Island

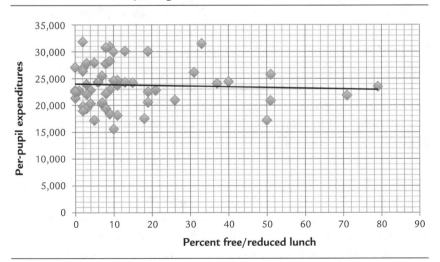

FIGURE 5.2   Relationship between school districts' average per-pupil expenditures and percentages of African American and Hispanic students in Nassau County, Long Island

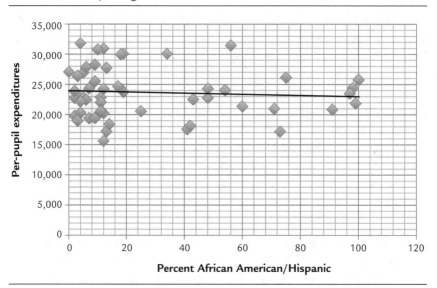

highly segregated local school districts in Nassau County. In other words, in a context such as this, where differences in tangible, per-pupil funding across school district boundaries are minimal, we wanted to measure what factored into peoples' housing choices. Thus, we designed a mixed-methods study that included *quantitative analysis* of census, New York State Education Department, and Nassau County data via GIS mapping, segregation indexes, and boundary discontinuity regression to measure segregation levels within and across boundaries.

In addition to this quantitative analysis, we conducted a *survey of recent home buyers and renters* in Nassau County, which we mailed to a weighted random sample of five thousand households drawn from 66,719 records of properties bought and sold from 2006 through 2011. The purpose of the survey was to ascertain the role that school district boundaries played in the choices of where people lived.

And throughout our study we collected *qualitative data*—namely interviews, observations, and case studies of school districts and schools—to learn how Nassau County residents and educators understood school district quality within and across boundary lines. In total, we conducted nearly four hundred interviews with officials, real estate agents, mayors, educators, parents, and recent home buyers or renters across the county as well as case studies of seven racially diverse schools. Here we draw mainly on qualitative data from the original five school case study districts on Long Island, which vary greatly in terms of student and local community wealth as well as racial/ethnic demographics.[20]

Our sampling of the five school districts began with our preliminary analysis of demographics, funding, and student outcome data across all the school districts on Long Island. We devised four categories of districts based on recent changes in their student populations:

1. *Category 1.* Districts that are predominantly (more than 75 percent) African American and/or Latino and low income (5 of the 56 districts)
2. *Category 2.* Districts that are predominantly (more than 75 percent) white and/or Asian and affluent (34 of the 56 districts)
3. *Category 3.* Districts that are racially and socioeconomically diverse, meaning they were less than 75 percent African American/Latino *or* white/Asian and not as poor as Category 1 (4 of the 56 school districts)
4. *Category 4.* Districts that are unstable and changing demographically and experiencing white flight (not more than 75 percent of any racial/ethnic group) and not as poor as Category 1 (13 of the 56 districts).

Using these categories, we selected five diverse districts on Long Island to capture the disparate experiences of children across unequal school district contexts (see table 5.1). Thus, these districts range from impoverished, all black, and Latino with large numbers of recent immigrant children who speak very little English (Grantsville; Category 1) to those enrolling very affluent, predominantly white students (Belvedere; Category 2). In the middle are three more racially/ethnically diverse districts, only one of which is stable (Clearview; Category 3). Two of these more diverse districts (Lakewood and Leesburg) fit into Category 4 because they have been losing their white and/or more affluent populations over the last ten years.

Table 5.2 provides information related to funding and student outcomes that speak to both the descriptions of the districts and the findings that emerged across them. What is most noteworthy about these five districts is the difference in per-pupil funding, which is not necessarily what would be expected given the distinctions across these communities in terms of wealth.

TABLE 5.1   Five Long Island school districts sampled for in-depth analysis

	Category	% White	% Black	% Latino	% Free lunch	% Reduced lunch
Grantsville	1	<1	53	46	65	7
Belvedere	2	97	1	<1	0	0
Clearview	3	64	12	20	15	4
Lakewood	4	14	50	19	27	15
Leesburg	4	43	20	30	20	8

TABLE 5.2   Input and outcome data on five sample Long Island school districts

District	Category	2012 Per-pupil funding	Percent of students scoring a 3 or 4 on the 8th grade math test	Percent going to four-year college
Grantsville	1	$24,312	18	32
Belvedere	2	$24,925	88	95
Clearview	3	$27,054	78	61
Lakewood* (grades K–6 only)	4	$16,303	n/a	n/a
Leesburg	4	$30,800	56	66

Note: *Lakewood is an "elementary school district" whose students feed into a larger, consolidated high school district. Elementary school districts usually have lower average per-pupil funding than K–12 or high school districts.

Because Lakewood is a K–6 school district with no high school, it has the lowest per-pupil expenditure of this sample. But the fact that Belvedere, the most affluent and white of the districts, ranks number three within this sample for per-pupil expenditure and is almost tied for fourth with Grantsville, which is the poorest district in the sample, speaks to the issue that public school funding in this county is not correlated to student demographics.

These case studies produced evidence-based findings that illustrate the subtle ways in which several critical resources not measured by per-pupil public funding formula vary tremendously across school district boundaries that separate students by race and social class. These factors include private funds, the academic culture, and political support for public education. These differences across school district boundaries are not easily measured and are generally not addressed in school finance equity cases, such as *Rodriguez* and the state court cases that followed. They are related, however, to the intangible factors noted in *Brown* and are the distinctions across school district boundaries that speak to the central reason why separate is inherently unequal in public education. These distinctions are the mechanisms by which the processes of exclusion and racial and social class segregation are perpetuated and are how they can affect not only the hearts and minds of students but also their life chances. They illustrate why a pro-equity, pro-plaintiff ruling in *Rodriguez* would have been helpful but insufficient.

FINDING 1: THE INTERPLAY OF PUBLIC AND PRIVATE RESOURCES

What we documented in our case studies of five districts that differ dramatically in student populations, if less so in terms of their public, per-pupil funding, are the multiple ways in which public resources and private wealth are often discretely commingled to give students who attend schools of concentrated privilege an almost immeasurable advantage. In other words, when private resources from parents and community members are added into the equation, the mounting inequities between rich and poor school districts are startling and are major factors in *separate and unequal educational opportunities.*

The Tale of Concentrated Privilege: Districts with the Most Public and/or Private Resources Serve the Most Affluent Families

The interaction, reinforcement, and intermingling of public and private resources is best illustrated in the most affluent school district we studied, the Belvedere Public Schools, where the educators and students are very clear that what makes their schools "good" is as much about what the people of Belvedere bring to the district as it is about the money these people generate in tax revenues.

The first part of the equation is this district's ample public funds for the regular operating budget of the schools. Belvedere ranks in the middle of our five-district sample in terms of its public funding level, at about $25,000 per pupil. But what is interesting about this district is that because it is such an elite residential enclave, it lacks a commercial tax base and additional federal or state funds for low-income or bilingual students. In spite of this, Belvedere homeowners generate enough property tax to maintain a per-pupil funding level that is close to the Long Island median. Indeed, a theme we heard from the faculty and students in this district is that they had more than enough resources—be it technology, art supplies, or science equipment—to do what they needed to educate their high-achieving students and prepare them for the competitive four-year college application process. But in reality, the official per-pupil funding is just the beginning of the story.

The Tangled Web of Public and Private Resources Within the "Good" Community.

In Belvedere, the lack of need when it comes to what the district provides for its educators and students is intertwined with what the parents and students already have. The most blatant example of this commingling of public and private resources is the size and scope of private donations parents and other community members make to the schools. When we were conducting site visits to Belvedere High School, the school was completing the construction of its second Astroturf athletic field. Both this new turf field and a second, slightly older one had been made possible through gifts from parents. The cost of the first field was $1 million; the estimated cost of the second field was closer to $2 million.

The high school's assistant principal explained, in the context of talking about how Belvedere is a "different" place, where the educators' needs are consistently met either through public funds or parents' generous donations to the district: "I know the first turf [field] was a million, and two parents gave $500,000 each. The next one is very close to two [million], because there's a parking area for a hundred cars." He said that in addition to the fields, the Booster Club donated items such as golf carts for the athletic director's, trainers', and coaches' use on the sprawling suburban campus. A district social worker noted that the enhanced athletic opportunities available in Belvedere are easily translated into tangible academic opportunities because more students are playing sports with better facilities and equipment than other schools, which translates into an advantage in the college application process.

The private funding prevalent in Belvedere also bonds community members in their shared sense of support for their schools, which is then credited to their superior values and beliefs about education. Indeed, the high school principal spoke at length about how well supported he feels at this school, noting that having abundant resources is "what makes working here incredible."

A portion of the private funds from wealthy donors goes into the principal's discretionary budget of $20,000 to $30,000 per year, which is supposed to help shape the culture of the school. The principal told us, "They don't put any restrictions on the money. It's what you want to spend it on for the good of the cause." He emphasized several times how beneficial it is to have complete flexibility with these donated funds, which he uses to help enhance school spirit, further solidifying the bond between the school and the local community by making the high school a better place to work and go to school. For instance, he used his discretionary money to buy several filtered water coolers, Smartboards, and decent food for the faculty meetings and to pay for registration to professional development conferences, superb pep rallies, and a special Senior Day, replete with a rented amusement park set up on campus. The relationship between these private, discretionary funds and intangible factors such as the high school's sense of community, commitment, and convergence is illustrated by the principal's favorite purchases for the pep rallies on the new turf fields: a $900 air gun to shoot 400 Belvedere High School t-shirts 500 feet into the student bleachers and a 13-foot blimp to hover over the football stadium, "The kids love it," he said. "Anything that makes [school] positive."

Blimps, air guns, and amusement parks aside, there are also many ways in which the abundance of private resources in the community enhances the already exemplary academic program at Belvedere High School. Indeed, there is a connection between the process of building the esprit de corps on the campus and furthering the reputation of the Belvedere public schools. For instance, the art department chair described the extra programs, equipment, field trips, and events as being possible only because of parental support. The school is awash with new technology that she uses for her media arts program. "It is a disservice," she said, "to not offer all this technology to kids." She explained that parents in this affluent community support the schools because they have the money to do so, and they see it as an important supplement to the rigorous, high-powered academic program at the school and a component of a well-rounded education and access to top universities. She noted that "getting into a lot of the big-name schools is very important to the students, their families. And the district understands that."

Supporting "Good" Schools by Supporting "Good" Students.   We also learned through our interviews with educators and students in Belvedere of the multiple and often subtle, or behind-the-scenes, ways private resources ensure greater academic success for not just the school as a whole but for individual students. While educational researchers have long documented the powerful relationship between parents' socioeconomic status and student outcomes, the insights from this highly privileged school demonstrate some of the more subtle and nuanced mechanisms of this home advantage and how it creates a set of norms or expectations about what it is parents provide for their children to help them in the competitive race toward a high-status college.[21]

For instance, the social worker at Belvedere High School, who previously worked with poor New York City students, noted that the main difference between the two contexts is not the kind of challenges students face in affluent versus poor communities but the types of support systems they have outside of school to help them through difficult times. In both contexts, he said, there are students who are socially awkward, in need of special education services, have parents divorcing, etc. "What I think is different," he offered, is that in Belvedere "families have the money to help them get through it." For example, he noted that in Belvedere, if your parents are divorcing, you have the financial means to go to a therapist. "If you're autistic, your family has gone to the best specialists and they have you with the best medications, and you're going to special camps over the summer to really develop your social skills, and I think that's what separates the districts."

In describing similarities in the conditions and problems facing students across these different contexts, we do not wish to downplay the privilege of Belvedere students and thus the many obstacles they do *not* face on a daily basis compared with their counterparts in poorer districts. As the assistant principal noted, "So, much of our job is done for us, as opposed to other schools." Still, the idea of similar, almost universal teen problems facing students across varied socioeconomic contexts and school districts also has some validity. And it is within these similarities that we see different safety nets available, as the home-school nexus highlights the tangible and intangible benefits of private resources. This distinction also emerged whenever Belvedere educators spoke of social challenges such as drug or alcohol abuse among their affluent students. The assistant principal explained, "These parents are intelligent. They'll realize, and they have the means . . . to deal with these problems in ways that other parents just couldn't. . . . If there's a drug problem that seems serious, they will put them in some sort of rehab."

These costly residential rehab centers serve a secondary purpose of keeping students' school records clean of suspensions or expulsions. As the assistant principal of discipline at Belvedere High School noted, there had been no expulsions from the school in more than a year. She said that the only infraction that could have led to one never made it to the superintendent's hearing because the parents pulled the student out of school and put him in a residential rehab center. She noted that once a child in this school district has a problem, be it drugs or alcohol or something else, the parents will act on it.

In this vein of "acting on" a problem, or a perceived problem, nearly everyone we interviewed in Belvedere said the private tutoring industry was thriving despite the stellar academic reputation of the high school and the quality of the teachers. The principal stated that some families spend $10,000 to $15,000 per child per year for tutors and SAT prep classes. Meanwhile, he noted, in the school where he used to work, most parents worked minimum-wage jobs and were just getting by. "They can't say, 'Let's give $150 to a tutor.' Or, even in that community, $80 for a tutor, or $50 . . . I mean, $50 is the difference between light and heat to them."

Buying the Best College Admissions Letters. This willingness of affluent Belvedere parents to write checks to help their children get ahead in an increasingly competitive educational system does not end with rehab centers or tutors. According to the high school guidance counselors, they also use their financial resources to buy their children a college admissions letter, which they go about doing in two strategic ways.

First of all, an increasing number of Belvedere families are outsourcing the college admissions process by hiring private admissions counselors or relying heavily on the high school's counseling office, with its 44:1 student-counselor ratio. As one guidance counselor noted, she has seen a sudden rise in the number of families who hire other people to help their children apply to college. She said this trend is prevalent even among the

large percentage of Belvedere families with one stay-at-home parent, usually the mother, who has the full-time "job" of supporting the highly paid
spouse by planning dinner parties for his associates, etc. The counselor
noted that this practice is another dimension of outsourcing in their lives,
much like hiring a housekeeper, gardener, child-care provider, and driver.
Still, even with their relatively low caseloads, the Belvedere counselors said
they are grateful when the parents hire a private college admissions counselor because it takes the pressure off them and frees their time to connect
with the colleges.

Thus, the private family outsourcing for college applications supports another critical factor in the Belvedere counseling office's strategy for getting
many students into competitive colleges: close relationships with college admissions officers. According to the Belvedere guidance counselors, while
other high schools try to get their students to attend crowded college fairs,
here, in one of the most affluent school districts within one of the most affluent counties in New York, the college admissions officers come to them.
In fact, many of the college admissions officers come to the high school and
spend a full period meeting with a small group of students, facilitating discussion, and getting to know students on a personal level. According to one
counselor, these tight bonds with admissions officers are extremely beneficial
because students are able to shake hands with the people who will review
their applications.

Through "personal" relationships with admissions officers from nearby,
competitive colleges and these social networks, even the more academically
borderline Belvedere students get into some of the top colleges and universities. For these students in particular, this counselor noted, private meetings
with admissions officers are critical for relationship building and for allowing
questions to be asked and answered. She said that she did not intend to dis-
credit her colleagues working in more low-income areas, who probably "have
a better relationship with maybe the social service workers[, but] I don't need
to maintain that relationship very much. . . . I don't have that number on
speed-dial. What I have is the admissions officer from Georgetown, Buck-
nell, University of Chicago, and many others on my school e-mail account
that I can find at any time."

The Belvedere students themselves note with great pride that many college
admissions officers come to them, that they do not need to seek them out.
The students seem to understand and accept the importance of relationship

building and networking as a part of the competitive process they must navigate. As one senior explained, having the admissions officers visit the school is invaluable because of the personal connection: "They'll have your name down, and they'll have your information and they'll know that you inquired about their school."

Another strategy employed by Belvedere parents trying to get their children into college is the "early decision" or "early action" application option for first-choice schools, which is limited to students from families that can afford to forego the option to request or negotiate financial aid. According to the Belvedere guidance counselors, applying "early decision" boosts students' chances of getting into the most competitive colleges. One of the counselors noted that she sees many upper-middle-class or more affluent white kids from Belvedere who are borderline in terms of getting into the most competitive colleges get "bumped over" into the accepted category by the early decision option, which shows the colleges how committed the student is to their university and signals that the applicant comes from a family that can pay full tuition. Thus, she advises students and their parents about the benefits of this strategy if they can afford to forego the financial aid, which most of them can. She noted that about 75 percent of Belvedere students utilize early action programs.

As the U.S. Supreme Court noted in its landmark *Brown* decision, it is not just the tangible factors such as resources and facilities that matter in public education, although they clearly do matter. The intangible factors—personal relationships, networks, status, reputation, and so on—are critical as well.

The Tale of Concentrated Poverty: Districts with Fewer Public and/or Private Resources Serve Families with the Least

Nassau County's school districts stand in sharp contrast to Belvedere in terms of what they lack in both tangible and intangible resources. When we factor in the social and emotional needs of the students served in low-income and predominantly African American and Latino districts such as Grantsville, the resource gap seems even wider. As Belvedere's social worker pointed out, it is not always the disparate problems facing students across these contexts but, rather, their parents' ability to help "solve" such problems with private resources.

Educators and students in the other districts in our study—even those with higher per-pupil expenditures than Belvedere—talked about numerous unmet educational needs due to a lack of private donations and familial support to augment the public funding. In particular, the need for better facilities came up frequently, especially in Grantsville, a poor district experiencing enrollment increases in its immigrant population. We learned through our interviews, for instance, that the school board had been ordered by the state to close two schools due to their states of disrepair (asbestos, falling ceilings, and the like). These school closures created overcrowding in other schools and classrooms, which in turn led to a greater reliance on portable classrooms. According to one report, there were seventy portable classrooms in use in the district, some of which were twenty years old.

The lack of facilities in places like Grantsville too often means that classes or programs which would greatly benefit the students are not offered or do not serve students very well. As one educator in that district noted, the preschool center is housed on the third floor of a building with no elevator—"So therefore, if you can, imagine these little four-year-olds going up to the top level every day." This interviewee noted several other projects that are supposedly in the works at the district office but have no resolutions in site. In terms of the preschool facility, there is a district-level committee working on it hoping to float a bond issue to raise money for it, but there are conflicting needs and demands on their time, energy, and resources.

In addition to a lack of preschool programs, the Grantsville elementary school we studied has no gifted education program because the only elementary-level gifted program is housed at another school, and students must be tested to gain access to this program, which consists of one class each for all the gifted fourth and fifth grade students in the district. The assistant principal noted that some of the children who qualify for the gifted class opt instead to remain in their home schools because the district does not transport them to the school housing the gifted program.

In this same elementary school, the assistant principal explained, they have only one part-time social worker and one part-time psychologist because they have to share them with other schools in the district. The lack of resources and support in Grantsville is also evident in smaller matters, such as basic school supplies. According to one of the administrators at the elementary school we studied, "We have to prioritize as to what we need most because we never have enough resources to order everything."

Our research revealed multiple reasons why the Grantsville schools lack basic resources despite having comparable public funding to other local districts. Not only are additional services needed to meet the needs of low-income students in the district, but also, due to political issues discussed below, the district often fails to allocate the resources in ways that best serve the students. To make matters worse, the families in the Grantsville district lack the private resources that the Belvedere families have to supplement their public school education. As one of the school administrators noted, the children served in this district lack basic supplies from home: "They'll come without a book, without a notebook, without paper, without pencils. . . . our children are coming with less and less."

Efforts to meet the needs of students in this mostly poor and all black and Latino district have become even more challenging according to many of the Grantsville educators as their district has become the destination of a large influx of immigrant families, mostly from Central America. These educators describe these immigrant families as "transient" and note that between mid-July and mid-September each year, they have hundreds of new families lined up outside the central district office trying to enroll their children. Most of these families, one official noted, do not stay more than a year or two. He said, "The enrollment issues are of serious concern because they come and go so much."

Indeed, in the Grantsville elementary school we studied, the number of Latino students (most of whom are recent immigrants from Central America) had surpassed the number of African American students. This demographic shift in less affluent districts on Long Island adds a new set of needs and required services. For instance, given the recent immigrant status of many of these students, the educators noted that they were even more disadvantaged than the black students. As one school administrator noted, "Many of the students come lacking skills. Some are new to the country, without having had any school experience. . . . their attendance fluctuates because they're going back and forth to their home countries. And that definitely interferes with the educational process."

The lack of "home advantage" that the Grantsville students bring with them to school each day is shocking in comparison to students in districts with far more advantages. The key point that educators here keep honing in on is that little things can have a big impact on students' school success. According to one administrator, "When your parents have not spoken to you because they're working two jobs, when you have not had somebody read a book to you, learn the alphabet—you know, they're coming to first grade and some of our children, who are bilingual particularly, still need to learn the alphabet."

Still, this is not to say that districts like Grantsville are completely lacking in private resources. The problem is that the private resources available have far less flexibility and are far less comprehensive than those supporting the Belvedere students. For instance, Grantsville has somewhat compensated for the families' lack of resources by garnering partnerships with local businesses and nonprofit organizations. But these partnership programs, unlike Belvedere's donations from community-based boosters, often do not address the most urgent needs of the Grantsville students. Furthermore, these private funds often come with many strings attached and are often as much about meeting the needs of the partnering organization as the students'.

One such partnership is between a Grantsville elementary school and a local bank. The program is a social studies–based curriculum called Junior Achievement in which a bank employee comes to the school for ninety minutes each week for ten weeks to teach "social studies." According to the school principal, as part of their participation in this program, the first graders color in a book titled *Our Community Partners,* which features the local bank, and the fifth graders learn about marketing and finance. While the educators said such programs are somewhat helpful, the partnerships do not really evolve around the needs of the students as much as they focus on what the bank wants students to know about their services.

There are other programs with local nonprofits and universities, but the benefits from such programs are still piecemeal and sometimes completely due to luck. For instance, one year the father of a student teacher at one of the elementary schools, who owned a big plumbing company, adopted the school, and gave laptop computers to every child in the school. While such donations are greatly appreciated, they are completely serendipitous and cannot be counted on, as can the Belvedere High School principal's annual discretionary fund.

Other private resources for Grantsville come from the educators themselves. We learned from several staff members of their regular practice of taking money out of their own pockets to spend on the students. For instance, there is the school nurse who buys clothes for students, and many teachers donate their own funds to help pay for field trips and supplies. These donations on the part of the school staff are meaningful for the children in this high-poverty school, but they cannot make up for what these

Grantsville students are *not* getting from their district, school, parents, and/ or local community.

This first theme to emerge from our data on the interplay of public and private funding illustrates the multiple ways in which information on public school expenditures and finances is missing some vital data about the broader context of the public schools. In some instances, the private resources supplement and even supplant the public funds to help students succeed academically. In other situations, those resources are not there, and students lack a safety net to catch them if they fall. And still, in other contexts, as we discuss below, there are ample public funds generated to support public schools, but those with greater political power use much of this funding to support their own private interests.

FINDING 2: THE EDUCATIONAL IMPACT OF SEPARATE AND UNEQUAL PUBLIC AND PRIVATE RESOURCES

Private resource inequalities across school district boundaries affect not just the quality of pep rallies but students' access to high-quality curriculum and educational opportunities and, more importantly, how students make sense of who they are and what their academic identities and potentials are and will be in the future.

In describing the tightly intertwined relationship between the different levels of curriculum offered across district boundaries and varied academic identities of the students who encounter these unequal academic experiences on a daily basis, we argue that these educational distinctions are significant at any moment in time. However, if we consider their cumulative impact across students' K–12 education—the educational debt accrued—these distinctions are frightening.[22]

Differentiated Curricula and Academic Identities Across District Lines

"Differentiated curriculum" is generally used to describe a process whereby teachers try to meet the individual needs, skill levels, and learning styles of different students within their classrooms. We are using the term here in a pejorative way to illustrate a serious consequence of structural inequality. What we learned in these school districts and talking to educators and students is that, despite the state standards, state exams, and definition of *proficiency* under No Child Left Behind and the Common Core State Standards, there is very little consistency across these five New York districts in the quality of education the students are receiving. The discrepancies have less to do with state mandates, however, than they have to do with local inequalities and the way they are reflected in the educational support systems available to students, educators' expectations of the students, students' sense of their academic identity, and the communities' understanding of their educational rights. Each of these, in turn, relates to the affluence, or lack thereof, of the constituents across these contexts.

For instance, we learned that in the affluent district of Belvedere, students are challenged and pushed by their parents and peers to achieve at extremely high levels, well above the state standards, which are more of an aside than a set of benchmarks. In contrast, in the poorer districts of Lakewood and Grantsville, this intense academic pressure is lacking, and the state mandates are the ceiling and not the floor. This phenomenon relates to the race/ethnicity and socioeconomic status of the students within these districts and tracks and the ways in which the adults in their lives come to define them.

State Mandates as the Maximum in Less-Privileged Contexts.

In the two school districts in our study serving the poorest students, Lakewood and Grantsville, educators talk about curriculum and instruction as driven by the state mandates, which for many students are the hurdles they strive to clear. From the perspective of educators, absent the kind of parental pressure central to the experience of educators working in more affluent districts, such as Belvedere, and in the midst of serving students who have been mostly disadvantaged in terms of their familial wealth and privilege, meeting the state standards is the goal; exceeding the standards, to the extent that they can simply be ignored, as Belvedere educators do every day, is difficult to fathom in these contexts.

The best example of this contrast comes from Lakewood, the diverse but increasingly nonwhite district with a growing percentage of immigrant students. In this district, which is a K–6, elementary school district, one of the principals talked about the themes that he asks the teachers to cover on a monthly basis to stay on schedule for the state tests. His goal is to get the teachers to cover certain skills at certain points in the year; this means that most of the curriculum covered in this school is dictated by the state mandates.

Lakewood students take practice exams for the state tests, and then the teachers sit down with the principal to go over the scores on those tests and plan curriculum accordingly. Based on the practice tests, the educators conduct an "item skills analysis" by examining which topics the children may be struggling with, and, in theory, the educators focus those topics to help students develop the specific skills they are lacking according to the state tests. According to the educators in the school, they do a lot of "tiered assignments so that the children receive the proper amount of scaffolding for each topic that's taught."

But, as the principal noted, doing the tiered assignments geared toward the needs of each student can be particularly challenging for more novice teachers, which are the only teachers Lakewood tends to attract. He also commented that the school is trying to move away from giving students too much test prep "busy work" and instead meet the students where they need to be met.

This is in stark contrast to what the educators in Belvedere see as appropriate for the needs of their students. The state tests in the Belvedere district are mere blips on the radar screen in the race for admissions to the best colleges and universities. There is virtually no discussion of them as salient to the work of educators in that district, who must administer the mandated tests that are far from high stakes in this context.

The Academic Press of Affluent Parents, Schools, and Classroom.

In sharp contrast to the other districts, in Belvedere, students, educators, and parents talk about how hard the students there are pushed to succeed far beyond state mandates. In this way, they tend to internalize and even embody the distinctions across the boundaries of Long Island school districts. Thus, the degree of privilege that students in the Belvedere district assume—and how it becomes their "common sense"—is quite remarkable but not completely surprising.

Virtually everyone we interviewed in Belvedere, including the parents themselves, attributed much of the pressure the students feel to their parents' anxiety. Indeed, the students and educators marveled at the degree to which the parents, advertently or inadvertently, influence their children's engagement in the educational process and their "academic identity." They noted that the parents play a central role in fostering a school environment described as an "academic pressure cooker." As one of the seniors we interviewed at Belvedere High School explained it, "There's more to lose when you go to a prestigious school like Belvedere and like you have very successful parents and it's like you want to live up to expectations both from your parents and yourself."

A Belvedere High School social worker said that for about 20 percent of the students, the anxiety of trying to live up to their parents' expectations is the main issue: "In this community where there's such a high-income lifestyle, the kids want that same lifestyle. The parents are like, 'You need to get good grades, you need to do this.' I mean, a lot of the parents come in in seventh grade and say, 'Okay, when can my child start AP classes?'" Indeed, the social worker and many of the counselors and educators noted that it is not unusual for students to take four and five Advanced Placement classes at one time or spend four, five, and six hours a night on homework. Students often arrive in the morning drinking coffee and reporting that they were up until three a.m. doing homework. According to the social worker, "[it's] that home influence of academic pursuit—be a doctor, be a lawyer, be a CEO—[that] drives that." Looking back on their fast-paced, high-stress high school careers and reflecting on why they did what they did, the senior boys we interviewed at Belvedere commented on their sense of academic identity within the context of a very affluent community. According to one, when your father is very rich, "you think, 'oh I'm going to be just like my dad. I'm going to do the things my father did and try to be just as great and successful as my father.'"

The pressure Belvedere parents place on their children leads to an understanding of high school as a "means to an end" on the part of many students. One senior explained his decision to take the hardest classes in high school: "If it was up to me, I'd be in all regular classes and do as little work as possible. But basically, like, my parents force me into everything . . . I mean, I really don't think in high school— like, I don't really care what we're learning here, but most of it's just so I can get into a good college."

In response to both the pressure from the parents and the academic success of the students, Belvedere school officials continue to add more AP courses—a different form of test prep than in Lakewood. One of the assistant principals noted that between the early 1990s and early 2000s, Belvedere High School doubled the number of AP courses offered to twenty-seven. Such responses to the pressures and demands of parents perpetuate the distinctions between Belvedere and the other districts we studied where the state mandates are more the ceiling than the floor.

In the two most racially/ethnically and socioeconomically diverse school districts, Leesburg and Clearview, the more affluent and well-educated parents, who were mostly white, did the same thing. The difference is that in those contexts such parents were distinct from other, less-involved, less-vocal parents. In Leesburg, for instance, the higher-income white parents are vocal and demanding of their children and the school. As a high school teacher there explained, "These parents expect their children to get 100 percent on every assignment. If the students receive a 99 percent, the parents want to know what they could have done to get a higher score."

It is clear, therefore, that Belvedere parents are not unique among affluent, white parents in terms of their expectations and the demands they place on their children and their educators. But what makes Belvedere unique among the districts we studied is the concentration of such parents in one school district, creating not only an exclusive enclave in which other students outside the district cannot participate in the high-status curriculum but also a pressure cooker environment in which the academic floor for the high school is higher than the ceiling is in most public high schools. And the fear of falling through that floor is great.

The relationship between students' academic identities and the curriculum offered in their schools—the high-pressure atmosphere of Belvedere or the less-involved communities of color in a diverse district such as Clearview—all shape their sense of themselves as students and their possibilities for the future. They, in turn, are likely to internalize this sense of where they "fit in" in a manner that can profoundly shape their future decisions. What these data suggest is that the curricular and educational distinctions across separate educational spaces shape not only what the students experience but also what they come to understand they *should* experience.

FINDING 3: THE POLITICAL FALLOUT OF SEPARATE AND UNEQUAL SCHOOL DISTRICTS

Another critical facet of public school inequality is the relationship between the highly unequal social contexts of school districts across Long Island and the democratic processes in public education systems. What we see here is that the local constituents in the poorer communities often lack the political power and the information needed to hold school officials and educators accountable for the quality of education they provide the students. Such lack of political clout—directly related to the concentration of families with limited economic and social capital across separate and unequal school districts—stunts the development of vibrant democratic institutions.

While such lack of accountability and voice is problematic in the context of a racially and ethnically diverse school district such as Clearview, at least the Clearview parents and students have greater access (in theory) to a more challenging curriculum and higher-quality teachers within the boundaries of their district and schools. The fact that their children are not always able to partake of these resources due to several social, political, and academic barriers is highly problematic, but it is a more easily solved problem than segregation across district lines. However, when the racial/ethnic and social class segregation transcends school district boundary lines, African American, Latino, and low-income families are more systematically removed from both tangible and intangible opportunities and they rarely have the political clout to demand or develop within the context of separate and unequal school systems.

School Districts with Poor and Disenfranchised Constituents Lack Political Accountability

Our conclusion after studying these five school districts is that in the context of communities characterized by high levels of poverty and large numbers of disempowered and recent immigrant families, public school systems too often serve a purpose other than educating the children. In the poorest district we studied, Grantsville, allegedly the public funding generated by the district is used to support school board members, allowing them to hand out jobs and contracts to people who need income and who are too often willing to pay kickbacks to the board members. In this local context, where there are few viable working- or middle-class jobs to be had, inside whistle-blowers complain that the school district and its funds too often support the most well-connected community members. Sometimes, some of these observers fear, such support comes at the expense of the Grantsville schools and students.

According to U.S. Census data on the residential population within the Grantsville school district, the parents and constituents in this district are for the most part poorly educated, low income, and recent immigrants. And, according to several officials in the Grantsville district, this leads to a situation in which many of these constituents lack the efficacy or legitimacy in the political system to hold the school board accountable. One Grantsville school board member who ran on an anticorruption platform noted that many of the parents in this district are busy surviving on low wages and long work hours, and they often come from a context and culture in which parents are not supposed to question educators or officials. Meanwhile, the more efficacious and affluent residents of this district put their children in private schools. This school board member noted that part of the problem of the corruption and lack of accountability in Grantsville is the lack of involvement and political pushback from the community.

The result of this lack of political vigilance within Grantsville, a political context of much poverty and scarce resources, is that corruption and malfeasance are not unusual.[23] This board member and others we interviewed know of people who have personally benefited from the corruption and kickbacks, of board members using their district-issued credit cards for personal expenses (including their magazine subscriptions, groceries, and non–district related cell phone charges), of friends of friends who got jobs they may or may not have been qualified to take.

Related to these issues of corruption and malfeasance and the subsequent whistle-blowing, there is a great deal of turnover in the central administration of the Grantsville school district. As one of the few long-time administrators in the Grantsville district noted, "I think if they could just get some permanent administration in here, you know, the district may be able to move. But when you get administration in here for six months, and you have this administration here for a year, you know, they come in and they wanna fix this. But [they] weren't here those prior years, so [they] don't know what happened. . . . you need stability to move forward."

What became increasingly clear to us during our data collection is that the type of corruption and malfeasance seemingly rampant in Grantsville would be unlikely to occur in a place like Belvedere. According to the Belvedere superintendent, the school board in this wealthy enclave is a group of highly educated adults who have a lot of information on what students need in an educational system to go on to high-status colleges and well-paying careers. They are also, as a political body, very responsive to the needs and demands of their constituents because there would be large political consequences if they were not. He also said, "I cannot tell you the level to which the Board members are actively involved in the education of the community. . . . They sit on committees. . . . we have Board members that go to the parent meetings so they know what's on the minds of the residents. They're very responsive to the residents. This is really just not, you know, a kind of a rubber stamp board or a board that is very removed from what's going on in the community. These people are on top of everything."

Similarly, the whistle-blower on the Grantsville school board member said that such corruption problems would not arise in more affluent contexts because there tends to be much more community involvement. "Parental involvement, community involvement is the difference." She said that communities with more of this kind of involvement would not "tolerate the fact that your buildings are in disrepair, that they're dirty, that your children don't have the proper learning environment. That your children are overcrowded and sitting in cardboard boxes by the roadside. I don't see any other community tolerating this."

Meanwhile, in Leesburg, the diverse school district experiencing a great deal of white flight in the last decade, there also appears to be a breakdown of the democratic process, because certain segments of that community may be too disenfranchised to fight the massive public funding for private schools. As a result of all the animosity, disconnection, and inequality within the Leesburg district, the democratic institution of public education does not function very well. Allegedly, people get bought off, and the minority parents are rarely involved and typically do not fight for their children's rights.

The lack of involvement and voice among the politically disenfranchised constituents of public education is not unique to Long Island. It appears to be a more universal phenomenon within low-income contexts with high concentrations of students of color and/or recent immigrant families. This is particularly a problem in Lakewood, where a large percentage of the population is recent immigrants who are not citizens, cannot vote, and may or may not speak English. According to one Lakewood school board member, these immigrants are often coming from countries or communities and settings where their vote was not important: "They don't feel that they have to be involved in that process. They're also coming from situations where you just picked your child up and you sent them to school and the school did what it had to do."

If the democratic process relies on some degree of efficacy, empowerment, and engagement on the part of its constituents, then the process of concentrating large percentages of people who lack these characteristics within distinct boundary lines seems highly detrimental to the creation of an effective public education system.

This section, in particular, highlights the political dimensions of inequality across school district contexts and the implications of that inequality for the functioning and success of democratic institutions such as public schools. Unless we explore all these many dimensions of inequality and their consequences for schools and students, we will not fully appreciate the effects of separateness and inequality in public education or the consequences of it for a democratic and increasingly diverse society.

CONCLUSION

We intended our research on Long Island to be a means for better understanding the ways in which the people who live within this separate and unequal public educational system make sense of it, how they help perpetuate it, and how both their perceptions and actions legitimize and reinforce it. Our findings speak to these understandings and their relationship to the structural inequalities illustrated in the quantitative data we collected on Nassau County, which documents the many facets and layers of inequality within the educational system and the central role that boundaries play in maintaining those inequalities, with white affluent students consistently on the more privileged side of the divide.

Our aim, therefore, is to present one way of making sense of the process by which tangible (material) and intangible (reputational) characteristics of school districts are intertwined in a manner that drives ongoing racial, ethnic, and social class segregation and stratification across place and space, particularly in highly fragmented areas such as Long Island.[24] In this way, tangible and intangible factors maintain an iterative relationship, often rising and falling together, creating sets of self-fulfilling prophecies as "bad" districts are both seen as bad and then become or remain bad due to lack of resources and high concentrations of poor students with relatively lower outcomes.

In our report from this study, we discuss several possible policy recommendations, including school district consolidation and interdistrict school desegregation plans.[25] We realize, however, that neither of these policies is likely to be implemented in the current political context in the aftermath of *Milliken*.[26] A more likely short-term strategy would be to build on the work being done across the country to support and sustain suburban communities that are racially, ethnically, and socioeconomically diverse in terms of their communities and public schools. This "diverse suburb" movement may be our best strategy to combat the creation of more school districts like Grantsville, for it is in places like this that we most clearly understand why, more than forty years ago, a different U.S. Supreme Court ruling in *Rodriguez* would have been much better than what we got but still not enough to ensure equal educational opportunity.[27]

PART II

Exploring Novel State Reforms That Support Equal Educational Opportunity

SIX

From *Rodriguez* to *Abbott*

New Jersey's Standards-Linked
School Funding Reform

DAVID G. SCIARRA
AND DANIELLE FARRIE

TEXAS HAS WITNESSED decades of school finance litigation, beginning with the United States Supreme Court decision in *Rodriquez* in 1973 and followed by three major lawsuits in state court, with several notable decisions by the Texas Supreme Court.[1] All of these cases challenged significant disparities in education resources between the state's high-wealth communities and its low-wealth communities. These resource gaps, so glaring in the late 1960s, have persisted through the decades and, despite some improvements in response to court intervention, remain firmly embedded in the state's finance structure. The bottom line: Texas provides substantially less funding to educate children in poor school districts than it does children in affluent, advantaged districts.

We contend that the persistent inequity in Texas school funding is not an anomaly; it both represents the enduring pattern of school finance in the United States over the last half-century and reflects the current condition in all but a handful of states. One state is New Jersey; we describe how that state broke through this pattern and achieved fair school funding, spurred by the state's supreme court rulings in *Abbott v. Burke*.[2] This effort culminated in the adoption of an unprecedented "standards-linked" finance formula in 2008 that connected school funding with the state's broader adoption of academic content standards and performance assessments.[3] We explore the challenges of and prospects for the New Jersey formula to serve as a model for a new wave of state finance reform explicitly intended to ameliorate resource disparities by aligning school funding to the actual cost of delivering rigorous academic standards to all students.

THE PERSISTENCE OF SCHOOL FUNDING DISPARITIES

Public education finance in the United States is controlled by the states, which, through school funding laws, account for the lion's share of education spending from state and local revenue. A lack of revenue data suitable for making comparisons both within and across states impedes analyzing overall funding levels and allocations relative to student poverty. The only comparative data is published by the National Center for Education Statistics (NCES), which measures the local and state revenue in each state on a per-pupil basis but does not account for student poverty or control for other factors that influence educational costs.

In 2010, a new set of measures was published that provides a more robust comparative analysis of state school finance. "Is School Funding Fair? A National Report Card" evaluates the states for funding "fairness," defined as a "system that ensures equal educational opportunity by providing a sufficient level of funding distributed to districts to account for additional needs generated by student poverty."[4] The Report Card, as it's known, measures state school finance fairness to evaluate whether these "systems ensure equality of educational opportunity for all children, regardless of background, family income, where they live, or where they attend school."[5]

The Report Card uses several measures as the foundational elements of a fair finance system. First, fairness requires varying levels of funding to provide equal educational opportunities to children with different needs. Specifically, funding levels should increase relative to the level of concentrated student poverty within a state. Schools and districts with high enrollments of poor students face a multitude of challenges that require additional educational resources. For example, high-quality preschool, full-day kindergarten, and afterschool and summer programs are all effective strategies for addressing achievement gaps between poor and not-poor students that require significant investments.[6] Districts with high poverty levels also require staff and programs to address the greater need for security, health and social services, and other programs. Student poverty is also correlated with a host of other factors that affect the costs of providing equal educational opportunity, such as racial segregation, English language proficiency, and student mobility.[7]

Second, fairness requires not just a fair distribution to account for student needs but also an overall funding level or base that is sufficient for all children statewide. Without sufficient base funding, even a system that allocates more for concentrated poverty will still be unable to provide equality of educational opportunities. Of course, sufficient funding alone does not lead to higher student outcomes; funding must be effectively used. Successful schools, however, do require a sufficient level of base funding to make investments in the foundational elements of schooling, including quality teaching, small class sizes, a rigorous curriculum in a wide range of content areas, and effective interventions for struggling students.[8]

The evidence is compelling that increasing overall funding and reducing inequities can lead to increased achievement, especially for low-income students. David Card and A. Abigail Payne have found that equalizing spending levels narrowed gaps in test score results in a multistate analysis.[9] More recently, C. Kirabo Jackson and colleagues found strong evidence that increased spending on education through court-ordered finance reforms provided long-term benefits in educational attainment, earnings, and a reduction in adult poverty.[10] Other studies of specific state reforms have found that court intervention improved educational outcomes, for example in Michigan, Kansas, and Massachusetts.[11]

Other research examines in more detail specific resources made available by increased funding that improves outcomes. The greatest proportion of school budgets is dedicated to teaching staff and other personnel. Two proven methods for improving outcomes are increasing staff levels and improving teacher quality through competitive wages. Research has also shown that smaller class sizes lead to better outcomes, particularly among low-income and minority students.[12] Similarly, higher overall and relative wages for teachers influence career choices, raise the quality of teachers, and boost achievement.[13] Recent longitudinal research tying twenty years of school funding and resource allocation data shows that variations in the level and distribution of funding have a predictable influence on access to these important resources and that these resources are associated with improved outcomes and smaller achievement gaps.[14]

The Report Card identifies two predominant features of public education that affect cost: decentralized governance and concentrated student poverty.

Decentralized governance means that school funding is determined and distributed through a non-uniform system to varying numbers of districts and charter schools. Further, there is also a growing population of at-risk students, many of whom are concentrated within a subset of districts. In the 2011–2012 school year, nearly half of all students in the United States were eligible for free or reduced-price lunch.[15] This marks nearly a decade of increasing poverty where the number of poor students grew from approximately eighteen million in 2000–2001 to over twenty-four million in 2011–2012.[16] The percentage of students in high-poverty schools (greater than 75 percent eligible for free/reduced lunch) grew from 12 to 19 percent in the last decade, and the number of students in majority-poor schools grew from 28 to 44 percent.[17] Of course, concentrated poverty is a significant barrier to educational progress in that it generates additional education costs.[18]

The Report Card categorizes states into three groups to describe the distribution of funding relative to student poverty: progressive, regressive, or flat (see figure 6.1). Progressive states provide higher district revenues as student poverty increases, while regressive states do the opposite; poor districts receive less than wealthy districts. In flat states there is no distinguishable relationship between funding and poverty. Though flat systems may not be as unfair as regressive systems, these systems also fail to meet the objectives of fair school funding. The Report Card also groups states

FIGURE 6.1   Funding profile

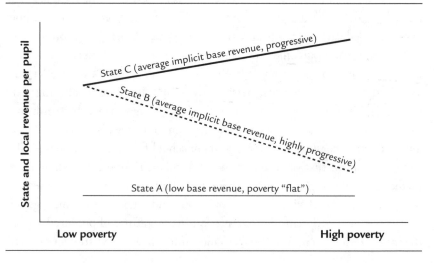

in small clusters or regions to allow for further comparison, such as the Mid-Atlantic Region.[19]

Figure 6.2 is illustrative of the pattern of funding disparities within and between states. In New Jersey and Delaware, funding increases with poverty level, giving high-poverty districts the capacity to provide students the extra resources necessary to ensure equality in educational opportunity. In New York and Maryland, funding levels are higher in low-poverty districts, and, correspondingly, high-poverty districts have less despite needing additional resources. While Delaware and New Jersey are progressive, funding in Delaware is far below New Jersey, after controlling for regional cost differences. In the Gulf Coast region, Mississippi is low-spending and does not provide additional funding to high-poverty districts (see figure 6.3). Louisiana is relatively low-spending but progressive, providing some additional funding to higher-need districts. Alabama and Texas are low-spending and regressive, a double disadvantage to students in poor districts who receive less funding than students in wealthy districts.

A map of the Report Card shows that fifteen states are progressive, fourteen are regressive, and the remaining are flat (see figure 6.4). New Jersey, whose school finance reform is the subject of this article, has a progressive

FIGURE 6.2   Funding profile: Mid-Atlantic

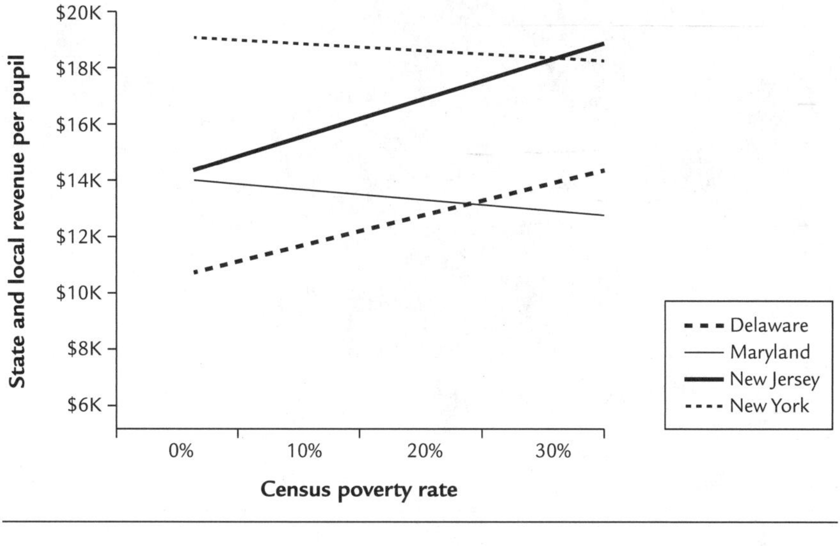

FIGURE 6.3 Funding profile: Gulf Coast

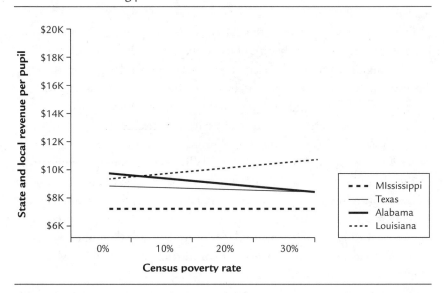

FIGURE 6.4 Funding distribution

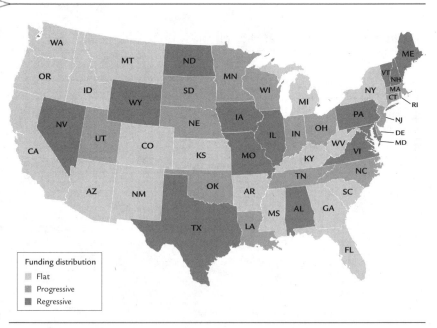

system in which the highest-poverty districts, on average, receive about $1.30 for every dollar in the lowest-poverty districts. In contrast, Nevada is the most regressive state; there, students in high-poverty districts receive only $.48 cents for every $1 in low-poverty settings.

Only a few states provide a sufficient level of base funding and also deliver greater resources as poverty increases. Consequently, most states do not ensure that districts have the resources needed to provide an equal educational opportunity for all students, regardless of socioeconomic background. Thus, four decades after *Rodriguez*, the Report Card documents continuing state resistance to providing sufficient education resources to give all students the opportunity to achieve rigorous standards prepared for current workforce and postsecondary education.

NEW JERSEY'S ROUTE TO FAIR SCHOOL FUNDING

In 1990, New Jersey was plagued by the same glaring disparities in funding between poor and wealthy districts that remain the dominant feature of state school finance. In 1984, the gap in per-pupil expenditures between the wealthy and poor districts was $1,140 per pupil, with poor districts receiving only 71 percent of the funding received in wealthy districts. These disparities were caused by New Jersey's overreliance on property taxes to fund education and the insufficiency of state aid targeted to property-poor communities. But by 2011, the state had both eliminated that disparity and also allocated more resources to the poor districts than to the more affluent ones.[20] Thus, in twenty years, New Jersey, unlike neighboring New York and Pennsylvania, transformed its school finance system from regressive to progressive, becoming one of the few states to provide sufficient base funding for all students and higher funding to districts with greater student need.

How did this transformation, elusive in so many states, take place? In the complicated educational and political context of school finance, many factors were at work over this two-decade span. Several, however, are central. First, the legislature's adoption of statewide standards-based education in 1996, and its subsequent implementation, played a pivotal role in New Jersey's school finance reform. Second, change was fueled by the supreme court's 1997 *Abbott IV* ruling, and the court also performed critical oversight and review of the new school finance formula adopted by the legislature ten years later.[21] Finally, the reform was supported by the concerted and sustained efforts of parents, education stakeholders, and citizens who advocated for fair funding in the Trenton statehouse and in communities across New Jersey.

These and other factors led to the enactment of a new statewide school funding formula, the School Funding Reform Act (SFRA), in January 2008. With the SFRA, New Jersey successfully transitioned from funding public education based largely on political considerations in the annual negotiations over the state budget to funding schools based on the actual cost of enabling all students, including low-income (at-risk) children, English language learners (ELLs), and students with disabilities, to achieve state academic standards.

1990 to 2004: Setting the Stage for School Funding Reform

The road to fair school funding begins with the New Jersey Supreme Court's 1990 *Abbott II* decision holding unconstitutional the Public Education Act of 1975, the finance formula at the time, as it applied to twenty-nine of the state's poorest urban, or "special needs," districts.[22] The court concluded that the act perpetuated deep disparities in funding between affluent suburban districts and the special needs districts, resulting in "tragically inadequate" education for students in those districts. Noting that the state had no substantive education standards on which to fashion a remedy, the court, without an alternative, utilized the educational program and funding levels in the successful suburban districts as the benchmark for "adequate" funding for the special needs districts. It ordered that the state must provide additional aid to bring the special needs districts to the average suburban district funding level, or "parity." The court also ordered the state to study the needs of students in the special needs districts for additional or "supplemental" programs and provide adequate funding for their implementation.

After an attempt at a statewide finance formula failed to comply with the court's remedial order for the special needs districts, the legislature, in 1996, adopted a second formula, the Comprehensive Educational Improvement and Financing Act (CEIFA).[23] At the heart of CEIFA was the legislature's adoption of the state's first academic standards in seven curriculum content areas, along with statewide assessments to measure student achievement of the standards. Further, the CEIFA formula was based on education costs derived from a single hypothetical school district constructed by the state education department, which the state claimed would provide the funding needed to deliver the academic standards to all students. As the state's supreme court observed, New Jersey, with enactment of the CEIFA formula, "appears to be the first state to try to base funding determinations on achievement standards."[24]

In the 1997 *Abbott IV* decision, the New Jersey Supreme Court held the CEIFA formula unconstitutional as applied to the special needs districts. The court made three critical rulings that dramatically shaped future school finance reform and altered the national educational landscape. First, describing the state legislature's adoption of standards-based reform as a "major step," the court held that the state's curriculum content standards and assessments are "facially adequate" and "a reasonable legislative definition of a constitutional thorough and efficient education" for all New Jersey students.[25] Second, the court made clear that content standards "themselves do not ensure any substantive level of achievement" and alone "cannot answer the fundamental inquiry" of whether the CEIFA financing formula "assures the level of resources needed to provide a [constitutional] education to children in the special needs districts."[26] As the court noted, "Real improvement still depends on the sufficiency of educational resources, successful teaching, effective supervision, efficient administration, and a variety of other academic, environmental, and societal factors needed to assure [*sic*] a sound education. Content standards, therefore, cannot answer the fundamental inquiry of whether the new statute assures the level of resources needed to provide a thorough and efficient education to children in the special needs districts."[27] Finally, the court determined that, to pass constitutional muster, the CEIFA funding formula must in a "concrete way attempt to link the content standards to the actual funding needed to deliver that content."[28]

Applying these principles, the court declared the CEIFA formula unconstitutional for several reasons. First, it cited the use of a "hypothetical" district cost model not based on the characteristics of the special needs districts or derived from the education costs in the successful suburban districts. Second, it underscored the state's failure to present evidence that the higher spending levels allowed in the suburban districts represented "excess" spending not necessary for the delivery of state academic standards. Finally, the court rejected the formula's use of funding levels based on a single set of education costs as "rest[ing] on the unrealistic assumption that, in effectuating the imperative of a [constitutionally] thorough and efficient education, all school districts can be treated alike and in isolation from the realities of their surrounding environment."[29]

Having found CEIFA unconstitutional, the New Jersey Supreme Court underscored the lack of "any constitutional measuring stick against which to gauge the resources needed [to deliver the] substantive educational opportunity" defined by the state's new education standards.[30] Consequently, the court found it "eminently reasonable" to maintain the parity remedy for the special needs districts given the "recipe for success" in suburban districts, at least "until experience under the new standards dictates otherwise."[31] It also made clear that parity funding was an "interim" remedy, imploring the executive and legislative branches of the state to "devise an adequate alternative funding remedy" that "convincingly" linked funding to the resources needed by all students to achieve state content standards, including the additional resources required for at-risk students, ELLs, and students with disabilities.[32]

The impact of these rulings cannot be overstated. The legislatively enacted curriculum standards and assessments—standards-based education—substantively defined the constitutional guarantee of a thorough and efficient education for all public school children. Further, to ensure that all students are afforded the opportunity to achieve those academic standards, the state finance system must be concretely linked to the actual funding necessary to deliver those standards to students in all districts, whether rural, urban, or suburban. These core constitutional principles set the stage for the enactment of the SFRA funding formula in 2008.

2004 to 2007: Developing Standards-Linked Funding Reform

In the wake of *Abbott IV,* New Jersey school funding took an unusual turn. For the special needs districts, with less than a quarter of public school enrollment, the state provided parity and supplemental funding under the order of the supreme court. All other districts, including districts with significant concentrations of poor, at-risk students, remained under the 1996 CEIFA formula declared unconstitutional in *Abbott IV* as applied to the special needs districts. As a practical matter, the legislature, beginning in 1999, abided by the court-ordered parity and supplemental funding remedies in the special needs districts but fell behind in funding the rest of the state under the CEIFA formula. Tensions arose between Abbott and non-Abbott districts over funding as special needs districts received annual increases under judicial branch order and funding shortfalls accumulated in rural areas, inner-ring suburbs, and mid-wealth communities.[33] As this dynamic intensified, so did political pressure to develop an alternative statewide funding formula to replace the *Abbott* parity remedy.

Against this political and legal backdrop, in 2003 New Jersey education officials began to develop a new formula. The first step involved conducting a "costing-out" study using the professional judgment methodology. Using the curriculum content and performance standards, upheld in *Abbott IV,* the state developed several prototypical districts to conform to New Jersey's diverse district and school size and student demographics, including varying concentrations of at-risk and ELL students. To identify the resources needed in these prototypical districts, three separate panels were convened, each building on the predecessor panel's work: educators within the State Education Department, educators and representatives selected by stakeholder groups, and, last, district-level administrators.[34] This costing-out process yielded a set of essential resources for an elementary, a middle, and a high school in each district model, including the additional staff, programs, and services identified as needed for at-risk and ELL students in the various district concentrations. Finally, the state calculated the costs of these resources using 2004–2005 cost data, which included a base per-pupil amount for general education students and the cost of programs and services for at-risk and ELL students.

School Funding Reform Act of 2008

On January 2008, the New Jersey State Legislature enacted SFRA. This statewide "weighted student formula" was designed to provide the resources (as determined through the lengthy development process) for all students—including at-risk students, ELLs, students with disabilities, and children in preschool—to achieve the state's academic standards. The base cost was set at $9,469 per pupil, with the weights and other costs as follows:

- *Grade-level weights*: Half-day kindergarten .5, elementary 1.0, middle school 1.04, high school 1.07
- *At-risk weights*: .47 for districts below 20 percent poverty and .57 for districts over 60 percent poverty, with a sliding scale in between English-language learners .5
- *Combination students*: Both ELL and at-risk receive the at-risk weight plus .125

Preschool children: Per-pupil amounts vary depending on the classroom setting at $11,506 in public schools, $12,934 in community
providers, and $7,146 in Head Start to augment federal funds

- *Students with disabilities*: $1,082 for students receiving special edu-
cation speech-only services and $10,898 for all other special educa-
tion pupils.[35]

Based on these cost amounts, the SFRA formula calculates each district's
funding target level, or "adequacy budget." This includes four cost components: the base amount for general education elementary, middle, and high
school students; the additional weights for at-risk, ELL, and combination
students; two-thirds of special education costs using a census-based methodology; and 100 percent of census-based speech-only costs.[36] The adequacy
budget is then "wealth equalized," which means that state aid is based on
the community's property wealth and income. Districts receive state "equalization aid," which makes up the difference between the district's "local fair
share," or the amount districts are expected to raise from local property taxes,
and the adequacy budget level. Aside from equalization aid, the SFRA has
only a few categorical aids, most notably one-third special education costs,
school security aid, preschool education aid, and hold-harmless aid to transition districts to the new formula. The formula also requires review by the state
education commissioner and the governor every three years, including recommended adjustments to the formula's costs and weights based on that review.

With enactment of the SFRA, the state still had to convince the supreme
court that it had finally, after three failures since 1990, constructed a formula that would satisfy the state constitution and render the interim parity
remedy moot. The court assigned a special master judge to conduct hearings
to review the formula and report on his findings and recommendations. After receipt of the special master judge's report, the court, in the 2009 *Abbott
XX* ruling, upheld the formula, lifted its remedial funding order, and authorized implementation. It acknowledged the long and arduous road traveled to
"reach the point where it is possible to say with confidence that the most disadvantaged school children in the State will not be left out or left behind."[37]

The State has constructed a fair and equitable means designed to fund the
costs of a thorough and efficient education, measured against the delivery of
the [state academic and performance standards]. The quality of the effort and

the good faith exhibited in the exercise of discretion over and over again at decision points during SFRA's development lead us to conclude that the legislative effort deserves deference. The Legislature and Executive have made considerable efforts to confront the difficult question of how to address the education needs of at-risk pupils, no matter where these children attend school. Those efforts are made all the more impressive due to the coordinate branches' collective will to do so during difficult economic times when there is extreme pressure on scarce State resources.[38]

2008 to 2014: Formula Implementation

A fair funding formula, although essential to the determination of education costs and funding amounts, does not itself ensure actual state aid at formula levels. Year-to-year funding requires the appropriation of aid, as calculated by the formula, in the annual state budget. The New Jersey Supreme Court had experience with the legislature not appropriating funds mandated by formulas in the past. The court was also concerned about whether the SFRA would actually work, noting that "until the formula has had time to function as intended, it is impossible to know precisely what its effect will be."[39] These concerns prompted the court, in giving the SFRA a constitutional green light, to impose two conditions on the state: to fully fund the formula for the first three years of implementation and to "diligently" review the formula after its initial three years of operation and adjust it "as necessary based on the results of that review," as required by the SFRA.[40]

The state provided almost all of the funding required by the SFRA in 2008–2009 and 2009–2010, the initial two years of operation. However, in 2010–2011, Governor Chris Christie cut $1.1 billion and refused to appropriate an additional $500 million increase required by the formula. In deciding an enforcement motion filed by the *Abbott* plaintiffs, the court found the state had deliberately violated one of two "express mandates" in *Abbott XX,* three-years of full formula funding:

> The State made a conscious and calculated decision to underfund the SFRA formula when enacting the FY 2011 Appropriations Act. It was not inadvertent or a mistaken exercise of governmental authority. It directly contravened representations made by the State when procuring relief from prior judicial remedial order . . . Thus, for the [special needs] districts, it was an action by the State that directly contravened the judgment in *Abbott XX,* which had authorized the State to substitute full SFRA funding for the parity remedy in those

districts . . . When we granted the State the relief it requested, this Court did not authorize the State to replace the parity remedy with some underfunded version of the SFRA.[41]

Based on this finding, the court ordered the Christie administration to calculate and provide aid for 2010–2011 in accordance with the SFRA, but only for the special needs districts. Funding was not restored for all other districts that year, and through 2014 the statewide shortfall in formula funding reached $5.1 billion.[42]

Finally, under the parity and other program remedies imposed under *Abbott IV* and *Abbott V*, and implemented from 1999 until 2007, the special needs districts saw measurable gains in the academic performance of their students. State assessments demonstrated a significant reduction in the fourth and eighth grade gap between Abbott districts and high-wealth districts in this time period. The National Assessment of Educational Progress (NAEP) also confirms this trend with greater growth in achievement for urban than suburban districts resulting in a shrinking achievement gap.[43] Other analyses show a significant positive impact on eleventh grade achievement in the Abbott districts, especially among minority students.[44] Further, a decade of universal access to high-quality preschool after 2001 has led to considerable gains. Two years of Abbott preschool resulted in increased achievement in fourth and fifth grade language arts and math and fourth grade science. The gains are equivalent to 20 to 40 percent of the achievement gap between minority and white students. Participation in Abbott preschool also resulted in lower special education classification rates and lower grade repetition rates.[45]

However, the state's failure to fully fund the SFRA formula since 2010 raises questions about whether the special needs districts can sustain these improvements and whether other low-income districts will realize academic benefits from the formula's targeted funding for at-risk students across the state.[46] The underfunding of the SFRA, if chronic, has the potential to jeopardize New Jersey's ability to maintain both fair funding and its overall high academic performance in comparison to other states.

Implementation of the SFRA formula from 2008 through 2014 has a mixed record. The formula's determinations of education costs and funding remain intact, despite efforts by the Christie administration to reduce spending by arbitrarily lowering the weights for at-risk and ELL students and other formula modifications, proposals that were rejected by the legislature.

However, the formula has been underfunded since 2011, resulting in substantial shortfalls of state aid. Even in the face of judicial exhortations for performance, SFRA implementation has proven difficult. The formula's promise of fair, consistent, and stable funding has yet to be realized for many students.

A WAY FORWARD: LINKING FUNDING TO STANDARDS

As the New Jersey Supreme Court noted in 1997, the state was the first to explicitly design a school finance formula based on the costs of the state-mandated curriculum standards. That initial effort failed because, as the court found, the state failed to show a concrete link between the CEIFA formula's costs and the funding necessary to deliver its own substantive education standards.[47] Sent back to the drawing board, and after almost a decade of work, the state finally accomplished this objective with the 2008 SFRA formula. As the court concluded in reviewing the formula in 2009, the record presented by the state on the development, components, and future operation of the formula "convincingly" demonstrated that the SFRA was designed to, and would, if properly implemented, deliver "adequate resources to provide the necessary educational programs consistent with state standards."[48]

The SFRA represents a bright light in the otherwise bleak landscape of state school finance since *Rodriguez*. The formula utilizes state curriculum standards not just in language arts and mathematics but also in science, social studies, arts, and other content areas as the basis for funding public education.[49] It recognizes not only the need for staff, programs, and services to enable individual at-risk students to achieve academic standards but also the need for greater resources generated by concentrated poverty. It is also the first formula to fund universal, high-quality preschool for all three- and four-year-olds in poor communities.[50] Finally, the SFRA is the nation's first formula where the linkage between resource costs and academic standards has withstood rigorous review, in this case intense judicial scrutiny under exacting constitutional principles. By delivering significantly more resources to students and schools with greater educational and educationally related needs, the SFRA can not only maintain equitable funding in the state's poor districts but also advance equity across the finance system, solidifying the New Jersey's high rankings on funding fairness.

The lessons from the New Jersey experience warrant close attention from policy makers, lawyers, parents, and others concerned with inequitable school funding and the significant impediment that inequity imposes on equal educational opportunity. The education policy landscape is littered with decades of failed efforts in statehouses and courtrooms to bring a modicum of equity and fairness into public education finance. There is an urgent need to reframe the discussion and debate over how to tackle the resource and funding inequities that have endured in most states over the last forty years.

The SFRA offers a new framework for fundamentally altering traditional approaches to state finance reform. The formula posits the need for reform by building on a simple logic consistent with current education improvement efforts: as states mandate curriculum content standards and impose test-based accountability to measure whether districts, schools, and students are meeting those standards, the states must also put in place a finance system driven by the actual cost of affording students a meaningful opportunity to achieve those standards. If states are defining the substantive content of what all students are expected to learn and measuring outcomes based on that content, the states must also provide students the resources needed to achieve those very same standards. This "standards-linked" frame for school finance reform upends the long-standing, business-as-usual way in which school funding is provided, where the debate starts and, by and large, ends with how much money is available and how to allocate that money among districts and schools to satisfy political interests, with little regard for what is needed to satisfy state education standards and performance goals.

It may well be that the SFRA will remain an anomaly among the states, driven by the uniquely sui generis *Abbott* rulings. There remains a stubborn resistance in many states to taking even the initial step of determining the actual cost of delivering mandated academic standards.[51] This resistance is motivated by how class and race stratifications, the vestiges of de jure segregation, and the realities of de facto segregation arising from housing and community wealth patterns play out in each state and how those factors impact political power in the statehouses. But it also arises from the fear—a realistic one—that the actual cost of standards-based education will significantly exceed the current level of investment in the public schools. What governors and legislators don't know cannot be used against them, or so the conventional wisdom goes.

There also exists a powerful and unchecked dynamic for states "under the guise of local autonomy," to delegate their affirmative constitutional responsibility to operate the nation's public education systems to their local constructs: districts and schools.[52] The roots of this modus operandi lie in the American tradition of local control of public education. In the current standards-based context, however, state delegation has transformed the promise of standards-based education into an unfunded mandate of significant dimension, as local districts and schools struggle to deliver more rigorous academic standards imposed by the state but without the requisite funding to afford students the opportunity to achieve those standards, particularly at-risk and ELL students and those high-poverty schools.

A recent federal report offers hope for building a new wave of state school funding reform, one grounded in SFRA-style standards-linked education finance. Authorized by Congress and established in February 2011, the Equity and Excellence Commission was charged with analyzing the condition of school funding in the states and making "recommendations for restructuring school finance systems to achieve equity in the distribution of educational resources and further student performance, especially for students at the lower end of the achievement gap."[53] The commission marked the first federal-level review of state education finance since 1972, when President Richard Nixon's Commission on School Finance documented the deep inequities resulting from overreliance on the property tax, the centerpiece of the unsuccessful challenge in *Rodriguez* to the Texas school finance system a year later.

The commission's February 2013 report, *For Each and Every Child: A Strategy for Education Equity and Excellence,* confirms the scant improvement in the level and distribution of school funding in the United States since Nixon's commission called for reform.[54] The Equity and Excellence Commission finds state reliance on local property taxes remains heavy, perpetuating the same disparities in funding between high- and low-poverty communities that figured so prominently in *Rodriguez*.[55] The commission also concludes that the resulting inequities in school finance across the states remain entrenched, exacerbated by the growing concentration of student poverty across the nation. Citing studies documenting inadequate funding in states over the last forty years, the commission finds this condition a key reason why the decentralized American education system has failed to properly educate so many children, especially low-income children and children of color, and contends that this failure "threatens the nation's ability to compete and retain leadership in the global economy."[56]

In calling for the states to reform their outmoded school finance systems, the Equity and Excellence Commission breaks new ground. Its diagnosis moves beyond variations in state spending and the level of spending in the United States as a whole, simplistic comparisons that dominate the public discussion of school funding. The commission also moves beyond the endless debates over whether money matters or whether districts already spend "too much" or can "cut" their way to equity through greater efficiencies.[57] Instead, the commission, in calling for states to overhaul education finance, lands firmly on the nexus between the state academic standards and the mechanism for public school funding:

> With few exceptions, states continue to finance public education through methods that have no demonstrable link to the cost of delivering rigorous academic standards and that can produce high achievement in all students, including but not limited to low income students, English-language learners, students with disabilities, students in high poverty and students who live in remote schools and districts. Few states have rationally determined the cost of enabling all students to achieve established content and performance standards, including the cost of achieving those standards across diverse student populations and geographic locations. Most states do not properly ensure the efficient use of resources to attain high achievement for all students. A meaningful educational opportunity requires that states make sure all students receive the resources to achieve rigorous academic standards and obtain the skills to compete in the economy and participate capably as citizens in a democratic society.[58]

The commission's call for "demonstrable linkage" between the substantive education content and the resources necessary for all students, including those with additional needs resulting from poverty, disability, or the need to learn English, mirrors the core principle articulated by the New Jersey Supreme Court in 1997 that undergirds the design of the SFRA formula enacted a decade later. As the *Abbott IV* ruling established the animating principles for New Jerseys' reform, the Equity and Excellence Commission provides specific recommendations to guide states in the development of a new generation of finance systems where funding levels are driven by the actual cost of delivering rigorous standards to all students.

First, the commission recommends that states begin by identifying the teaching staff, programs, and services necessary to provide all students the opportunity to achieve academic standards and to determine and report the actual cost of those essential resources. Second, it urges the states to adopt and implement a school finance system designed to provide equitable and sufficient funding for all students to achieve state content and performance standards. Here the commission emphasizes the point crucial to standards-based reform: students have differing needs that must be addressed, and, correspondingly, states must finance the additional resources to address the extra-educational needs of at-risk students, students in concentrated poverty, ELLs, students with disabilities, and students in remote areas.

Third, the commission calls for the states to do more than enact a standards-linked funding formula; they must also ensure that these systems are supported by stable and predictable sources of revenue to give all students a meaningful opportunity to reach established achievement goals. As so often occurs, and as the New Jersey experience shows, no matter how carefully a formula may be constructed, or how realistic the formula's cost determinations may be, unless the formula is actually funded as calculated from year to year, it will have no impact on whether students actually have the resources, driven by student and school need, to achieve prescribed standards.

Fourth, the commission confronts the reality that standards-based finance systems must be continuously adjusted to address changes in student demographics; changes in standards, assessments, and programs; and advances in practice and research. To meet these dynamics, states must periodically review and update their finance systems to maintain the opportunities for student achievement. As the New Jersey Supreme Court aptly observed, a school funding formula "is not an occurrence at a moment in time" but a "continuing obligation," citing the SFRA's required three-year review with the expectation that elected officials will "address whatever adjustments are necessary to keep the SFRA operating at its optimal level."[59] The commission's endorsement of ongoing formula review and adjustment mirrors these critical considerations.

Finally, the Equity and Excellence Commission emphasizes the pivotal point at which standards-linked finance systems must move past the confines of the typical formula: determining the level and distribution of funding to districts and schools. Rather, these systems must also include mechanisms to ensure the effective and efficient use of all education funding to enable students to achieve state academic standards. This recommendation embodies the principle so forcefully articulated in *Abbott IV,* namely, that adequate funding "will not, without more, solve the chronic problems of educating students" in high-poverty districts and schools.[60] "Equally important, if not more so, is the manner in which money is spent"—to effectuate this imperative, *Abbott IV* placed on the state the "essential and affirmative role" of ensuring that all funding is spent "effectively and efficiently" to enable students to achieve state academic standards.[61] The Equity and Excellence Commission places squarely on states the concomitant responsibility to provide fair funding and adopt and implement measures to ensure its effective and efficient use by districts and schools.

The decades since *Rodriguez* have witnessed countless policy efforts and recurring rounds of litigation to ameliorate the stubborn inequities so prominent in state school finance. Throughout this period, Congress has remained on the sidelines, ceding the issue, as the U.S. Supreme Court did in *Rodriguez,* as a matter within the sole province of the states. The Equity and Excellence Commission acknowledges this by noting that federal education policies "have not addressed the fundamental sources of inequities" in the states and have "continue[d] to allow for, and in many ways encourage, inequitable and inadequate funding systems and inefficient and ineffective resource allocation."[62] The commission also recognizes that a dramatic shift in the federal-state relations is needed, a shift built on the emerging consensus that education is central to confronting the national, twenty-first-century challenges of growing diversity, rising poverty, wage stagnation, and global economic competition. The No Child Left Behind Act (NCLB) has a narrow focus: conditioning state receipt of federal funds on implementation of content standards, assessments, and accountability regimes to measure district, school, and student performance. NCLB does not demand that states reform their finance systems to deliver the resources students and schools need to achieve its standards-based education objectives. By requiring states to adopt educational standards while ignoring the stark reality that state school funding is too often inequitable, the federal funds provided through NCLB and other programs—a relatively small share of overall education spending—has the effect of subsidizing the resource deficits experienced by many districts.[63] These resource deficiencies, the direct consequence of unfair state funding, impose a significant barrier to accomplishing NCLB's main objective: boosting achievement among academically at-risk student subgroups.[64]

The Equity and Excellence Commission proposes a greater federal role in financing K–12 education, noting that while *Rodriguez* refused to review unequal funding under the U.S. Constitution, there is no constitutional barrier to the enactment of federal policies to address the issue. The commission

recommends that the federal government assume this greater role by utilizing federal funds to provide incentives to states to adopt standards-linked finance systems and to demonstrate progress in the implementation of these
systems. It also calls on Congress to enact new "Equity and Excellence" legislation to provide significant new federal funding targeted at high-poverty
schools with achievement gaps and to offer states incentives to enhance their
own funding of such schools. The legislation should also include mechanisms
to enable the federal government to "monitor and enforce the ongoing performance of its new equity and excellence investments to make sure those investments are, in fact, enhancing student achievement."[65]

These recommendations represent a paradigm shift in federal education policy, one built on investing in strengthening standards-based education in the
states. The Equity and Excellence Commission wants federal policy to move
beyond its current, limited formulation by recognizing, as the New Jersey Supreme Court did in 1997, that standards alone do not ensure any substantive
level of education and student achievement; that making gains in student
achievement also depends on the sufficiency of teaching staff, programs, services, and other educational resources; and that, in the standards-based context, fair funding demands that states demonstrate a concrete linkage between
funding and the actual cost of delivering those standards to students with differing needs and in diverse school and district settings.

It may well be that congressional action on the commission's proposals
are not promising in the short term, given the staunch resistance to measures
that would be viewed as "federalizing" education and eroding the tradition
of local control. Yet, the commission has set the stage for what could be the
beginning of a long-term effort to enact federal legislation that provides increased funding tied to standards-linked finance reform. The touchstone of
this change is a federal focus on the overarching objective of enforcing the
right to education guaranteed to all students under their respective state constitutions by pressing the states to put in place the fair and equitable systems
of public education that serve every student, without regard to community
wealth or household income.

CONCLUSION

Rodriguez held that, under the Equal Protection Clause, education is not a
fundamental right, either explicit or implicit, in the language of the United

States Constitution. The U.S. Supreme Court also held that poverty is not a suspect classification for purposes of examining the disparities in school funding resulting from Texas's reliance on local property taxes in its finance law. The significance of these rulings on public education cannot be underestimated. *Rodriguez* insulated the states from federal constitutional review of school funding no matter how unequal that funding may be for students in high-poverty schools, or what the impact such funding disparities have on the quality and quantity of teaching staff, curriculum, course offerings, class size, kindergarten, or other resources in those schools and on the educational outcomes of students. *Rodriguez* effectively slammed the courthouse door shut to challenging unequal school funding under the U.S. Constitution.

Rodriguez also solidified the centrality of the state's role in and responsibility for public education. As the Supreme Court makes clear, with no explicit right or fundamental interest under the Constitution, education is the ultimate state right, ensconced as an affirmative, substantive guarantee to children in each of the fifty state constitutions. Yet, in the post-*Rodriguez* era, as the United States grapples with the impact of globalization, deindustrialization, advancing technology, and increasing racial and ethnic diversity, education is vital to national, and not just local, interests. These interests include workforce preparation, economic productivity, and civic engagement. In the face of these national concerns, the *Rodriguez* legacy has confined the federal government to the margins, as Congress struggles to enact policies in limited areas where lawmakers are able to reach consensus, such as the NCLB requirements for state adoption of content standards in language arts and mathematics.[66]

National education imperatives, however, have been growing in strength since the 1990s, allowing Congress to condition federal funding on the implementation of standards-based education in the states, albeit uneven, bumpy, and altogether unfinished. It is important to consider that, when *Rodriguez* was argued before the Supreme Court in 1973, Texas had neither academic content standards nor uniform assessments to measure the extent to which children were achieving those standards. At that time, matters related to academic content and student proficiency were delegated by Texas to its local instrumentalities—the districts. *Rodriguez* was decided on an evidentiary record consisting almost exclusively of the differences in spending levels between property-poor and -wealthy districts permitted under the Texas finance regime, with almost no proof of the impact of those differentials on

the educational program offered in the poor districts, much less the achievement levels of the predominately poor and minority children attending those
districts' schools. As the Court noted, Texas was able to "repeatedly assert"
in *Rodriguez* that its funding system allowed all districts to "have at least an
adequate program of education" and that "no proof was offered at trial persuasively discrediting or refuting the State's assertion."[67]

The establishment of standards-based education in the mid-1990s, acceler-
ated by the enactment of the NCLB in 2001, has profoundly altered this landscape. Even though states have had, and still have, de jure control over public
education, they historically left much of the financing, delivery, and quality
to the local communities. This tradition, as the *Rodriguez* Court acknowledged, has a "persistence of attachment" so strong as to sanction, at least under federal equal protection analysis, wide gaps in education spending within
states, such as those in Texas documented in the uncontested record before
the U.S. Supreme Court.[68] The adoption of uniform curriculum content standards, along with assessments, was the first significant step by states to assume direct control over the substance of education delivery and performance
by local districts and schools. As the New Jersey Supreme Court noted, prior
to 1997 there was no "valid legislative implementation" of the state's "constitutional education clause," leaving it to the court "to devise appropriate remedies to ameliorate the deprivation of an adequate education" for poor and
minority schoolchildren in the special needs districts.[69] With the enactment of
standards-based education, however, "the Legislature has now taken a major
step to spell out and explain the meaning of a constitutional education. The
content and performance standards prescribed by the new statute represent
the first real effort on the part of the legislative and executive branches to define and implement the education required by the [New Jersey] Constitution.
It is an effort that strongly warrants judicial deference."[70]

Legislatively prescribed standards are now firmly embedded in the states.
State standards also increasingly include disaggregated student data, school
report cards, and other accountability measures to assess the performance of
students in achieving those standards and, in turn, the success or failure of
districts, schools, and the state itself. From this lens, the stage is set to advance a new argument for fair and equitable school funding, one grounded in
the stark reality that the way most states fund education is an anachronism, a
relic of a bygone era. These outmoded finance systems are wholly unresponsive to current national education imperatives. The flaw in these traditional

finance systems is plain: the absence of any concrete relationship between school funding and the actual cost of meeting substantive state standards and performance goals, along with turning a blind eye toward the manner in which funding is used by districts and in schools and classrooms.

The correction of this fundamental flaw is what makes New Jersey's SFRA formula ground breaking. The formula closes the loop in a standards-based system, connecting state-mandated academic and performance standards to the resources needed to achieve them. The SFRA offers a real-world model of how to construct, enact, and implement a system of standards-linked school funding explicitly designed to fulfill the state's constitutional guarantee to all of its students, especially the increasing numbers of disadvantaged children in high-poverty schools. In approving the SFRA, the New Jersey Supreme Court's stirring "constitutional vision" is both a testament to the distance traveled since *Rodriguez* and a clarion call to the nation to redouble the decades-long struggle to build strong, equitable systems of public education in all fifty states:

> Our Constitution requires that public school children be given the opportunity to receive a thorough and efficient education. That constitutional vision irrefutably presumes that every child is potentially capable of attaining his or her own place as a contributing member in society with the ability to compete effectively with other citizens and to succeed in the economy. The wisdom giving rise to that vision is that both the child and society benefit immeasurably when that promise is realized.[71]

SEVEN

Bridging the Teacher Quality Gap

Notes from California on the Potential and Pitfalls of Litigating Teacher Quality

WILLIAM S. KOSKI

TEACHERS MATTER. Nearly all agree that the quality of a child's teachers affects her performance and life chances.[1] Yet, despite this widespread consensus, schools with economically disadvantaged, African American, and Latino children tend to be staffed by the least-experienced teachers, the lowest-paid teachers, and those who are most likely to be laid off for budgetary reasons.[2]

Researchers and policy makers have not ignored this yawning "teacher quality gap." In the past decade, Congress and the states have passed initiatives aimed at attracting and retaining high-quality teachers and fairly distributing those teachers among all schools. These efforts include offering incentives to teach in underperforming schools, establishing multiple pathways to the classroom, and evaluating teachers based on student performance. Most recently, legislators in some states have targeted teacher employment laws and collective bargaining rules that they believe hamstring administrators from dismissing poor teachers or making appropriate classroom assignments. Still, some advocates remain frustrated with the pace and scope of reform and are turning to the courts in an attempt to ensure that all children have access to a high-quality teacher.

In this chapter, I consider several recent litigation strategies designed, at least in part, to close the teacher quality gap in California, identify the pitfalls of each of the strategies, and discuss the potential of a comprehensive, yet modest, "all-of-the-above" litigation approach to ensuring that economically disadvantaged children have access to high-quality teaching. I discuss how traditional school finance litigation has employed—or could employ— evidence of the teacher quality gap to demonstrate the insufficiency and inequity of educational finance systems. Despite the fact that money buys teachers, school finance litigation's focus on dollars and distribution formulas has proven too blunt an instrument to address the teacher quality gap. I then assess two California lawsuits aimed directly at improving the quality of classroom teachers by seeking to ensure that all children have access to teachers with certain qualifications or attributes. This approach—like those policy approaches aimed at defining the minimum qualifications for classroom teaching—is hampered by our limited ability to assess and measure teacher quality or the characteristics of high-quality teachers. Finally, I discuss two recent California lawsuits that do not directly address the quality of teaching but, rather, claim that teacher employment rules, such as teacher due process protections, create the teacher quality gap by burdening disadvantaged children with ineffective teachers. While carefully designed and tested reforms to teacher employment rules should be pursued, using litigation to simply strike down employment rules will miss the mark and may create perverse outcomes. I conclude with some preliminary thoughts on modest, targeted litigation aimed at single schools and districts that not only seeks to break down the legal barriers to closing the teacher quality gap but also ensures that disadvantaged schools have the resources and support to attract and retain high-quality teachers. With this incrementalist, all-of-the-above approach tailored to specific school districts and the needs of their children, we can begin to create policy models for closing the teacher quality gap.

CLOSING THE EDUCATIONAL RESOURCE GAP TO CLOSE THE TEACHER QUALITY GAP

In 1971, California's *Serrano v. Priest* decision launched the school finance litigation movement.[3] Finding that education was a fundamental right and poverty a suspect classification, the California Supreme Court held that the state's highly unequal local property tax–based school finance system should be subjected to strict scrutiny under the U.S. Constitution's Equal Protection Clause. Of course, two years later, the *Rodriguez* Court decided that strict scrutiny would not be applied to the Texas school finance system under the Equal Protection Clause, but in 1976 the California Supreme Court re-affirmed its first *Serrano* decision under the California Constitution's equal protection provision and struck down the state's school finance scheme.[4] The *Serrano II* court specifically found that the state's school finance scheme "gives high wealth districts a substantial advantage in obtaining higher qual-ity staff, program expansion and variety, beneficial teacher-pupil ratios and class sizes, modern equipment and materials, and high quality buildings."[5] In other words, the court found what seems intuitively obvious: schools with fewer dollars are less likely to afford high-quality teachers.

In theory, then, educational finance litigation and reform should be an ef-fective method to close the teacher quality gap. More money for poor school districts should allow those districts to attract high-quality teachers because teachers, like most of us, consider salary a significant factor in choosing among job opportunities. Though many factors affect a prospective teach-er's choice of assignment, research on teacher preferences can be grouped into three broad categories: working conditions, student characteristics, and legal, bureaucratic, and contractual teacher assignment rules. Because cer-tain student characteristics (socioeconomic status and race/ethnicity) may be highly correlated with working conditions (schools with white, affluent chil-dren tend to have better working conditions), researchers cannot always parse out the effects that specific working conditions and terms have on teacher preferences. Nonetheless, research suggests that the following working con-ditions are important to teachers and are likely to impact the distribution of teachers among schools: salary, class size, administrative support, and school facilities.[6] Many improvements in working conditions are things that money can buy. Accordingly, litigation aimed at increasing funding for disadvan-taged schools should have the effect of improving teacher quality at a school or district by making the schools in the district more attractive and boosting teacher compensation.

But the *Serrano* litigation has not ensured a high-quality teaching force in California, nor has it closed the teacher quality gap. One 2005 study showed that intern teachers in California are eighteen times more likely to work in the quarter of California schools with more than 90 percent minority stu-dents than they are to work in the quarter of schools with less than 30 per-cent minority students.[7] Similarly, schools serving 91 to 100 percent minority students have an average of 20 percent underprepared and/or novice teachers, while those serving few or no minority students have an average of 11 percent underprepared or novice teachers. The same goes for low-achieving schools, where one of every five teachers (21 percent) are underprepared and/or novice, compared with only one in ten teachers (11 percent) in the highest-achieving schools.[8]

Of course, there are many reasons that the teacher quality gap exists and has persisted in the Golden State, despite the pathbreaking *Serrano* decisions and the legislature's responsive efforts to close the revenue gap between wealthy and poor school districts. *Serrano*'s equitable principles have slowly eroded over the past four decades as wealthy school districts have end-run *Serrano* through local parcel taxes and private educational foundations while the population of students in poor school districts became more educationally needy with increasing numbers of English-language learner (ELL) students and economically disadvantaged students. Moreover, the state underfunds most of its schools, as California's cost-adjusted per-pupil funding ranks forty-ninth in the nation and its teacher and staff to student ratios are at the bottom of national rankings.[9]

Scholars and policy makers have long recognized that California's school finance system has become irrational, inequitable, and inadequate. The 2007 "Getting Down to Facts" research project, which included some twenty-two studies of California's educational finance and governance system, resoundingly concluded that the school finance system is "inequitable by any measure" and "confusing and requires substantial and costly compliance work by school districts."[10] In 2007, the governor's own Committee on Education Excellence concluded that "California's K through 12 education system is fundamentally flawed. It is not close to helping each student become proficient in mastering the state's clear curricular standards, and wide disparities persist . . . Our current system is simply not preparing every student to be successful in college or work; it is not producing the results that taxpayers and citizens are counting on and that our children deserve."[11]

Recognizing that better fiscal conditions are necessary for improving student performance, a broad coalition of children, parents, grassroots organizations, school districts, school administrators and governing boards, and the largest teacher union in the state sued the state and governor in 2010 in two separate cases—*Robles-Wong v. California* and *Campaign for a Quality Education v. California (CQE)*—in a California superior court.[12] The suits ask the court to declare the state's educational finance system unconstitutional because it results in a violation of children's rights to an education guaranteed by the California Constitution's education article.[13] These cases are no *Serrano* redux. They do not seek to merely reshuffle the already inadequate educational dollars; they aim to ensure that the state's school funding system is designed and funded so that all children have an opportunity to be successful as the state defines it through its educational content standards. While the cases are not specifically and exclusively targeted at improving the quality of the teaching force and closing the quality gap, the goal is to create the fiscal conditions that allow all school districts to attract and retain high-quality teachers. For the time being, however, the cases are on appeal to the California appellate court, as the trial court dismissed the complaints.

To be fair, the California legislature and governor have not completely ignored the inequities of the school funding system. In 2013, the legislature passed the governor's Local Control Funding Formula, which consolidates many of the restrictive categorical funding streams, provides all school districts with a base funding amount per pupil, and, importantly, provides extra funding for each economically disadvantaged or ELL student with a further "concentration" grant for those school districts with high populations of such children.[14] To be sure, there are many details left to be worked out—such as how the state will ensure that the new monies flow to the schools and classrooms with needy children—but this weighted student funding formula is a step in the direction of closing the teacher quality gap. Yet there remain significant flaws in California school funding. The system is still not designed to achieve any goal, much less the goal of ensuring that all children have an opportunity for proficiency on the state-adopted Common Core standards. Nor will this funding formula increase school funding to the level necessary to give all students an opportunity for success.

That said, even if the new school funding formula actually targets funding to poor schools, and even if plaintiffs prevail in the *Robles-Wong* and *CQE* litigations, will the teacher quality gap automatically close and will all students have access to a high-quality teacher? Of course not. School finance litigation and reform are very blunt policy instruments that have historically operated at the level of the school district. California's funding formula and the school finance cases are no different. Neither prescribes how a local school district should spend its money. Neither requires a certain level of teacher quality or that teachers in all California classrooms meet certain qualifications. And neither ties teacher and administrative incentives to student performance and outcomes. Stated simply, school finance reform, while a necessary condition for closing the teacher quality gap, is hardly sufficient.

LITIGATING FOR A QUALITY TEACHER IN EVERY CLASSROOM

If school finance litigation is a bludgeon, perhaps a more surgical approach is in order. Perhaps the most straightforward route to ensuring the equitable distribution of teachers would be to argue that each child is entitled to a high-quality teacher or that the inequitable distribution of effective teachers violates antidiscrimination and equal protection principles. The trick here is twofold: to establish the doctrinal theory and cause of action that provides the right to an equitable distribution of teacher quality or the right to a high-quality teacher and to identify the appropriate measure of teacher quality, whether it be certain teacher characteristics; certain credentials, training, and experience; or certain measures of performance.

Two California lawsuits, *Williams v. California* and *Renee v. Duncan,* specifically sought to define the quality of teaching to which every student is entitled, though both were ultimately stymied by our current inability to directly measure teacher quality or teacher performance in any tractable way.[15]

A Minimally Qualified Teacher in Every Classroom

In 2000, hundreds of students in dozens of schools in California's low-income communities sued the state for its failure to provide them even the basic educational necessities—quality teachers, adequate facilities, and appropriate instructional materials and curricula.[16] *Williams v. California,* the most significant educational rights litigation in California since *Serrano,* was settled before trial. The settlement agreement reformed the state's system for monitoring and ensuring the provision of educational resources—including adequate instructional materials, clean and safe facilities, and qualified teachers—to all children in the state.

Firmly grounded in *Serrano*'s equal protection theory, the plaintiffs' complaint sought to bring California into line with the modern adequacy litigation movement, which posited that state constitutional education articles should be read to provide children a qualitative right to education, some basic level of educational opportunity.[17] The equal protection theory was well-grounded in precedent and straightforward: children in certain disadvantaged schools—primarily economically disadvantaged children and certain minority children—were being denied basic educational equity because they systematically received less-qualified teachers, poorer school facilities, and fewer and lower-quality instructional materials than their peers in more affluent schools. Under *Serrano* and the 1992 *Butt v. California* litigation, plaintiffs would have to demonstrate that the state denied the plaintiff schoolchildren "basic educational equality" by showing that the maldistribution of teachers had a "real and appreciable" impact on their fundamental right to an education and that the quality of teaching they received fell below the "prevailing statewide standard."[18] The equal protection doctrinal path was thus well established.

The plaintiffs' education article claim, however, was both novel (in California) and underspecified: "Defendants have violated [the plaintiffs'] right, pursuant to Article IX, Sections 1 and 5 of the California Constitution, to learn in a 'system of common schools' that are 'kept up and supported' such that children may learn and receive the 'diffusion of knowledge and intelligence essential to the preservation of the[ir] rights and liberties.' These constitutional provisions impose on the Defendants . . . the nondelegable duty to provide to each [Plaintiff] the opportunity to obtain a basic education."[19] Plaintiffs did not specify what constitutes a basic education, but they did specify what does not. In addition to inadequate and low-quality instructional materials and unclean and unsafe facilities, an education that falls below the basic standard is one in which the child is being taught by an unqualified teacher. In their complaint, the plaintiffs also did not explain which teachers were unqualified, but they seemed to suggest that it was a teacher lacking a credential: "Almost 90 percent of California's teachers have full, nonemergency teaching credentials, yet the schools the student Plaintiffs . . . attend have twice to five times as many uncredentialed teachers as this statewide norm."[20] The implication was that a credential might make a teacher "qualified" for purposes of providing a "basic" education.

But that's the rub. How can we decide who is a "qualified" teacher for purposes of litigating the denial of educational resources and the resulting denial of a student's right to an education? Social science does not help much. Although there is a solid consensus that teaching affects student outcomes, there is little agreement on which specific teacher characteristics are related to student outcomes. Some evidence suggests that teachers' experience levels (at least after the first few years of teaching), general academic and verbal abilities, educational attainment, and certification status are related to student outcomes.[21] But nearly all of these findings are contested by other studies.[22] Thus, any single measure of "teacher quality" may not capture the specific characteristics of teachers that produce student achievement gains.

Perhaps fortunately for the *Williams* plaintiffs, they never had to convince a judge that a "qualified" teacher was a "certified" teacher. After four years of intense and sometimes bitter litigation, a settlement was reached. The major terms of the deal included over $800 million in funding for facilities in the lowest-performing schools, $138 million in aid for instructional materials, and timetables for ensuring that "highly qualified" teachers as defined by the federal No Child Left Behind Act (NCLB) are available to all students. Thus, *Williams* established the proposition that the state of California must at least ensure that children are taught by an NCLB-defined highly qualified teacher. The meaning of highly qualified and the specific qualifications of such a teacher were the subject matter of another California lawsuit, *Renee v. Duncan,* more than a decade later.

A "Highly Qualified" Teacher in Every Classroom

The ultimate goal of Congress's landmark No Child Left Behind Act was for all students to be "proficient" in reading and math by 2014.[23] To reach this goal, NCLB required that states test students regularly to assess their progress and that states and districts be held accountable when students were not making "Adequate Yearly Progress" according to those assessment results.[24] In particular, NCLB held states accountable for closing the achievement gap between low-income and minority students and their more affluent, white peers.[25]

Central to NCLB's strategy of obtaining universal proficiency was the requirement that all classrooms be staffed by highly qualified teachers; accordingly, it contained numerous provisions relating to "highly qualified" teachers. At the foundation of those provisions were NCLB's mandates that every child be taught by a highly qualified teacher in her core classes and that poor and minority students not be taught by inexperienced, non–highly qualified teachers at higher rates than other students. To meet these mandates, NCLB required that every state and local school district develop plans to deliver highly qualified teachers in all core academic classes and to provide for equitable distribution of these teachers. Notably, NCLB did not require that school districts fire and stop hiring teachers who are not highly qualified. Rather, it only required transparency and accountability should districts choose to hire such teachers by publicly reporting that a classroom is being taught by a non–highly qualified teacher and ultimately holding districts accountable for ensuring student proficiency.[26]

NCLB defined a highly qualified teacher as someone who "has obtained full State certification . . . or passed the State teacher licensing examination and holds a license to teach."[27] The then secretary of education, Margaret Spellings, and her U.S. Department of Education promulgated a regulation, however, that deemed as highly qualified those teachers who were still "participating in an alternative route to certification" and who had not yet obtained their full teaching credential.[28] California similarly defined as "highly qualified" intern teachers who did not possess full certification but were participating in programs that provide an alternative route to certification.[29] Those policy decisions provoked a lawsuit that was perhaps the first federal statutory suit to ensure all students the right to a "quality" teacher as defined by certain criteria.

Renee v. Spellings (later renamed *Renee v. Duncan*) was brought by a coalition of grassroots organizations, students, and parents to challenge the Department of Education's definition of highly qualified on the grounds that it was not consistent with congressional intent. The designation of thousands, perhaps tens of thousands, of teachers was at stake. While many novice teachers, particularly those from traditional teacher credentialing programs, have earned their licenses, are certified under state law, many other novice teachers, particularly those from so-called "alternative route" teacher training and credential programs, are placed in classrooms as interns without having earned their credential. Plaintiffs alleged that intern teachers tended to be disproportionately concentrated in low-income and minority schools. This, they argued, was precisely the kind of inequitable distribution of teacher quality at which NCLB was aimed.

Although the lawsuit was not a full-scale assault on alternative route credential programs like the vaunted Teach For America (TFA), it was clear that the lawsuit would make such alternative route teachers less attractive to schools and potentially hinder the efforts of intern providers to place their interns in schools. Most TFA teachers were not fully credentialed under state law; rather, they were—and are—only *participating* in an alternative route to certification. Put bluntly, the lawsuit could have been viewed as a proxy war between traditional teacher credentialing programs and TFA. But the underlying policy issues—Does a teacher credential matter? Are uncredentialed, alternative route teachers of the same quality as traditionally credentialed teachers?—were just below the surface and continue to be debated.

At the heart of the plaintiffs' position was the belief that a teacher who is fully credentialed—not merely participating in a credential program—is a more highly qualified (and high-quality?) teacher. There is a significant body of research which supports the position that fully credentialed teachers raise their students' test scores more than not-fully-certified teachers.[30] Others, however, have shown that teachers participating in high-quality alternative route programs (like TFA) perform no worse and may, in fact, perform better than their traditionally certified peers.[31] What can be concluded from the research is that possessing full certification or a license or some other evidence of having completed the courses and training—including coursework in education philosophy, pedagogy and teaching methods, and content knowledge—prescribed by a state agency does not guarantee that a teacher is either highly qualified or of a high quality, nor can it be said that those in intern programs are not of a high quality.[32]

But the *Renee* court's job was not to determine what makes for a quality teacher. Rather, it had the relatively straightforward responsibility of determining whether merely making progress toward a credential is the same as having obtained full certification or a license to teach. On appeal from a district court decision to uphold the U.S. Department of Education's regulation, the Ninth Circuit concluded that it "is invalid because it is inconsistent with the 'unambiguously expressed intent of Congress.' *Chevron*, 467 U.S. at 843. We emphasize that our holding is based on the difference between the meaning of 'has obtained' in 20 U.S.C. § 7801(23) and the meaning of 'demonstrat[es] satisfactory progress toward' in § 200.56(a)(2)(ii). Our holding is not based on the meaning of 'full State certification' in § 7801(23)."[33]

That ruling makes sense. But the final sentence of the holding points the way toward a possible loophole: to designate interns as highly qualified, California (or any other state) need only redefine the meaning of "full State certification" to include participation in an alternative route program and making progress toward a preliminary credential. As it turns out, California did not have to make that logically and linguistically dubious move because Congress stepped in and defined highly qualified as the Department of Education had defined it: participation in an alternative route credential program and satisfactory progress toward that credential (this provision expired at the end of the 2012–2013 school year). However, neither the Ninth Circuit nor Congress settled the question of whether certification equals quality.

To be sure, the *Renee* plaintiffs would contend that affluent schools would have the same proportion of intern-credentialed teachers as poor schools if certification did not really matter. And parents of children in affluent schools would likely object to swapping their experienced teachers for interns. Perhaps perception alone is enough and we need not worry about proving that a certification gap actually is a quality gap. But for those seeking to ensure that all children have access to a high-quality teacher, the quest for defining teacher quality has shifted from teacher characteristics to teacher performance.

The Prospects of Measuring (and Litigating) Teacher Quality and Teacher Performance

When reporters at the *Los Angeles Times* obtained and analyzed student test score data from the Los Angeles Unified School District (LAUSD) that were linked to specific teachers, the resulting articles sparked a public debate in California about whether we can measure good teaching and isolate a teacher's value added to student performance (at least on standardized tests).[34] In that series of articles in 2010, the *Times* analyzed seven years of student test scores linked to some six thousand elementary school teachers and found what it characterized as "huge" disparities among teachers' performance as measured by scores of their students on the math and English portions of the California Standards Test.[35] The *Times* followed that series with the publication of an interactive database that allows taxpayers, parents, and students to access the value-added rating of more than 11,500 LAUSD teachers.[36]

What ensued was a very public argument among the United Teachers of Los Angeles (UTLA) teacher union, the LAUSD, and the *Times* over whether the release of the data violated teachers' privacy rights, over the reliability and methods of the *Times* analysis, and over the possibility of using the value-added data to evaluate teachers in the district. That argument spilled into the legislative chambers, the courtroom, and eventually some California classrooms.

First, the education policy and advocacy group EdVoice sued the LAUSD pursuant to often-ignored language of California's teacher evaluation statute, the Stull Act.[37] That language seemed to require school districts to consider the "progress of pupils" in evaluating the performance of teachers and administrators.[38] A Los Angeles Superior Court judge agreed and issued a writ of mandate compelling the LAUSD to use student performance measures when evaluating teachers and principals.[39]

Nearly simultaneously, the state legislature took up legislation that would have explicitly required districts to use student performance in evaluating individual teachers.[40] Although that bill was ultimately withdrawn by its author in the face of an epic battle between the state's largest teacher union and the organizations representing school boards and administrators, several school districts and their local union affiliates quietly negotiated to either adopt or pilot evaluation systems that included student performance.[41] Notably, this recent activity in the nation's second-largest school district and the legislature of the state in which about 12 percent of America's children are educated dovetails with a national movement to develop better methods for evaluating teachers, methods that will include some measure of student performance.

The fact that management and unions are beginning to agree that teacher performance can be measured and that some are even raising the stakes by tying teacher retention and pay to these evaluations might provide advocates a new strategy for closing the teacher quality gap. Rather than attempting to identify the characteristics and experiences of teachers that are tied to effective teaching, perhaps teacher quality can be measured by results, by identifying those teachers who produce better student results and ensuring that those teachers are fairly distributed among students. From a litigation advocacy perspective, the legal strategy can be taken directly from *Williams*, *Robles-Wong*, and *CQE*: an equal protection theory that would require that no identifiable group of students (such as African American students, ELLs, or students in a particular school) be denied basic educational equality by being disproportionately taught by lower-performing teachers as measured by value-added measures; or an education article–based adequacy theory that would require all students to be taught by a teacher who has met minimum performance standards based on value-added measures.

The difficulty, of course, is that although there are many promising teacher evaluation methods on the horizon, those methods that are based on or at least include value-added measures are not yet reliable enough to ensure that their measures can be equated with teacher quality.[42] The reasons are manifold. Because there are so many factors that influence student performance, and because those factors may vary for even an individual child

from year to year, it is difficult to isolate the contribution of the teacher
to the student's performance. In many schools, especially middle and high
schools, it is difficult to separate the effects of the many teachers and instruc-
tors who contribute to a student's or classroom's performance in any given
year. Experience with value-added measures has shown that they are quite
unstable over time and should be used to evaluate teachers only in combination with other performance indicators, including traditional classroom
observations and even student evaluations. And perhaps most concerning
about value-added measures are the perverse incentives that they might create, ranging from narrowing the curriculum to only those subjects and topics assessed, to teaching to tests that might not capture higher-order, critical
thinking, and problem-solving capacities, to outright cheating by teachers
and others whose livelihood is tied to the test scores.

This is not to say that the project of litigating the teacher quality gap directly—either by ensuring that teacher experience and those characteristics
associated with good teaching are fairly distributed or ensuring that teachers whose students have measurably improved are fairly distributed—should
be abandoned. Rather, this is to say that legal theory has outpaced the social
science and technology of measuring teacher quality, and any advocacy strategy should understand the proper role for measures of teacher quality when
attempting to close the quality gap.

Others, however, might argue that the entire enterprise is doomed and
that we may never develop reliable measures of teacher quality. Instead, we
should trust the professionals who are trained and experienced in evaluating
teacher quality and ensure that they have the maximum discretion to hire,
fire, and assign teachers in a way which ensures that all students have access
to a high-quality teacher. For proponents of this approach, breaking down
the barriers to administrative discretion is the most effective route to closing
the teacher quality gap.

REMOVING LEGAL BARRIERS TO CLOSE THE QUALITY GAP

From politically conservative leaders to the reform progressives, many have
pointed at a troika of constraints to improving teacher quality and closing
the teacher quality gap: teacher employment and tenure laws that protect
the jobs of poor performing teachers; collective bargaining laws and the restrictive contracts that are the product of bargaining; and the teacher unions

that enjoy outsized political clout in state capitols, local school boardrooms, and the collective bargaining table. Some deemed politically liberal, such as the Washington, DC, schools former superintendent, Michelle Rhee, have taken on teacher unions. Even President Barack Obama and his secretary of education, Arne Duncan, infused their centerpiece education-improvement efforts, the Race to the Top grants, with incentives to improve teacher effectiveness based on performance, despite collective bargaining agreements that eschew performance pay schemes.

Moreover, many state legislatures have pursued reforms to teacher employment laws and collective bargaining, including reforms aimed at lengthening the time it takes to achieve tenure; streamlining teacher dismissal procedures; and eliminating seniority as the basis for laying off teachers for budgetary reasons. Some state legislators have sought to remove entire topics from collective bargaining or to eliminate collective bargaining for teachers entirely.

Some advocates, however, have turned to the courts to break down the legal and contractual barriers that they blame for burdening poor children with ineffective teachers. Untie administrators' hands, the theory goes, and they will hire and reward the best teachers to teach in the hardest-to-staff classrooms and, at the same time, fire those ineffective teachers who are harming students. Again, two suits in California are at the leading edge of this strategy.

How Law and Collective Bargaining Might Widen the Quality Gap

Much of the teacher–school district employment relationship is governed by state statutes that provide due process protections for teachers, a pension system, certification requirements, and the like. Moreover, many other employment rules affecting a teacher's working conditions, such as the teaching load, length of workday, and evaluation procedures, may be governed by locally negotiated collective bargaining agreements. The teacher–school district employment relationship is unusual because the terms governing teachers' work implicate the state's plenary power over education. This means that the employment terms established through legislation or across bargaining tables not only constrain the decision making of school administrators and school boards, they affect the educational services and resources children receive. The reverse is also true. The policies established by school boards and state legislatures aimed at serving schoolchildren may seriously affect the workaday lives of teachers.

Some argue that this tension between educational policy—some of which might be aimed at improving teaching and closing the teacher quality gap—on the one hand, and teacher employment and collective bargaining rules, on the other, might shortchange students. Put simply, the interests of individual teachers and the organizations that collectively represent teachers in state-houses and at the bargaining table may not be aligned with the interests of students. Whether it's the collectively bargained and rigid step-and-column salary schedules that reward teachers only for years of service and level of education (rather than their classroom performance or the difficulty of their assignments) or the "seniority preference" provisions of collective bargaining agreements that give senior teachers priority in filling teaching vacancies, some reformers believe that the teacher quality gap is caused, or at least facilitated, by teacher employment protections.

In California, union detractors allege that at least three of those employment protections—so-called last-in, first-out (LIFO) layoff processes for reduction-in-force (RIF) layoffs; teacher tenure provisions that grant teachers due process protections and are less rigorous than those in other states; and the due process protections themselves that allegedly make it difficult for administrators to fire incompetent and even dangerous teachers—are individually or collectively denying certain California children their right to an education or, according to two recent lawsuits, basic educational equality.

Removing the Barriers Through Litigation

Reduction in Force Rules: **Reed v. California.**   In *Reed v. California,* children in poor schools in the LAUSD who suffered the direct and serious consequences of the district's implementation of California's RIF law brought suit in state court.[43] As a result of the state's budget cuts during the 2008–2009 academic year, thousands of teachers in the LAUSD received pink slips letting them know that they were being laid off. Because these teachers were at the bottom of the seniority ladder, and because California state law prescribes a LIFO layoff process, those layoffs disproportionately affected low-performing schools that had higher concentrations of junior teachers. This meant that those schools would have a much higher turnover rate than other schools and that teacher turnover would result in a lower-quality education.

The complaint focused on three middle schools, one of which lost 70 percent of its faculty, while the other two lost more than 40 percent. Some schools lost no teachers.

Consequently, the children in the three disadvantaged schools alleged that the budget-based layoffs violated their right to an education and their right to equal protection under the California Constitution, and the plaintiff students moved to preliminarily enjoin the district from laying off teachers in those schools. The court granted that injunction, and the parties ultimately reached a settlement that would ensure that future reduction-in-force layoffs would not harm students in the lowest-performing schools and would be spread fairly among the schools in the district. That court-approved settlement, however, was stayed after the California appellate court ruled that the UTLA had been improperly excluded from the litigation and the settlement negotiations, which some argued was less than arm's-length given LAUSD's board and the superintendent's and Los Angeles mayor Antonio Villaraigosa's frustration with the teacher union.

Reed is a discrete case in which a rigid employment rule adversely affected an identifiable group of children. It should be noted, however, that the RIF rules employed by LAUSD probably made layoff decision making more efficient and less contentious in that district of more than 694,000 students and 45,000 teachers. In colloquial terms, "it takes two to tango." It is entirely possible that, even if the interests of teachers and their unions are not aligned with those of students, the interests of administrators and school districts as organizations may not be aligned with students either. Moreover, the elimination of the LIFO system does not guarantee that its replacement will return any better results. If rigid rules are adopted—as was the case with the proposed *Reed* settlement agreement—some lowest-performing schools will be protected from layoffs, but those layoffs might be displaced to those only marginally better off (and soon to become worse off). It is also possible that such a rigid rule protects junior, poor-performing teachers in low-performing schools (the very teachers who could have been easily released under the LIFO rule). Nuance and context seem important in making layoff decisions, and any statewide, rigid rule could cause problems.

But if rules are not reformed and we are left with greater administrative discretion as a result of successful litigation, it is still not at all clear that low-performing schools would fare any better. Simply put, there is no guarantee that principals of those schools would have the capacity to identify and resources to retain their best performers, even if they want to do so. In other words, merely removing the barrier of LIFO rules may not be a sufficient condition for ensuring that low-performing or economically disadvantaged schools are not saddled with lower-quality teachers.

Teacher Tenure, Teacher Evaluation, and RIF Rules: **Vergara v. California.** Much of the complaint in the novel and potentially landmark *Vergara v. California* litigation reads like the perfect marriage between *Serrano*'s and *Butt*'s equal protection theory and a modern policy treatise on the importance of high-quality teachers.[44] It alleges that "recent studies have confirmed what students and parents have always known: The key determinant of educational effectiveness is teacher quality. . . . Students assigned to effective teachers are more likely to attend college, attend higher-quality colleges, earn more, live in higher socioeconomic-status neighborhoods, save more for retirement, and are less likely to have children during their teenage years."[45] It goes on to point out that certain California students, particularly those who are economically disadvantaged, are disproportionately burdened with "grossly ineffective" teachers and that these students are denied basic educational equality under *Serrano* and *Butt.* So far, so good. But here is the causal leap and the novel departure from traditional educational equity litigation in California.

> The hiring and continued employment of such grossly ineffective teachers in the California public school system is the direct result of the continued enforcement of five California statutes (the "Challenged Statutes") that confer permanent employment on California teachers, effectively prevent the removal of grossly ineffective teachers from the classroom, and, in economic downturns, require layoffs of more competent teachers. The Challenged Statutes prevent school administrators from prioritizing—or even meaningfully considering—the interests of their students in having effective teachers when making employment and dismissal decisions. By forcing these critical decisions to be made primarily or exclusively on grounds *other* than students' need for effective teachers, . . . these laws infringe upon California students' fundamental right to education.[46]

The conspiracy among teacher tenure laws, teacher due process protections, and LIFO RIF rules is (alone?) causing "grossly ineffective" teachers to be assigned to certain (usually economically disadvantaged) schools, who in turn are (alone?) causing poor performance among those students, which in turn denies those students their fundamental right to an education.

On June 10, 2014, in a surprisingly slim sixteen pages, a Los Angeles trial court judge agreed that the "Challenged Statutes" violated children's—particularly economically disadvantaged children's—equal protection rights.[47] According to the court, "Evidence has been elicited in this trial of the specific effect of grossly ineffective teachers on students. The evidence is compelling. Indeed, it shocks the conscience."[48] With that, the *Vergara* case sent shockwaves throughout the nation and potentially established a tectonic shift in educational equity litigation, as copycat litigation has already been brought in New York and is being contemplated elsewhere.

Meanwhile, the decision is being appealed and will undoubtedly find its way to the California Supreme Court. And while there are myriad legal-factual matters on which the *Vergara* decision can be challenged, I focus here on the political and policy challenges this case faces. On the political front, the case fits squarely within the reform movement in education that seeks to break down legal and bureaucratic barriers to administrative discretion, focus on the performance of teachers in enhancing student outcomes (read: test scores), and inject market-style rewards and incentives into the management of schools and districts. A group called Students Matter that is bankrolled by a wealthy Silicon Valley entrepreneur is driving the case, and the case is sympathetic with the technology world's ethos of disrupting the status quo and the project of bringing market-style accountability and flexibility to schools.[49]

Naturally, that formula does not sit well with California's teacher unions and those who would prefer that reform come from within the public schools, not from the external shock of litigation and deregulation of teacher employment. As a result, the California Teachers Association joined the state in defending the teacher employment laws, and it is entirely possible that the case could serve as a rallying point for rank-and-file teachers, entrenching their opposition to any legislative or bargaining table reform of teacher employment rules, no matter how sensible. Contrast this potentially charged path to reform with the broad coalition of labor, management, grassroots organizations, school districts, children, and parents in the plaintiff coalition supporting the *Robles-Wong* and *CQE* litigations. This is not to say that any reform and advocacy strategy aimed at closing the teacher quality gap must enjoy universal or even widespread political support, but it does point to a potential flaw in any strategy that does not take a more nuanced, incremental, and stakeholder-inclusive approach to reform.

Perhaps more troubling, however, are the institutional capacity and policy implications of the *Vergara* matter. While the lawsuit merely asks the court to declare unconstitutional the so-called Challenged Statutes, it does raise serious concerns about judicial-institutional competence. If these statutory education and employment policies can cause the denial of the fundamental right to an education, what other legislative policies could be placed in the crosshairs of litigation or demanded as constitutional remedies? Universal, high-quality preschool? Standards-based testing? And are courts the best forum to make such specific policy choices? Courts may be better suited to resolving localized disputes and damages from legislative policy choices (as in the *Reed* litigation), but courts might want to be wary of plunging into the thicket of crafting the specifics of state-level education policy.

Attacking statewide policies that focus on narrow subjects—such as teacher due process protections—may have unforeseen and potentially perverse consequences. If the Challenged Statutes are struck down in *Vergara,* the immediate result will be displacing all of the decision making on tenure, discipline, and layoffs to the collective bargaining table, which means bilateral (not multilateral) stakeholder negotiation behind closed doors, where the prior regime could simply be replaced by a less favorable regime. If the legislature steps in to design a new system, all the political rancor in the courtroom will be transferred to the capitol building, where teacher unions still hold sway. It is also possible that any statewide solution will simply push the problem to different schools and classrooms.

More specifically, *Vergara*'s assault on teacher employment protections makes two heroic policy assumptions. First, it assumes that unfettered administrators will make employment decisions in the best interests of children. This may not be true. While one could imagine a carefully designed statewide teacher employment policy that would give administrators greater leeway in staffing decisions *and* sufficiently protect teachers from arbitrary decision making, it seems plausible that many administrators may not have the capacity or time to identify good teachers and good teaching. Or they may prioritize efficiency and cost-effectiveness (keep the cheapest teacher whenever possible) over quality. Or, more benignly, they may simply continue to honor those teacher employment protections in the breach because they want to avoid confrontation, because they come from the same culture of teaching and administration as the teachers themselves, or because they do not have the time or ambition to gather the information to make tough and necessary decisions.

Second, the theory underlying *Vergara* assumes that there is a ready bullpen of would-be teachers who want to teach in low-performing classrooms filled with economically disadvantaged and/or ELLs. This seems unlikely. The latest figures from the California Commission on Teacher Credentialing show that enrollment in teacher preparation programs plunged 74 percent since 2001–2002.[50] With the ongoing exodus of baby boomers from the teaching force, California needs to attract and retain high-quality millennials, and that is not happening. *Vergara* will do nothing to attract young people to the profession and may, in fact, deter would-be teachers who value job security.

Yet, none of this is to say that there is no room for targeted and nuanced local reform of teacher employment rules and policies. That seems necessary. But even those narrow and incremental reforms should not be pursued in isolation from other advocacy strategies.

CONCLUSION

So, should we abandon litigation strategies to close the teacher quality gap? Not so fast. We ought to consider an incremental, modest, and all-of-the-above litigation approach that focuses on the school or district, rather than the state, as the unit of analysis for litigation purposes; an understanding of all stakeholders' interests, because the design and implementation of any remedy is rife with politics; and a focus on the outcome—an equitable distribution of high-quality teachers (or at least the assurance that ineffective teachers are not concentrated in poor-performing, economically disadvantaged schools).

In California, as in many states, the state has the ultimate responsibility to provide basic educational equity and ensure that all children receive the constitutionally required education. But the denial of that education, particularly any such denial based on low-quality teaching, is best demonstrated at the school site or district level, and any remedy to the problem should be crafted at the district and school site.

First, in approaching the teacher quality gap as a failure of the state to provide adequate resources, it may be necessary to first demonstrate that the maldistribution of teachers is not a product of local malfeasance. Indeed, the state itself will seek to place responsibility on local school district mismanagement and probably join those districts as necessary parties (as the state of California did in the *Williams* litigation). If student advocates can demonstrate that the district has efficiently deployed its resources but still cannot close the quality gap, the case for additional state resources is made easier.

Second, if the problem is burdensome teacher employment rules, it is important to be sure that those rules are actually operating (being implemented) in a way that causes problems in the local district. This is a lesson from the *Reed* litigation. It was clear in the three schools that were identified in the lawsuit that the LIFO RIF rules were causing extreme turnover and that turnover was harming children. In other schools or districts, however, those rules may have had no concentrated effect on the distribution of teacher layoffs and may even be a useful and relatively uncontroversial method to lay off teachers during times of fiscal stress. Thus, a statewide injunction could have caused more problems than it was worth. The challenge of demonstrating causation between the employment statute and the quality gap is only exacerbated when addressing far more complicated teacher employment rules such as due process protections, teacher evaluation, and tenure rules. Put simply, though statewide, facial challenges to teacher employment rules are possible (witness the *Vergara* litigation), an as-applied analysis seems prudent from both an evidentiary/causal analysis perspective as well as a policy perspective. Better to target the litigation on those schools and districts where the problem exists than to destabilize those districts in which statewide rules do not have an adverse effect.[51]

And why should we focus on the remedy at the local level? Because the remedy must be as complex as the cause of the quality gap. And those causes differ across districts. The causes of the teacher quality gap likely include an inequitable or insufficient distribution of resources coupled with undue regulatory burdens placed on administrators. It's not just the money, and it's not just the rules. For instance, what principal wouldn't want to reward effective teaching, or what superintendent wouldn't want to use financial incentives to attract teachers to and retain them in the most disadvantaged schools? In both of those cases, however, it may be the combination of a lack of money *and* collectively bargained salary formulas that prevent the administrators from closing the quality gap through financial incentives.

Instead of focusing on specific causes, then, the liability theory and the remedy should focus on the indicators of teacher quality (not the specific means of achieving quality and equity), leaving the specifics of the remedy to stakeholder bargaining in the shadow of legal liability for continued failure to meet teacher quality indicators. The state's liability should be tied to the evidence (albeit imperfect) of a denial of quality teaching to an identifiable school or group of children. No single measure currently can capture quality, so multiple measures of quality, including teacher attributes such as experience and training, as well as teacher performance measures such as value-added data and qualitative performance reviews, should be used to measure both liability and the efficacy of the remedy.

Then, the remedy itself should be tied to improvement toward outcome goals, such as the equitable distribution of teacher quality as measured by those same indicators. But that remedy should not be dictated by a court. Rather, it should be the product of stakeholder negotiation, including not only the parties but also any other stakeholders who will be necessary to implement a local remedy (for example, the local teacher union). The remedy might include some increased flexibility for administrators in the hiring, firing, assignment, and rewarding of teachers. The remedy may also look like that in traditional adequacy litigation, increased funding from the state. Or the remedy may include specific resources to build capacity among the teachers, including technical assistance and training. Moreover, because conditions may change as the district and state work toward the goal of quality teaching for all students, the design and implementation of any proposed remedies should be transparent and should be subject to modification as the organization and stakeholder community learn from implementation. Specifically, the state and district should be committed to reporting progress on the outcome indicators to the public and the stakeholder community. There should be periodic opportunities to assess that progress and propose modifications to the remedial measures.

This process, which is outcomes based, transparent, and dynamic, parallels the "experimentalist" principals espoused by James Liebman, Charles Sabel, and William Simon, in which courts first destabilize the institutional status quo (that has not served the needs and interests of disadvantaged children) and work toward reform through ongoing stakeholder negotiation, evolving measures of performance to address dynamic conditions on the ground, and transparency to the stakeholders and the public.[52] Equally important, this process reflects not only judicial modesty but also the limitations of using policy and law to reform complex educational institutions. Modesty—or "tinkering," as David Tyack and Larry Cuban so aptly describe the school reform process—may be the best policy.[53]

EIGHT

It Takes a Federalist Village

A Revitalized Property Tax as the Linchpin for Stable, Effective K–12 Public Education Funding

MILDRED WIGFALL ROBINSON

The property tax is one of the most maligned and least understood subjects of public and official discussion today.

—Ralph Nader,
testimony before the Senate Subcommittee
on Intergovernmental Relations, May 9, 1972

AMERICAN PUBLIC EDUCATION is a big business. In 2011, more than 55.5 million students from kindergarten through grade 12 were expected to enroll in the nation's public schools at a total cost of $595,078,949,000.[1] Though a service provided by local governments, education's cost is borne by local, state, and federal taxpayers.[2] Providing public education is a massive undertaking which costs more than one level of government can bear.

Each governmental level taps into own source revenue in bearing its cost. Local governments tap into property tax revenues; state funding comes primarily from individual income or retail sales taxes; federal contributions are primarily from income taxes. Funding has been further complicated by the 2008 recession; most states have reduced funding for public education in its wake. Diminished funding must be reversed. To do this, policy makers must accommodate differences among funding sources; property, income, and retail sales taxes do not have the same characteristics.

However, the U.S. Supreme Court's 1973 watershed school finance decision, *San Antonio Independent School District v. Rodriguez,* muddies the water.[3] The Court found that a public school financing system based on local property taxes did not violate the Fourteenth Amendment's Equal Protection Clause, stark resultant funding disparities notwithstanding. In so doing, the Court contributed to the intensifying focus on the elimination or modification of the tax as the heart of the funding disparities. Justice Lewis Powell, in concluding the majority opinion, noted that the Court in *Rodriguez* had not placed its "judicial imprimatur on the status quo." He continued, "The need is apparent for reform in tax systems *which may well have relied too long and too heavily on the local property tax.*"[4]

This is understandable. First, the property tax contributed substantially to the financial support for K–12 public education nationally when *Rodriguez* was decided.[5] Second, the tax was already drawing taxpayer vitriol as a result of ongoing litigation in California. Challenges to disparities stemming from reliance on property tax revenues for funding were at the heart of California's *Serrano* cases, which both preceded and followed *Rodriguez.* Further, nationwide anti–property tax sentiment was very much a part of political discourse during the 1970s, including congressional hearings in 1973 incident to failed Senate Bill 1255. The bill, if passed, would have assisted state governments in reforming their property tax laws.[6]

Cumulatively, this broadly targeted opposition has affected the perceived range of options for school finance in the four decades since *Rodriguez.* The tax has been increasingly hobbled both by limitations intended to reduce taxpayer burden and economic incentives unrelated to taxpayer relief. Both practices adversely affect funding efforts and merit reexamination. While the tax remains an important and indispensable part of the funding calculus, its thoughtful reform could stabilize and increase productivity without sacrificing tax relief.

To accomplish this, policy makers must be attuned to policy possibilities and revenue capacities at each level of government and must understand especially how financial practices and decisions across governmental levels are related. Property tax administration must be highlighted and streamlined in order to maximize the tax's revenue potential, and policy makers at each level of government must respond appropriately to the challenges of this reimagined effort.

LESSONS FROM FISCAL FEDERALISM

Fair market value annually determined is the base for the property tax. The cyclical nature of base determination means less revenue volatility. Though an economic downturn may cause reduced property values, such declines will not show up for a cycle or two. As such, revenues from property taxes will remain more stable during recessionary periods and, if recessions are short lived, not decline at all.

Retail sales taxes and income taxes are comparatively much more volatile. When employment levels stagnate or unemployment rises, incomes diminish resulting in both reduced sales and income tax collections. State revenues correspondingly decline. Further, the decline is likely to be both more immediate and precipitous than with the property tax. In short, the property tax is more inelastic and less volatile than income and retail sales taxes.

As states assumed increased funding responsibility for public education after *Rodriguez,* the realignment of funding sources brought with it risks inextricably a part of greater revenue volatility. Property tax funding had proven relatively stable but inadequate because of variations in the value of taxable property. State funding often proved more generous but also more volatile. Reliance on state sources of revenue thus simultaneously provided increased funding for public education and introduced unanticipated funding instability as state economies expanded and contracted.

THE PRESENT LOCAL-STATE FUNDING ENVIRONMENT

Ideally, state and local governments could as partners renegotiate the terms of public school finance, predicating that effort on informed accommodation of the comparative characteristics of revenue sources. Doing so could finally begin to address in an effective and sustainable fashion funding inadequacies that remained unresolved after *Rodriguez* and that were made worse by the revenue shortfalls incident to the 2008 recession. Easy accommodation is, however, presently impossible. Since *Rodriguez,* monumental shifts have occurred in the fiscal relationship between and the relative political power of state and local governments. Both of these factors now profoundly affect the way forward.

First, taxpayer opposition to the property tax has been and remains an issue. U.S. taxpayer resistance to the property tax ran deep during the 1970s, and Californians were at the epicenter of that unrest. California's *Serrano* decisions, ultimately holding unconstitutional reliance on the tax to fund public education, are thought by many to have played an important role in fomenting the taxpayer resistance that ultimately led to Proposition 13 in 1978, which amended the California Constitution to impose significant limitations on property tax use for funding local government in general.[7] California ignited a movement that spread nationwide; comparable state-based taxpayer activity was ubiquitous during the early 1970s.[8]

The movement resonated in Congress. During his 1972 State of the Union address, President Richard Nixon declared that "the property tax is one of the most oppressive and discriminatory of all taxes" and later that year pledged to "make my final recommendation for relieving the burden of property taxes."[9] During 1973 congressional hearings, the importance of the tax was reiterated.[10] Local governments then relied almost exclusively on the tax for revenues. It is also clear, however, that the tax was a misunderstood administrative disaster, was deeply resented by taxpayers, was characterized by administrative misfeasance (if not malfeasance), and had little transparency. During an earlier set of hearings, Ralph Nader, summarizing the litany of complaints, "charged that 'the property tax is one of the most maligned and least understood subjects of public and official discussion today.'"[11] He contended that the property tax had become oppressive to homeowners because, among other things, as applied it was "rife with corruption, favoritism, antiquated laws, and secrecy."[12]

In short, proactive taxpayers in California catalyzed a national debate that made property tax limitation an urgent agenda item.[13] The resistance became manifest in legislative activity that throughout this period featured the enactment of expansive tax and expenditure limitations (TELs) that cumulatively diminished revenues. Overall, TELs have now been enacted in virtually every state and have been both general—limits on millage, rate increases, and assessments—and specific, such as relief targeted by age, disability, or military status.[14] In addition, thirty-six states now impose limits on local jurisdictions' ability to generate revenues beyond some specified point or to make expenditures.[15] These changes have, in varying combination, limited property tax revenue potential, eroded the tax base, or undermined local ability to meet expenses. Moreover, TELs relieve only taxpayers who own property in richer districts. Taxpayers in property-poorer districts that are already utilizing maximum allowable rates receive neither relief nor adequate public services.

In addition to these broadly cast limitations and targeted provisions, states have enacted a pastiche of laws enabling a mélange of practices and initiatives linked to economic revitalization. Some result in locally based initiatives; others may originate from state agencies. They, too, compromise property tax revenue production.

Tax increment financing (TIF) schemes provide the best example of local projects having this effect. TIFs may be "the most widely used local government program for financing economic development in the United States and the District of Columbia," having been implemented in forty-nine states and the District of Columbia and across all kinds of communities.[16] Though there are no available national data, one commenter suggests that the number of such districts is likely to "reach well into the thousands."[17] Briefly, these programs subsidize public infrastructure improvements incident to economic revitalization in depressed areas.[18] Property owners continue to bear liability for the tax even as values increase, but these increases are diverted to bonds floated to finance the public infrastructure improvement. Increased collections are unavailable to local governments.

Foreclosing financial benefit to other entities has been characterized as "by far the greatest moral hazard posed by TIFs."[19] Amounts involved may be significant. In Chicago, for example, where former mayor Richard M. Daly declared tax incentive financing "the only game in town," there were 162 TIF schemes in 2010 covering approximately 30 percent of the city's area, affecting roughly 10 percent of the tax base, and collecting in excess of $500 million in both 2010 and 2011.[20] Some percentage of this amount could be made available for funding education.

State-approved programs permitting local governments to abate property tax liability entirely are even more problematic. Abatement is the key element under stand-alone property tax abatement programs (SAPTAPs) as well as other more broadly cast programs where qualifying business property is accorded partial or complete forgiveness of property tax liability for some predetermined period.[21]

Nationally, such initiatives have become ubiquitous. In 2005, thirty-five states permitted some form of SAPTAP, and, including programs more broadly cast, forty-two did in 2007.[22] These incentive programs remain controversial;

data have not yet definitively established their effectiveness.[23] That debate cannot be resolved here, but this much is certain: local taxpayers may bear significant additional costs and realize little or no benefit.[24] Importantly, states (with some exceptions) rarely hold localities financially harmless under these schemes, in spite of the anticipated overall enhancement in economic activity. Success may enhance state revenues through increased individual income and retail sales tax collections, but local governments are left holding the financial bag.

Equally troubling, such incentives may be counterproductive. Numerous studies have consistently identified a well-educated employee base as an important state attribute for businesses. Limiting or waiving property tax liability undermines a state's ability to invest in a resource—education—that has consistently proven important to the effort to stimulate economic activity.[25] States would seem well advised to refrain from this kind of myopic bargaining.

From what had been a source of revenue exclusively under the control of local government, the property tax has devolved into a source of revenue over which states have assumed significant political control. Neither states nor local governments are being well served by the tax's relative stability. Instead, the tax is consistently less productive in overall percentage terms because of limitations imposed on its use.[26]

Public education is generally *not* protected from the negative effect of measures like these. TELs' revenue-related losses adversely affect metrics generally considered indicative of the quality of education. For example, data support a strong inference that increased student-teacher ratios, lower teacher salaries, and loss of experienced teachers follow in the wake of TEL-related funding reductions.[27] A handful of states have safeguarded school districts from the effects of TIFs and SAPTAPs; four of the SAPTAP states protect revenues to be spent for public schools, as do eight of the TIF states.[28] Overall, however, state policy makers (and, perhaps, incompletely informed voters) have failed to provide ex ante global protection for school districts in particular as TELs are enacted.

Several ex post protective strategies intended to hold schools financially harmless also presently exist. First, the majority of states that subject schools districts to TEL provisions also give affected voters the power to override limitations.[29] The few studies available report quite limited voter success with such efforts, however.[30] This difficulty is unsurprising in light of changing demographics. Voters with school-age children quite likely no longer constitute a majority coalition in many school districts.[31] It is one thing for a voter to support public education as a theoretical matter and quite another to support referenda cutting against personal economic interests. Indeed, limitations may exacerbate preference differences.

Override provisions, thus, may simply not be enough. For example, and practically, if the twin demographic trends toward greater childlessness and increasing population age continue, override provisions may become increasingly ineffectual for many identifiable subgroups, including voters with children. The political clout of persons with school-age children will wane through sheer lack of numbers. In this scenario, and very superficially, the preferences of an aging demographic for services of particular interest to them and their families will likely take precedence for those voters over the need to provide public education, a service that may be seen to be of only indirect benefit.

Other provisions are similarly flawed. A few states give schools boards veto power over property tax abatement or TIF-based diversion, a concession that at least allows school board input.[32] Again, however, the few studies available suggest that the power is rarely used by school boards in defense of school funding.[33] Finally, and only occasionally, an enterprise may agree to make a payment in lieu of taxes (PILOT).[34] PILOTs, however, have two shortcomings: they are voluntary payments, and they rarely fully compensate school districts for taxes that might otherwise have been paid.[35] At the end of the day, most school districts will not be adequately reimbursed (if at all) for revenues forgone as a result of TIFs or SAPTAPs. Greater attention should be paid to ex ante protections.

Without question, funding disparities exist because of wide variances in the value of underlying property. Legal challenges to those variations were warranted. The argument against using the property tax to finance public education in the last several decades has been only partially correct, however. The much-vilified property tax is presently much better administered.[36] It is quite probable that as currently administered, the property tax would bring a quantum of greatly needed stability to public school finance. Moreover, TELs, TIFs, and SAPTAPs and comparable economic initiatives could be modified to permit school districts to share in any increased economic activity. The latter point is of particular import in light of the political dynamics and economic pressures that presently characterize state politics.

On the state level, difficulties stem from the broadening spectrum of increasingly expensive financial demands. Most recently, states' rapidly increasing health-care costs have placed enormous pressure on state budgets.[37] Available data report that the most expensive items at present are health care and education, in that order. Health care, K–12 education, and higher education presently account for more than half of most state budgets.[38]

Public education will have its advocates in the battle for limited state funds. Realistically, however, it will likely be disadvantaged by the political realities of this fierce competition for funding. Public education simply has not been accorded the primacy that would be likely on the local level.

THE WAY FORWARD

The present reality is that state and local governments provide 90 percent of public school funding. Shared financial burden is not, however, the product of shared local/state governance. All parameters of local governance, including financial matters, are controlled by state legislatures. Though local governments are clearly stakeholders in local finance matters, they have not played an influential role in formulating policy. If changes are to be made in the way in which public education is funded, and the role of the property tax in that effort, states and locales must act in tandem.

Presently, the only realistic source of replacement for lost state funds is the property tax. There is little likelihood, however, that the property tax as currently limited can generate significant additional resources. Further, even if the property tax is restructured, a revenue gap between available funds and funds needed for an adequate and equitable education will remain. Persisting intrastate funding differentials stemming from variations in the values of underlying properties in the respective school districts preclude exclusive or even primary reliance on the property tax for funding purposes. As such, many school districts will continue to be compelled to look to the state for financial assistance. The financial role played by the property tax, however, can be more robust than it is presently. That part of the property tax revenue stream allocable to public school funding should be so earmarked. If this is to happen, state and local financial and policy roles must be complementary.

Even assuming that states move to immunize and stabilize the property tax, wide variations in the value of districts' taxable property will continue to make the task of generating funding substantially equivalent to that provided by richer school districts impossible for poorer school districts. States must make funding public education from general sources of revenue a priority and must do so primarily from revenues generated through retail sales and income taxes.[39]

General revenues are necessarily available to defray the overall expenses of the state as they arise, and state legislatures generally refrain from earmarking with regard to general revenues. The monies are treated as fungible.

Excise tax collections, however, have been more routinely earmarked. The most notorious excise taxes are the "sin" taxes imposed on the sale of alcoholic beverages, tobacco products, and, most recently, gaming.[40] All states and the District of Columbia tax the sale of alcoholic beverages and tobacco products. Further, forty states and the District of Columbia currently use lotteries as a revenue source.[41] States occasionally (often in response to the urging of interest groups) earmark taxes collected through the sale of alcoholic beverages or tobacco products for specific programmatic purposes. In general, however, such initiatives have been relatively few in number. In contrast, the earmarking of gaming proceeds for support of public education seems to have gained significant political traction; a number of states presently dedicate at least some part of these collections to support public education.[42] The decision has usually been driven by economic considerations; proceeds from gaming have often been viewed as a growing source of revenue that would provide a stable and increasing source of funding.[43]

While earmarking gaming proceeds for education is still relatively recent and remains somewhat exceptional, it has already raised a number of vexing issues. First, how stable is this source? It is simply not evident that gaming will continue to be the financial bonanza for states that it was originally projected to be. The fact is, as more and more states enact legislation that enables gaming, overall collections are spread more thinly. Gaming proceeds simply will not, over the long term, have the financial heft critical to provide stable and effective public school funding.[44] Further, who bears the burden of this tax? The majority of available studies conclude that the implicit gaming tax, like excise taxes on alcohol and tobacco, falls disproportionately on less-affluent taxpayers.[45] In other words, these taxes are regressive in effect. To the extent, however, that gaming proceeds are in fact earmarked for public education, regressive effect may be an acceptable cost. Earmarking would ensure that poorer individuals benefit from gaming revenues—important since this is the demographic most heavily engaged in the taxed activity.[46] Essentially, this demographic would self-finance its use of public education.

Unfortunately, it is not clear that states in which earmarking has been the practice have sustained increases in funding. More often, data establish that this source of funding has simply displaced support that would otherwise have been provided from general revenues.[47] Further, as gaming proceeds have declined, general revenues have not been allocated in order to redress the shortfall. In short, earmarking excise taxes could prove an important way to *supplement* public school funding but no more than that. Revenues from excise taxes may prove to be a welcome windfall for cash-strapped states appropriate for ad hoc use.

While some earmarking from specific revenue sources might be exploited to *supplement* funding for education, states must refrain from exclusive reliance on such sources, almost certainly a questionable policy choice.

Realistically, states will face periods of financial exigency over which they have no control. Such volatility is inevitably a part of being in a federalist system of government. A modified and revitalized property tax should, however, provide some protection from possible reductions in state support as long as such recessions are not prolonged. The combination of property tax revenues and secured funding primarily from state general source revenues supplemented as appropriate from excise taxes is most likely to be the most effective combination for public school finance if stable funding is to be achieved.

THE FEDERAL ROLE

Funding Everyday Operations

Direct federal financial support for schools has been both limited and designated for particular purposes. Despite continuing calls for increased direct, regularized, and unrestricted support, there is little evidence that such increases will be forthcoming.

Additional federal support, however, might be indirectly provided. Tax expenditures are revenue losses, subsidies, attributable to tax provisions that result from using the tax system to achieve policy goals without incurring direct expenditures. The deduction for state and local taxes provides general indirect support for local government through the Internal Revenue Code deduction for specified state and local taxes (the SALT deduction) paid or incurred by the taxpayer.[48] This deduction (indirect subsidy) has historically included the property tax among those taxes for which the deduction is allowed. One commenter estimated that the property tax deduction generated approximately $16.5 billion to $17.1 billion for public K–12 education in 2009 as it was then (and is currently) structured.[49]

The deduction is limited, however; only individual taxpayers who are property owners, who have paid the tax, and itemize can take it. The majority of individual taxpayers do not itemize, however, and nonitemizers use the standard deduction in determining taxable income.[50] Thus, for nonitemizing taxpayers, the availability of a deduction for property taxes paid is irrelevant.

The inability to deduct forecloses the possibility of observable indirect support for subnational governmental entities. In short, though some percentage of non-itemizers may well bear a property tax burden, nonitemizers treat any property tax burden as they do any other nondeductible personal expense: it becomes a nondeductible outlay. As such, the $16-plus billion is exclusive of that part of property tax borne by non-itemizers. Because nonitemizers take no deduction, their very real liability provides no additional indirect federal expenditure for support of local government.

Support for public education could be indirectly increased by expanding, for federal income tax purposes, the availability of a deduction or credit for property tax liability imposed to support public schools. A more universally available deduction solely for property taxes paid to support public education might be one way of accomplishing this.[51] Through the indirect subsidy, the federal government would assume a greater share of the cost of funding education. As such, more generous treatment for federal income tax purposes might lessen local-level taxpayers' resistance to property tax increases.

A deduction available to both itemizers and nonitemizers would, however, prove an administrative challenge to implement and could be quite expensive if it were taken without limit by upper-income, itemizing taxpayers. Yet, a capped credit for a specified percentage of the tax liability has much to recommend it. Unlike an income tax deduction, a credit is a dollar-for-dollar reduction of federal tax liability that would otherwise be borne. The credit would be available to all taxpayers bearing the expense and would replace the income tax deduction presently available insofar as property taxes are concerned. Importantly, all taxpayers eligible to take the credit would be equally advantaged regardless of income levels. Thus, a capped credit will not provide a disproportionate benefit to more affluent taxpayers. Assuming that preferential treatment for state and local taxes is appropriate, a credit is also more protective of the federal fisc.[52] It can be capped at levels deemed appropriate by federal policy makers. Hence, total cost to the treasury of a subsidy provided through a credit can be more easily controlled. This distinguishes a credit in an important way from an income tax deduction; the cost to the treasury of a deduction is not so easily contained. Finally, a capped credit for that percentage of property tax liability earmarked for support of public K–12 education would signal a powerful federal preference for state use of a more stable source of revenue for financing this important public good.[53]

This approach could also prove to be a boon for local officials, who would formulate policy and determine the required levels of support. The credit would be available for the federally capped property tax liability. This scheme would indirectly provide additional resources to local school districts through the federal government but would preserve local policy control. An available credit may also make increased property tax liability more politically palatable for taxpayers. The universally available character of the credit does this work; the outlay would enable any taxpayer bearing this cost to have it taken into account for tax purposes without the need to itemize on the tax return. Thus, senior, childless, nonitemizing taxpayers would be able to take the credit in the appropriate amount as well as the taxpayer in a household including school-age children. It would be available at the level deemed to constitute acceptable federal cost to all qualifying taxpayers having positive tax liability.

Finally, a comparable approach might be taken for federal tax purposes for qualifying charitable contributions. Under present law, itemizing taxpayers are able to deduct contributions to public schools, school districts, or foundations. For example, a credit against tax liability could be permitted for charitable contributions made to foundations or state-administered agencies that serve schools or school districts in which a disproportionately high percentage of poorer children are enrolled. Alternatively, a deduction might only be allowed if the taxpayer contributes to a fund or to schools serving less affluent families.[54] A source of funding providing additional support for such schools would likely be a financial boon. Of equal importance, without this kind of incentive for contribution, supplementary assistance of this kind would almost certainly be unavailable to poorer districts. This credit as structured would be altruistic in flavor and entirely in keeping with the policy underlying the charitable contributions deduction.

In short, an income tax credit especially for property taxes could be specifically crafted in order to support public education. That concept could be extended to include charitable contributions by disinterested donors to funds administered solely for the support of officially designated public schools. In both cases the credit would be an important way to increase federal funding for public education without a corresponding increase in federal direct cost, control, or oversight. The concept could be replicated by states.

As is the case with any indirect expenditure, there would likely be an additional cost to the affected treasury if the property tax credit is more broadly available than is the present deduction for property taxes paid. Similarly, a new credit for designated charitable deduction would carry with it some additional expense to the federal fisc. Support of public education in this fashion, however, is consistent with the congressional policy that underlies both the deduction for qualifying state and local taxes as well as for charitable contributions. Allowing the property tax deduction in either its original or restructured form effectively subsidizes an important state undertaking—indeed, one having state constitutional stature. Though this deference is not compelled under the federal constitution, it is entirely permissible as a matter of policy. In like manner, Congress provides the charitable deduction as an incentive to taxpayers to provide support for charitable and educational purposes.[55] Support of public education as suggested here fits neatly into these categories. And if properly structured, additional cost to the federal government could be kept within acceptable bounds.

Federal Financial Assistance During Economic Exigencies

Income taxes are the primary sources of all federal revenue (generating more than 60 percent). Because of this reliance on income taxes, the business cycle will affect revenue ebb and flow at the national level. There is, however, an important difference between federal and state governments. The federal budget need not be balanced. As such, in times of recession, and given its superior access to capital markets, the federal government can borrow in order to maintain governmental services until the economy recovers. This enables the national government to extend financial assistance to subnational governments during periods of economic exigency, as occurred during the recent recession when the American Recovery and Reinvestment Act authorized approximately $48 billion in State Fiscal Stabilization Funds to support local education in 2010.

The obvious difficulty is the ad hoc nature of this assistance; these distributions are not cyclical. Arguably, however, the federal government did precisely what it should do in such circumstances: provide assistance limited in time and amount to help state and local governments, including school districts, through a difficult financial period.

CONCLUSION

Public education is arguably *the* most important service provided by government. Its importance has been touted time after time by various courts. The language in *Serrano* is illustrative: "Education is essential in . . . preserving an individual's opportunity to compete successfully in the economic marketplace . . . is universally relevant [and] is unmatched in the extent to which it molds the personality of the youth of society."[56] There is little question that an educated populace is critical to an effectively functioning democratic society. The necessary education cannot be accomplished without financial support that is sufficient and stable. All levels of government must be involved in this effort.

Neither school districts nor state governments acting alone possess the necessary fiscal capacity to meet even the minimal challenge of adequacy. On the local level, school districts have been deeply disadvantaged by voter- and state-imposed limitations on the ability to generate revenues from property taxes. As lawmakers for local government, state legislators and policy makers must take steps to reverse the effect of these limitations by rethinking the structuring of economic initiatives. States must refrain from imposing limitations or engaging in initiatives that undermine locals' ability to be as self-sufficient as possible. The local property tax remains the best way to raise local revenue for public education. Further, local power to impose the tax for this limited purpose should not be abrogated by TELs or other measures of overly broad property tax relief. States can begin to revitalize the tax by crafting economic initiatives that protect public education from diversions or abatement incident to incentives for development.

Even assuming that states adopt this stance, wide variations in the value of districts' taxable property will continue to make the task of generating funding substantially equal to that provided by richer school districts impossible for poorer school districts. State assistance to poorer districts will be critical if adequate and equitable funding is to be a reality. In providing this support, states must make funding from general source revenue a priority. While some earmarking from specific revenue sources might be exploited to supplement general source funding for education, states must refrain from relying exclusively on such sources. Earmarking from excise taxes such as tobacco, alcohol, or gaming should not, in any case, be the primary source of funding. Realistically, states will occasionally face periods of financial exigency over which they have no control. A modified and revitalized property tax should provide some protection from possible reductions in state support as long as recessions are not prolonged.

The assistance of the federal government remains critically important to achieving stable, efficient funding. Federal assistance directly subsidizing particular purposes such as Title I and the Individuals with Disabilities Education Act (IDEA) should be continued. Additional federal financial assistance for unrestricted use need not be in the form of direct subsidies; a credit available to all taxpayers bearing this cost provided through the Internal Revenue Code would work well for this purpose. The credit could contribute significantly to stabilizing revenues over time.

Treating that part of the property tax liability earmarked for support of public education as a credit against what would otherwise be income tax liability would signal a powerful federal preference for a more stable source of funding for public education. A credit is also particularly attractive from the federal point of view in light of Congress's ability to control its ultimate cost to the federal treasury while according to all taxpayers bearing this cost some measure of relief. It could well shore up routine financing and make the cost of supporting public education more politically palatable. Finally, the role of the federal government during periods of economic exigency would be clearer; the federal government will likely need to provide critical bridge support during recessionary periods, as it did subsequent to the Great Recession.

Local, state, and federal governments must act in tandem if meaningful progress is to be made in restoring, stabilizing, and increasing funding for possible education. The continuing quest for new revenue sources is likely to continue to be elusive. That reality does not, however, foreclose the possibility of more effectively using presently available funding sources with a reconceived and revitalized property tax as the linchpin of that effort.

Determining how best to provide stable and effective funding for public education is a demanding task. In the quest to provide a publicly supported education to American children that is adequate, equitable, and second to none, a stable and effective foundation is indispensable. And failure is not an option.

NINE

Tearing Down Fences

School Boundary Lines and Equal Educational Opportunity in the Twenty-First Century

GENEVIEVE SIEGEL-HAWLEY

We deal here with the right of all of our children, whatever their race, to an equal start in life and to an equal opportunity to reach their full potential as citizens. Those children who have been denied that right in the past deserve better than to see fences thrown up to deny them that right in the future.

—Justice Thurgood Marshall, *Milliken v. Bradley* (1974)

IN 1972, TWO FEDERAL district court judges many states apart—one in the Midwest, one in the South—authored strikingly similar opinions that stood poised to dramatically alter the landscape of school desegregation. Each ruling recognized the power of political boundaries in structuring patterns of school and residential segregation, and each sought to eliminate them through school district consolidation. Tearing down the proverbial fences that separated city and suburban school systems for the purposes of desegregation, in light of trends that a popular band from the era described as "chocolate cities" and "vanilla suburbs," would directly address the profoundly racialized nature of U.S. metropolitan settlement.[1]

In the Detroit area case, Judge Stephen Roth first determined that school district officials had contributed to de jure segregation through school construction decisions and transfer policies. He then ordered a metropolitan remedy—to the shock and dismay of many white residents who believed the suburbs exempt from desegregation—due to state responsibility for public education.[2] On the subject of the powerful but invisible boundaries dividing city and suburban schools, Roth wrote, "School district lines are simply matters of political convenience and may not be used to deny constitutional rights."[3]

Down South, in a federal district court in Richmond, Virginia, Judge Robert Merhige also reached the conclusion that district lines could and should be crossed in order to achieve meaningful school desegregation. Beginning in 1969, area civil rights lawyers began to argue that the elimination of racially identifiable education could not occur in a city school system that was already 70 percent black and surrounded by suburban districts that were more than 90 percent white.[4] Merhige eventually agreed and, like Roth in Detroit, determined that the state's role in fostering segregation justified a cross-district remedy. His ruling, penned in the months prior to Roth's, contained comparable reasoning: "The proof here overwhelmingly establishes that school division lines between Richmond and the counties here coincide with no natural obstacles to speak of and do in fact work to confine blacks on a consistent, wholesale basis within the city, where they reside in segregated neighborhoods."[5]

These two cases steadily made their way up to the U.S. Supreme Court around the time of the 1973 *Rodriguez* decision. All three came before a Court significantly altered by President Richard Nixon's judicial appointees. Justices Lewis F. Powell, Jr., and William Rehnquist joined the court in 1972, close on the heels of two other Nixon appointments. Powell hailed from Virginia, where he had served as chairman of both the Richmond and Virginia school board. He was no advocate of school desegregation; just two black students attended schools with whites when he stepped down from the Richmond school board in 1961.[6] Meanwhile, Rehnquist openly flouted the notion of integrated schools. As a clerk on the Supreme Court in 1953, he wrote a sharply worded memo stating that he thought *Plessy v. Ferguson*'s separate but equal principle should be reaffirmed.[7]

The addition of Nixon's four appointees radically shifted a Court that had just begun to clarify what the landmark 1954 *Brown v. Board of Education* decision looked like in terms of desegregation standards and to provide districts with the tools needed to implement it.[8] The reconfigured Supreme Court now faced the vital issue of boundary lines: could metropolitan school desegregation remedies legitimately overcome the government-sponsored racial divides between city and suburb? In a heavily urbanized country, this was a central remaining question to be resolved before the full realization of *Brown*.

In 1973, the Supreme Court justices tied 4-4 in the Richmond case, with Justice Powell abstaining due to his prior role on the city's school board. The tie left standing an appellate ruling striking down the city-suburban merger.[9] School desegregation would proceed absent suburban involvement in Richmond. Yet the split decision left the legality of other metropolitan desegregation remedies unsettled, which meant that the Detroit case continued to move forward.

One year later, the U.S. Supreme Court handed down its momentous ruling in the Detroit-based *Milliken v. Bradley* case. In a 5-4 decision, the majority found that cross-district desegregation remedies were not permissible unless all affected districts were found guilty of intentional interdistrict discrimination. Building a comprehensive case documenting constitutional violations in multiple school districts was difficult for numerous reasons. After *Brown*, governmental units were aware that segregating policies were illegal and were therefore more careful not to create documents that would serve as evidence against them. Without direct evidentiary material, plaintiffs needed to collect a vast amount of information showing the history of school and public housing construction and outlining decisions about the formation of district and school attendance boundary lines, among other things. This was often beyond the reach of civil rights groups and lawyers, already pressed for time and resources.[10] Given such difficulties, *Milliken* was the first major judicial setback to school desegregation efforts since the *Brown* decision.[11]

Like *Rodriguez*, the *Milliken* decision dealt squarely with issues of equal educational opportunity. Many different and important goals underlie school desegregation, but efforts to ensure that a diverse group of children learn together are driven in part by an awareness that disparate resources and opportunity structures remain tightly linked to race and class.[12] Advocates believed that desegregation policy could address such disparities, emphasizing that sending black and white students to the same schools would increase the likelihood of more equal educational investment (fiscal and otherwise) across all schools. It would become much more difficult, the thinking went, to elicit community support for policies or actions that unfairly disadvantaged some schools over others when children of diverse backgrounds were evenly distributed across a school system. In short, desegregation was and continues to be about the equalization of resources, as emphasized in *Rodriguez*, among other deeply worthy goals like improved race relations and access to advantaged social networks.

Over the years, though, as integration efforts stalled, a narrower emphasis on "desegregating the money" emerged.[13] School finance litigation refocused attention on making separate schools equal by emphasizing the need for additional resources in segregated educational settings. Yet a wealth of evidence indicates that, even with an influx of extra money, the quality of education in racially and economically isolated schools still suffers.[14] It is thus likely that both *Milliken* and *Rodriguez* needed to be decided differently in order to provide equal educational opportunities to all students.

THE 1973 *RODRIGUEZ* defeat in federal court did not represent the end of efforts to equalize funding. Attorneys and advocates regrouped and began to wage similar battles in state courts throughout the nation. What may be less widely recognized, however, is that the *Milliken* decision in 1974 did not represent the absolute demise of metropolitan school desegregation. Such efforts proceeded, under different circumstances, in a number of communities.

Lawyers representing plaintiffs in several places, like Wilmington, Delaware, and Indianapolis, Indiana, took careful note of what *Milliken* required for proof of an interdistrict violation of the Fourteenth Amendment and designed their federal lawsuits accordingly.[15] Civil rights advocates were victorious in both instances, yielding important city-suburban remedies for generations of students.

State courts have offered another avenue for the pursuit of metropolitan school desegregation. Connecticut's long-running *Sheff v. O'Neil* case, first opened in 1996, hinges on the state's constitutional requirement that all children be provided with equal educational opportunity. In *Sheff,* the Connecticut Supreme Court held that providing equal educational opportunity required the state to remedy the racial and ethnic isolation in the schools regardless of its cause.[16] Over and over again, a powerful combination of grassroots activism and careful legal reasoning has yielded slow but steady advances in the contemporary city-suburban remedies—mainly in the form of interdistrict magnet schools—required by the *Sheff* case.[17]

The de facto legal victories in Connecticut, Delaware, and Indiana notwithstanding, most communities that implemented metropolitan remedies were located in the de jure segregated South. Along with a handful of court-ordered metropolitan mergers, several states in the southern region of the United States operate under laws that facilitate city-suburban school consolidation. These regional characteristics create an ideal backdrop for understanding the potential impact of metropolitan desegregation remedies. Doing so is vital, because the issues confronting Judge Roth and Judge Merhige endure. Patterns of racial and economic isolation in schools continue to be heavily driven by jurisdictional boundaries that separate multiple school districts in the same metropolitan area, just as they are also influenced by attendance zone boundaries within a single district.

In this chapter, I explore the contemporary relationship between school-related boundary lines and segregation in the metropolitan South and offer a vision for the contemporary pursuit of educational equity. Analyzing policies designed to integrate students across broad metropolitan communities in the South calls attention to tested—but in many cases discarded—strategies for equalizing educational and life opportunities. Evidence indicates that comprehensive city-suburban desegregation plans continue to be linked to lower levels of both school and housing segregation, underscoring the importance of revisiting the lessons of an earlier era and updating them for the twenty-first century. In that vein, I also present innovative and specific policy options for a more regional pursuit of educational equity.

METROPOLITAN SCHOOL DESEGREGATION: PRIOR RESEARCH AND THEORY

Metropolitan school desegregation strategies encompass broadly defined communities that include major portions of both the central city and surrounding suburbs. During the 1970s, despite the limitations of *Milliken*, these strategies gained particular favor due to their perceived ability to both stem long-standing patterns of white flight to the suburbs and to promote stable, integrated schools and neighborhoods.[18] Earlier research does in fact show that districts with comprehensive metro desegregation plans—including city-suburban transfers and magnet schools—have the most stably integrated schools.[19] Past studies also indicate that between 1970 and 1990 regions with metro-wide school desegregation plans experienced decreases in residential segregation at more than twice the national average.[20]

The dynamics behind the success of metropolitan school desegregation plans are clear. A school assignment policy that encompasses a hefty portion of a metro area's housing market helps disentangle residential choices from school choices. Home buyers know that they can move virtually anywhere in the metro and remain connected to high-quality schools serving student bodies that reflect the demographics of the broader community.[21]

In places without metropolitan school desegregation plans, the common practice of drawing school attendance boundaries to encircle nearby neighborhoods ensures that existing patterns of residential segregation will be reflected in the school enrollment.[22] This matters because more than half a century of social science research continues to link separate education to unequal opportunities and outcomes.[23] At the same time, a growing body of evidence indicates that carefully structured integrated schools are linked to profound benefits for all children.[24]

Beyond attendance zones, district boundaries send signals about entire systems of education by creating artificial barriers to educational opportunities that are still strongly associated with race and class. Families with children moving to or across the typical metro thus face a series of racialized decisions when choosing between attendance zones and school districts. And while those choices are often billed as free and open, for many families they are constrained by race and/or income level.[25]

OVERCOMING FENCES BETWEEN SCHOOL DISTRICTS: ANALYZING METROPOLITAN SCHOOL DESEGREGATION TODAY

Three southern metro areas—Richmond, Virginia; Louisville–Jefferson County, Kentucky; and Charlotte-Mecklenburg, North Carolina—were identified as key sites for an analysis of the contemporary impact of metropolitan school desegregation in 1990 through 2010.

Given the higher courts' rejection of Judge Merhige's district consolidation plan, the Richmond metro area exemplifies the more common metropolitan arrangement of separate city and suburban school systems. After the failed merger, formal school desegregation efforts were confined to Richmond Public Schools until a unitary status declaration in 1986.[26]

In contrast to circumstances in the Richmond area, Louisville–Jefferson County carried out a court-ordered 1975 merger and continues to implement a student assignment plan dedicated to promoting diverse schools across the metropolitan school district.[27] Earlier, mandated efforts to desegregate the district have been conducted on a voluntary basis since the late 1970s. The

school system is currently in the process of implementing a new student assignment plan that strives to ensure a balance of students from different
neighborhood contexts in each school.[28]

The merger of the city of Charlotte and Mecklenburg County's school
systems occurred more than a decade prior to the court-ordered events that
unfolded in Virginia and Kentucky. Dating back to the late 1940s, North
Carolina promoted the consolidation of city and county districts as a means to
improve the quality of rural school systems.[29] As Charlotte sought to expand
its outer limits through an annexation process in 1957, city leaders and stakeholders recognized that the operation of two distinct school systems would
impede future expansion efforts and disadvantage students in the more rural
Mecklenburg system (where the tax base continually shrank with each annexation). In 1959, Charlotte residents approved the school district merger by
a 3-1 margin.[30] Just two years later, the struggle for meaningful school desegregation began across a consolidated system—replete with the demographic
advantages of a merged city-suburban student population. Today, the district
continues to operate as a metropolitan school system. But in the aftermath
of a unitary status decision in 1999, the Charlotte-Mecklenburg district adopted a Family Choice Plan that heavily prioritized neighborhood schools.[31]

Each of these metropolitan communities represents a different experience
with desegregation policy and school district boundary lines. Though only
one district, Louisville–Jefferson County, continues to implement a comprehensive city-suburban desegregation strategy, Charlotte-Mecklenburg
did employ similar prior practices, with a policy shift occurring during the
time period under study. As such, the Charlotte area offers an important
before-and-after portrait of a site that engaged with and then retreated from
the goals of *Brown*. Meanwhile, the Richmond area adheres to the model of
desegregation limited to the central city. These three sites, therefore, offer a
critical comparative perspective on the relationship among district boundary
lines, desegregation policy, and racial patterns in the metropolitan South.

The first key lesson that emerged from the study of three southern metropolitan areas indicates that the presence of city-suburban district boundaries
was linked to more extreme patterns of racial isolation in schools.[32] An analysis of federal enrollment data shows that levels of school segregation in the
merged systems of Louisville–Jefferson County and Charlotte-Mecklenburg
(prior to unitary status) were dramatically lower than segregation levels in
the Richmond area. According to a commonly used empirical measure of

segregation, just 20 to 25 percent of white students in the Louisville and Charlotte areas needed to transfer schools to ensure that black and white students were evenly distributed across the district in 1992, compared with 66 percent of white students in the broader Richmond metro.[33] Another way of looking at these patterns is to consider the fact that, in 1992, virtually no students of any race attended intensely segregated schools (where underrepresented minority students make up 90 to 100 percent of the enrollment) in the merged Charlotte and Louisville systems. By contrast, nearly 37 percent of the Richmond area's black students were enrolled in intensely segregated settings in 1992. Again, it is worth noting that figures from this earlier year reflect a time period in which the Charlotte-Mecklenburg district was still pursuing widespread integration efforts.

Twenty years later, Louisville–Jefferson County was the only metro school system still operating under a comprehensive school desegregation policy, as well as the only district without substantial shares of students in intensely segregated settings. Meanwhile, after the Charlotte-Mecklenburg district implemented a neighborhood-based assignment plan in 2002, school segregation skyrocketed. Recall that roughly 25 percent of white students needed to transfer schools so that black and white students were spread evenly across schools in the district in 1992, a figure that more than doubled to 57 percent in 2008.

An arguably even more important finding from the study was that metropolitan school desegregation continues to be associated with swifter decreases in housing segregation. Figure 9.1 illustrates how school desegregation policy helps disconnect school and residential segregation. In contrast to the Richmond metro, where school and housing segregation levels were both high and intertwined, Louisville and Charlotte (pre-unitary status) reported much lower levels of school segregation. And by decoupling school considerations from housing decisions, contemporary metropolitan desegregation efforts helped hasten the demise of long-standing patterns of residential segregation.

Figure 9.2 illustrates the percentage change in residential segregation over the twenty-year period. Importantly, the metro area with the comprehensive city-suburban school desegregation plan, Louisville–Jefferson County, reported the fastest declines in black-white housing segregation—fully two times the rate of Richmond's decrease over the same time period. Moreover,

FIGURE 9.1 School and residential black-white/white-black dissimilarity index, three metropolitan areas, 1990–2010

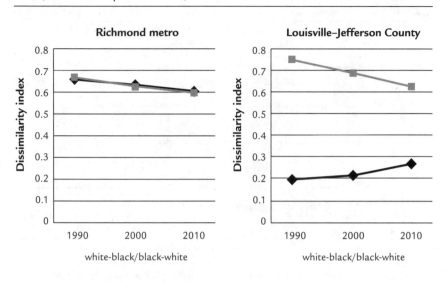

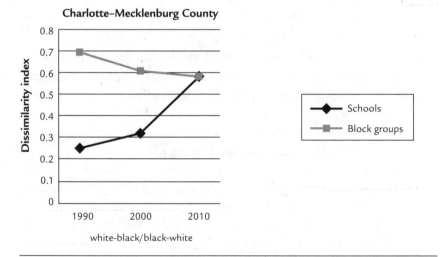

Sources: National Center for Education Statistics, *Common Core of Data*, 1992–1993, 1999–2000, 2008–2009, http://nces.ed.gov/ccd/; U.S. Census 1990, 2000, 2010, http://www.census.gov /prod/www/decennial.html.

FIGURE 9.2   Percent change in black-white/white-black residential dissimilarity index, three metropolitan areas, 1990–2000, 2000–2010, and 1990–2010

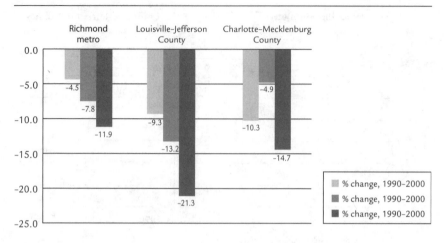

Sources: National Center for Education Statistics, *Common Core of Data*, 1992–1993, 1999–2000, 2008–2009, http://nces.ed.gov/ccd/; U.S. Census 1990, 2000, 2010, http://www.census.gov/prod/www/decennial.html.

between 1990 and 2000 Charlotte-Mecklenburg's black-white housing segregation was falling at a pace similar to Louisville's. But once the district abandoned its comprehensive school desegregation policy, levels of residential segregation between blacks and whites began to decline much more slowly. Though not illustrative of a causal relationship, these results do suggest that, in some ways, school policy can become housing policy.

Findings also showed the dramatic consequences associated with the dismantling of desegregation policy. Once a pioneering district that modeled innovative and successful desegregation efforts for the rest of the country, Charlotte-Mecklenburg is now eleven years into the radical resegregation of its school system and is experiencing stalled progress on housing integration. Developments in Charlotte-Mecklenburg highlight the critical importance of maintaining a strong commitment to school desegregation strategies. Even across a merged city-suburban school system, where enrollment trends make within-district desegregation more feasible, the presence of desegregation policy is critical to facilitating pro-integrative movement. In other words, while city-suburban school district consolidation is a policy development in its own right, it should be accompanied by specific efforts targeting school integration.

Where school district boundary lines remain intact, they give structure to regional patterns of school and housing segregation. Conversely, when those boundaries are subverted, patterns become less distinct. Regional district arrangements, then, accompanied by the presence of school desegregation policy, can significantly alter the contours of both school and housing segregation trends.

In the fragmented Richmond area, however, virtually nothing has been done over the past two decades to foster school integration. And ongoing segregation *between* Richmond metro districts has recently been accompanied by sharply increasing levels of school segregation *within* the separate city and suburban school systems.[34] The rise of this type of segregation signals the need for a renewed focus on boundaries both among and within school systems.

OVERCOMING FENCES WITHIN DISTRICTS

Over the past two decades, Henrico County, Virginia, one of the two suburban school systems slated for consolidation with Richmond public schools under Judge Merhige's order, has grown substantially more diverse. Rising levels of racial diversity in Henrico have largely been fueled by an increase in the share of black students attending schools in the county: in 1992, black students made up just over one in four students; that number climbed to nearly two out of five students by 2008. But even though integration remains a possibility in this suburban district, the lack of leadership and policy harnessing the potential of changing demographic characteristics has made it difficult to facilitate.

A recent school redistricting process in Henrico County, for example, created and maintained numerous racially isolated high school attendance zones.[35] The boundaries that were eventually adopted resulted in a situation where fully 17 percent of the county's black students were zoned to attend an intensely segregated high school, compared with 0 percent under the original attendance zones.[36] Nearly 10 percent of Latino students were similarly zoned under the newly adopted boundaries. Moreover, three high school zones remained more than 80 percent white in the final redistricting scenario.

The politics of school rezoning in Henrico, as in other documented cases, were decidedly contentious.[37] In this and other instances, the end result catered to parents and stakeholders resistant to an increase in the racial diversity of their zoned school.[38] Perhaps such a development is not surprising in light of the racially driven relationship between school and housing decisions. As long as neighborhoods are tightly linked to school enrollments, communities will be defined narrowly in the eyes of families and home buyers. But it is precisely because of these parochial political interests that strong, ethical leadership and policy seeking to broaden our notions of community—and tear down the fences that divide us—is sorely needed.

It is critical to understand that school redistricting processes present both challenges and opportunities. Because they occur any time a school opens or closes, among other reasons, school systems confront with some frequency the possibility of either enhancing diversity or extending segregation through rezoning. Importantly, the law has recently and clearly stated that districts are permitted to consider the general demographic characteristics of neighborhoods, to include racial composition, when drawing school-related boundaries.[39] In 2011, joint guidance from the Departments of Education and Justice reaffirmed this strategy.[40] It is also worth remembering that the law still prohibits school officials from intentionally drawing attendance boundaries in a way that exacerbates segregation.[41]

POLICY SOLUTIONS

Tearing down the fences that wall off children from educational opportunities both within and between districts is one of the most urgent tasks facing our nation today. There is clear evidence to support the still-nascent movement toward more regional solutions for educational inequalities. Most of these solutions involve efforts to subvert boundary lines through municipal consolidation or annexation processes, heightened regional cooperation, rezoning for diversity, or student assignment policies that break the link between school and housing segregation.

Federal and State Efforts to Promote Regionalism

At the federal level, government should provide unequivocally strong leadership supportive of regional efforts to combat metro area inequalities. The creation of a high-profile commission or task force to investigate innovative, regionwide school and housing integration strategies would be a positive first step. Federal funding for a regional schools and housing initiative would also signal high-level leadership and interest in promoting more equitable metropolitan areas, already begun under President Barack Obama's Sustainable Communities Initiative.[42]

State legislatures should also work to support regionalism, either through the enactment of policy that stimulates municipal and school district consolidation or annexation or through incentives to promote metropolitan-wide cooperation. Virginia, for example, passed a law (now shelved) in 1996 that provided money for municipalities to collaborate through regional partnerships. Regions were most heavily rewarded for plans to cooperate around education, revenue sharing, human services, local land use, and housing.[43] Yet even with these financial incentives, the politics linked to regional cooperation proved difficult.

Given the contentious politics, state courts may need to provide strong leadership around issues of equal educational opportunity. State constitutional language regarding the right to education that has led to the state-level pursuit of school finance litigation could also be applied to school desegregation litigation. In Connecticut, civil rights lawyers won a crucial legal victory in *Sheff* by arguing that schools segregated by both race and class were discriminatory and unequal and failed to provide a minimally adequate education.[44] Though the vast majority of state constitutions do not contain Connecticut's explicit prohibition of de facto segregation, experts assert that lawyers could mount desegregation cases in other states by defining educational equity or adequacy not simply in terms of dollars but in terms of integration.[45] Given the scope and scale of contemporary school segregation, this is surely an option worth exploring.

Getting the Politics Right

The task of framing the political debate surrounding annexation or consolidation in terms agreeable to populations that have often been pitted against one another is immense but not insurmountable.[46] City-county consolidation efforts require that narrow notions of neighborhood and community be expanded to include a diverse cross-section of interests and needs. Referendum campaigns that explore the fundamental interests of the local community and devise their political strategy accordingly have a higher probability of winning public support. Strong local leadership and agenda setting from business, media, and community stakeholders is also critical.[47]

Despite the political difficulty linked to mergers, in the current fiscal climate, conversations around school district consolidation have emerged with some frequency. Many recent consolidation efforts have been spurred by the potential financial benefits that may come with the elimination of duplicative bureaucracies.[48] The governor of New York, for instance, has continually urged the state's fragmented school districts and municipalities to consolidate in order to save costs.[49]

If Not Consolidation, at Least Cooperation

Of course, in the absence of efforts to actually eliminate boundary lines, other alternatives that ease any segregating effects of those lines should be considered. With respect to efforts to promote educational opportunity across regional boundaries, a number of options beyond actual consolidation are available. For example, eleven school districts in the Omaha, Nebraska, metropolitan area recently joined together to form a regional learning community, an entity defined by revenue sharing, increased aid to underresourced, high-needs schools and efforts to promote socioeconomic balance in the student enrollment.[50]

Other methods of cooperation might include pairing nearby city and suburban schools (or inner suburban and outer suburban schools) or finding ways to leverage school choice across boundary lines. The nation's eight long-standing interdistrict transfer programs could and should be expanded. Regional magnet or charter schools, imbued with appropriate civil rights protections, might offer integrative possibilities. Indeed, the interdistrict remedy ordered in the Connecticut case has led to the establishment of several successful networks of regional magnet schools in the state's major metropolitan areas.[51]

Finally, the student transfer provision in the Elementary and Secondary Education Act (ESEA), while currently underutilized, may deliver interdistrict possibilities if it is revised and strengthened accordingly.[52] Under the existing ESEA framework, students may transfer from low-performing schools to higher performing ones in the same district. Yet research has indicated that fewer than 2 percent of eligible students actually transferred, with eligible students of color transferring at even lower rates.[53] One possible explanation for the extremely low shares of students taking advantage of the transfer provision is that markedly better options are not available within the same district. Offering students a meaningful option to transfer to a higher-performing school outside of their district, however, may yield more participation. A study modeling the effects of a shift in the current law, from intradistrict to interdistrict choice, found that, if nationally implemented, interdistrict choice could expand access to higher-performing schools for students in more than 80 percent of eligible schools, compared with the 95 percent of eligible schools that currently do not have meaningful access to higher-performing schools under the intradistrict transfer provision.[54] It seems clear, then, that expanding the current policy—either through reauthorization or with the next round of waivers—to allow students to transfer to other districts could help alleviate the constraints presented by district boundaries. Though, as with magnet, charter, and existing interdistrict programs, extensive outreach and the availability of free transportation are key considerations for equity and access.

The Urgency of Fair Housing Efforts

While the *Milliken* decision presents a difficult legal barrier to crossing school district lines, fair housing law, if proactively enforced, could advance regional housing opportunities—which, in turn, would positively influence school diversity efforts. The federal government should heighten its efforts to expand and implement the 1968 Fair Housing Act. In addition to fair housing enforcement possibilities, the federal government could work to broaden the five existing Moving to Opportunity programs, which help low-income residents move to low-poverty neighborhoods. All levels of government, including state and local officials, could and should help ensure that Section 8 and the Low Income Housing Tax Credit are disbursed in ways that promote affordable housing in high-opportunity areas throughout a region.[55] State and local laws and policies should also guarantee that new metropolitan development contains a certain share of affordable housing.[56]

Within-District Strategies

Within demographically changing school systems, educational stakeholders should make the promotion of stable, diverse schools and neighborhoods an absolute priority. Systematic and legal within-district efforts to reduce racial isolation and advance the benefits of diverse schools include making diversity a goal during school closures, site selection for new schools, and rezoning. Controlled-choice policies offer a range of school options to parents but leave the final assignment decision to the school system, with diversity as one of the assignment criteria. Likewise, magnet schools may help promote voluntary integration by enticing a diverse range of families to schools offering unique themes or programmatic options.[57]

Joint School and Housing Integration Efforts

Each of these policy options should be crafted with an eye toward jointly disrupting patterns of school and housing segregation. For many decades, school desegregation policy bore much of the responsibility for interrupting underlying patterns of residential isolation. Given the success of those one-dimensional efforts in the Louisville and pre-unitary Charlotte areas, it is difficult to comprehend the power of a joined school and housing desegregation strategy. Early, pre-1990s evidence from the same two metro areas provided extremely rare examples of coordinated school and housing desegregation efforts.[58] The programs did not continue, but they offer ideas for how regional communities might begin to design united housing and school policy. For instance, voluntary school integration programs should consider transportation exemptions for families making integrative residential moves, in addition to providing exceptions for residents of stable, diverse communities. There is also a need for expertise in the areas of housing and schools to flow across metropolitan districts and agencies. Local housing programs and proposals for new developments grow and shift—as do student assignment plans and building and redistricting decisions—with little knowledge or discussion about the two related processes within the different sectors.[59] Public officials and policies should be put into place that can help bridge these gaps.

CONCLUSION

Over the past half century, rapid growth and demographic change in metropolitan areas has been accompanied by a dearth of policy seeking to harness the potential of those transformations. Yet, in many ways, law and policy has instead cemented tremendous racial and socioeconomic inequities into the structure of our cities.

In Charlotte, where desegregation plans have been significantly altered, or dropped altogether, school and housing segregation levels tell a story of what was lost—but also of what might still be regained. Areas like Louisville that continue to operate under comprehensive metropolitan school desegregation policies are decidedly more likely to display integrated schools and residential communities. Richmond, along with other locales that have not yet experimented with policies designed to lessen the impact of boundaries and promote desegregation, must examine the consequences of inaction and be spurred toward greater commitment.

PART III

Creating Innovative Federal Avenues for Promoting Equal Access to an Excellent Education

TEN

How Reconstructing Education Federalism Could Fulfill the Aims of *Rodriguez*

KIMBERLY JENKINS ROBINSON

THE *RODRIGUEZ* PLAINTIFFS, Mexican American schoolchildren who resided in districts with a low property tax base, challenged the Texas school finance system in federal court because they sought educational opportunities that equaled those of their more affluent and white peers in a nearby neighborhood. Although state school finance litigation and reform has resulted in some reform of school finance systems, the educational opportunity gap that the *Rodriguez* plaintiffs sought to remedy in the early 1970s remains one of the persistent challenges that plague the American education system. Today, it relegates at least ten million students in low-income neighborhoods and millions more minority students to poorly performing teachers, substandard facilities, and other inferior educational opportunities.[1]

Why have the disparities that the *Rodriguez* plaintiffs attempted to remedy continued to burden the public school system in the United States? Although these disparities have broad roots, they persist in part because the United States invests more money in high-income districts than in low-income districts, a sharp contrast to other developed nations.[2] Scholars and court decisions also have documented the sizeable intrastate disparities in educational opportunity. In addition, interstate inequalities represent the largest component of disparities in educational opportunity. The harmful nature of interstate disparities falls hardest on disadvantaged schoolchildren who have the most educational needs, and states do not possess the resources and capacity to address the full scope of these disparities.[3]

The central aim of the *Rodriguez* plaintiffs—equal educational opportunity—remains an essential goal of the U.S. education system. Yet it has never been realized. The United States relies heavily on schools to overcome the influence of a child's circumstances, such as family income and structure, on life opportunities despite evidence that schools are not effectively serving this function. Fulfilling the goal of equal educational opportunity will become increasingly important to the nation's interests given the growing need for more highly skilled workers to supply jobs that meet the economy's demands.[4]

As policy makers, scholars, and reformers continue to search for new ideas for how to fulfill the aims of the *Rodriguez* litigation, we must identify all of the root causes for these disparities. I believe that one of the overlooked causes is the nation's approach to education federalism—a balance of power across the federal, state, and local governments that emphasizes substantial state autonomy over education—which has played a significant and influential role in undermining federal reforms that address disparities in educational opportunity. Indeed, in a recent article I analyzed how the nation's approach to education federalism served as one of the principal obstacles to three of the most comprehensive federal attempts to advance equal educational opportunity: school desegregation, federal school finance litigation, and the No Child Left Behind Act of 2001 (NCLB).[5]

In the *Rodriguez* decision, the U.S. Supreme Court held that the plaintiffs did not have a right under the Constitution's Equal Protection Clause, which required the state of Texas to remedy disparities in funding for schools in high-wealth and low-wealth school districts. One of the principal reasons that the Court rejected the plaintiffs' claims was the need to maintain the current balance of power between the federal and state governments over education. Indeed, the Court acknowledged in *Rodriguez* that even though all equal protection claims implicate federalism, "it would be difficult to imagine a case having a greater potential impact on our federal system than the one now before us," because upholding the plaintiffs' claims would ultimately lead the Court to invalidate the school systems in all fifty states. Although some contend that these decisions and results are driven more by a lack of political will rather than education federalism, the consistency with which federalism has arisen as a real or imagined obstacle to reforms aimed at ensuring equal educational opportunity suggests that federalism is a significant contributing factor, even if other factors also adversely influenced these reforms.[6]

I contend that the United States should strategically restructure and strengthen the federal role in education to establish the necessary foundation for a national effort to ensure equal access to an excellent education. This restructuring and strengthening of the federal role in education would require shifting some power away from the state and local governments and toward the federal government. The United States would then need to adopt a new understanding of education federalism that embraces the federal government as the guarantor of equal opportunity, because it is the only government with the capacity and sufficient incentive to lead a national effort to achieve this widely supported, yet persistently elusive, goal. Although this would not require federalizing the nation's education system as at least one scholar has recommended, it would require acceptance of a larger federal role in education to hold the states accountable for ensuring that all students receive equal access to an excellent education.[7]

I define equal access to an excellent education as the opportunity for all students to attend a high-quality school that enables them to effectively pursue their life goals, to become engaged citizens, and to develop their abilities to their full potential.[8] Equal access to an excellent education enables all students to receive "a real and meaningful opportunity to achieve rigorous college- and career-ready standards."[9] If the United States pursues equal access to an excellent education as the primary goal for its education system, it will break the traditional link between low-income and minority status and inferior educational opportunities. This goal recognizes that educational opportunities should be tailored to meet the individual needs of students that may vary dramatically depending on a variety of factors, including family structure and stability, students' health and nutrition, and neighborhood climate. This goal also embraces closing the opportunity gap as an essential prerequisite for closing the achievement gap. Furthermore, embracing racially and economically diverse schools is essential for achieving this goal given compelling research regarding the harms of racial and class isolation, the benefits of diversity, and evidence of diverse schools providing important educational benefits that cannot be duplicated by alternative reforms.[10] An excellent education for all schoolchildren should be the nation's ultimate education goal, because all families ultimately want a first-rate education for their children and because the United States would benefit economically, socially, and politically from providing such an education.

My proposal for disrupting education federalism is particularly timely. First, the United States is undergoing an unprecedented expansion of the federal role in education and an accompanying shift in its approach to education federalism. The American Recovery and Reinvestment Act of 2009, also known as the stimulus bill, authorized an unprecedented $100 billion to invest in education funding, tuition tax credits, and college grants. President Barack Obama trumpeted this as "the largest investment in education in our nation's history." The stimulus bill included $4.35 billion for the Race to the Top (RTTT) program, which represented far more discretionary funding than all of Secretary of Education Arne Duncan's predecessors. Although RTTT has its shortcomings, it has sparked significant education reform, including greater state support for the Common Core State Standards, charter schools, and revisions to state laws regarding the use of student testing data to evaluate teachers. In a number of states and districts, the two years following the creation of RTTT sparked more reform than those locations had seen in the preceding twenty years.[11] The stimulus bill built on the expansion of the federal role in education established in the No Child Left Behind Act of 2001. NCLB represents the most expansive federal education reform law in the history of the United States. For example, the law's far-reaching provisions require annual testing in math and reading in grades 3 through 8 and once in grades 10 through 12 and periodically in science. NCLB also instituted public reporting of results of student assessments on the content of state standards; launched disaggregation of this data for a variety of student characteristics, including race and ethnicity; created accountability interventions for Title I schools; and set minimum requirements for highly-qualified teachers.[12]

Second, there is currently a national focus on improving educational performance of poor schoolchildren and reducing the achievement and opportunity gaps. For instance, a 2013 report from the Equity and Excellence Commission, a panel of education policy experts convened by President Obama, proposed a variety of far-reaching reforms that would greatly expand federal responsibility for equal educational opportunity.[13] Scholars similarly have offered a variety of thoughtful proposals for how to reduce the opportunity gap that would require greatly expanding federal authority over education and thereby restructuring education federalism.[14] Here I strengthen these calls for reform by explaining why disrupting education federalism is necessary for a successful national effort to ensure equal access to an excellent education and identifying the essential elements for a successful comprehensive effort to achieve this goal.

In offering a proposal for restructuring education federalism, I build on Yale Law professor Heather Gerken's argument that scholars developing and critiquing federalism theory should consider the appropriate balance of institutional arrangements for a specific context.[15] Therefore, I only propose a shift in the balance of federal, state, and local authority in order to strengthen the federal role in ensuring equal access to an excellent education.

UNDERSTANDING THE CURRENT STRUCTURE OF EDUCATION FEDERALISM AND ITS BENEFITS

Historically, the hallmarks of education federalism in the United States have been decentralized state and local control over public schools and a limited federal role. The constitutional foundations for this approach lie in the omission of education from the purview of federal authority and the Tenth Amendment's reservation of authority for the states in all areas that the Constitution does not assign to Congress.[16]

However, three trends are noteworthy to understand the current structure of education federalism. First, the federal role in education has grown exponentially from its original narrow role. After *Brown v. Board of Education* in 1954, Congress passed several statutes that fostered federal responsibility for equal educational opportunity, including the Elementary and Secondary Education Act of 1965 (ESEA). In the last two decades, Congress has expanded the federal role to encourage higher standards and greater accountability for the education of all children, most recently through NCLB and its waivers and the RTTT program.[17]

Second, state control over education has risen substantially over the last half century or more of school reform. School finance litigation and reform encouraged centralization of education authority with state officials who eventually became the primary funders of public schools.[18] States currently contribute 45.2 percent of school funding, and local government provides 44.6 percent. The federal government provides 10.2 percent of funds for education, and this represents an increase in federal education funding over the last decade, although not a steady one.[19] The increase in the state proportion of funding led to an increase in state authority over schools. State-created standards and tests also have expanded state influence over the curriculum.[20]

Finally, the third trend necessarily follows from the first two. The rise in federal and state authority over education has led to a substantial decrease in local control of schools for the last half century. Local authority over education is primarily focused on the daily administrative responsibilities for running schools, including implementing federal and state categorical programs and court orders; hiring and supervising staff; constructing, acquiring, and maintaining school buildings; managing vendor contracts; and transporting students. Most local school boards also may raise funds for public schools through property taxes.[21]

The nation's current approach to education federalism has been praised for its ability to reap several benefits. Some find this approach superior, based on Justice Louis Brandeis's view that state and local governments may serve as experimental "laboratories" that can help solve the nation's economic and social challenges. States and localities have adopted a diverse array of governance structures for education that are designed to respond to state and local interests and preferences. This decentralized approach also allows state and local governments to adopt a variety of curricula, teaching, and learning approaches.[22]

Others praise the current structure of education federalism for its ability to produce the most effective outcomes. For example, proponents of localism contend that local decision making can produce more effective policy reforms because those most affected by the decision shape the reform. Still others contend that a decentralized approach to education is more effective at identifying the most successful educational approaches given the existing uncertainties regarding how best to educate children. Localism also can create an efficient allocation of goods and services by allowing local governments to compete for citizens by offering an attractive array of public services. When localities offer diverse learning options, some citizens can shop for the best schools or relocate so that their children can attend schools that best serve their educational needs.[23]

Additionally, state and local control over education is commended for its ability to foster greater accountability to citizens. Individuals exert greater influence over local government policy than over federal or state government. Local control can enable parents to become involved in and influence their child's education and school. Many parents regularly interact with and monitor their child's school, and this involvement can improve student performance.[24]

The tradition of local control of education also remains an important value for many within the American public. Many view state and local control over public elementary and secondary education as a central component of state and local government. While public opinion polls reveal an increasing comfort with federal involvement in education, the polls continue to indicate that Americans generally prefer state and local control over education. In addition, state and local authority over education has resulted in diversity in education governance that influences the impact the federal government can have on education.[25]

REASONS FOR REEXAMINING EDUCATION FEDERALISM

Given these benefits, why should the nation reexamine the structure of education federalism and consider increasing federal authority over education as part of a national plan to ensure equal access to an excellent education? This reexamination is needed for at least five reasons.

The Inconsistencies in the Benefits of Education Federalism

Although education federalism undoubtedly reaps some of the benefits that it is designed to accomplish, the current approach does not consistently yield the benefits that it is supposed to secure. For instance, education federalism has been praised for its ability to allow the state and local governments to serve as "laboratories" of reform. However, research reveals that in the area of school finance reform, most reforms have been fairly limited in scope and that the reliance on property taxes to fund schools remains the prevailing approach to local school funding.[26] This approach has continued despite the Supreme Court's 1973 call for school finance reform in *Rodriguez*: "The need is apparent for reform in tax systems which may well have relied too long and too heavily on the local property tax. And certainly innovative thinking as to public education, its methods, and its funding is necessary to assure both a higher level of quality and greater uniformity of opportunity."[27]

Even when plaintiffs have prevailed in litigation that sought to reform school finance systems, most states typically have maintained the same fundamental and unequal structure for school finance. Additionally, in a substantial majority of the states, funding inequities between wealthy and poor districts and schools persist.[28] In 2012, only fifteen states provided more funding to districts with high concentrations of poverty than those with low concentrations of poverty, despite consistent research that low-income students require more resources for a successful education than do their more affluent peers. The 2013 Equity and Excellence Commission report notes that substantial reform is needed because, apart from a few exceptions, states fail to link their school finance systems to the costs that they would need to invest to educate all children in compliance with state standards.[29] Given decades of reforms that have not made consistent and substantial inroads on these challenges, the states are not serving as effective laboratories for school finance reform.

Education federalism also is supposed to yield an efficient and effective education system. However, the U.S. education system regularly falls short of achieving these goals. The substantial percentage of poorly educated students inflicts substantial costs on the nation, resulting in numerous inefficiencies. For example, substantially increasing the high school graduation rate could save the nation $7.9 to $10.8 billion annually in food stamps, housing assistance, and welfare assistance. The nation forfeits $156 billion in income and tax revenues during the life span of each annual cohort of students who do not graduate from high school. This cohort also costs the public $23 billion in health-care costs and $110 billion in diminished health quality and longevity. By increasing the high school graduation rate by 1 percent for men age twenty to sixty, the nation could save $1.4 billion each year from reduced criminal behavior.[30]

Local participation in the governance of school districts also is quite low and thus does not accomplish the accountability that it is supposed to secure. The growing federal and state influence over education has led some scholars to contend that "local control" no longer exists in American education and, in fact, has not existed for quite some time. Typically, no more than 10 to 15 percent of voters participate in school board elections, and school board meetings also often experience low citizen attendance. In low-income communities in particular, community participation regularly can yield little influence due to the lack of political power and financial means of residents. Although the quality of schools certainly influences where many families purchase homes, low-income families typically lack the financial ability to choose the best schools because such schools are zoned for more expensive housing options.[31]

In noting that education federalism does not consistently yield the benefits that it is designed to secure, I am not suggesting that it does not yield some important benefits. Certainly, the decentralized nature of the American education system fosters some state and local experimentation and innovation, such as curricular reform, teaching innovations, and other state and local reforms. The current structure of education federalism undeniably fosters more state and local control and accountability for state and local decisions than does a completely federalized system of education.[32] Although these benefits are worth preserving, the inconsistency in reaping these benefits suggests that it is worth reexamining how education federalism could be restructured to more reliably secure such benefits.

Education Federalism as a Roadblock to Equal Educational Opportunity

Elsewhere I have analyzed how a preference for local control and a limited federal role in education have functioned as one of several critical roadblocks to three of the primary reforms that promote equal educational opportunity: school desegregation, school finance litigation in federal court, and NCLB. The Supreme Court relied on education federalism as one of the primary justifications for rejecting a federal right to education in *Rodriguez*. Similarly, key Supreme Court decisions, from the 1974 decision in *Milliken v. Bradley* to the 1995 decision in *Missouri v. Jenkins,* have relied on the structure of federalism and the American tradition of local control of education as one of the reasons for severely curtailing effective school desegregation. In so doing, these opinions clung to a form of dual federalism which insisted that education was solely a state and local function. However, dual federalism had already been eschewed in prior Court decisions that prohibited segregated educational systems and in federal legislation and enforcement that provided additional federal funding for low-income students and that required equal educational opportunity for girls, women, disabled students, and English language learners.[33] Even when Congress was adopting NCLB, the nation's long-standing approach to education federalism insisted that states decide the standards for students and teachers, which resulted in many states failing to adopt rigorous standards for either students or teachers.[34]

Certainly, education federalism does not stand alone as an obstacle to these reforms. Numerous other obstacles, including state and local backlash against court-ordered desegregation, the challenges of court-mandated school reform, and inadequate funding for NCLB, also undermined the effectiveness of these reforms.[35] Nevertheless, education federalism was one of the central obstacles to the effectiveness of these reforms.

Education Federalism Allows States to Make Equal Educational Opportunity a Low Priority

Throughout this nation's history—even acknowledging state reforms in education and school funding—the states have not taken sustained and comprehensive action to ensure that all students receive equal access to an excellent education. Redistributive goals and equity concerns are simply not consistent state priorities for education.[36] Indeed, the 2013 report from the Equity and Excellence Commission found that "any honest assessment must acknowledge that our efforts to date to confront the vast gaps in educational outcomes separating different groups of young Americans have yet to include a serious and sustained commitment to ending the appalling inequities—in school funding, in early education, in teacher quality, in resources for teachers and students and in governance—that contribute so mightily to these gaps."[37] Furthermore, intrastate reforms cannot address significant and harmful interstate disparities in funding.[38]

The limited scope of many reforms also reveals that the United States has lacked the political will and investments in enforcement to adopt and implement the type of reforms that would make equal access to an excellent education a reality.[39] Given this generally consistent failure to undertake comprehensive and sustained reform, the United States should not expect different results from a system that has failed to ensure equal access to an excellent education for many generations of schoolchildren. Instead, an assessment of how education federalism could be restructured to support a comprehensive national effort to achieve this goal is long overdue.

Education Federalism Invites Inequality

Primary state and local control over education essentially invite inequality in educational opportunity because of pervasive state insistence that local governments raise education funds and state funding formulas which do not effectively equalize the resulting disparities in revenue. Although some influential victories have occurred, school finance litigation has mostly failed to change the basic organizational structure of school finance systems and their reliance on property taxes to fund schools. Instead, this litigation at best has obtained limited increases in funding for property-poor districts while allow-ing property-rich districts to maintain the same funding level or to raise their funding rate at a slower pace.[40]

Evidence of the persistent inequalities in school funding can be found in the 2013 Equity and Excellence Commission report. The report found that "no other developed nation has inequities nearly as deep or systemic; no other developed nation has, despite some efforts to the contrary, so thor-oughly stacked the odds against so many of its children." These dispari-ties are due in substantial part to the continued state reliance on property taxes to fund schools. As a result, many predominantly low-income and minority schools predictably produce poor outcomes because they typically lack both the resources to ensure that their students obtain an effective ed-ucation and the capacity to undertake effective reforms even when these reforms are well conceived.[41]

The harms from persistent and pervasive disparities in educational oppor-tunity are not limited to schoolchildren, their families, and their commu-nities. These disparities also harm nationwide interests in a strong economy and a just society. The United States needs to maintain international aca-demic competitiveness to attract businesses and prevent the loss of jobs to other, more educated nations. Research reveals that the long-term vigor of the U.S. economy will depend on the advanced skills that are typically pro-vided in higher education and that are needed for upper-level technical oc-cupations. Yet, international assessments reveal that the performance of U.S. students is often average or below average when compared with students from other countries, which will make it difficult for American students to com-pete successfully.[42] Eric A. Hanushek, Paul E. Peterson, and Ludger Woess-man summarize the lackluster performance of U.S. students on international assessments, noting that "the evidence of international comparison is now clear. American students lag badly and pervasively. Our students lag behind students not just in Asia, but in Europe and other parts of the Americas. It is not just disadvantaged students or a group of weak students who lag, but also American students from advantaged backgrounds. Americans are badly underrepresented among the world's highest achievers."[43]

Although some scholars challenge such conclusions from international as-sessments as overblown and simplistic, others conclude that these less-than-stellar outcomes indicate that the U.S. education system is failing to prepare many of its students to compete successfully for jobs with other students from around the world.[44] The nation also has a strong interest in ensuring that entire segments of the public are not denied the American Dream due to their family income and racial/ethnic background.

Education Federalism Should Be Guided by Research Rather Than Politics

The expansion of the federal role in education has largely been guided by politics, and politics, indisputably, will continue to play an influential role in education reform. Nevertheless, the expanding federal role should be guided primarily by rigorous research regarding the strengths of federal policy making, just as research about the importance of educational opportunities for disabled students informed Congress's passage of the Education for All Handicapped Children Act of 1975. Although federal education law and policy are also influenced by politics, the federal government has demonstrated a willingness to leverage politics and research to address the needs of the disadvantaged within American society when politics has prevented effective reform at the state and local levels.[45]

A THEORY FOR DISRUPTING EDUCATION FEDERALISM

Education federalism should be restructured to embrace greater federal leadership and responsibility for a national effort to provide equal access to an excellent education. Any substantial strengthening and reform of the federal role in education will transform the nature of education federalism, because substantive changes to federal authority over education directly affect the scope of state and local authority over education. These shifts in education federalism have occurred throughout U.S. history, including federally mandated school desegregation and NCLB.[46] This broad theory could be used to guide development of federal legislation, new initiatives by the Department of Education, or, most likely, a combination of the two. I focus here on future action by Congress and the executive branch, rather than doctrinal reform through the courts, because the legislative and executive branch enjoy numerous policy-making strengths over courts.[47]

The following six policy-making areas identify how the federal government's role in education should be expanded to ensure equal access to an excellent education:

1. Prioritizing a national goal of ensuring that all children have equal access to an excellent education and acknowledging that achieving this goal will require disrupting education federalism.[48]

2. Incentivizing development of common opportunity-to-learn (OTL) standards that identify the education resources states must provide.[49]

3. Focusing rigorous research and technical assistance on the most effective approaches to ensuring equal access to an excellent education.[50]

4. Distributing financial assistance with the goal of closing the opportunity and achievement gaps.[51]

5. Demanding continuous improvement from states to ensure equal access to an excellent education through federal oversight that utilizes a collaborative enforcement model.[52]

6. Establishing the federal government as the final guarantor of equal access to an excellent education by strengthening the relationship between federal influence and responsibility.[53]

Each of these elements either suggests how to leverage existing strengths of federal policy making more effectively or fills in important gaps of federal policy making and enforcement.[54]

Prioritizing a National Goal of Ensuring Equal Access to an Excellent Education

Some national leaders already have noted the importance of a national goal of ensuring that all children are provided equal access to an excellent education.[55] However, some key points are missing from this rhetoric that must be emphasized to support the type of comprehensive reforms I envision. For instance, the nation's top education leaders, including the president, the secretary of education, and members of Congress, must initiate a national conversation on why the United States should no longer tolerate long-standing disparities in educational opportunity and why federal action is needed to address them. Initiating such a conversation also requires the federal government to prioritize equal access to an excellent education on its national policy-making agenda.

Federal and national education leaders also must make the case that the entire nation would benefit from ending inequitable disparities in education, because research reveals that reforms to help those who are disadvantaged typically do not succeed unless they benefit more privileged Americans.[56]

Therefore, the federal government must convince the more affluent segments of American society that a more equitable distribution of educational opportunity would inure to their benefit. This could be accomplished in part by publicizing existing research which quantifies the myriad high costs that the United States pays for offering many schoolchildren a substandard education and which acknowledges that even many advantaged children are not competing effectively with their international peers.[57]

Federal leadership also must explain why a reexamination and restructuring of education federalism is warranted. This discussion should highlight federal willingness to shoulder greater responsibility for leading the national effort to achieve this goal. It also should emphasize that effective, comprehensive reform must involve a shoulder-to-shoulder partnership among the federal, state, and local governments.

Fortunately, the federal government has proven its ability to herald the importance of new educational goals and approaches in the national interest. Research and history confirm that agenda setting serves as one of the strengths of the federal government in education policy making. For instance, President Lyndon Johnson successfully convinced Congress to advance equal educational opportunity for low-income schoolchildren through the ESEA, which includes Title I, and the Economic Opportunity Act, which includes programs like Head Start and Upward Bound. President George W. Bush championed NCLB and its insistence on proficiency for all children in math and reading, public reporting of testing data disaggregated by subgroups, and a range of accountability interventions for failing schools.[58] Therefore, a federal call to implement a comprehensive plan to ensure equal access to an excellent education should build on the lessons learned from these and other federal reforms that set the nation's education agenda.

Incentivizing Development of Common Opportunity-to-Learn Standards

A federal effort to ensure equal access to an excellent education should incentivize the states to develop common opportunity-to-learn standards that would identify the in-school and out-of-school resources students should receive in order to meet rigorous achievement standards. Most states are implementing the Common Core standards, which were developed by a group of assessment specialists and academics in response to a request from the Council of Chief State School Officers and the National Governors

Association. The standards are intended to provide a clear set of math and English language and literacy standards for kindergarten through twelfth grade that would prepare all public school children to complete their high school education and be ready to enroll in college or participate in the workforce.[59] OTL standards are essential for ensuring equal access to an excellent education because, as Linda Darling-Hammond has noted, two decades of high standards and testing implementation have revealed that "there is plentiful evidence that—although standards and assessments have been useful in clarifying goals and focusing attention on achievement—tests alone have not improved schools or created educational opportunities without investments in curriculum, teaching, and school supports."[60] Common OTL standards would identify both what educational resources should be offered and the quality of the resources needed to effectively implement standards.

I recommend the adoption of common OTL standards to set a floor of equal educational opportunity, so that state adoption of high academic standards can have the intended effect of improving outcomes. During its inception, the standards and accountability movement recognized that the success of academic standards depended on ensuring that students receive an equal opportunity to acquire the knowledge within high standards. OTL standards were tested, but proved politically unsustainable, in the mid-1990s. In 1994, Congress passed the Goals 2000: Educate America Act, and this law provided for two options for the creation of OTL standards that established the conditions and resources needed throughout the education system to provide students the opportunity to learn the content set forth in voluntary national or state content standards. The Improving America's Schools Act of 1994 (IASA) also conditioned Title I funds on state development of rigorous content and performance standards. It included a requirement that state plans must describe how states will help districts and schools "develop the capacity" to achieve high standards and that state plans could include OTL standards. However, shortly after the passage of these laws, a Republican-controlled Congress repealed the federal power to establish OTL standards and the mandate that states should establish such standards.[61]

My theory has the states serving as the primary architects of the standards, because this approach fosters greater cooperation in implementing the standards and reduces criticism that the standards represent a federal takeover of education. Common OTL standards would preserve the ability of states to adopt a variety of educational governance, funding, and policy-making structures. Once the states develop the standards, states would implement plans to identify the gap between existing resources and the OTL standards, determine the cost of bridging the gap, and raise funds and implement reforms to close the gap. Any federal support for common OTL standards should encourage state-level innovation and experimentation regarding how each state implements the standards, thus preserving the states as laboratories for education reform.

Others also have called for OTL standards and proposed possible content, including the Schott Foundation's National Opportunity to Learn Campaign and education law scholars Michael Rebell and Jessica Wolff.[62] In contrast to these proposals, I recommend that the federal government provide incentives for states to develop common OTL standards. As a result, these standards would not be federally defined, as the National Opportunity to Learn Campaign and Rebell and Wolff recommend, or designed individually by each state, as with Goals 2000 and IASA.

Although securing federal support to incentivize the states to adopt common OTL standards will likely involve a tough political battle, the battle would begin with greater ammunition and more favorable conditions than did the previous effort. When OTL standards were first considered in the mid-1990s, vigorous debates were ongoing about the content and implementation of academic standards and the appropriate federal role regarding those standards. Today, although some states have chosen not to adopt the Common Core standards, and some opposition has arisen regarding concerns such as the pace of implementation, all states have adopted academic standards, and the states are far closer to adopting common academic standards than ever before. These standards provide a foundation for the states to engage in a joint effort to identify what educational resources student need. State leadership also could draw on the lessons from school finance litigation that define the educational opportunities students must receive to meet state constitutional obligations for education, which was not available when OTL standards were first introduced through federal legislation.[63]

The Need for Additional Federal Research and Technical Assistance

Although the federal government currently provides research and technical assistance to states and school districts, I recommend that federal research and technical assistance should be refocused to help identify the most effective approaches for ensuring equal access to an excellent education and to expand state capacity to achieve this goal. Substantial variations exist in the educational, economic, and administrative capacities of states. One of the principal hindrances to NCLB's success is insufficient capacity at the state and local levels to implement the required changes. Therefore, federally supported research and technical assistance must help state and local governments develop the capacity to implement effective reforms.[64]

Congress has begun to recognize the need for federal support for high-quality education research to enable the United States to reach its essential educational goals, as evidenced by passage of the Education Sciences Reform Act of 2002 (ESRA). Rigorous, objective research that supports a national effort to ensure equal access to an excellent education should build on this success while also establishing an agenda that identifies the critical research states need to understand as they enact reforms to achieve this goal. Federal research should examine the essential characteristics of an excellent education and the most cost-effective and efficient state funding approaches, including models from other nations. A federal research agenda also should identify the primary state and local impediments to ensuring equal access to an excellent education and how to overcome them.[65] Establishing a federal research agenda such as this would capitalize on the federal government's substantial comparative advantage over states and localities in conducting and supporting research while eliminating the inefficiencies and costs of each state conducting its own research.[66]

In addition to research assistance, the federal government should build on its current technical assistance by offering states support for implementing reforms that ensure equal access to an excellent education. This technical assistance is essential for expanding the limited capacity of state education agencies that typically have focused on distributing and monitoring funds and that typically "possess little expertise in actually working on substantively important education initiatives."[67] States may need federal technical assistance on the most effective and efficient funding mechanisms and how to develop data collection systems that enable states and localities to document the scope of opportunity gaps and the effectiveness of efforts to reduce those gaps. Federal technical assistance should help to avoid any unnecessary diversion of resources and duplication of effort that would occur if each state had to develop such technical expertise on its own.[68]

Federal Financial Assistance to Close Opportunity and Achievement Gaps

Federal financial assistance will be essential for expanding the capacity of states to participate in a comprehensive national effort to ensure equal access to an excellent education. The federal financial contribution should include both incentives and assistance to address opportunity and achievement gaps. Financial incentives would draw attention to this critical issue and motivate states to implement reforms, just as incentives motivated reform through RTTT. Financial assistance also would expand the potential reform options beyond what states could implement with their own state resources and would supply political cover for politicians who support reform.[69]

The federal government should generously increase its contribution to education costs while continuing to share these costs with the state governments. Additional financial support for education would leverage the federal government's superior ability to redistribute resources among the states. Past experience reveals that federal resources can be an effective means for influencing state and local education policy. Generous federal financial assistance would fund a larger percentage of the costs of reforms than it did with past education reforms, which typically failed to deliver the substantial funds anticipated when the laws were enacted. The level of generosity of federal funding should be based on the disparate capacities of states to close opportunity and achievement gaps. Additionally, a blend of federal and state funding would encourage greater efficiency than full federal funding because it should encourage both governments to contain costs.[70]

Demanding Continuous Improvement Through a Federal Collaborative Enforcement Model

A federally led effort to ensure equal access to an excellent education should include federal monitoring of, and accountability for, state progress. In addition to fostering improvement, such oversight also would enable the federal government to identify states' needs for research, technical, and financial assistance.[71]

Federal monitoring should focus on a collaborative enforcement approach to resolve any disputes regarding how states achieve this goal. The theory I propose here should be implemented by including a collaborative enforcement model similar to the one I proposed in a 2007 article.[72] With such an approach, the federal government would establish a periodic, state reporting obligation that would describe progress on achieving the goal, identify any impediments to progress, and note plans for reform. Input also would be sought from education reform organizations, civil rights groups, and citizens so that the federal government would have a full picture of state efforts.

A panel or commission would then assess state reforms and provide recommendations, not mandates, for how states could improve their efforts. In addition, the collaborative enforcement approach would view penalties as an undesirable last resort and would embrace flexibility in negotiating compliance with federal funding conditions when warranted by unique state and local conditions. A collaborative enforcement model also would require the Department of Education to develop systems to ensure consistency in federal oversight so that the inconsistent enforcement that undermined NCLB's implementation and prior authorizations of the ESEA is not repeated.[73]

The Federal Government as the Final Guarantor of Equal Access to an Excellent Education

By enacting federal legislation, programs, and initiatives that embrace the elements discussed above, the federal government would reestablish itself as the final guarantor of equal access to an excellent education. Historically, ensuring equal educational opportunity was one of the principle rationales for federal involvement in education by assisting vulnerable groups when the states have failed to act in the national interest. Yet, an increasing focus on standards and accountability has shifted federal attention away from issues of educational equity, while federal reforms have unsuccessfully attempted to ensure a quality education for all schoolchildren.[74] Although the federal government consistently should aim to maintain excellence, it also needs to reassert itself as the final guarantor of equal educational opportunity. In making this recommendation, I join with other scholars, such as Michael Rebell and Goodwin Liu, whose proposals call on the federal government to guarantee some form of equal educational opportunity.[75]

History suggests that the federal government is likely to be the only level of government to engage in the leadership and substantial redistribution of resources that equal access to an excellent education will require. Local politics often hinders substantial efforts to redistribute resources. Thus, it is not surprising that it took federal legislation to initiate numerous past reform efforts that addressed disparities in educational opportunity, such as those that assist disadvantaged students, girls and women, and disabled children. The federal government possesses an unparalleled ability to mobilize national, state, and local reform when the nation is confronted with an educational crisis.[76] Therefore, my call for a stronger federal role in education builds on the historical federal role in advancing educational equity and the superior ability of the federal government to accomplish a redistribution of educational opportunity.

By focusing its attention on the policy-making areas identified above, the federal government would shoulder the primary burden for a national effort to ensure equal access to an excellent education and draw on its strengths in education policy making. Federal leadership would incentivize the states to engage in a collaborative partnership with the federal government to achieve this goal. At the same time, states, facing compelling incentives to join the national effort, would retain substantial control over education in choosing among a wide array of reforms.

Some may argue that the states should bear the primary burden for ensuring equal access to an excellent education because education remains primarily a state function. I reject this dualist understanding of education and highlight here the long history that reveals that the states will not rectify opportunity and achievement gaps on their own. Embracing federal leadership on these issues builds on the growing consensus reflected in NCLB and other federal education legislation: the federal government should exercise a substantial role in education law and policy.[77]

Others may contend that the federal government should rein in its growing role in education. In some ways, this criticism points to the failures of past initiatives as evidence that the federal government's role in education should be curtailed. Most recently, some scholars condemn the shortcomings and implementation of NCLB and RTTT. Undeniably, the federal government has undertaken a variety of unsuccessful education reforms.[78] Yet, an established track record in education over the last fifty years has given the United States ample evidence to identify the strengths and weaknesses of federal education policy making. My theory embraces a variety of federal policy-making strengths and builds on the federal government's superior and more consistent reform record on issues of educational equity in the face of inconsistent and overwhelmingly ineffective state reform.[79]

Today, although the federal government invests in education, this investment is quite limited relative to state and local investments. Increasing federal demands for its limited contribution have enabled the federal government to avoid shouldering a substantial portion of the costs and burdens associated with accomplishing the nation's education goals while still enjoying the ability to set the education agenda and demand results.[80] Having the federal government as the final guarantor of equal access to an excellent education would strengthen the relationship between growing federal influence in education and greater federal responsibility for accomplishing national objectives. This transformation would greatly improve on the nation's current cooperative federalism approach to education.

Finally, even though the U.S. Supreme Court, for the first time, has placed limitations on Spending Clause legislation in *National Federation of Independent Business v. Sebelius* (*NFIB*), that decision still leaves the executive branch and Congress ample constitutional room to restructure and expand their authority over education.[81] I agree with scholars Samuel Bagenstos and Eloise Pasachoff, who contend that for the Court to find a statute unconstitutional under the Spending Clause after *NFIB*, a federal education program would have to take an existing, large, well-entrenched program, add new and unforeseen conditions that are so substantial as to constitute an independent program, and present the possibility of losing all funds for both the old and new programs as conditions for any state not wanting to follow the new conditions.[82] The need to run afoul of multiple concerns simultaneously will leave Congress with ample room to enact far-reaching education legislation.

RECONSTRUCTING EDUCATION FEDERALISM WOULD EMPOWER STATE AND LOCAL CONTROL, ACCOUNTABILITY, AND INNOVATION

In this chapter, I offer ways to reduce harmful aspects of state and local control of education while simultaneously empowering beneficial and collaborative aspects. States admittedly would lose some control over education because they would be accountable to the federal government for ending long-standing disparities in educational opportunity. At the same time, other aspects of state and local control of education would remain. States would retain authority to control education policy making through education governance, the nature and content of a school finance system, state assessments

and graduation standards, and a wide variety of teaching and curricular decisions. Localities would continue to administer education, manage the daily
operation of schools, hire teachers and staff, build and maintain schools, and
transport students.[83] Maintaining these functions under state and local authority fosters continuance of most of the existing levels of state and local
control, accountability, and innovation for education.

Most importantly, placing primary responsibility on the federal government for leading a national effort to close the opportunity and achievement
gaps would foster new types of state and local control over education. Currently, substantial disparities exist in each state's capacity to offer high-quality
educational opportunities. With the federal government in the lead role, state
and local governments would both have a greater and more equal capacity
to offer all children an excellent education.[84] This enhanced capacity would
empower states and localities to engage in innovative reforms previously hindered by capacity limitations; they would decide how they want to achieve
equal access to an excellent education and thus continue to function as laboratories of reform—but with new federal research, technical expertise, and
financial assistance to support the identification and implementation of appropriate reforms.

Such reforms might diminish some state and local accountability for education. Federal accountability is more diffuse and less effective than state
and local accountability because federal officials are more removed from state
and local electorates and are held accountable for a wider range of decisions.[85]
However, it is important to note two responses to this concern. First, the
public has not effectively held state and local officials accountable for closing
the opportunity gap; therefore, adding an additional layer (even if diffuse)
of accountability could facilitate achievement of this objective. Second, state
and local officials would be charged with designing and implementing plans
to achieve this goal, and thus critical aspects of state and local accountability
would be preserved.[86] Federal leadership and support to accomplish this goal
ultimately would increase total government accountability.

CONCLUSION

Disrupting the nation's long-standing approach to education federalism
and reconstructing it in ways that support the nation's education goals will
be essential to successful education reform. My theory for reconstructing

education federalism envisions the federal, state, and local governments joining together in a shoulder-to-shoulder partnership to build an education system in which all schoolchildren receive equal access to an excellent education. In recommending the federal government as the final guarantor of equal educational opportunity, I offer innovative ways to incentivize and empower state and local governments to close opportunity and achievement gaps.

Though we continue to seek new ways to expand educational opportunity and improve educational quality, and support for federal involvement in education has been growing, the United States has lacked a theory for how the federal role should evolve.[87] And while the nation currently lacks sufficient political will to adopt all aspects of my theory, the pioneering ideas I present here seek to contribute to the growing momentum for reform by moving our national dialogue away from educational paralysis and toward educational excellence.

ELEVEN

Leveraging Federal Funding for Equity and Integration

DEREK W. BLACK

FOR MANY, THE HOPE of a significant federal role in ensuring educational equity, particularly with regard to funding, came and went with the Supreme Court's decision in *San Antonio Independent School District v. Rodriguez*.[1] Today, many believe the federal government is irrelevant to school-funding equity. This view makes a certain amount of sense given the extensive school finance victories that have occurred under state law since *Rodriguez*. To the extent that funding gaps have narrowed over the past four decades, it is a result of changes at the state, not the federal, level. These state changes, however, have been insufficient to entirely close the gap. Equally troubling is the fact that some states are so poor that closing the funding gap would not mean a high-quality education for all students but an equally mediocre education for most. If our public schools are to provide equal and high-quality opportunities for all, the federal government must reassert itself in the process. Fortunately, it already has the tool at its fingertips—the Elementary and Secondary Education Act (ESEA)—and a roadmap for using it—its 1960s and 1970s policies.

Title I of ESEA, the federal government's antipoverty program, is the sleeping giant of education equity and integration. Through Title I, the federal government distributes around $15 billion a year to public schools. This is not an enormous sum, but it has been enough to buy huge influence in the states over the past several decades. Most recently, Congress reauthorized Title I through the No Child Left Behind Act of 2001 (NCLB) and was able to impose a host of changes. All fifty states were forced to adopt curriculum standards, to test students yearly to assess whether they were meeting those standards, and to impose severe sanctions on those schools that failed to make Adequate Yearly Progress toward those standards. States also signed on to the requirement that all teachers be "highly qualified." While NCLB is riddled with numerous serious flaws, no one can question that it produced enormous change—good or bad—in the way that education is delivered across the United States.

The time is now for Congress to use its leverage under the ESEA to achieve equity and integration. The Education Trust's 2006 report revealed that the national funding gap between high-poverty districts and low-poverty districts was nearly $1,000 per pupil.[2] In some states the gap was twice that amount. In a typical elementary school of four hundred students, this amounts to a funding gap of $400,000 to $800,000 a year—enough to drastically increase teacher salaries, lower classroom sizes, and offer a panoply of support services to needy students. A 2010 report by the Education Law Center found that only seven states distributed funds fairly.[3] Our schools are faring even worse in terms of segregation. Numerous reports by the Civil Rights Project have shown a steady trend of resegregation since the 1980s. Now, the segregation levels in our schools are as high as they were in the late 1960s and early 1970s, when mandatory desegregation began in earnest. Congress watches this segregation and inequality from the sidelines, suggesting that there is no problem to address or that Congress is powerless to fix it. Neither is true.

As much as policy makers may ignore it, the problems of segregation and inequality are the key obstacles to ensuring quality educational opportunities for poor and minority students. Students in predominantly poor and minority schools tend to receive a generally low-quality curriculum, have limited access to highly qualified teachers, and find that the good teachers their schools manage to hire quickly depart for other schools once they get some experience.[4] At the root of this problem is the fact the racial and socioeconomic characteristics of schools significantly influence where teachers decide to teach.[5] But regardless of which teachers schools hire, concentrated poverty would still negatively affect student achievement. Research shows that a student in a predominantly poor and minority school, even if the student is from a middle-income family himself, will routinely achieve much lower than students in predominantly middle-income schools.[6] These basic facts tend to make educational success an exception to the rule in our high-poverty, racially isolated schools.

When Congress has been willing to acknowledge and tackle these problems, it has proven capable of achieving important measures of success. During the 1960s and 1970s, the ESEA's Title I funds were crucial in creating the carrot that enticed many school districts to voluntarily desegregate. At the same time, those funds offered much-needed assistance to a narrow subset of the neediest schools. Since then, however, Congress has allowed Title I to get sidetracked into a state entitlement program that makes attempts at general education reform. Most notably, NCLB does almost nothing to ensure equity or integration. Rather, it assumes that by simply setting high achievement standards for all schools, disadvantaged schools can overcome the structural segregation and inequality they have faced for decades. When segregated and unequal schools fail to overcome these barriers and achieve at the same level as all other schools, NCLB effectively punishes poor and segregated schools for being poor and segregated. Characterizing this as willful ignorance is generous; characterizing it as cruel and unusual punishment is probably more accurate.

Offering these students and schools a meaningful chance at success requires realigning Title I with its original mission, which includes, at a minimum, making three major changes to ESEA. First, Title I funds should be focused on the neediest schools and create incentives for states to do the same through their funding formulas. Second, Congress must once again set rigorous standards demanding that all states devote equal resources to the neediest schools. Third, Title I should explicitly incentivize school policies that promote integration while penalizing policies that increase segregation.

TITLE I'S LOST MISSION AND FUNDAMENTAL FLAWS

The History and Purpose of Title I

Gradual changes during the last three decades have come to undermine Title I's core mission. Its original intent was to assist poor children, remedy inequity, and incentivize integration. Those goals, although still implicit in the ESEA, are now far from clear. Today, the act's focus is more on general educational reform and accountability for all schools than on equity and integration for needy schools. In addition, Title I funds are no longer targeted or conditional in any meaningful sense. Instead, its funds now resemble state and local entitlements that the federal government is scared to take away or condition on fundamental change. Although improving education generally is a laudable goal, that goal cannot come at the expense of, or be indifferent to, equal opportunity for the neediest schools and students.

Congress enacted the ESEA in 1965, during the height of the civil rights movement and the war on poverty. Extra money through Title I was intended to provide supplemental funding to meet the special needs of poor students and presumably close the achievement gap. These funds were directed to schools serving poor children living in areas of concentrated poverty. Congress recognized that these students needed far more resources than they were receiving and that by extending funds to public schools it could demand compliance with antidiscrimination principles. Most notably, by accepting federal funds, schools became subject to Title VI of the Civil Rights Act of 1964, which prohibits discrimination in federally funded programs and directs federal agencies to implement regulations to enforce Title VI.

The Supreme Court's decision in *Brown* initially accomplished very little desegregation. A decade later, desegregation had not even begun in most school districts. But by extending federal dollars to school districts through the ESEA and attaching conditions to those funds, the federal government could systematically desegregate schools instead of relying on the piecemeal, halting approach of litigation. This notion proved immediately effective. Once financial consequences were attached to desegregation, the number of schools implementing *Brown*'s mandate increased exponentially.

The threat of losing federal money played an enormous role in this integration shift, but whether districts spent this money responsibly was far less clear. Rather than using the money to provide extra resources for low-income students, some states and districts appeared to be using federal dollars to replace state dollars. As a result, the resources available for many low-income students remained relatively flat. In response, Congress imposed additional conditions and restrictions on the receipt of ESEA funds. In particular, it conditioned the receipt of Title I funds on the concepts of comparability and supplemental funding.[7]

The comparability standard required that the state and local funds available at Title I schools be equal or comparable to the state and local funds at non–Title I schools in the district. In effect, school districts could not use

Title I funds to make up the difference or hide the inequality that the states and districts themselves had created. The supplemental funding standard indicated that school districts could only use federal dollars to supplement the state and local funds that they were already spending. They could not use federal dollars to supplant existing state or local funds. In short, raising poor schools to a level of comparability with other schools was not enough; states and districts had to use Title I funds to increase the opportunities and resources in poor schools above that of other schools.

Unfortunately, the ESEA's equality and integration goals have been diluted in some instances and, in others, outright undermined. Starting in the late 1970s and early 1980s, Congress and the executive branch altered the standards that had previously ensured equity among schools. Most important, they consistently diluted Title I's comparability requirements. Title I regulations originally required that the funding available at Title I schools be within 5 percent of the available funding at other schools, which over time was expanded to a 10 percent variance.[8] During the Reagan administration, quantifiable measures of comparability were eliminated altogether and replaced with the ambiguous standard of "substantial comparability," which also included significant exemptions.[9]

The ESEA's shift in regard to segregation is less obvious because the act never included any specific integration mandate. ESEA funds merely created the carrot by which to entice states and districts into compliance with anti-discrimination statutes. Congress still requires schools to comply with these statutes, but both Congress and the Department of Education increasingly expect less and less of districts in terms of racial equality and integration. Today, the lever that Congress and the executive once used to force integration has nearly gone out of use. For instance, the Department of Education maintains disparate impact regulations, but routinely absent from the Office for Civil Rights' recent reports to Congress is any mention of enforcing those regulations. In some respects, the tacit acceptance of segregation is a response to unfavorable Supreme Court cases during the late 1980s and 1990s that limited the desegregation obligations of school districts, but the problem is equally attributable to the federal legislative and executive branches, whose interest drifted elsewhere. The executive has the power to more aggressively enforce desegregation through Title VI but chooses not to. Likewise, instead of using ESEA Title I funds to desegregate schools or ensure racial equity, Congress now uses those funds to further general educational reform efforts. General efforts certainly have wider political appeal, but they divert much-needed attention and funding away from Title I's core mission. In short, Title I of the ESEA has morphed from an engine to meet the needs of poor and minority children into one that pushes the general education policy reforms of any given congressional cycle. This shift in educational mission becomes even more obvious considering how the distribution of Title I funds has changed over time.

The Deconcentration and Limited Impact of Title I Funds

The current way in which Congress disburses Title I funds undermines ESEA's ability, regardless of intent, to meet student need. By distributing Title I funds to a relatively small number of schools, the impact of Title I funding was maximized in its initial years. This focus and impact, however, are gone today because so many schools receive funding. In fact, over 90 percent of school districts receive Title I funds today.[10] Such a high number of districts receive funds because any locality with the existence of a mere 2 percent poverty qualifies.[11] As a result, Title I funds are dispersed across a wide cross-section of schools. If all of these schools were predominantly poor, spreading funding to so many might be defensible. But they are not. In effect, Congress is helping to ensure a national constituency for its general education policy rather than addressing concentrated poverty and segregation.

For needy schools, the practical effect of diluting Title I funds is to decrease its per-pupil grants. To be clear, Title I funding is substantial in many high-poverty districts and is crucial to their ability to operate, but larger grants could better give these districts the ability to make a serious impact on the education of the neediest students. The consensus among educational experts is that poor students need 40 percent more resources than other students to receive equal educational opportunities.[12] Congress, of course, has no obligation to meet this need, but if that were its goal, spreading funds across so many schools would cause it to fall far short. For instance, in 2006, in states like Arkansas, South Carolina, and Nevada, the Title I supplement amounted to a mere 17, 16, and 14 percent increase in funding, respectively.[13] These averages, however, do not tell the full story of individual schools and districts. Goodwin Liu's research has shown that the problem may be even worse at the school level in many localities. As a result of various irrational weights built into the ESEA funding formulas, the poorest schools, on average, must stretch their Title I dollars further than wealthier schools. The average Title I aid per student in low-poverty schools is $773, while that number is only $475 in high-poverty schools.[14] In short, Congress's dilution of Title I funds across so many districts reduces their impact as a general matter. Congress then compounds the problem through funding formulas that fail to drive disproportionately higher funds to the places that need them the most.

The Inequitable and Irrational Distribution of Title I Funds

The practical results of Title I's funding practices are so poor that one might wonder how they could even be possible. The answer is not that Congress necessarily intends to disadvantage poor children, or that Title I has mechanisms that create facial inequalities for poor districts. Rather, the problem lies in the practical difficultly of devising a funding formula that accounts for relevant factors and cancels out irrelevant ones. Some aspects of the current Title I formulas are well-intentioned efforts to address relevant factors, but most often they are based on assumptions that do not match reality. This disconnect is a major reason why the ESEA is ineffective in directing funds to states and schools that serve the neediest students.

The problem begins with the fact that Congress distributes Title I funds through no less than four different funding formulas and grants. Previously, Title I distributed funds through two formulas. Rather than revise those formulas, Congress simply added two more during the 1994 reauthorization of the ESEA. The result is a set of funding formulas with different assumptions and goals, which often work against one another. The only obvious coordination among the formulas appears to be those aspects that expand inequality rather than eliminate it. In at least four distinct ways, the Title I funding formulas ignore or expand inequality.

Ignoring the Negative Effects of High Concentrations of Poverty.   Title I's funding formulas do not fully account for the negative effects of concentrated poverty. The bottom end of eligibility for Title I funding is so low—2 percent poverty—that nearly all districts are eligible, which drives funds away from high-poverty districts to wealthy districts. Equally troubling is the cap that the two newest formulas place on the weight they afford to concentrated poverty. Beginning with James Coleman's seminal 1966 study for the U.S. Department of Health, Education, and Welfare, data have consistently shown that as the concentration of poverty increases, the negative educational effects of poverty on student achievement are compounded.[15] In other words, a student's chance of educational success, regardless of her own race and socioeconomic status, will decline as the percentage of low-income students in her school increases.

Two of Title I's funding formulas generally recognize this principle but still draw inexplicable distinctions between schools. The formulas increase the per-pupil Title I grant as the percentage of poor students in a district rises, but the increase flattens once the poverty level reaches approximately 30 percent in a district.[16] In other words, the formulas distinguish between a school with 20 percent poverty and a school with 30 percent poverty, but they treat all poverty above the 30 percent poverty level as equivalent. This cap makes little sense; the effects of poverty do not flatten at 30 percent. In fact, low levels of poverty concentration do not necessarily have a negative effect on a school as a whole. Rather, the negative effects of concentrated poverty become manifest as the poverty level in a school approaches or passes 50 percent.[17] At that point, the effects become deleterious for both poor and middle-class students in the school. In short, the only two Title I formulas that even take poverty concentration into account focus on the wrong tipping points. By doing so, they drive funds toward schools on the low end of the poverty concentration scale—which may not even warrant significant funding—when those funds are desperately needed by high-poverty districts that struggle with the serious negative effects of concentrated poverty.

Basing Grants on States' Per-Pupil Expenditures Rather Than Need.   All four funding formulas rely on the same base multiplier: each state's per-pupil expenditure. The more a state spends, the higher its Title I grant will be; the less it spends, the smaller its Title I grant. Two facially reasonable premises underlie Congress's reliance on state per-pupil expenditures, but both prove false in practice. Most likely, Congress's intent was to identify some factor that would account for varying geographic costs. One might reasonably assume that local expenditures would reflect those local costs. A few states do reflect that assumption, but, overall, state per-pupil expenditures do not closely correlate with geographic costs.[18] As a result, in terms of actual costs, some states are overcompensated while others are undercompensated. For this very reason, the General Accounting Office (GAO) recommended that Congress eliminate state expenditures as a factor in Title I funding formulas.[19]

Alternatively, Congress may have intended to incentivize states with low per-pupil expenditures to increase their expenditures. In practice, however, basing Title I grants on state expenditures creates almost no incentive because federal funds are such a small part of states' education budgets. Moreover, states with low per-pupil expenditures are often those with the least capacity to increase funding.[20] As a group, states with low per-pupil expenditures already tend to tax themselves at higher levels than the states with high per-pupil expenditures. Thus, even if Title I grants were large enough to incentivize additional educational spending, rich states would be the only ones capable of taking advantage. In other words, basing Title I grants on state per-pupil expenditures penalizes poor states for being poor and aggravates inequality between states. Rather than rewarding effort, it rewards wealth.

Title I's formulas may, as a practical matter, also inadvertently reward inequality in several states. Those states spending the most money on education often spend it unfairly. Figure 11.1 plots each state based on its statewide average per-pupil expenditures versus its per-pupil expenditures in high-need districts. Here I term proportionally higher spending in high-poverty districts as "progressive funding," or "progressivity." Figure 11.1 reveals a small correlation between high average state expenditures and progressivity, but

FIGURE 11.1   Progressivity vs. education spending

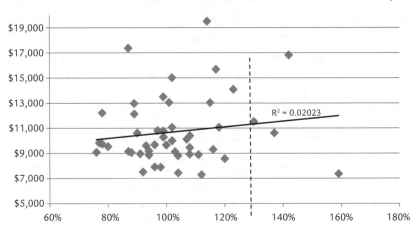

Progressivity (spending in high-poverty districts as a percentage of spending in low-poverty districts)

Source: Baker, Sciarra, and Farrie, *Is School Funding Fair?*

it also reveals tremendous outliers. Of the six highest spending states, only one meaningfully addresses student need (based on a generous standard of whether high-need districts receive 30 percent additional funding in comparison to other districts). Conversely, of the four states that progressively fund high-need districts with 30 percent additional funding, only two are high-spending or wealthy states. The other two progressive states include one that is right at the national per-pupil funding average and one that ranks among the very bottom in the nation in average per-pupil expenditures. In fact, that low-spending state has the most progressive funding formula in the country. Thus, the heavy weighting of average state per-pupil expenditures can do a serious disservice to those states trying their best to achieve equitable results for students in concentrated poverty and also fails to hold the rest of the states accountable.

To be fair, one Title I formula does purport to reward progressivity, but the formula's definition of progressivity is so permissive that it is functionally pointless. To qualify for funding under the formula, a state need only show that, after discarding the school districts with the top and bottom 5 percent per-pupil expenditures, the remaining schools' per-pupil expenditures are within 25 percent of one another.[21] The exemption allows limitless inequities at the top and the bottom, and the 25 percent variance allowance for the remaining districts permits gross disparities in its own right. Even the most regressive states can qualify under a 25 percent variance standard. Moreover, the weighting for progressivity is so weak in comparison to other weightings in the other formulas that it offers no incentive for a state to progressively fund its schools. In fact, as the trend line on figure 11.2 reveals, the size of Title I grants remains flat as state funding formulas become more regressive.

Awarding Grants Based on School District Size.   The third major flaw in Title I is that one of the funding formulas heavily weights school district size. In fact, that formula places more weight on district size than the other two formulas place on poverty concentration.[22] Under the district-size weighting, Title I grants per pupil significantly increase as the size of the school district increases. While such a formula would make sense if district size corresponded with population density and locale costs, district size actually has little relation to either of these things. Nor does the size of a school district have any correlation with the percentage of poor students a district serves. In fact, more than half of the nation's poor children attend school districts

FIGURE 11.2   Progressivity vs. federal support (as percentage of education expenditures)

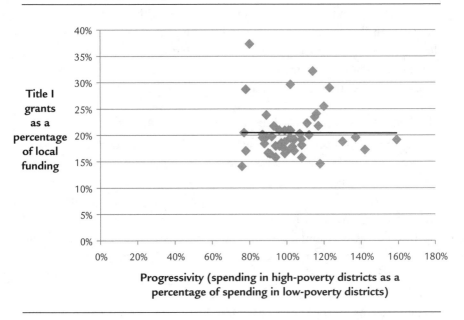

Title I
grants
as a
percentage
of local
funding

**Progressivity (spending in high-poverty districts as a
percentage of spending in low-poverty districts)**

Source: Baker, Sciarra, and Farrie, *Is School Funding Fair?*; Education Trust, *Funding Gaps 2006*.

with fewer than fifty thousand students.[23] Nevertheless, under the formula, a medium-sized school district with over 90 percent poverty would be disadvantaged in relation to a larger school district with a lower percentage of poverty. In short, favoring large school districts does not target additional funds to poor students. It creates arbitrary inequalities and takes funds away from districts that need them and gives them to those that may not.

Awarding Statutory Minimum Grants Regardless of Need.   Finally, all of Title I's funding formulas include a statutory minimum that provides a base level of funding to all states regardless of need, poverty level, or other factors, such as geographic cost.[24] This ensures that every state gets a substantial piece of the pie, but it is not clear why every state would need a substantial piece. The more likely explanation is that these statutory minimums create the incentive for senators from small states to support the ESEA. Even if one gave some credit to that motivation, the statutory minimums are too generous. They are substantial enough that they provide relatively large Title I grants to districts in small states, even though they tend to have smaller percentages of poor students.[25] For instance, South Dakota and Rhode Island receive Title I grants that exceed the per-pupil amount that two-thirds of the other states receive, even though most of those states have higher percentages of poor students.[26] In short, the small state minimums provide funds to some states that bear no relation to the number of poor students they serve and, thus, drive funds to small states that more appropriately belong elsewhere.

The Federal Disregard for Inequitable State Practices

While Congress exacerbates inequality and fails to meet student need, states are not innocent. School finance victories in more than half of the states demonstrate many states' complacent and willful violations of students' rights to equal and adequate educational opportunities. States that have escaped liability are often no better; their courts simply have been unwilling to hold them accountable. The point here is not to detail these state failures but to point out how Congress is complicit in these violations. As David Sciarra recently characterized the relationship, Congress is the "great enabler."[27] He and various others point out, during its bailout of state education systems during the recession of 2008, that Congress gave state education systems billions of dollars but then, in the face of blatant violations, did not enforce the equity rules put in place for those funds.[28] This one-time failure, however, comes as no surprise considering that the previous three decades of ESEA enforcement were marked by a virtual absence of any equity standards to even enforce.

Current Title I standards are so flexible that they do not prevent states and school districts from reducing their own education funds and replacing them with federal funds. The problem arises both from changes to the standards themselves and underenforcement of those standards. First, Title I includes a maintenance of effort standard that is designed to prevent states and districts from drawing down their local expenditures on education.[29] But the numerical benchmark in the current maintenance of effort standard no longer provides any real check on school budgets. The current maintenance of effort standard only requires that school districts maintain their funding at 90 percent of the previous year. Because the federal government provides less than 10 percent of educational funds, it would not be very hard for a district to subvert the standard's purpose, particularly if a district drew down its funds and replaced them with federal funds over a two- or three-year period.

The prohibition on supplanting funds is designed to prevent this, but the U.S. Department of Education has stopped enforcing the requirement. In the department's defense, the prohibition on supplanting funds requires speculation regarding future budgets and is labor intensive to monitor. Finding that those tasked with enforcing the standard are understandably confused by it, a 2003 GAO report recommended eliminating the supplement-not-supplant standard altogether, concluding that the more effective solution to state manipulation of federal funding would be to tighten the maintenance of effort standard.[30] In the meantime, evidence suggests that some states and districts have taken advantage of the lax maintenance of effort standard and the department's underenforcement of the supplanting prohibition. A study of Texas and Colorado schools, for instance, found that "federal and other categorical funds, which were intended to provide additional opportunities, are used to fill in for inequitable distribution of foundational funds."[31] In other words, states and school districts were funding schools unequally and using federal funds to hide it.

The practical ineffectiveness of the supplement-not-supplant and maintenance of effort standards could largely be overcome if Title I included strict equity requirements. Like other standards, however, Title I's comparability standards are currently meaningless. Its regulations initially required that per-pupil funding at Title I schools be within 5 percent of non–Title I schools in the same district. Title I's statutory language now explicitly rejects this requirement, stating that "nothing in this subchapter shall be construed to mandate equalized spending per pupil for a state, local education agency, or school."[32] Title I, at best, expresses a symbolic commitment to equity with its general indication that "services . . . taken as a whole" at Title I schools must be "comparable" to those at non–Title I schools.[33] But the absence of any numerical benchmark for comparability leaves too much to interpretation and renders enforcement practically impossible.

Even if these standards were subject to strict construction and enforcement, they are robbed of any potential vitality by Title I's major exemptions and limitations. First, the comparability standards do not apply at all between school districts; rather, the current standards apply only within school districts. Yet, the largest inequities exist between districts, not within them. By limiting the comparability standards to within districts, our national funding gap for high-poverty districts of nearly $1,000 per pupil and gaps in excess of $2,000 per pupil in the worst offending states evades all scrutiny.

Second, within districts, the largest portions of school budgets are exempt from even meeting the weak requirement of substantial comparability. Title I exempts teacher salaries from comparability analysis, even though teacher salaries regularly account for 80 to 90 percent of school budgets.[34] To be deemed comparable in regard to teacher salaries, a school district need only maintain a single salary schedule that applies to all schools in the district.[35] Yet, real inequities arise not from variations in salary schedules but from the unequal distribution of teachers among schools. Under Title I's comparability standard, all of the twenty-year teachers with advanced degrees in a district could be placed at a single school and all the first-year teachers at another without violating comparability. Assume that a district had two elementary schools with twenty-five teachers at each school, that the salary gap between the experienced teachers and the new teachers was $30,000, and that half of the district's teachers were highly experienced. If the district assigned seventeen of its of twenty-five experienced teachers to one school, the district would have created a $270,000 funding gap between the schools, and Title I would call it "comparable" because the teachers at both schools were compensated on the same salary schedule. While this scenario may seem far-fetched, data indicates that it is a prevailing reality.[36]

Although not as significant in terms of money, central administration expenditures—such as gifted and talented, tutoring, and prekindergarten programs—also evade scrutiny because school districts generally fund these programs out of their central budgets rather than through individual school budgets.[37] Consequently, school districts are free to distribute these funds and programs among their schools any way they see fit. The result is two-fold. First, high-end programs for the "top" students are disproportionately available at middle-income schools. Students in high-poverty schools may still have the opportunity to participate in those programs, but their participation may require more personal initiative and come with higher transportation and time commitment burdens. Second, when middle-income schools see the success of supplemental Title I programs at other schools, they can petition their central administration to fund similar programs at their schools. This is not to suggest that middle-income schools should be deprived of these programs but that a district should be prohibited from pushing the cost of special programs for high-poverty schools onto the federal government while, at the same time, using local funds to supply those same programs at other schools. The result is that rather than receiving extra resources, high-poverty schools need federal money just to break even with other schools. In summary, Title I entirely ignores the most significant resource inequities, which occur between school districts, and sanctions the inequities that occur within districts by exempting the most important expenditures and permitting wide variances for the others.

REENVISIONING TITLE I AS AN ENGINE OF EQUALITY AND INTEGRATION

Correcting Title I's flaws is not without its challenges. Political opposition would surely arise on several fronts. Some would object to federal intervention in state school finance and education policy as a general matter. Others would object because they have vested interests in maintaining the status quo. Still others would object because they claim to doubt the efficacy of more money and integration. None of these, however, are legitimate reasons for maintaining segregated and unequal schools. In the end, these objections would largely amount to grandstanding and partisan politics—although both have been known to achieve dubious victories. The public, however, also instinctively understands basic equality. Title I is currently so far from equitable that the public need not understand the nuances of its formulas to understand that they need to be changed.

If that hurdle can be crossed, the solutions are relatively simple. First, the current formulas need to be eliminated. Second, new formulas should distribute funds based on three simple principles: concentrated poverty, rewarding progressive state funding policies, and rewarding fiscal effort. Third, Title I should require any state or district that receives a Title I grant to fund its high-poverty schools and districts equal to others. Finally, states and localities that take segregative actions should forfeit any Title I funding increases, and those that take integrative actions should be rewarded.

Phase Out Current Funding Formulas

The first step in leveraging federal funding for equity and integration is to eliminate the counterproductive aspects of current funding formulas. But, because so many states and school districts have operated in ways that expand inequity, immediately reversing these structures in their entirety would exact significant costs on some districts. States and school districts would be expected to redirect funds and may face the prospect of losing funding.

To eliminate any undue hardship suffered by states, districts, and schools—which would ultimately be visited on children—Congress should gradually transition to new funding patterns. A gradual transition would mean flattening expenditures in the existing formulas immediately and drawing them down over time. As those funds draw down, the excess funds would be moved to new formulas.

Heavily Weight Concentrated Poverty, Progressive State Funding Distributions, and Fiscal Effort in Funding Formulas

The new formulas should not include any measure that distributes funds based on state expenditures, nor should they attempt to approximate costs through some other measure—because no good measure exists. In the absence of a metric that accurately reflects locality costs and student need, the most effective approach would be to focus on incentivizing particular state policies and targeting funds to particular categories of districts and states. In particular, Title I funds can meet student need directly as well as incentivize states to meet student need with their own funds. ESEA could meet student need itself by narrowing the number of districts that receive funding and by using the available funds to focus on the neediest districts. A funding formula could do this by heavily weighting concentrated poverty. As opposed to the current weights (where the graduated weights increase funding as concentrated poverty rises from 0 percent to 30 percent), only districts in excess of 30 percent poverty should receive substantial Title I funds. And among those districts, the funding per pupil should steadily increase as poverty approaches 90 percent.

In combination with the federal government meeting student need, Title I should incentivize states to meet student need by heavily weighting progressivity and fiscal effort. Heavily weighting progressivity would have two effects. First, it would reward those states that devote a higher amount of state funds to high-need districts, as well as offset some of a state's cost of progressive funding. Second, it would indirectly penalize states with regressive funding practices. A state would effectively forgo or lose money, and have a smaller overall education budget, if its funding practices were regressive. If the lion's share of Title I funds were subject to this weighting, this measure alone would work substantial change in the way states fund schools.

The only potential drawback of heavily weighting progressivity might be the creation of some inequity between poorer and wealthy states. As a general matter, wealthier states would find it easier to ensure both progressivity and adequacy across all districts, whereas some poorer states might only achieve progressivity at the expense of overall adequacy. Implicit in this concern is the recognition that wealthy states do not necessarily need significant Title I funds; they need fiscal incentives. To offset the possibility of interstate inequity and to drive resources toward poor states that are trying hard to do the right thing, Title I should reward fiscal effort. The result would be that poorer states would be eligible to receive higher per-pupil grants than rich states, but both groups would be rewarded for progressivity.

Enforce Strict Equity Standards Within and Between Districts

These funding incentives are not a substitute for affirmatively demanding equity. Some states and districts may not respond to fiscal incentives. Title I and the Department of Education must return to their core mission and once again monitor and enforce strict equity provisions. Congress can ensure this by including explicit numerical measures of comparability, as opposed to the current inherently subjective and unquantifiable standards. At the very least, Congress should condition Title I funds on both inter- and intradistrict equality for high-poverty schools and districts. In other words, the availability of state and local funds in high-poverty school districts should be at least equal to those available in other districts. Likewise, the availability of state and local funds in Title I schools should be equal to or greater than those in non–Title I schools within the same district.

To make these standards meaningful, the equity provisions must apply to the entire education budget, not just portions of it. The exemptions for teacher salaries and supplemental programs funded through central administration budgets must be eliminated. To be clear, these equity standards would amount to a drastic step forward in several states and districts, but these measures are relatively mild. Fully equal and adequate educational opportunities in high-poverty districts require progressive funding. Strict equity standards would only prohibit regressive funding practices.

These equity standards must also include a private right of action. Title VI of the Civil Rights Act of 1964, Title IX of the Education Amendments of 1972, the Individuals with Disabilities Education Act, the Equal Educational Opportunities Act, and the McKinney-Vento Homeless Assistance Act all include a private right of action. Title I of the ESEA should be no exception to the general rule. While regulations and agency enforcement with all these statutes have been key to global-level compliance, a private cause of action is an individual child's, or group of children's, only guarantee that education rights will be honored. The specter of litigation has always been instrumental in prompting reluctant—and even recalcitrant—school districts to voluntarily comply with the law. Without a private cause of action, aggressive new Title I provisions would run the risk of becoming merely aspirations rather than effective drivers of educational equity.

The best policing of standards sometimes comes at the local level, not from the distant oversight of a federal agency. A private right of action empowers communities to serve this policing function. Moreover, even when the U.S. Department of Education finds a violation, it can be hesitant to use its blunt tool of fund termination as a solution, because doing so will harm innocent students. In most instances, the threat of administrative action alone is sufficient to secure compliance. But some districts and states do not always take the department's threats seriously. One need look no further than the waivers and flexibility in 2012 and 2013 for all but five states that failed to meet NCLB's achievement mandates.[38] The most obvious solution to this problem is a private cause of action to enforce Title I's equity requirements in court.

Incentivize Integration and Penalize Segregation

Money alone will not ensure a high-quality education for the neediest students in the neediest districts. To be sure, money can make matters better, but it will not address the fundamental underlying problems of racial and economic segregation that motivate middle-income families and high-quality teachers to avoid or flee the neediest schools. In addition, if Title I's funding formula heavily weighted concentrated poverty, it could incentivize states and districts to maintain, if not increase, their poverty concentrations. Guarding against this possibility and encouraging integration requires that the ESEA monitor changes in poverty concentration from year to year and respond to them. Of course, some increases in poverty concentration are attributable to forces unconnected to school policy, such as demographic shifts, private industry decisions, and downturns in the economy. Increases in poverty concentration due to these forces would not affect states' and districts' Title I eligibility. But districts and states that make changes to their student assignment policies, district boundaries, or other relevant policies that increase poverty concentration would forfeit the additional Title I funding to which they would otherwise be entitled.

This forfeiture of additional funds would not be enormous, but it would send a strong message to districts regarding federal goals and expectations. Likewise, the psychological effect of losing money cannot be understated in its capacity to encourage good behavior. Recently, when Wake County, North Carolina, was first debating whether to abandon its integration plan and revert to neighborhood schools, the possibility of losing federal funds was an important point of consideration. But once the district found that no threat existed, it moved forward with its neighborhood schools plan. North Carolina state law, however, did contain another measure that conditioned the receipt of high-need district funds on districts refraining from acts that might increase segregation.[39] New Hanover County School District apparently did not realize this until after it had implemented a school assignment policy that increased segregation. When a school board member was later required to sign an affidavit of compliance with the segregation standard, she realized the problem and refused to sign the affidavit.[40] As a result of the segregative action, the school district stood to lose $750,000 in state funds. Presumably, the district's decision-making process would have been far more cautious had it recognized the consequences in advance, particularly given the other serious budget shortfalls it was experiencing. In short, penalties matter, and in some instances they may have an effect greater than or equal to incentives.

In penalizing segregative acts, Title I must be careful to also incentivize integration and reverse, not just stop, the resegregation trend of the past two and a half decades. First, Title I must include a hold-harmless provision whereby any district that takes integrative action would retain its prior ESEA funding level for a period of years. Otherwise, a district or state would stand to lose Title I funds if it heavily weights concentrated poverty because integration necessarily means deconcentrating segregation in some schools and districts. The ability to retain prior funding levels, however, is a relatively mild incentive. A real incentive would only come from a state's or school district's recognition that integrated schools are economically efficient and result in overall cost savings, which many districts may not fully appreciate. Thus, in addition to retaining their prior Title I funding levels for a period of years, the ESEA should offer one-time integration grants to these districts or states. In the long term, Congress could expect to recoup these upfront costs, as the integrating districts' Title I grants would revert to normal levels after a period of years and the districts would not be eligible for increases due to their own resegregative actions.

Title I, however, must go one step further and incentivize those schools and districts that receive students from high-poverty districts or schools. At the very least, the receiving school or district should be entitled to funding based not on its own lower level of concentrated poverty but on the higher level of concentrated poverty whence the student came. For example, a district with a high percentage of poor students might be receiving $3,000 per pupil in Title I aid, whereas a neighboring affluent district might be receiving less than $1,000 per pupil. If the affluent district agreed to take five hundred low-income students from the other district, the per-pupil Title I funding for those students would drop from $3,000 to $1,000 (or slightly more than $1,000 if the added students sufficiently drove up the affluent district's poverty concentration). Likewise, if Title I monitored and accounted for segregation changes within districts—which I advocate—the same problems would arise in regard to districts that reassigned low-income students to new schools within a district. But if, for instance, an affluent district received $3,000 per pupil in Title I aid for the low-income students it enrolled from another district, rather than the lower amount it would otherwise receive, its incentive to integrate would significantly increase.

CONCLUSION

Title I once provided the hope of a nation to make good on the promise of integration and education as the means of economic mobility for the disadvantaged. It pumped new funds into the poorest areas of the country and acknowledged that poor children need more resources than the average student if they are to succeed on a consistent basis. These efforts radically changed the opportunities poor students received and also played a huge role in fostering racial equity. Today, a casual observer would struggle to recognize this rich history in the text and effect of Title I. At best, he would recognize a general education reform tool preoccupied with standardizing education and expanding its constituency.

When Congress next reauthorizes Title I of the ESEA, it should recognize the act for what it is: the sleeping giant of educational equity and integration. Achieving those ends will be no small political feat. Without strong leadership from Congress and the executive branch, the act will continue on its misguided trajectory. But with leadership, straightforward solutions are available. The old formulas can be replaced with a simpler and more cohesive formula that distributes funding based on concentrated poverty, progressive state funding practices, and fiscal effort. Where this formula is insufficient to incentivize states to meet the additional needs of high-poverty schools, Title I would at least prohibit inequitable and regressive funding practices.

Finally, we cannot just throw money at education when the underlying problem is segregation. Title I must also incentivize integration and penalize segregation. Nearly fifty years ago, social science indicated that this was a key factor in the achievement gap. Nothing since has ever suggested otherwise. While many challenges to student learning involve experiences outside school and may be somewhat beyond schools' reach, whether students attend racially and socioeconomically isolated schools remains well within Congress's, states', and local districts' power.

TWELVE

Remedying Separate and Unequal

Is It Possible to Create Equal Educational Opportunity?

ERWIN CHEMERINSKY

ON MAY 17, 2014, the nation celebrated the sixtieth anniversary of the Supreme Court's landmark decision in *Brown v. Board of Education*.[1] The simple and tragic reality is that American public education is separate and unequal.[2] Schools today are more segregated than they have been for decades, and segregation is rapidly increasing. Wide disparities exist in funding for schools. In *Brown*, Chief Justice Earl Warren spoke eloquently of the importance of education and how separate can never be equal.[3] More than a half century later, in an even more technologically complex society, education is even more essential.

The causes for this tragedy are easy to recite. There never has been the political will to pursue equal educational opportunity. No president since the 1960s has devoted any attention to decreasing segregation or to equalizing school funding. The Supreme Court refused to allow the needed steps to deal with the problem in its holding that metropolitan school districts can be created as a remedy only in very limited circumstances and that disparities in school funding do not violate the Constitution.[4] Moreover, Supreme Court decisions in the 1990s have required the lifting of even successful desegregation orders, causing the resegregation of schools.[5] The Court's most recent decision about school desegregation, *Parents Involved in Community Schools v. Seattle School District No. 1,* greatly limited the ability of school boards to pursue voluntary desegregation plans, such as by considering race as one factor in assigning students so as to enhance diversity.[6]

In this essay, I look behind these explanations and argue that the central problem in achieving equal educational opportunity has been the lack of a unitary system of education. Desegregation will not occur in most cities so long as parents can move their children to suburban or private schools. Adequate, let alone equal, funding for schools will not occur so long as wealthy parents can send their children to private or suburban schools, where far more is spent on education than in inner cities. A crucial aspect of *Brown's* wisdom was the importance of a unitary system of education. Minority children are far more likely to receive quality education when their schooling is tied to that of wealthy white children. The failure to create truly unitary systems is the core explanation for the inequalities in American schools today.

Consider a simple analogy: the dual system of medical care. If wealthy people had to receive their medical treatment in public hospitals, is there any doubt that the quality of those hospitals would be dramatically different? But so long as the public hospital system is just for poor people, and often predominately racial minorities at that, they never will be of the same quality as top private hospitals. The same is true of schools.

Therefore, I propose a radical solution: the abolition of private and parochial schools in the United States and the creation of large metropolitan school districts. Under this proposal, every child will be required to attend these public schools. In this way, there truly would be a unitary system of education and, as a result, equality of school funding and meaningful desegregation. Desegregation and equalization of funding can be achieved through this approach, but probably not otherwise.

I do not pretend that this is likely to happen. The rich and powerful will perceive that they have far too much to lose if they cannot send their children to private and parochial schools or to separate, wealthy public school systems. A Supreme Court that is untroubled by the current unequal educational system is not about to find a compelling interest in eliminating separate schools. But at the very least, I suggest that the goal should be to maximize the creation of a unitary system of education. From this perspective, reforms such as school vouchers are moves in exactly the wrong direction, as they allow parents to opt out of public schools and thus further frustrate the goal of a unitary system.

SEPARATE AND UNEQUAL SCHOOLS

A study by Gary Orfield, *Schools More Separate: Consequences of a Decade of Resegregation*, carefully documents how, during the 1990s, America's public schools became substantially more segregated. In the South, for example, "from 1988 to 1998, most of the progress of the previous two decades in increasing integration in the region was lost. The South is still much more integrated than it was before the civil rights revolution, but it is moving backward at an accelerating rate."[7]

The statistics presented in Orfield's study are stark. For example, the percentage of African American students attending majority white schools has steadily decreased since 1986. In 1954, at the time of *Brown*, only 0.001 percent of African American students in the South attended majority white schools.[8] In 1964, a decade after *Brown*, it was just 2.3 percent. From 1964 to 1986, there was significant progress: from 13.9 percent in 1967, to 23.4 percent in 1968, to 37.6 percent in 1976, to 42.9 percent in 1986, to 43.5 percent in 1988. But since then the percentage of black students attending majority white schools has gone in the opposite direction. By 1991 the percentage of black students attending majority white schools in the South had decreased to 39.2 percent, and over the course of the 1990s it went to 36.6 percent in 1994, to 34.7 percent in 1996, to 32.7 percent in 1998.[9]

Orfield shows that nationally the percentage of African American students attending majority black schools and schools where over 90 percent of the students are black also has increased. In 1986, 63.3 percent of black students attended schools that were 50 to 100 percent minority students; by 1998–1999, this had increased to 70.2 percent.[10]

And the problem is getting worse.[11] Supreme Court decisions ending successful desegregation orders are causing substantial increases in segregation.[12] In several cases, the Supreme Court concluded that school systems had achieved "unitary" status and thus that federal court desegregation efforts were to end. The result was that remedies that were in place and working were ended. Resegregation resulted. Many lower courts followed the lead of the Supreme Court and have likewise ended desegregation orders. The result has been predictable: the increase in segregation Orfield documents.

In several cases, the Supreme Court considered when a federal court desegregation order should be ended. In *Board of Education of Oklahoma City v. Dowell* in 1991 the issue was whether a desegregation order should continue when its end would mean a resegregation of the public schools.[13] Oklahoma schools had been segregated under a state law mandating separation of the races. It was not until 1971, seventeen years after *Brown,* that desegregation was ordered in Oklahoma City. A federal court order was successful in desegregating the city's public schools. Evidence proved that ending the desegregation order would result in dramatic resegregation. Nonetheless, the Supreme Court held that once a unitary school system had been achieved, a federal court's desegregation order should end even if it will mean resegregation of the schools. The Court did not define unitary system with any specificity.

In *Freeman v. Pitts,* the Supreme Court held in 1992 that a federal court desegregation order should end when it is complied with, even if other desegregation orders for the same school system remain in place.[14] A federal district court ordered desegregation of various aspects of a school system in Georgia that previously had been segregated by law. Part of the desegregation plan had been met; the school system had achieved desegregation in pupil assignment and in facilities. Another aspect of the desegregation order, concerning assignment of teachers, had not yet been fulfilled. The school system planned to construct a facility that likely would benefit whites more than blacks. Nonetheless, the Supreme Court held that the federal court could not review the discriminatory effects of the new construction because the part of the desegregation order concerning facilities had already been met. The Court said that once a portion of a desegregation order is met, the federal court should cease its efforts regarding that part and remain involved only in those aspects of the plan that have not been achieved.

Finally, in 1995, *Missouri v. Jenkins* ordered an end to a school desegregation order for the Kansas City schools.[15] Missouri law once required the racial segregation of all public schools. It was not until 1977 that a federal district court ordered the desegregation of Kansas City's public schools. The federal court's desegregation effort made a difference. In 1983, twenty-four schools in the district had an African American enrollment of 90 percent or more. By 1993, no elementary student attended a school with an enrollment that was 90 percent or more African American. At the middle school and high school levels, the percentage of students attending schools with an African American enrollment of 90 percent or more declined from about 45 percent to 22 percent.

The Court, in an opinion by Chief Justice William Rehnquist, ruled in favor of the state on every issue. There were three parts to the Court's holding. First, the Court ruled that the district court's order which attempted to attract nonminority students from outside the district was impermissible because there was no proof of an interdistrict violation. Second, the Court ruled that the district court lacked authority to order an increase in teacher salaries. Although the district court believed that an across-the-board salary increase to attract teachers was essential for desegregation, the Supreme Court concluded that it was not necessary as a remedy. Finally, the Court ruled that the continued disparity in student test scores did not justify continuance of the federal court's desegregation order. It concluded that the Constitution requires equal opportunity and not any result, and therefore any disparity between African American and white students on standardized tests was not a sufficient basis for finding that desegregation had not been achieved.

The three cases together have given a clear signal to lower courts: the time has come to end desegregation orders, even when the effect will be resegregation. Lower courts have followed this lead. The U.S. Court of Appeals for the Fourth Circuit has ended the desegregation remedy for the Charlotte-Mecklenburg schools.[16] The Eleventh Circuit ended the desegregation order for the Hillsborough County schools in Tampa, Florida.[17] The Eleventh Circuit rejected the district court's conclusion that unitary status had not been reached. Notwithstanding that conclusion, at thirteen Hillsborough Schools, Latino students outnumber whites and blacks combined.[18] As Orfield explains, "We're going back to a kind of *Plessy* separate-but-equal world. I blame the courts. Because the courts are responsible for the resegregation of the South."[19]

At the same time, there is substantial disparity in school funding. A 2002 study by the General Accounting Office (GAO) describes the importance of this disparity:

> Factors that may relate to student achievement differed between inner city and suburban schools in our study. Research has shown a positive relationship between student achievement and factors such as teacher experience, lower

enrollment, more library books, and computer resources, and higher levels of parental involvement. Among the 24 schools we visited, the average student achievement scores were generally lower in inner city than in suburban schools. Along with lower achievement scores, these inner city schools were more likely to have a higher percentage of first-year teachers, whose lack of experience can be an indicator of lower teacher quality. In addition, in comparison to the suburban schools, inner city schools generally were older, had higher student enrollments, and had fewer library books per pupil and less technological support.[20]

In some cities, the disparities are enormous. For example, the GAO report notes how in Fort Worth, Texas, the lowest spending suburban school had per-pupil expenditures 21 percent higher than the highest-spending inner-city school.[21] Of course, this does not begin to account for the disparity between spending in public schools and private schools, which are predominately attended by wealthier students. Studies show the continuing disparities in school funding.[22]

Ironically, the area of society that remains most segregated, where the Supreme Court has most failed, is the one that was the focus of *Brown*: public school education. American public schools are racially separate, and this segregation is increasing at an accelerating rate. The overall statistics for major city public schools could not be more discouraging for those who believe in desegregation. In the 2008 to 2009 school year in Boston, only 13.3 percent of the children in the public schools were white. In Chicago, just 8.9 percent of children in the public schools were white. In Dallas, only 4.6 percent of children in the public schools were white. And in Los Angeles, 8.7 percent of the students were white.[23]

The simple and tragic reality is that American schools are separate and unequal. To a very large degree, education in the United States is racially segregated. By any measure, predominately minority schools are not equal in their resources or their quality. Wealthy suburban school districts are almost exclusively white; poor inner-city schools are often exclusively comprised of African American and Hispanic students. Studies have shown that across the United States, significantly more is spent on the average white child's education than on the average black child's.[24] Moreover, disproportionately more white children than minority children attend private schools with more resources and far better student-faculty ratios. According to recent national statistics, private schools were 71.4 percent white in the fall of 2011.[25]

THE CAUSE: THE LACK OF A UNITARY SYSTEM

My central thesis is that the current inequalities in educational opportunities are a result of the failure to create unitary systems of education and, in fact, Court decisions preventing this from occurring. By the 1970s, a crucial problem had emerged: white flight to suburban areas. Whites left the cities—in part to avoid school desegregation and in part as a result of a larger demographic phenomenon—and this endangered successful desegregation. In virtually every urban area, the inner city became increasingly comprised of racial minorities. By contrast, the surrounding suburbs were almost exclusively white, and what little minority population did reside in suburbs was concentrated in towns that were almost exclusively black.[26] And school district lines paralleled town borders; racial separation of cities and suburbs resulted in segregated school systems. For example, a decade later, by 1980, whites constituted less than one-third of the students enrolled in the public schools in Baltimore, Dallas, Detroit, Houston, Los Angeles, Miami, Memphis, New York, and Philadelphia.[27]

Thus, by the 1970s it was clear that effective school desegregation required interdistrict remedies. There were simply not enough white students in most major cities to achieve desegregation. Likewise, suburban school districts could not be desegregated via intradistrict remedies because of the scarcity of minority students in the suburbs. As Theodore Smedley explains, "Regardless of the cause, the result of this movement [of whites to suburban areas] is that the remaining city public school population became predominately black. When this process has occurred, no amount of attendance zone revision, pairing and clustering of schools, and busing of students within the city school system could achieve substantially integrated student bodies in the schools, because there are simply not enough white students left in the city system."[28]

But in *Milliken v. Bradley,* in 1974, the Supreme Court imposed a substantial limit on the courts' remedial powers in desegregation cases.[29] A federal district court had imposed a multidistrict remedy to address de jure segregation in one of the districts. The Supreme Court ruled this impermissible and held that "before the boundaries of separate and autonomous school districts may be set aside by consolidating the separate units for remedial purposes or by imposing a cross-district remedy, it must first be shown that there has been a constitutional violation within one district that produces a significant segregative effect in another district."[30] Thus, the Court concluded that "without an interdistrict violation and interdistrict effect there is no constitutional wrong calling for an interdistrict remedy."[31]

Milliken has had a devastating effect on the ability to achieve desegregation in many areas. In a number of major cities, inner-city school systems are substantially black and are surrounded by almost all-white suburbs.[32] Desegregation obviously requires the ability to transfer students between the city and suburban schools. There simply are not enough white students in the city, or enough black students in the suburbs, to achieve desegregation without an interdistrict remedy. Yet, *Milliken* precludes an interdistrict remedy unless there is proof of an interdistrict violation. In other words, a multidistrict remedy can be formulated for those districts whose own policies fostered discrimination or if a state law caused the interdistrict segregation. Otherwise, the remedy can include only those districts found to violate the Constitution. Such proof is often not available, although there have been some cases where the requirements of *Milliken* have been met.[33]

The segregated pattern in major metropolitan areas—blacks in the city and whites in the suburbs—did not occur by accident but, rather, was the product of myriad government policies. Moreover, *Milliken* has the effect of encouraging white flight. Whites who wish to avoid desegregation can do so by moving to the suburbs. If *Milliken* had been decided differently, one of the incentives for such moves would be eliminated. The reality is that in many areas *Milliken* means no desegregation.

By the 1970s, it also was clear that there were substantial disparities in school funding. In 1972, Christopher Jencks estimated that, on average, 15 to 20 percent more was being spent on each white student's education than on each black child's.[34] This was true throughout the country. For example, Chicago's public schools spent $5,265 for each student's education; but just north of the city, Niles Township's school system, spent $9,371 on each student's schooling.[35] Camden, New Jersey, spent $3,538 on each pupil, while Princeton, New Jersey, spent $7,725 per student.[36] These disparities also correspond to race: in Chicago, 45.4 percent of the students were white and 39.1

percent were African American; in Niles, the schools were 91.6 percent white and 0.4 percent black.[37]

There, of course, is a simple explanation for the disparities in school funding. In most states, education is substantially funded by local property taxes. Wealthier suburbs have significantly larger tax bases than poor inner cities. The result is that suburbs can tax at a low rate and still have a great deal to spend on education. Cities must tax at a higher rate and still have less to spend.

The Court had the opportunity to remedy this inequality in education in 1973 in *San Antonio Independent School District v. Rodriguez*.[38] But the Court profoundly failed and concluded that the inequalities in funding did not deny equal protection. *Rodriguez* involved a challenge to the Texas system of funding public schools largely through local property taxes. Texas' financing system meant that poor areas had to tax at a high rate but had little to spend on education; wealthier areas could tax at low rates but still had much more to spend on education. One poorer district spent $356 per pupil, while a wealthier district spent $594 per student.[39]

The plaintiffs challenged this system on two grounds: it violated equal protection as impermissible wealth discrimination and denied the fundamental right to education. The Court rejected the former argument by holding that poverty is not a suspect classification and that, therefore, discrimination against the poor only needs to meet rational basis review.[40]

The Court also rejected the claim that education is a fundamental right. Justice Lewis Powell, writing for the majority, concluded, "Education, of course, is not among the rights afforded explicit protection under our Federal Constitution. Nor do we find any basis for saying it is implicitly so protected."[41] Although education obviously is inextricably linked to the exercise of constitutional rights such as freedom of speech and voting, the Court nonetheless decided that education itself is not a fundamental right.[42] It also noted that the government did not completely deny an education to students; the challenge was to inequities in funding.[43] The Court concluded that strict scrutiny was inappropriate because there was neither discrimination based on a suspect classification nor infringement of a fundamental right and found that the Texas system for funding schools met the rational basis test.

The combined effect of *Milliken* and *Rodriguez* cannot be overstated. *Milliken* helped to ensure racially separate schools, and *Rodriguez* meant that those separate schools would be unequal. American public education is characterized by wealthy, white, suburban schools that spend a great deal on education surrounding much poorer, black, city schools that spend much less on education.[44]

CREATING A TRULY UNITARY SYSTEM OF EDUCATION

At this point, there seems neither the political nor the judicial will to deal with the growing segregation and inequalities in American schools. No political candidate is addressing the issue. Since court decisions are causing the problem, not solving it, it seems appropriate to begin thinking of new solutions, even if at this point they seem unlikely to ever be implemented. I believe that the only answer to separate and unequal schools is a truly unitary system, where every child—rich and poor, of color and white—will receive education in the same school system.

My proposal is simple, although unrealistic at this point in American history. First, every child must attend public school through high school. There will be no private schools, no parochial schools, no home schooling. Second, metropolitan school districts will be created for every metropolitan area. In each metropolitan area, there will be equal funding among the schools, except where educational needs dictate otherwise, and efforts will be taken to ensure desegregation. Third, states will ensure equality of spending among metropolitan school districts within their borders.

How could this happen? One possibility would be through the Supreme Court, though certainly not with the current Court. The Supreme Court could find that the existing separate and unequal schools deny equal protection and could order the creation of a unitary system as a remedy. Another way to achieve this would be by legislative action. Congress could adopt a law to achieve these goals, using its power under Section 5 of the Fourteenth Amendment, or state legislatures could do so within their borders.

For the Supreme Court to do this, it would need to find that there is a fundamental right to education and that equality of educational opportunity is a compelling government interest. Education is the key to the exercise of many other constitutional rights, ranging from freedom of speech to voting. The Court has held that spending money in election campaigns is speech protected by the First Amendment because money facilitates speech. But education, too, facilitates speech and communication. Freedom of the press is meaningless unless there is literacy, and literacy cannot occur without education.

Congress could act even in the absence of judicial decisions. Congress has broad power under Section 2 of the Thirteenth Amendment to eradicate the "badges and incidents" of slavery. The educational disparities between white children and black children are a legacy of slavery and racism. In fact, Congress could act to create unitary school systems through its spending power and conditions on grants, or even under its commerce power because of the close relationship between education and the economy.

I do not minimize the radical nature of this proposal. But this is the way in which equal educational opportunity can be achieved. If wealthy parents must send their children to public schools, then they will ensure adequate funding of those schools. However, they have no incentive to care about funding in public schools so long as their children are in private or suburban schools. Moreover, desegregation can be meaningfully achieved in metropolitan school systems that include suburbs and cities, especially if white students cannot flee to private schools.

The most significant objection to this proposal is that it is unconstitutional under current law. In *Pierce v. Society of Sisters*, the Supreme Court held that parents have a fundamental right to send their children to parochial schools, declaring unconstitutional an Oregon law that prohibited parochial school education.[45] The Court based this on the right of parents to control the upbringing of their children and thus to send their children to a religious rather than a secular school.

However, this right, like other fundamental rights, is not absolute. I would argue that strict scrutiny is met and that therefore interference with the parents' right to control the upbringing of their children is justified. There is a compelling interest in achieving equality of educational opportunity, and the means are necessary because no other alternative is likely to succeed.

Parents desiring religious education for their children would claim a violation of their free exercise of religion. Of course, under the Supreme Court's decision in *Employment Division v. Smith,* the free exercise clause would not be violated by such a neutral law of general applicability.[46] I do not minimize the interests of parents in providing religious instruction for their children. However, parents could still do this through afterschool and weekend programs. This is not the same as education where religion permeates instruction, but it does provide a way in which parents can provide religious education for their children.

Perhaps the Court would need to reconsider *Wisconsin v. Yoder* as well, to the extent that it is read as creating a right of parents to isolate their children from the influences of public education.[47] In *Yoder*, the Court held that Amish parents had the right to exempt their fourteen- and fifteen-year-old children from compulsory school requirements so as to preserve the special Amish culture. Read broadly, parents could invoke *Yoder* to justify a right to home schooling if parents wanted to insulate their children from the influences of public education. Simply put, the courts should hold that the compelling need for equal schooling outweighs this right of parents.

One criticism of this proposal is that it can be circumvented as wealthy parents will provide supplemental classes for their students, after school and on weekends. Certainly nothing in this proposal limits what occurs outside of school hours. But this type of inequality is not a reason to abandon unitary schools. Wealthier children always will have the chance to attend nicer summer camps, go on better vacations, and take more enrichment classes. But, if anything, all of these other inequalities make it even more important that schools be equal for all.

I have repeatedly emphasized that I do not see this proposal as having the slightest chance of implementation for the foreseeable future. But it does point toward the goal: a unitary system of education. Even if the proposal never is fully implemented, the goal must be to work toward a unitary system. Therefore, measures that move in this direction—metropolitan school districts, desegregation orders, equalization of funding—should be aggressively pursued.

At the same time, efforts that push away from unitary schools should be disfavored. Most notably, voucher systems are undesirable because they are the antithesis of a unitary system. Vouchers encourage parents to send their children to private and parochial schools and to abandon public schools. Vouchers will only exacerbate segregation and inequalities in educational opportunity. In large cities, top private schools often cost over $25,000 a year; a voucher worth $2,500 does not give poor children the ability to attend these schools. Instead, vouchers take money away from the public school, leaving poor children with the choice of attending even worse public schools, lesser private schools, or religious schools. My central point is that the focus should be on how to ensure that all children are in the same school system; vouchers have exactly the opposite effect.

CONCLUSION

As *Brown* has now passed its sixtieth anniversary, it is easy to be discouraged by the failure to create integrated, equal public schools. All institutions share responsibility. The Supreme Court deserves a great deal of the blame for its decisions precluding metropolitan-wide desegregation efforts and for not finding that disparities in school funding are unconstitutional. Presidents and Congress deserve the blame for ignoring the issue for so long.

The underlying problem is that as long as parents can opt out of public schools in cities, by sending their children to private and suburban schools, there never can be desegregation and never will be equalization of resources for education. The only solution is to make sure that every child must attend the public schools. Then, and only then, will parents have the incentive to ensure adequate education for all. Put another way, if schools for the poor are regarded as a welfare program, they always will be inadequately funded. But if education is an insurance program, affecting and benefiting all, then their quality will be assured.

Ultimately, if American society will ever be more equal, it will be through education. But the reality is that the American educational system is terribly unequal and thus an engine for widening, not closing, the gap between whites and racial minorities and between rich and poor. And the problem of segregation and inequality in education is getting worse, not better. The Supreme Court in *Brown* got it right: providing equal educational opportunity requires a unitary system of schools. But the justices in *Brown* could not have imagined the white flight to suburban and private schools that would frustrate desegregation. Nor could they have imagined that less than two decades later the Supreme Court would hold that education was not a fundamental right. Creating equal educational opportunity requires creating school systems where all children—rich and poor, white children and children of color—are all present. That is what I try to imagine and propose in this essay.

Creating New Pathways to Equal Educational Opportunity

CHARLES J. OGLETREE, JR.
AND KIMBERLY JENKINS ROBINSON

BY EXPLORING THE impact of *San Antonio Independent School District v. Rodriguez,* we have highlighted one of the pivotal Supreme Court decisions that has enabled disparities in educational opportunity to persist. We also have invited policy makers, educators, scholars, and the public to reexamine the broken foundations of our nation's education system. We believe that this reexamination is long overdue and that too much education reform merely tinkers at the margins of a system built on fundamentally flawed premises and assumptions. In this book we have collected a diverse array of tools that law and policy makers, educators, and reformers could employ to fulfill the aims of the *Rodriguez* plaintiffs even without access to the federal courts to enforce a constitutional right to education. The chapters analyze how much of the current law and policy governing educational opportunity perpetuates and entrenches opportunity and achievement gaps and thus provide the foundational understanding needed to successfully employ these new tools.

In this concluding chapter, we consider how the insights and lessons in this book change the way we understand the issues that confronted the *Rodriguez* Court and chart new pathways for closing opportunity gaps.

MAKING SENSE OF *RODRIGUEZ* AND THE CAUSES OF DISPARITIES IN EDUCATIONAL OPPORTUNITY

Each of the contributing authors in this book recognizes the indisputable fact that the *Rodriguez* plaintiffs' goals remain unfulfilled. *Rodriguez* foreclosed a powerful avenue for reducing educational opportunity gaps by holding that the U.S. Constitution does not recognize a right to education. In the United States, the federal courts have served as one of the most important protectors of the rights of minorities and the disadvantaged. The persistence of the educational opportunity gap leads us to believe that the *Rodriguez* decision has greatly hindered the work of reformers who sought to use school finance litigation as a means of ensuring equal educational opportunity and completing the unfinished work of school desegregation. Understanding *Rodriguez* and its unfortunate legacy is essential for comprehending why so many American schoolchildren do not have equal access to a high-quality education.[1]

Given the substantial negative impact of the *Rodriguez* decision on efforts to narrow educational opportunity gaps, we wholeheartedly agree with Michael Rebell's persuasive analysis, which argues that *Rodriguez* was wrongly decided. Over four decades of experience since *Rodriguez* has demonstrated that state courts and legislatures alone will not consistently close opportunity gaps throughout the United States.[2] A federal remedy is needed for greater consistency of access to a forum for reform. Furthermore, the federal role in education has expanded in ways that make it tenable for the federal courts to serve as that forum.

This book also provides important research and analysis for understanding whether the decision will, in fact, be reversed. For instance, Camille Walsh's chapter reveals that the anticommunist sentiments that influenced Justice Powell resulted in the plaintiffs' claims carrying the weight of the Cold War battles that infiltrated U.S. law and policy making for many decades. Her research raises important questions regarding potential outside influences that might guide the decision if a *Rodriguez*-like case ever reaches the Supreme Court. Would the Court view the enduring nature of disparities in educational opportunities as evidence that its confidence was misplaced in trusting states to address them? Would evidence of the high costs of inadequate education and the sometimes struggling economy encourage greater Court interest in reducing educational disparities in the face of robust evidence that such disparities are hindering the United States in maintaining its economic competitiveness?[3] Or would the Court continue to believe that the federal courts are not appropriate venues in which to resolve essential debates over education policy?

There is compelling evidence that even if *Rodriguez* is reversed, the United States will still need effective policies to tackle the harmful effects of socioeconomic and racial isolation. Amy Stuart Wells, Lauren Fox, and Alana Miles find that racial and socioeconomic segregation continues to perpetuate tangible and intangible inequalities between school districts even when funding levels are relatively equal. Genevieve Siegel-Hawley contrasts communities that engage in metropolitan school desegregation with those that have been prevented from integrating city and suburban schools, finding reduced school and housing segregation only after broad, metropolitan-wide school desegregation. Given the persistent ineffectiveness of racially and socioeconomically isolated schools, Siegel-Hawley recommends that metropolitan areas, as well as state and federal officials, employ a variety of integration tools, including regional integration strategies, cooperative agreements among districts, and controlled choice plans within districts.[4] Similarly, our foreword author, James Ryan, convincingly argues in his 2010 book that, given the persistence of low academic performance in urban districts with high concentrations of minorities and poor students even when funding levels are high, the United States should resume the unfinished business of racial and socioeconomic integration in schools.[5] Thus, the recommendations for creating socioeconomically and racially integrated schools made here by Wells, Fox, and Miles and Siegel-Hawley, Derek Black, and Erwin Chemerinsky are essential for winning the battle against the educational opportunity gap. Reducing racial and class isolation also will better prepare all students to be, among other things, engaged and compassionate citizens and to enter the increasingly diverse and international workforce.

The Enduring Legacy of Rodriguez also tackles the complex issue of how education federalism and federal law have contributed to educational inequalities. For instance, Kimberly Jenkins Robinson analyzes how education federalism has both hindered past efforts to ensure equal educational opportunity and invited educational inequalities.[6] Black evaluates how Title I of the Elementary and Secondary Education Act has directed funds to districts with low concentrations of poverty in spite of the far greater need for such funding in districts with high concentrations of poverty. Chemerinsky identifies both an array of Supreme Court precedent and the ability of some families to opt out of public schools as root causes of today's separate and unequal schools. These chapters expand our understanding of how the nation should view disparities in educational opportunity, and their insights can serve as guideposts for the design and implementation of future reforms.

MOVING BEYOND "DOES MONEY MATTER?"

The *Rodriguez* Court identified ongoing debate about whether money influences educational opportunity, and its inability to resolve this debate, as one of several reasons not to invalidate the Texas finance system.[7] Since *Rodriguez,* that question has consistently engaged the attention of scholars, policy makers, and courts. This book does not rehash this debate. Instead, it recommends legal and policy theories and reforms that must be considered for an effective comprehensive effort to achieve equal educational opportunity in the United States. It is these fundamental legal and policy theories and reforms that far too often are missing from discussions about how to achieve this goal.

As shown in these pages, there is no need to revisit this debate, because sufficient compelling evidence has emerged that money spent well does, in fact, make a difference. For instance, Michael Rebell explains that since *Rodriguez* a consensus has emerged in the state school finance decisions that money does indeed matter. As the Ohio Supreme Court explained in *DeRolph v. State,* "Although a student's success depends upon numerous factors besides money, we must ensure that there is enough money that students have the chance to succeed because of the educational opportunity provided, not in spite of it."[8] Other courts have reached similar conclusions and have noted the importance of ending inequitable funding disparities while acknowledging the variety of other factors that also influence student outcomes.[9]

David Sciarra and Danielle Farrie also highlight compelling research confirming that raising funding levels and reducing funding inequities can improve student outcomes. They cite studies that have found improved educational outcomes from finance reforms that raised spending and from money spent on such reforms as smaller class sizes and improving teacher quality.[10] Similarly, Rebell describes studies which conclude that increased school funding can improve student outcomes. He also explains why Eric Hanushek's contentions that key educational resources are not consistently linked to improved student achievement has been criticized as misleading and underinclusive. Researchers at the University of Chicago conducted a meta-analysis of research similar to that conducted by Hanushek that eliminated some of the studies Hanushek relied on as inappropriate and included other relevant studies. These researchers found that a variety of student inputs have a positive relationship with student outcomes and that "moderate increases in spending may be associated with significant increases in achievement."[11]

The conclusion that money does matter has also been confirmed by a recent and comprehensive review of major studies on this question by education law and policy scholar Bruce Baker, who reached three conclusions important for understanding this research. First, his research reveals that money matters, in that overall per-pupil spending is "positively associated with improved or higher student outcomes." He acknowledges that effect sizes vary and that funding may influence some student outcomes more than others. Thus, careful investment strategies are needed to leverage the positive impact of financial investments. Second, the resources that money can buy, such as increasing teacher salaries and reducing class sizes, also are positively related to student results. Here, too, effect size can vary. Finally, he finds that "sustained improvements to level and distribution of funding across local public school districts can lead to improvement in the level and distribution of student outcomes." In other words, more equitable funding systems also can raise student achievement.[12]

In addition to the emerging consensus that, at a minimum, money spent well matters, we note that scholarly attention and energy appear to be shifting toward how school finance policies can be reformed to improve student achievement. For instance, Sciarra and Farrie use the New Jersey Supreme Court's *Abbott* decisions as a template for recommending that states should link funding for education to what must be provided for all students to achieve high academic standards.[13] Other scholars also are focusing on how reforming school finance systems can raise student outcomes. For example, Eric Hanushek, who was a prominent advocate for the position that money does not matter, recently commented that "while there is some uncertainty about the specific details of programs, the most promising school finance policies and institutions are ones that promote higher achievement (instead of simply providing more resources to schools). The modern way to view school finance is how the support of schools relates to incentives."[14] Similarly, prominent education scholar W. Norton Grubb has observed that improving school finance reform should focus on ensuring that the broad constellation of resources that influence student achievement are provided, including "the compound, complex, and abstract resources that must be constructed rather than bought."[15]

Therefore, it is time to move past debate about whether money matters. It does. Our book offers new directions for research and analysis about the foundational assumptions, laws, and policies that entrench inequality and the theories, laws, policies, and reforms that could chart new pathways toward greater equality and improved quality of educational opportunity.

LESSONS AND CAUTIONARY TALES FROM SCHOOL FINANCE LITIGATION

For those contemplating how to engage states in school finance litigation or other state reform through litigation, there are several lessons and cautionary tales offered here. The litigation efforts analyzed by David Hinojosa in Texas, Sciarra and Farrie in New Jersey, and Rebell in New York reveal that successful school finance litigation has yielded important victories. State school finance litigation has called public attention to the scope and persistence of educational opportunity gaps and how school finance systems contribute to, and often exacerbate, such gaps. For instance, Hinojosa highlights how the most recent plaintiff victory in Texas led the trial court to charge Texas with failing to even attempt to assess "the cost of providing all students with a meaningful opportunity to acquire the essential knowledge and skills reflected in the state curriculum and to graduate at a college and career-ready level."[16]

Successful state school finance litigation also has clarified for legislatures and the public what must be provided to meet the requirements for education within state constitutions. For instance, Rebell explains that a consensus has emerged that state education clauses guarantee students an education which prepares them to be capable citizens and to be effective competitors in today's global employment market. In addition, successful school finance litigation has demanded reform of fundamentally broken finance systems that were not designed to meet the educational needs of students. Sciarra and Farrie describe the supreme court of New Jersey's pathbreaking *Abbott* decisions, which found that funding must be directed toward enabling all students to learn the content of state standards.[17]

What is remarkable about the *Abbott* decisions is that they are noteworthy at all. The fact that most funding systems are not designed to equip all students with the content within state standards should be both unacceptable and appalling to the American public. Yet, the National Commission on Equity and Excellence in Education has found that "with few exceptions, states continue to finance public education through methods that have no demonstrable link to the cost of delivering rigorous academic standards and that can produce high achievement in all students."[18] We agree with Sciarra and Farrie that all states should implement funding systems which enable all students to achieve high academic standards. Indeed, such reforms are long overdue given the decades that have passed since the rise of the standards and accountability movement in the late 1980s and 1990s.[19]

The analyses by Hinojosa, Rebell, and Sciarra and Farrie also reveal that judges have the authority and expertise to understand the adverse effects of school funding disparities and to require state legislatures to develop remedies to address them, despite the *Rodriguez* majority's suggestion to the contrary. Undoubtedly, the schoolchildren in states in which plaintiffs successfully challenge school funding systems would be experiencing even greater disparities of educational opportunity without the persistent efforts of these and other reformers, as Hinojosa acknowledges. Furthermore, Hinojosa astutely argues that state courts often remain the only avenue for many communities that lack influence in state legislatures. Thus, state courts will remain on the frontlines of school finance reform absent a consistent federal forum.

These scholars and advocates also provide important cautionary insights from state school finance litigation. State school finance victories repeatedly have encountered entrenched resistance by state legislatures and the public and thus often require decades of litigation to achieve any results. In addition, James Ryan, among others, also notes the limited impact of even successful school finance litigation due to political opposition and the reluctance of courts to require equalization of funding, to abolish property taxes, and to insist on redrawing of attendance zones.[20] Further evidence of the failures of state school finance litigation can be found in Sciarra and Farrie's analysis of the *Is School Funding Fair?* report in which they find that even after decades of such litigation, only a few states deliver enough of funding and provide additional resources when student poverty increases.[21] Therefore, even if *Rodriguez* is overturned, as Rebell predicts, the actual reform of school finance systems will require political support and cooperation by state legislatures that are willing to disrupt the status quo and to overcome the opposition of those who benefit from it.

We believe Rebell's acknowledgment that "it also is clear . . . that there are limits to what can be accomplished through state by state litigation" is important for understanding what reforms must be undertaken to make consistent and sustained progress on ensuring equal access to a high-quality education. When we consider the lessons and cautionary tales presented in these chapters, we conclude that state school finance litigation cannot effectively close all educational opportunity gaps in the United States. Instead, comprehensive and coordinated federal, state, and local reform is needed to close these gaps.

THE IMPORTANCE OF DIVERSE REFORM MECHANISMS

The entrenched opportunity gaps in the United States demand federal, state, and local reforms that supplement and reinforce one another. Several scholars propose reforms in these pages that focus on new and innovative federal interventions to promote equal educational opportunity, and we believe such reforms are essential for an effective comprehensive effort to close opportunity gaps. For instance, Mildred Wigfall Robinson recommends indirect federal support for education by expanding the deduction or credit for any property taxes paid to support public schools. This additional federal support would particularly benefit communities with relatively lower property tax bases. Both Chemerinsky and Rebell contend that the Supreme Court or Congress could guarantee a right to equal educational opportunity by overturning prior decisions or by adopting new legislation.

Kimberly Robinson's reconstruction of education federalism would increase the federal role in education by reestablishing the federal government as the guarantor of equal educational opportunity and raising federal investment in and responsibility for education reforms that ensure equal access to an excellent education. She contends that this enhanced federal role should incentivize states to adopt common opportunity-to-learn standards, augment federal research and technical and financial assistance, and implement a collaborative enforcement model in which the federal and state governments engage in a supportive partnership to close opportunity and achievement gaps.

However, the invoking of additional federal authority to remedy opportunity gaps undoubtedly would encounter substantial obstacles. First among them might be the lack of political will to engage in far-reaching and progressive federal reform. In addition, many states would likely resist substantial additional federal involvement in an arena they have dominated for generations. Most of these reforms also would necessitate an increase in federal funding for education, which would require education to prevail over competing policy making priorities. Therefore, these proposals raise important questions about how to build congressional and judicial consensus for progressive reform, the drawbacks of increasing federal involvement in education, and the ways to structure federal intervention in education policy making to optimize effective reforms that aim to guarantee equal educational opportunity.

Moreover, even if additional federal support for closing opportunity and achievement gaps was developed, effective federal reform will be unsuccessful unless fundamental reforms are not undertaken within states and localities. Litigation remains a potential avenue for addressing disparities in educational resources. For those considering this avenue for reform, William Koski highlights the potential benefits and pitfalls of litigation to address disparities in access to qualified teachers. Litigation that challenges the laws regarding the placement and retention of teachers represents a recent shift focusing on one critical resource disparity rather than all resource disparities. Koski explains how this new approach has embraced a more focused attempt to tinker with education policy that embraces judicial modesty in shaping targeted reforms. He recommends litigation that seeks local reforms to provide quality teachers, because the cause of the teacher quality gap varies across districts and thus the remedies for such gaps should vary accordingly. This approach can avoid disrupting teacher placement and retention rules where they do not cause a negative impact. In assessing such efforts, it is helpful to ask, Will these reform efforts enjoy greater success because they do not attempt to reduce all educational disparities simultaneously, or will they run the risk of leaving other critical, harmful disparities untouched in perpetuity?

We believe that federal, state, and local reforms can and must complement and support one other. This is evidenced in part in Siegel-Hawley's recommendations for greater federal and state efforts to support local metropolitan-wide desegregation plans. Similarly, Black counsels revisions to Title I that would focus federal funds on the neediest schools, incentivize states to focus on these schools, establish meaningful federal requirements for equalizing resources between schools, and create incentives for states to integrate public schools. Kimberly Robinson proposes a more robust federal role in education to create a more effective marriage between federal influence and responsibility in education as well as a more impactful federal-state partnership that could ensure equal educational opportunity. These and other reform proposals presented here offer synergistic federal, state, and local reforms to close opportunity gaps.

CREATING NEW PATHWAYS TO EQUAL EDUCATIONAL OPPORTUNITY

Increasingly, reformers are challenging business as usual and insisting that fundamental change must occur so that educational opportunity and quality do not depend on a family's income, race, or place of residence.[22] This book is intended to help broaden the ongoing reform conversation to include reforms that will overturn the foundational laws and policies that entrench educational inequality. *Rodriguez* is an important part of this foundation and thus should be overturned. This collection of essays also shows that overturning *Rodriguez* alone would not be enough to end educational inequality and that many additional pathways exist that could lead the United States to equal educational opportunity.

We look to policy makers, educators, reformers, and scholars to adopt these recommendations to implement fundamental reforms. However, such reforms can only be implemented if the public demands that the United States abolish an education system that routinely fails to produce the educated citizens that are essential to an effective democracy. Comprehensive, effective reform will require rejecting the belief that disparities in educational opportunity are inevitable. Furthermore, the nation must embrace a willingness to engage in bold experiments that demand what has never been provided in the United States: equal access to a high-quality education. Our future economic prosperity depends on this.[23] Yet, it is not clear that the more privileged sectors of the American public are willing to relinquish the entrenched expectations and advantages offered by the status quo.

We hope that *The Enduring Legacy of* Rodriguez will become an important part of a toolkit that will dismantle the broken foundation of our nation's education system and then rebuild a more equitable and excellent one. We can end the stranglehold of the *Rodriguez* decision and other adverse laws and policies that perpetuate an inequitable education system, but this will require transforming the U.S. education system from an engine for maintaining privilege and advantage to a launch pad for our common prosperity.

School Finance Litigation Cases

IN TWENTY-THREE STATES, plaintiffs have prevailed in the state's highest court at least once. Listed below are the initial plaintiff wins for each state. An asterisk (*) denotes a plaintiff loss in that state's highest court.

Alabama
Opinion of the Justices, 624 So.2d 107 (Ala. 1993)
*Ex parte Governor Fob James, 836 So.2d 813 (Ala. 2002)

Arizona
Roosevelt Elementary School District No. 66 v. Bishop, 877 P.2d 806 (Ariz. 1994)
*Shofstall v. Hollins, 515 P.2d 590 (Ariz. 1973) (en banc)

Arkansas
Lake View School District No. 25 v. Huckabee, 91 S.W.3d 472 (Ark. 2002)
DuPree v. Alma School District No. 30, 651 S.W.2d 90 (Ark. 1983)

California
Serrano v. Priest, 557 P.2d 929 (Cal. 1976) (en banc)

Connecticut
Sheff v. O'Neill, 678 A.2d 1267 (Conn. 1996)
Horton v. Meskill, 376 A.2d 359 (Conn. 1977)

Idaho

Idaho Schools for Equal Educational Opportunity v. State, 129 P.3d 1199 (Idaho
   2005)

*Thompson v. Engelking, 537 P.2d 635 (Idaho 1975)

Kansas

Gannon v. State, 319 P.3d 1196 (Kan. 2014)

Montoy v. State, 120 P.3d 306 (Kan. 2005)

*Unified School District No. 229 v. State, 885 P.2d 1170 (Kan. 1994) (upholding
   the state funding system after legislative modifications in response to a lower
   court ruling requiring equal educational opportunity)

Kentucky

Rose v. Council for Better Education, Inc., 790 S.W.2d 186 (Ky. 1989)

Massachusetts

McDuffy v. Secretary, 615 N.E.2d 516 (Mass. 1993)

Commonwealth v. Dedham, 16 Mass. 141 (1819)

*Hancock v. Commissioner of Education, 822 N.E.2d 1134 (Mass. 2005)

Montana

Columbia Falls Elementary School District No. 6 v. State, 109 P.3d 257 (Mont.
   2005)

Helena Elementary School District No. 1 v. State, 769 P.2d 684 (Mont. 1989)

New Hampshire

Claremont School District v. Governor, 703 A.2d 1353 (N.H. 1997)

New Jersey

Abbott v. Burke, 575 A.2d 359 (N.J. 1990)

Robinson v. Cahill, 303 A.2d 273 (N.J. 1973)

New York

Campaign for Fiscal Equity, Inc. v. State, 801 N.E.2d 326 (N.Y. 2003)

*Reform Educational Financing Inequities Today v. Cuomo, 655 N.E.2d 647
   (N.Y. 1995)

*Board of Education, Levittown v. Nyquist, 439 N.E.2d 359 (N.Y. 1982)

North Carolina

Hoke County Board of Education v. State, 599 S.E.2d 365 (N.C. 2004)

North Dakota

Bismarck Public School District v. State, 511 N.W.2d 247 (N.D. 1994)

Ohio
DeRolph v. State, 677 N.E.2d 733 (Ohio 1997)
*Board of Education of Cincinnati v. Walter, 390 N.E.2d 813 (Ohio 1979)

South Carolina
Abbeville County School Board v. State, 767 S.E.2d 157 (S.C. 2014)
*Richland County v. Campbell, 364 S.E.2d 470 (S.C. 1988)

Tennessee
Tennessee Small School Systems v. McWherter, 851 S.W.2d 139 (Tenn. 1993)

Texas
Edgewood Independent School District v. Kirby, 777 S.W.2d 391 (Tex. 1989)
*Neeley v. West Orange–Cove Consolidated Independent School District, 176
    S.W.3d 746 (Tex. 2005)

Vermont
Brigham v. State, 692 A.2d 384 (Vt. 1997)

Washington
McCleary v. State, 269 P.3d 227 (Wash. 2012) (en banc)
Seattle School District No. 1 v. State, 585 P.2d 71 (Wash. 1978) (en banc)
*Federal Way School District No. 210 v. State, 219 P.3d 941 (Wash. 2009) (en banc)
*Northshore School District No. 417 v. Kinnear, 530 P.2d 178 (Wash. 1974) (en
    banc)

West Virginia
Pauley v. Bailey, 324 S.E.2d 128 (W. Va. 1984)

Wyoming
Campbell County School District v. State, 907 P.2d 1238 (Wyo. 1995)
Washakie County School District No. 1 v. Herschler, 606 P.2d 310 (Wyo. 1980)

Plaintiffs have lost and never prevailed at the state's highest court in nineteen states:

Alaska
Matanuska-Susitna Borough School District v. State, 931 P.2d 391 (Alaska 1997)
Although some analyses of school finance litigation have classified Alaska as a win
    state due to two school funding cases that settled without an appeal to the state
    supreme court (Kasayulie v. State, 3AN-97-3782 Civ. (Alaska Super., September 1, 1999); Moore v. State, 3AN-04-9756 Civ. (Alaska Super., June 21, 2007))

we do not classify Alaska as a winning state because plaintiffs have not prevailed in the state's highest court.

Colorado
Lobato v. State, 304 P.3d 1132 (Colo. 2013)
Lujan v. Colorado State Board of Education, 649 P.2d 1005 (Colo. 1982) (en banc)

Florida
Coalition for Adequacy and Fairness in School Funding, Inc. v. Chiles, 680 So.2d 400 (Fla. 1996)

Georgia
McDaniel v. Thomas, 285 S.E.2d 156 (Ga. 1981)

Illinois
Carr v. Koch, 981 N.E.2d 326 (Ill. 2012)
Lewis E. v. Spagnolo, 710 N.E.2d 798 (Ill. 1999)
Committee for Educational Rights v. Edgar, 672 N.E.2d 1178 (Ill. 1996)

Indiana
Bonner v. Daniels, 907 N.E.2d 516 (Ind. 2009)

Maine
School Administrative District No. 1 v. Commissioner, 659 A.2d 854 (Me. 1995)

Maryland
Maryland State Board of Education v. Bradford, 875 A.2d 703 (Md. 2005)
Hornbeck v. Somerset County Board of Education, 458 A.2d 758 (Md. 1983)

Michigan
Milliken v. Green, 212 N.W.2d 711 (Mich. 1973)

Minnesota
Skeen v. State, 505 N.W.2d 299 (Minn. 1993)

Missouri
Committee for Educational Equality v. State, 294 S.W.3d 477 (Mo. 2009)

Nebraska
Nebraska Coalition for Educational Equity and Adequacy v. Heineman, 731 N.W.2d 164 (Neb. 2007)
Gould v. Orr, 506 N.W.2d 349 (Neb. 1993)

Oklahoma
Oklahoma Education Association v. State, 158 P.3d 1058 (Okla. 2007)
Fair School Finance Council of Oklahoma, Inc. v. State, 746 P.2d 1135 (Okla. 1987)

Oregon
Pendleton School District 16R v. State, 200 P.3d 133 (Or. 2009) (Although the court found school funding to be unconstitutionally low, it denied the plaintiffs relief.)
*Coalition for Equitable School Funding, Inc. v. State, 811 P.2d 116 (Or. 1991)
*Olsen v. State, 554 P.2d 139 (Or. 1976)

Pennsylvania
Pennsylvania Association of Rural and Small Schools v. Ridge, 737 A.2d 246 (Pa. 1999)
Marrero v. Commonwealth, 709 A.2d 956 (Pa. 1998)
Danson v. Casey, 399 A.2d 360 (Pa. 1979)

Rhode Island
Woonsocket School Committee v. Chafee, 89 A.3d 778 (R.I. 2014)
City of Pawtucket v. Sundlun, 662 A.2d 40 (R.I. 1995)

South Dakota
Davis v. State, 804 N.W.2d 618 (S.D. 2011)

Virginia
Scott v. Commonwealth, 443 S.E.2d 138 (Va. 1994)

Wisconsin
Vincent v. Voight, 614 N.W.2d 388 (Wis. 2000)
Kukor v. Grover, 436 N.W.3d 568 (Wis. 1989)

In Delaware, Hawai'i, Iowa, Mississippi, Nevada, and Utah, a court has not decided a lawsuit challenging the constitutionality of the school funding system.

In 2002, plaintiffs in Iowa filed suit in *Coalition for a Common Cents Solution v. State* in the district court for Warren County challenging the constitutionality of the school funding formula because it provides unequal and inadequate resources to "non-retail-rich" counties. After the legislature amended the funding statutes, the parties reached a settlement and the plaintiffs withdrew the suit without prejudice.

In Louisiana, plaintiffs have lost and never prevailed in lower state appellate courts. Jones v. State Board of Elementary and Secondary Education, 927 So.2d 426 (La. Ct. App. 2005) and Charlet v. Legislature of the State of Louisiana, 713 So.2d 1199 (La. Ct. App. 1998).

In August 2014, school districts in Mississippi filed suit against the state for failure to pay the districts the funding required by the Mississippi Adequate Education Program. This case remains pending.

In New Mexico, in Zuni Public School District v. State (CV-98-14-II, District Court of McKinley County (October 14, 1999)), the plaintiffs prevailed with a partial summary judgment in the trial court in a challenge to the constitutionality of funding for school facilities. The court ordered the state to uniformly fund capital improvements and to remedy prior inequities.

Please note that in states with a court decision at the highest court, we do not include litigation that settled. Additional information on lower court cases and settlements for all states is available at the National Education Access website http://www.schoolfunding.info.

This appendix was last updated on May 6, 2015.

NOTES

CHAPTER 1

1. San Antonio Independent School District v. Rodriguez, 411 U.S. 1, 40, 54–55 (1973).
2. Brown v. Board of Education, 347 U.S. 483, 493 (1954); James E. Ryan, *Five Miles Away, a World Apart: One City, Two Schools, and the Story of Educational Opportunity in Modern America* (New York: Oxford University Press, 2010), 55, 59.
3. Greg J. Duncan and Richard J. Murnane, *Restoring Opportunity: The Crisis of Inequality and the Challenge for American Education* (Cambridge, MA: Harvard Education Press, 2014), 2.
4. "*Rodriguez* at 40: Exploring New Paths to Equal Educational Opportunity," http://law.richmond.edu/events/rodriguez.html.
5. Paul A. Sracic, San Antonio v. Rodriguez *and the Pursuit of Equal Education* (Lawrence: University Press of Kansas, 2006), 20–21, 26.
6. Rodriguez v. San Antonio Independent School District, 337 F. Supp. 280, 281–282 (W.D. Tex. 1971); *Rodriguez*, 411 U.S. at 9–10.
7. *Rodriguez*, 337 F. Supp. at 282.
8. Ibid. at 282–284.
9. *Rodriguez*, 411 U.S. at 4–59.
10. Stewart published a concurring opinion that briefly echoed the key points of the majority opinion. Ibid. at 59–62 (Stewart, J., concurring).
11. Ibid. at 70–133 (Marshall, J., dissenting). Douglas joined Marshall in his dissent.
12. Ibid. at 63–70 (White, J., dissenting).
13. Ibid. at 62–63 (Brennan, J., dissenting).
14. Sracic, *Pursuit of Equal Education*, 152–153; William Celis III, "One Man's Legal Odyssey," *New York Times*, April 10, 1994, http://www.nytimes.com/1994/04/10/education/one-man-s-legal-odyssey.html; Elaine Ayala, "Rodriguez, Who Fought for Equality, Dies at 87," *MySanAntonio.com*, April 23, 2013, http://www.mysanantonio.com/news/local_news/article/Rodriguez-who-fought-for-equality-dies-at-87-4456618.php.
15. *Rodriguez*, 411 U.S. at 37.
16. See, for example, Michael A. Rebell, "The Right to Comprehensive Educational Opportunity," *Harvard Civil Rights–Civil Liberties Law Review* 47 (2012): 93; Susan H. Bitensky, "We 'Had a Dream' in *Brown v. Board of Education*," *Detroit College of Law at Michigan State Law Review* 1996 (1996): 12; Missouri v. Jenkins, 515 U.S. 70, 99–102 (1995); Papasan v. Allain, 478 U.S. 265, 283–289 (1986).

17. See Plyler v Doe, 457 U.S. 202, 210, 215, 221–224, 228–230 (1982) (citing *Rodriguez*, 411 U.S. at 35).

18. Powell v. Ridge, 189 F.3d 387, 394, 396, 397–403 (3d Cir. 1999).

19. Alexander v. Sandoval, 532 U.S. 275, 288–293 (2001); "Fact Sheet and Dear Colleague Letter from the Office for Civil Rights of the U.S. Department of Education on the Requirement of Resource Comparability under Title VI of the Civil Rights Act of 1964" (2014), http://www2.ed.gov/about/offices/list/ocr/letters/colleague-resourcecomp-201410.pdf.

20. *Rodriguez*, 411 U.S. at 42, 58–59.

21. See, for example, Jeffrey S. Sutton, "*San Antonio Independent School District v. Rodriguez* and Its Aftermath," *Virginia Law Review* 94 (2008): 1970, 1971–1972, 1977; Ryan, *Five Miles Away*, 149–151.

22. Ryan, *Five Miles Away*, 149–150.

23. Bonner *ex rel.* Bonner v. Daniels, 907 N.E.2d 516, 522 (Ind. 2009).

24. Oklahoma Education Association v. State *ex rel.* Oklahoma Legislature, 158 P.3d 1058, 1065–1066 (Okla. 2007); Committee for Educational Rights v. Edgar, 672 N.E.2d 1178, 1189 (Ill. 1996); Ryan, *Five Miles Away*, 147.

25. See, for example, Davis v. State, 804 N.W.2d 618, 639–640 (S.D. 2011); Vincent v. Voight, 614 N.W.2d 388, 411–412 (Wis. 2000); Ryan, *Five Miles Away*, 148.

26. See, for example, Abbott v. Burke, 575 A.2d 359, 384–386, 391–394 (N.J. 1990).

27. Campaign for Fiscal Equity v. State, 655 N.E. 2d 661, 666 (N.Y. 1995); Campaign for Fiscal Equity v. State, 801 N.E.2d 326, 331 (N.Y. 2003).

28. Vergara v. State, Superior Court of the State of California, Case No. BC 484642 (2014).

29. Ryan, *Five Miles Away*, 145, 175.

30. Michael A. Rebell, "*CFE v. State of New York*: Past, Present and Future," *NYSBA Government, Law and Policy Journal* 13 (2011): 26–27; Michael Rebell, "Cuomo's Obligation to Your Kids," *New York Daily News*, January 6, 2014.

31. See, for example, David Hurst et al., *Overview and Inventory of State Education Reforms: 1990 to 2000* (Washington, DC: U.S. Department of Education, National Center for Education Statistics, 2003), 47, http://nces.ed.gov/pubs2003/2003020.pdf; Michael A. Rebell, *Courts and Kids: Pursuing Educational Equity Through the State Courts* (Chicago: University of Chicago Press, 2009), 30–31 ("Virtually all of these studies have concluded that the litigations have resulted in a narrowing of interdistrict expenditure disparities and an increase in educational spending"); Kim Rueben and Sheila Murray, *Racial Disparities in Education Finance: Going Beyond Equal Revenues* (discussion paper, the Urban Institute, Washington, DC, 2008), 4–5, http://www.taxpolicycenter.org/UploadedPDF/411785_equal_revenues.pdf. But see also Christopher Berry, "The Impact of School Finance Judgments on State Fiscal Policy," in *School Money Trials: The Legal Pursuit of Educational Adequacy*, ed. Martin R. West and Paul E. Peterson (Washington, DC: Brookings Institution, 2007), 214 ("In contrast to much of the rhetoric about the revolutionary impact of school finance judgments, I find that they have had relatively small or no effects on most school finance outcomes. On a variety of fiscal measures, ranging from total spending to spending inequality, I find substantively small or statistically insignificant effects of school finance judgments. The most important effect, according to this analysis, has been to accelerate the centralization of school funding to the state level").

32. Compare Sheila E. Murray, William N. Evans, and Robert M. Schwab, "Education-Finance Reform and the Distribution of Education Resources," *American Economic Review* 88, no. 4 (1998): 806 (finding a 19 to 34 percent decrease in spending disparities within states after litigation), with Christopher Berry, "The Impact of School Finance Judgments on State Fiscal Policy," in *School Money Trials: The Legal Pursuit of Educational Adequacy*, ed. Martin R. West and Paul E. Peterson (Washington, DC: Brookings Institution, 2007), 214, 223, 233 (finding a 16 percent reduction after litigation and that the net effect from litigation on spending disparities is typically limited because increased spending by states is often offset by decreased local spending).

33. Rebell, *Courts and Kids,* 31; Deborah A. Verstegen and Teresa S. Jordan, "A Fifty-State Survey of School Finance Policies and Programs: An Overview," *Journal of Education Finance* 34, no. 3 (2009): 224.

34. *See* Ryan, *Five Miles Away*, 153–155, 174; Benjamin Michael Superfine, *The Courts and Standards-Based Education Reform* (New York: Oxford University Press, 2008), 123; Douglas S. Reed, *On Equal Terms: The Constitutional Politics of Educational Opportunity* (Princeton: Princeton University Press, 2001), 16; Derek Black, "Unlocking the Power of State Constitutions with Equal Protection: The First Step Toward Education as a Federally Protected Right," *William & Mary Law Review* 51 (2010): 1371; William J. Glenn, "School Finance Adequacy Litigation and Student Achievement: A Longitudinal Analysis," *Journal of Education Finance* 34 (2009): 262–263; Christopher Roellke, Preston Green, and Erica H. Zielewski, "School Finance Litigation: The Promises and Limitations of the Third Wave," *Peabody Journal of Education* 79, no. 3 (2004): 105.

35. The Equity and Excellence Commission, *For Each and Every Child: A Strategy for Education Equity and Excellence* (Washington, DC: ED Pubs Education, 2013), 19 (emphasis added).

36. Ryan, *Five Miles Away*, 153, 174.

37. *See* Grace Kena et al., *The Condition of Education 2014* (Washington, DC: U.S. Department of Education, National Center for Education Statistics, 2014), 86, http://nces.ed.gov/pubs2014/2014083.pdf.

38. Milliken v. Bradley, 418 U.S. 717 (1974).

CHAPTER 2

1. The exact number of students and protestors is unknown. See, for example, Cynthia E. Orozco, "Rodriguez v. San Antonio ISD," *Texas State Historical Association*, http://www.tshaonline.org/handbook/online/ articles/jrrht (estimating 400 protestors); Ron White, "3000 Ask Reforms in Walkout," *San Antonio Light*, May 16, 1968, 1 (estimating 3,000 protestors); Doris Wright, "Edgewood Students Protest," *San Antonio Express News*, May 17, 1968, 1 (estimating 300 protestors).

2. Diana Herrera (class of 1969), phone interview with author, June 26, 2013; Louis H. Martinez (class of 1968 and senior class president), phone interview with author, June 28, 2013. Joe Muriel (class of 1968), said in a phone interview on June 27, 2013, that the students ate on a warped ping-pong table because there was no room in the "cafetorium" (a room doubling as the cafeteria and auditorium). Teachers also held class there due to a lack of classroom space. Rebecca Felan (class of 1969), stated in a phone interview on July 5, 2013, that the inequities between Edgewood High and other high schools had been discussed among the students as early as her sophomore year. As an

example, she reflected on scholastic typing competitions with other schools, where the Edgewood students were at a disadvantage with the electric typewriters because they were trained on old, manual typewriters.

3. Ron White, "Curbstone Class at Edgewood," *San Antonio Light*, May 17, 1968, 1.

4. See Neeley v. West Orange–Cove Consolidated Independent School District, 176 S.W.3d 746, 792 (Tex. 2005) (*Edgewood V*), showing that 95 percent of all revenue was captured under the Foundation School Program and that 85 percent of all school districts were in the equalized funding system; Edgewood Independent School District v. Kirby, 917 S.W.2d 717, 731 (Tex. 1995) (*Edgewood IV*), noting that the disparities in yield per penny of tax effort during the *Edgewood I* trial between property-rich and property-poor school districts was 2:1 compared with 1.36:1 after SB 7 was adopted in 1993. Compare, for example, Rodriguez v. San Antonio Independent School District, 337 F. Supp. 280, 282 (W.D. Tex. 1971) (noting that property-wealthy Alamo Heights ISD received twice as much from state and local funding as property-poor Edgewood ISD), with The Texas Taxpayer and Student Fairness Coalition v. Williams, No. D-1-GN-11-003130, 2014 WL 4254969, *215 (D. Tex. 2014) (*Edgewood VI*) (noting that property-wealthy Alamo Heights ISD received $6,666 while taxing at $1.04 compared with Edgewood ISD, which received $5,809 while taxing at $1.17).

5. Frank Trejo, "Board Promises Solution to Grievances," *San Antonio Light*, May 24, 1968, 39.

6. Rodriguez v. San Antonio Independent School District, 337 F. Supp. 280, 281 (W.D. Tex. 1971).

7. Ibid. at 281–282.

8. Peter Irons, *The Courage of Their Convictions* (New York: The Free Press, 1988), 292.

9. San Antonio Independent School District v. Rodriguez, 411 U.S. 1, 71 (1973) (Marshall, J., dissenting).

10. Ibid. at 64–65.

11. Ibid. at 133 n.100.

12. The education clause states, "A general diffusion of knowledge being essential to the preservation of the liberties and rights of the people, it shall be the duty of the Legislature of the State to establish and make suitable provision for the support and maintenance of an efficient system of public free schools." Tex. Const. art. VII, § 1.

13. José A. Cárdenas, *Texas School Finance Reform: An IDRA Perspective* (San Antonio: IDRA, 1997), 221.

14. Kirby v. Edgewood Independent School District, 761 S.W.2d 859 (Tex. App. 1988).

15. Edgewood Independent School District v. Kirby, 777 S.W.2d 391, 397 (Tex. 1989) (*Edgewood I*).

16. J. Steven Farr and Mark Trachtenberg, "The Edgewood Drama: An Epic Quest for Education Equity," *Yale Law and Policy Review* 17 (1999): 635.

17. *Edgewood I*, 777 S.W.2d at 398.

18. Ibid. at 395 n.4.

19. Ibid. at 397.

20. Ibid. at 393.

21. Ibid.

22. Ibid. at 397.

23. Albert H. Kauffman, "The Texas School Finance Litigation Saga: Great Progress, Then Near Death by a Thousand Cuts," *St. Mary's Law Journal* 40 (2008): 533.

24. Edgewood v. Kirby, 804 S.W.2d. 491, 498 (Tex. 1991) (*Edgewood II*).

25. For instance, Glen Rose ISD, a property-wealthy district due to the oil lying underground, taxed at $.235 and generated $9,500 per student.

26. *Edgewood II*, 804 S.W.2d at 496–497.

27. Kauffman, "The Texas School Finance Litigation Saga," 535–536.

28. *Edgewood II*, 804 S.W.2d 491.

29. Kauffman, "The Texas School Finance Litigation Saga," 536.

30. *Edgewood II*, 804 S.W.2d at 501 (Doggett, J., concurring).

31. Kauffman, "The Texas School Finance Litigation Saga," 537; see also Cárdenas, *Texas School Finance Reform*, 13, 15. But see Carrolton-Farmers Branch Independent School District v. Edgewood Independent School District (*Edgewood III*), 826 S.W.2d 489, 511–512 (contending that the prior opinions never sanctioned a system like Senate Bill 351).

32. Ibid. at 493.

33. Ibid. at 523.

34. *Edgewood IV*, 917 S.W.2d at 727–729.

35. Ibid. at 725.

36. Ibid. at 729 (quoting *Edgewood I*, 777 S.W.2d at 397).

37. Kauffman, "The Texas School Finance Litigation Saga," 539. The source discusses Justice Cornyn's concurrence in *Edgewood III,* where he raised a number of issues not previously addressed in the *Edgewood* opinion or even raised in the *Edgewood III* case.

38. *Edgewood IV*, 917 S.W.2d at 731.

39. Ibid. at 731–732.

40. Ibid. at 731 n.12.

41. Ibid. at 732.

42. Ibid. at 726.

43. See West Orange–Cove Consolidated Independent School District v. Alanis (*Edgewood V-A*), 107 S.W.3d 558, 562 (Tex. 2003).

44. Ibid. at 574.

45. Ibid. at 575–576.

46. Ibid. at 583.

47. *Edgewood V*, 176 S.W.3d at 752.

48. Ibid. at 751 n.5.

49. Ibid. at 751 n.6.

50. Ibid. at 751.

51. West Orange–Cove Consolidated Independent School District v. Neeley, No. GV-100528, 2004 WL 5719215, *18 (Travis County Dist. Ct., 250th Jud. Dist., Tex. Nov. 30, 2004).

52. *Edgewood V*, 176 S.W.3d at 755.

53. See *Neeley*, 2004 WL 5719215, at *90.

54. Ibid. at *90, 109–110.

55. *Edgewood V*, 176 S.W.3d at 762.

56. Ibid.

57. Ibid. at 790 (citing *Edgewood IV*, 917 S.W.2d at 726).

58. Ibid. at 792.

59. Ibid.

60. Ibid.

61. Ibid. at 787.

62. Ibid. at 765, 769.
63. Ibid. The bilingual weight is set at .10 (10 percent) of the adjusted basic allotment, and the compensatory education allotment is set at .20 (20 percent). These weights were arbitrarily lowered to their respective numbers following a study conducted by the School Finance Working Group in 1984, which conservatively recommended that both weights be set at .40 (40 percent) of the adjusted basic allotment. *Neeley*, 2004 WL 5719215, at *72–73, 83.
64. *Edgewood V*, 176 S.W.3d at 757.
65. Ibid. at 789. The court apparently disregarded the fact that Texas ranked thirty-seventh among states.
66. Ibid. at 789–790.
67. Ibid. at 794.
68. Ibid. at 796–797.
69. Ibid. at 790.
70. Ibid. at 798.
71. Ibid. at 790.
72. Because this case is currently in litigation, I refer here only to facts and arguments made publicly in the case.
73. Some Houston-area school districts can raise their tax rates above the $1.17 tax cap, which is not the result of any education-related reason but pure political compromise.
74. Donna Clapp, "The Lone Star State Shines Bright in a Dark Economy," *Business Facilities*, March 2009, http://www.nxtbook.com/nxtbooks/groupc/bf_200903/index.php?startid=25#/26.
75. *Edgewood VI*, at *28.
76. Ibid. at *25, 90.
77. Ibid. at *24.
78. Ibid.
79. Ibid. at *31–32 and n.28.
80. David Hinojosa, "Closing Argument of Edgewood I.S.D., et al.," MALDEF, February 4, 2013, slide 35, http://www.maldef.org/assets/pdf/texas_school_finance_case_closing_arguement_PPT.pdf.
81. At the urging of MALDEF, the equal protection claim was eventually dropped. Although MALDEF believed in the soundness of the legal argument, it did not feel that this claim should be brought at this time.
82. *Edgewood VI*, at *2.
83. Ibid. at *210.
84. Ibid. at *202.
85. Ibid. at *187, 225–226.
86. Ibid. at *6, 90–96.
87. Ibid. at *231.
88. Ibid. at *244.
89. Ibid. at *230.
90. Ibid at *230–231.
91. Ibid. at *231.
92. Ibid. at *49–54.
93. Hinojosa, "Closing Argument of Edgewood I.S.D., et al.," 35.
94. *Edgewood VI*, at *5.

/

95. Ibid. at *49.
96. Texas Taxpayer and Student Fairness Coalition v. Williams, No. D-1-GN-11-003130, 2013 WL 459357, *5 (D. Tex. 2013).
97. *Edgewood VI*, at *2.
98. Ibid. at *12.
99. Ibid. at *9.
100. Kauffman, "The Texas School Finance Litigation Saga," 512.
101. See, for example, Michael A. Rebell, "Educational Adequacy, Democracy, and the Courts," in *Achieving High Educational Standards for All: Conference Summary*, ed. Timothy Ready, Christopher Edley, Jr., and Catherine E. Snow (Washington, DC: National Academies Press, 2002), 224, which cites *McInnis v. Shapiro*, 293 F. Supp. 327 (N.D. Ill. 1968), where the plaintiffs argued that the Illinois school funding system's minimum foundational funding was inadequate for disadvantaged urban students.
102. Ibid., 218.
103. Jeffrey S. Sutton, "*San Antonio Independent School District v. Rodriguez* and Its Aftermath," *Virginia Law Review* 94 (2008): 1972.
104. Ibid., 1972–1973.
105. Rebell, "Educational Adequacy, Democracy, and the Courts," 226.
106. Ibid., 227.
107. 790 S.W.2d 186 (Ky. 1989); 769 P.2d 684 (Mont. 1989).
108. Please see the appendix for this list of cases.
109. See William S. Koski, "Courthouses vs. Statehouses?" *Michigan Law Review* 109 (2011): 926, which reviews Eric A. Hanushek and Alfred A. Lindseth, *Schoolhouses, Courthouses, and Statehouses: Solving the Funding-Achievement Puzzle in America's Public Schools* (Princeton: Princeton University Press, 2009), and discusses the usefulness and uselessness of the courts judging the merits of school finance claims.
110. Serrano v. Priest, 557 P.2d 929, 951, 958 (Cal. 1976).
111. Rebell, "Educational Adequacy, Democracy, and the Courts," 227.
112. Robinson v. Cahill, 303 A.2d 273 (N.J. 1973).
113. Ibid. at 295.
114. "The History of Abbott v. Burke," Education Law Center, http://www.edlawcenter.org /cases/abbott-v-burke/abbott-history.html, accessed July 10, 2013.
115. In 1982 the Colorado Supreme Court denied an equity claim in *Lujan v. Colorado*, relying heavily on *Rodriguez*. See Lujan v. Colorado State Board of Education, 649 P.2d 1005 (Colo. 1982).
116. Lobato v. State, 218 P.3d 358 (Colo. 2009).
117. "Major MALDEF Victory in Landmark Colorado School Finance Case," MALDEF, http://www.maldef.org/news/releases/victory_lobato_colorado/ (findings available through link at bottom of press release).
118. Lobato v. State, 304 P.3d 1132, 1151–1160 (Colo. 2013) (Hobbs, J., dissenting); ibid. at 1140.
119. Ibid. at 1144 (Bender, C. J., dissenting).
120. Ibid. at 1147–1148.
121. But see Dwyer v. Colorado, No. 2014CV32543 (Colo. D. Ct. 2014). *Dwyer* is a lawsuit filed by parents and school districts charging that the state has failed to maintain funding levels at 1988 funding levels as required by a constitutional amendment. Although not a traditional school finance lawsuit, the claim does seek to force the

state to provide additional resources for public schools. See Jenny Brundin, "Parents, School Districts, File Lawsuit Asking State to Enforce Amendment 23," *Colorado Public Radio*, June 27, 2014, http://www.cpr.org/news/story/ parents-school -districts-file-lawsuit-asking-state-enforce-amendment-23.

122. Sutton, "*Rodriguez* and Its Aftermath," 1977.
123. Jonathan Kozol, *Savage Inequality, Children in America's Schools* (New York: Harper Perennial, 1992), 209.
124. See, for example, Lynn Huntley, foreword to *No Time to Lose: Why America Needs an Education Amendment to the US Constitution to Improve Public Education* (Atlanta: Southern Education Foundation, 2009), 1.
125. María "Cuca" Robledo Montecel, "Holding on to the Goal of Quality Education for Every Child," in *Courage to Connect: A Quality Schools Action Framework,* ed. María "Cuca" Robledo Montecel and Christie L. Goodman (San Antonio: Intercultural Development Research Association, 2010), xiii.
126. Irons, *The Courage of Their Convictions*, 302.

CHAPTER 3

1. Lani Guinier, "From Racial Liberalism to Racial Literacy: *Brown v. Board of Education* and the Interest-Divergence Dilemma," *Journal of American History* 91, no. 1 (2004): 92–118.
2. Peter Irons, *The Courage of Their Convictions: Sixteen Americans Who Fought Their Way to the Supreme Court* (New York: Penguin, 1988), 284; Richard R. Valencia, *Chicano Students and the Courts* (New York: New York University Press, 2008), 93; Richard Schragger, "*San Antonio v. Rodriguez* and the Legal Geography of School Finance Reform," in *Civil Rights Stories,* ed. Myriam E. Gilles and Risa L. Goluboff (St. Paul, MN: Foundation Press, 2008), 91, 92.
3. Gochman, Complaint Brief, Rodriguez v. San Antonio Independent School District, 337 F. Supp. 280 (W.D. Tex. 1971), reversed, 411 U.S. 1 (1973).
4. Rodriguez v. San Antonio Independent School District, 337 F. Supp. 280 (W.D. Tex. 1971), reversed, 411 U.S. 1 (1973); brief of ACLU et al. as amici curiae supporting respondents, San Antonio v. Rodriguez (No. 71-1332).
5. Testimony of Dr. Jose A. Cardenas, U.S. Senate Select Committee on Equal Educational Opportunity, *Part 4: Mexican American Education* (Washington, DC: Government Printing Office, 1970), 2443; affidavit of Dr. Jose A. Cardenas, Plaintiff's Exhibits in *Rodriguez,* available through the Curiae Project, Yale Law School, New Haven, CT; testimony of Sarah Carey, U.S. Senate Select Committee, *Part 16B: Inequality in School Finance* (Washington, DC, Government Printing Office, 1970), 6870, 6872.
6. U.S. Commission on Civil Rights, *Mexican-American Education Study, Report I: Ethnic: Isolation in the Public Schools of the Southwest* (Washington, DC: Government Printing Office, 1971), 7–8; Steven H. Wilson, "*Brown* Over 'Other White': Mexican Americans' Legal Arguments and Litigation Strategy in School Desegregation Lawsuits," *Law and History Review* 21, no. 1 (2003): 145; Guadalupe San Miguel, Jr., *"Let All of Them Take Heed": Mexican Americans and the Campaign for Educational Equality in Texas, 1910–1981* (Austin: University of Texas Press, 1987), 175; brief of Jack Greenberg et al. for NAACP Legal Defense Fund as amici curiae supporting respondents, Curiae Project.

7. Larry Hammond to Powell, memorandum, October 2, 1972, *San Antonio v. Rodriguez*, Series 10.6, Supreme Court Case Files, box 8-153, Lewis F. Powell, Jr., Papers, Washington and Lee University School of Law, Lexington, VA; brief of Wendell Anderson et al. for State Governors as amici curiae supporting respondents, Curiae Project; Arthur Gochman et al., Appellee's Motion to Affirm, filed May 17, 1972, 5, 7–8, Curiae Project; Irons, *The Courage of Their Convictions*, 325.

8. Powell to J. Harvie Wilkinson III, memorandum, August 30, 1972, *Rodriguez*, Powell Papers; undated conference notes, *Rodriguez*, Powell Papers.

9. Initial Vote Chart, *Rodriguez*, Powell Papers.

10. Undated revisions, *Rodriguez*, Powell Papers.

11. Camille Walsh, "Erasing Race, Dismissing Class: *San Antonio Independent School District v. Rodriguez*," *Berkeley La Raza Law Journal* 21 (2011): 133–171. See also Neil Gotanda, "A Critique of 'Our Constitution Is Color-Blind,'" *Stanford Law Review* 44 (1991): 17, 18.

12. Brief of Armando De Leon et al. for La Raza/ACLU as amici curiae supporting respondents, Curiae Project.

13. Guinier, "From Racial Liberalism to Racial Literacy," 7.

14. Melvyn P. Leffler, *The Specter of Communism: The United States and the Origins of the Cold War, 1917–1953* (New York: Hill & Wang, 1994), 24; Morton J. Horwitz, *The Warren Court and the Pursuit of Justice* (New York: Hill & Wang, 1999), 57; Dennis v. United States, 341 U.S. 494 (1951). See William M. Wiecek, "The Legal Foundations of Domestic Anticommunism: The Background of *Dennis v. United States*," *Supreme Court Review* 2001 (2001): 375.

15. For a discussion of the Jenner-Butler bill, see Barry Friedman, "'Things Forgotten' in the Debate over Judicial Independence," *Georgia State University Law Review* 14, no. 737 (1997–1998): 751–752.

16. Brief for the United States, *Brown v. Board of Education* 347 U.S. 483 (1954) (Nos. 1, 2, 4, 10).

17. Mary Dudziak, *Cold War Civil Rights: Race and the Image of American Democracy* (Princeton: Princeton University Press, 2001); Gerald N. Rosenberg, *The Hollow Hope: Can Courts Bring About Social Change?* (Chicago: University of Chicago Press, 2008), 162; Martha Biondi, *To Stand and Fight: The Struggle for Civil Rights in Postwar New York City* (Cambridge, MA: Harvard University Press, 2006), 182–183.

18. Lewis F. Powell, Jr., to Eugene B. Sydnor, Jr., "Attack on American Free Enterprise System," August 23, 1971, box 51-167, Powell Papers; Lyman Johnson, "Justice Powell and Free Enterprise," *Richmond Times-Dispatch,* August 24, 2011, http://www.timesdispatch.com/news/johnson-justice-powell-and-free-enterprise/article_81f16d98-369f-502a-b84c-55835324d612.html.

19. John C. Jeffries, Jr., *Justice Lewis F. Powell, Jr.: A Biography* (New York: Fordham University Press, 2001), 166–167, quoted in Paul Sracic, "The *Brown* Decision's Other Legacy: Civic Education and the *Rodriguez* Case," *PS: Political Science and Politics* 2 (2004): 214, 217.

20. Powell to Hammond memorandum, October 9, 1972, 1–3, *Rodriguez*, Powell Papers.

21. Brief by George W. Liebmann et al. as amici curiae supporting respondents, 6, Curiae Project; brief by Shale C. Stiller et al. for State Government Representatives as amici curiae supporting respondents, 68, Curiae Project.

22. John E. Coons, William H. Chine III, and Stephen D. Sugarman, *Private Wealth and Public Education* (Cambridge, MA: Harvard University Press, 1970); Stiller et al. brief, 37, 47, citing James Coleman, "The Struggle for Control of Education," in *Education and Social Policy* 64 (1970): 77–78 .

23. Stiller et al. brief, 83–88.

24. JWZ to Blackmun, memorandum, October 4, 1972, box 161, folder 5, *Rodriguez* file, Papers of Harry Blackmun, Library of Congress, Washington, DC; oral arguments in *San Antonio v. Rodriguez,* presented October 12, 1972, http://www.oyez.org/oyez /resource/case/343/audioresources.

25. N. Peters to Powell, March 26, 1973, *Rodriguez*, Powell Papers.

26. "Abolishing the Department of Education Is the Right Thing to Do," Julie Borowski, September 19, 2011, *Tea Party Tribune*, http://www.teapartytribune.com/2011/09/19 /abolishing-the-department-of-education-is-the-right-thing-to-do/.

27. Kimberlé Crenshaw, "Mapping the Margins: Intersectionality, Identify Politics and Violence Against Women of Color," *Stanford Law Review* 43 (1993): 1298.

28. Michael Klarman, "An Interpretive History of Modern Equal Protection," *Michigan Law Review* 90 (November 1991): 281, 282, 287, 290.

29. McDonald v. Board of Election Commissioners, 394 U.S. 802, 807 (1969).

30. Van Dusartz v. Hatfield, 334 F. Supp. 870 (D. Minn. 1971); Serrano v. Priest, 487 P.2d 1241 (Cal. 1971), *cert. denied*, 432 U.S. 907 (1977); Robinson v. Cahill, 287 A.2d 187 (N.J. 1972), *cert. denied*, 414 U.S. 976 (1973).

31. See, for example, *Skinner v. Oklahoma*, 316 U.S. 535 (1942) (ruling that forced sterilization of habitual criminals unconstitutional for impinging on fundamental right to procreate); *Edwards v. California*, 314 U.S. 160 (1941) (ruling a state statute prohibiting bringing an indigent person into the state unconstitutional because interstate travel constituted a fundamental right); *Boddie v. Connecticut*, 401 U.S. 371 (1971) (ruling that filing fee for divorce imposed on a fundamental right of marriage for indigent people).

32. Kenneth Karst, "Foreword: Equal Citizenship under the Fourteenth Amendment," *Harvard Law Review* 91 (November 1977): 60, 66.

33. Larry Hammond to Powell, March 21, 1973, *Rodriguez*, Powell Papers.

34. Lewis Powell to William Brennan et al., memorandum, January 30, 1982, box 154, folder 6, *Plyler* file, Blackmun Papers; Klarman, "Interpretive History," 288.

35. Testimony of Mario Obledo, U.S. Senate Select Committee, *Part 4: Mexican American Education*, 2522.

CHAPTER 4

1. San Antonio Independent School District v. Rodriguez, 411 U.S. 1 (1973).

2. Ibid. at 30.

3. Shapiro v. Thompson, 394 U.S. 618 (1969).

4. Brown v. Board of Education, 347 U.S. 483, 493 (1954).

5. The Court implicitly acknowledged this reality when, incongruously, it pointed out in *Rodriguez* that not only in *Brown* but also in a long list of other cases it had emphasized the critical role education plays in our society. *Rodriguez,* 411 U.S. at 29–30.

6. Plyler v. Doe, 457 U.S. 202 (1982).

7. Current information on the status of these litigations nationwide is available from the National Education Access Network, http://www.schoolfunding.info.

8. David C. Long, *"Rodriguez:* The State Courts' Response," *Phi Delta Kappan* 64 (1983): 481–482.

9. Serrano v. Priest, 557 P.2d 929, 949–952 (Cal. 1976).

10. Robinson v. Cahill, 303 A.2d 273 (N.J. 1973); Horton v. Meskill, 376 A.2d 359 (Conn. 1977); Pauley v. Kelly, 255 S.E.2d 859 (W. Va. 1979).

11. For a detailed discussion and analysis of the state court education adequacy cases, see Michael A. Rebell, *Courts and Kids: Pursuing Educational Equity Through the State Courts* (Chicago: University of Chicago Press, 2009).

12. Ga. Const., art. VIII, § 1; N.Y. Const., art. XI, § 1. The specific language in the New York constitutional provision states that "the legislature shall provide for the maintenance and support of a system of free common schools, wherein all of the children of this state may be educated." The New York court of appeals has interpreted the concept of "educated" in this provision to mean "a sound basic education." Levittown v. Nyquist 439 N.E.2d 359, 368–369 (1982); N.J. Const., art. IV, § 1; Mont. Const., art. X, § 1.

13. See Mass. Const., pt. 2, ch. 5, §2; McDuffy v. Secretary of Education, 615 N.E. 2d 516, 545 (Mass. 1993).

14. Robinson v. Cahill, 303 A.2d 273, 295 (N.J. 1973); Campaign for Fiscal Equity, Inc. v. State, 801 N.E.2d 326, 330–331 (N.Y. 2003) (*CFEII*).

15. Williams v. California, First Amended Complaint, ¶ 280 (No. 312236, Cal. Sup. Ct, 2000).

16. *CFE II*, 801 N.E.2d at 334 n.4.

17. National Commission on Excellence in Education, *A Nation at Risk: The Imperative for Educational Reform* (Washington, DC: U.S. Department of Education, 1983), 5.

18. 20 U.S.C.A. § 6301 et. seq. (2001).

19. Eric A. Hanushek, "The Quest for Equalized Mediocrity: School Finance Reform Without Consideration of School Performance," in *Where Does the Money Go? Resource Allocation in Elementary and Secondary Schools,* ed. Lawrence O. Picus and James L. Wattenbarger (Thousand Oaks, CA: Corwin Press, 1996), 26–27.

20. Richard J. Murnane, "Interpreting the Evidence on 'Does Money Matter," *Harvard Journal on Legislation* 28, no. 2 (1991): 457, 458; Corrine Taylor, "Does Money Matter? An Empirical Study Introducing Resource Costs and Students Needs to Education Production Function Analysis," in *Developments in School Finance, 1997* (Washington, DC: U.S. Department of Education, National Center for Education Statistics, 1998), 75, 78.

21. David Card and Alan B. Krueger, "Does School Quality Matter? Returns to Education and the Characteristics of Public Schools in the United States," *Journal of Political Economy* 100, no. 1 (1992): 1–2.

22. Richard Laine et al., "Does Money Matter? A Research Synthesis of a New Universe of Education Production Function Studies," in *Where Does the Money Go? Resource Allocation in Elementary and Secondary Schools,* ed. Lawrence O. Picus and James L. Wattenbarger (Thousand Oaks, CA: Corwin Press, 1996), 44, 46–47.

23. Rob Greenwald, Larry V. Hedges, and Richard D. Laine, "The Effect of School Resources on Student Achievement," *Review of Educational Research* 66, no. 3 (1996): 362.

24. See, for example, C. Kirabo Jackson, Rucker Johnson, and Claudia Persico, "The Effect of School Finance Reforms on the Distribution of Spending, Academic Achievement and Adult Outcomes" (working paper 20118, National Bureau of Economic Studies, Washington, DC, 2014), http://www.nber.org/papers/w20118. This finds that

a 20 percent increase in annual per-pupil spending for K–12 low-income students leads to almost one more year of completed education, 25 percent higher earnings, and a 20 percent decrease in adult poverty.

25. Montoy v. State of Kansas, No. 99-C-1738, 3003 WL 22902902963 (Kan. Dist. Ct. Dec. 2, 2003), *aff'd*, 112 P.3d 923 (Kan. 2005). See also, for example, Rose v. The Council for Better Education, 790 S.W.2d 186, 197 (1989) ("Achievement test scores in the poorer districts are lower than those of rich districts and expert testimony clearly established that there is a correlation between those scores and the wealth of the district").

26. For a specific discussion of these cases, see Michael A. Rebell, "Poverty, 'Meaningful Educational Opportunity' and the Necessary Role of the Courts," *North Carolina Law Review* 85 (2007): 1476–1487.

27. Ibid. The one exception was City of Pawtucket v. Sundblum, 662 A.2d 40, 62 n.10 (RI 1995), which relied on a vaguely referenced study which claimed that parental involvement was the most influential aspect of a child's educational opportunities and that dollars expended did not have an impact on the education a child received. Rebell, "Poverty, 'Meaningful Educational Opportunity,'" 62 n.10.

28. *Montoy*, 3003 WL 22902902963, *49 n.31.

29. "Courts can navigate well through (disputed) social science arguments regarding educational outcomes, educational inputs (the education production function), and the deployment of teacher inputs. Moreover, rulings themselves can offer useful guidance to researchers on what fields of inquiry are important for resolving key public policy concerns, on what empirical evidence and which methodologies are deemed most valid, as well as indicate new areas for academic interest." Clive R. Belfield and Henry M. Levin, "The Economics of Education on Judgment Day," *Journal of Education Finance* 28 (Fall 2002): 182, 205.

30. New State Ice Co. v. Liebmann, 285 U.S. 262, 311 (1932) (Brandeis, J., dissenting).

31. These figures are drawn from National Education Access Network, http://www.school funding.info.

32. See, for example, Gordon MacInnes, *In Plain Sight: Simple, Difficult Lessons from New Jersey's Expensive Effort to Close the Achievement Gap* (New York: Century Foundation Press, 2009*)*, 35–37; William N. Evans, Sheila E. Murray, and Robert M. Schwab, "The Impact of Court-Mandated Finance Reform," in *Equity and Adequacy in Education Finance: Issues and Perspectives*, ed. Helen Ladd et al. (Washington, DC: National Academies Press, 1999), 72, 77 (a study of ten thousand school districts from 1972 to 1992 found that court-ordered reform leveled up disparities and increased overall spending on education); Peter Schrag, *Final Test: The Battle for Adequacy in America's Schools* (New York: New Press, 2003) (finding that litigation in Kentucky, Massachusetts, and other states has led to noticeable improvements in student achievement); Margaret Goertz, Susanna Loeb, and Jim Wyckoff, "Recruiting, Evaluating and Retaining Teachers: The Children First Strategy to Improve New York City's Teachers," in *Education Reform in New York City: Ambitious Change in the Nation's Most Complex School System*, ed. Jennifer A. O'Day, Catherine S. Bitter, and Louis M. Gomez (Cambridge, MA: Harvard Education Press, 2011), 157, 166 (in New York City, as a result of the *CFE* litigation, "the qualifications of teachers in the schools with the greatest proportion of poor students improved dramatically between 2000 and 2005").

33. See, for example, Larry J. Obhof, "DeRolph v. State and Ohio's Long Road to an Adequate Education," *Brigham Young University Education and Law Journal* 2005 (2005): 83–149.
34. Jonathan Kozol, *The Shame of the Nation: The Restoration of Apartheid Schooling in America* (New York: Random House, 2006), 249.
35. National Commission on Equity and Excellence in Education, *For Each and Every Child: A Strategy for Education Equity and Excellence* (Washington, DC: U.S. Department of Education, 2013), 17. I was a member of this commission.
36. Ibid.
37. Ibid., 12.
38. Ibid., 17.
39. Ibid., 18–19. The commission also called for major reforms in the recruitment, retention, preparation, evaluation, and compensation of teachers, a guarantee of universal access to high-quality pre-K programs for all low-income children, and health, extended day, parent engagement, and other comprehensive, wraparound services to meet the needs of at-risk students.
40. Ibid., 9 (such an opportunity "should be the birthright of each and every American child").
41. For further discussion of these recommendations, see David G. Sciarra and Danielle Farrie, "From *Rodriguez* to *Abbott:* New Jersey's Standards-Linked School Funding Reform," chapter 6, this volume.
42. Susan H. Bitensky, "Theoretical Foundations for a Right to Education under the U.S. Constitution: A Beginning to the End of the National Education Crisis," *Northwestern University Law Review* 86 (1992): 552–553.
43. *Rodriguez*, 411 U.S. at 24 (citations omitted).
44. Papasan v. Allain, 478 U.S. 265, 285 (1986).
45. Quoted in Bitensky, "Theoretical Foundations," 615 n.378.
46. Almost all of the courts that have found for defendants have, however, done so on justiciability or separation of powers grounds, dismissing the complaints before they went to trial or without purporting to review the trial evidence that had been presented. See Rebell, *Courts and Kids*, 22–29.
47. Rodriguez, 411 U.S. at 36–37.
48. Ibid. at 36–37.
49. See, for example, Shaw v. Reno, 509 U.S. 630, 639 (1993) (avowing the principle that the right to vote is essential to democracy); Burdick v. Takushi, 504 U.S. 428, 441 (1992) ("the right to vote is the right to participate in an electoral process that is necessarily structured to maintain the integrity of the democratic system"); Board of Estimate of New York v. Morris, 489 U.S. 688, 698 (1989) ("the personal right to vote is a value in itself"); Harper v. Virginia Board of Elections, 383 U.S. 663, 670 (1966) ("wealth or fee paying has, in our view, no relation to voting qualifications; the right to vote is too precious, too fundamental to be so burdened or conditioned"); Wesberry v. Sanders, 376 U.S. 1, 17 (1964) ("no right is more precious in a free country than that of having a voice in the election of those who make the laws under which, as good citizens, we must live. Other rights, even the most basic, are illusory if the right to vote is undermined"); Reynolds v. Sims, 377 U.S. 533, 567 (1964) ("to the extent that a citizen's right to vote is debased, he is that much less a citizen"); Yick Wo v. Hopkins, 118

U.S. 356, 370 (1886) ("[the right to vote] is regarded as a fundamental political right, because preservative of all rights").

50. 719 N.Y.S.2d 475 (N.Y. Sup. Ct. 2001), *aff'd*, 801 N.E.2d 326 (N.Y. 2003). I was co-counsel for plaintiffs in this litigation.

51. Campaign for Fiscal Equity, Inc. v. State, 719 N.Y.S.2d 475, 485 (N.Y. Sup. Ct. 2001).

52. See, for example, Philip B. Kurland, "The Privileges or Immunities Clause: Its Hour Come Round at Last?" *Washington University Law Quarterly* (1972): 405, 419 (finding a federal right to education in the privileges and immunity clause); Penelope A. Preovolos, "*Rodriguez* Revisited: Federalism, Meaningful Access, and the Right to Adequate Education," *Santa Clara Law Review* 20 (1980): 75–76 (distinguishing *Rodriguez* as a federalism case that does not preclude the existence of a federal right to education); Julius Chambers, "Adequate Education for All: A Right, an Achievable Goal," *Harvard Civil Rights–Civil Liberties Law Review* 22 (1987): 69–72 (setting forth a number of constitutional and international law bases for recognizing a federal right to education); Bitensky, "Theoretical Foundations for a Right to Education under the U.S. Constitution," 552–553 (finding a variety of constitutional anchors for a right to education in the Fourteenth Amendment's Due Process Clause, the Privileges or Immunities Clause, the First Amendment's Free Speech Clause, the right to vote, and other implied constitutional rights); Nicholas A. Palumbo, "Protecting Access to Extracurricular Activities: The Need to Recognize a Fundamental Right to a Minimally Adequate Education," *Brigham Young University Education and Law Journal* 393 (2004): 408–412 (arguing that the decision in *Lawrence v. Texas*, 539 U.S. 558 (2003) provides relevant precedent for the existence of fundamental interests that are not explicitly mentioned in the Constitution); Kimberly Jenkins Robinson, "The Case for a Collaborative Enforcement Model for a Federal Right to Education," *UC Davis Law Review* 40 (2007): 1712–1716 (proposing that Congress recognize a more than minimal right to education based on the International Covenant on Economic, Social and Cultural Rights, and the Convention on the Rights of the Child); "A Right to Learn? Improving Educational Outcomes Through Substantive Due Process," *Harvard Law Review* 120 (2007): 1341–1344 (arguing that the compulsory nature of public education provides a substantive due process right to education based on the precedent of *Youngberg v. Romeo*, 457 U.S. 307 (1982)).

53. Goodwin Liu, "Education, Equality and National Citizenship," *Yale Law Journal* 116 (2006): 333; Akhil Reed Amar, *America's Unwritten Constitution: The Precedents and Principles We Live By* (New York: Basic Books, 2012). Liu is an associate justice of the California Supreme Court and was a professor of law at Boalt Law School at the University of California, Berkeley. Amar is a professor of law and political science at Yale University.

54. Liu, "Education, Equality and National Citizenship," 357.

55. *Congressional Globe,* 41st Cong., 2d Sess., app., 478 (1870) (statement of Rep. Hoar); H.R. 1326, 41st Cong. (2d sess. 1870).

56. Liu, "Education, Equality and National Citizenship," 378.

57. 83 U.S. 36 (1872); 109 U.S. 3 (1883).

58. Amar, *America's Unwritten Constitution.*

59. Ibid., 408: "Later amendments often contain powerful although unwritten, gravitational pull that invite reinterpretation of earlier amendments so that the constitution as a whole coheres as a sensible system of rules and principles."

60. Ibid., 108.
61. Carl F. Kaestle, "Equal Educational Opportunity, the Federal Government, and the United States Constitution: An Interpretive Synthesis" (working paper, Southern Education Foundation Study Group, Atlanta, 2006), 38; Ted Shaw, former executive director, NAACP Legal Defense Fund, quoted in Kozol, *The Shame of the Nation*, 254.
62. 147 Cong. Rec., 26,593 (2001) (statement of Sen. Russ Feingold).
63. Ibid. at 26,601 (statement of Sen. Blanche Lincoln).
64. Ibid. at 26,134 (statement of Rep. John Boehner).
65. 20 U.S.C. § 6301 (2006). For a full discussion of this point, see Michael A. Rebell, "The Right to Comprehensive Educational Opportunity," *Harvard Civil Rights–Civil Liberties Law Review* 47 (2012): 64–71.
66. Lawrence A. Cremin, *American Education: The National Experience 1783–1876* (New York: Harper & Row, 1980), 3.
67. For a detailed discussion of this point, see Michael A. Rebell, "Safeguarding the Right to a Sound Basic Education in Times of Fiscal Constraint," *Albany Law Review* 75 (2012): 1920–1956.
68. See, for example, *No Time to Lose: Why American Needs and Education Amendment to the U.S. Constitution to Improve Public Education* (Atlanta: Southern Education Foundation, 2009).

CHAPTER 5

1. Milliken v. Bradley, 418 U.S. 717, 741–742 (1974).
2. San Antonio Independent School District v. Rodriguez, 411 U. S. 1, 40, 55 (1973).
3. See, for example, Margaret E. Goertz and Michael Weiss, "Assessing Success in School Finance Litigation: The Case of New Jersey," *Education, Equity, and the Law* 1 (2009), http://www.equitycampaign.org/i/a/document/11775_edequitylawno1.pdf; Jennifer Imazaki and Andrew Reschovcky, "School Finance Reform in Texas: A Never Ending Story?" in *Helping Children Left Behind: State Aid and the Pursuit of Educational Equity*, ed. John Yinger (Cambridge, MA: Massachusetts Institute of Technology Press, 2004), 1–42; Juliana Herman, *School-Finance Reform: Inspiration and Progress in Colorado* (Washington, DC: Center for American Progress, 2013), http://cdn.americanprogress.org/wp-content/uploads/2013/06/HermanCOschoolFinance-1.pdf.
4. Molly McUsic, "The Law's Role in the Distribution of Education: The Promises and Pitfalls of School Finance Litigation," in *Law and School Reform: Six Strategies for Promoting Educational Equity*, ed. Jay P. Heubert (New Haven: Yale University Press, 1990), 88–159.
5. Gary Orfield, John Kucsera, and Genevieve Siegel-Hawley, *E Pluribus . . . Separation: Deepening Double Segregation for More Students* (Los Angeles: UCLA Civil Rights Project, 2012), http://civilrightsproject.ucla.edu/research/k-12-education/integration-and -diversity/mlk-national/e-pluribus...separation-deepening-double-segregation-for-more -students/orfield_epluribus_revised_omplete_2012.pdf.
6. William Frey, "Melting Pot Suburbs: A Study of Suburban Diversity," in *Redefining Urban and Suburban America*, ed., Bruce Katz and Robert E. Lang (Washington, DC: Brookings Institution, 2003), 155–180; Elizabeth Kneebone and Alan Berube, *Confronting Suburban Poverty in America* (Washington, DC: Brookings Institution, 2013); Barrett A. Lee et al., "Beyond the Census Tract: Patterns and Determinants of Racial Segregation at Multiple Geographic Scales," *American Sociological Review* 73, no. 5

(2008): 766–791; Chrisopher B. Leinberger, "The Next Slum?" *The Atlantic Monthly*, March 1, 2008, http://www.theatlantic.com/doc/200803/subprime.

7. Alan Ehrenhalt, *The Great Inversion and Future of the American City* (New York: First Vintage Books, 2013).

8. James E. Farley and Gregory D. Squires, "Fences and Neighbors: Segregation in 21st-Century America," *Contexts* 4, no. 1 (2005): 33–39; Kneebone and Berube, *Confronting Suburban Poverty*; Patrick Sharkey, *Stuck in Place: Urban Neighborhoods and the End of Progress Toward Racial Equality* (Chicago: University of Chicago Press, 2013).

9. Orfield, Kucsera, and Siegel-Hawley, *E Pluribus;* John Yun and Sean Reardon, "Patterns of Multiracial Private School Segregation," in *School Choice and Diversity: What the Evidence Says,* ed. Janelle Scott (New York: Teachers College Press, 2005); George Galster and Jason Booza, "The Rise of the Bipolar Neighborhood," *Journal of the American Planning Association* 73, no. 4 (2007): 421–435.

10. Lee et al.,"Beyond the Census Tract"; Kendra Bischoff and Sean F. Reardon, *Segregation in Suburban Schools: Changing Demographics and School District Fragmentation* (working paper, Stanford University, Palo Alto, CA, 2009).

11. R. Burke Johnson, "Knowledge," in *Sage Encyclopedia of Qualitative Research Methods*, ed. L. M. Given (Thousand Oaks, CA: Sage, 2007), 478–482.

12. Amy Stuart Wells et al., *Divided We Fall: The Story of Separate and Unequal Suburban Schools 60 Years after* Brown v. Board of Education (New York: Center for Understanding Race and Education, Teachers College, Columbia University, 2014), http://www.tc.columbia.edu/cure/.

13. Kendra Bischoff, "School District Fragmentation and Racial Residential Segregation: How Do Boundaries Matter?" *Urban Affairs Review* 44, no. 2 (2008): 197.

14. Ibid.

15. Charles T. Clotfelter, "Public School Segregation in Metropolitan Areas," *Land Economics* 75, no. 4 (1999), http://www.jstor.org/stable/pdfplus/3147061.pdf?acceptTC =true; Douglas Ready, *Inter-District and Intra-District Segregation on Long Island* (Garden City, NY: Long Island Index, The Rauch Foundation, 2012), 6.

16. Bruce Baker, David Sciarra, and Danielle Farrie, *Is School Funding Fair? A National Report Card* (Newark: Education Law Center and Rutgers Graduate School of Education, 2012), 12–15, http://www.schoolfundingfairness.org/National_Report_Card_2012.pdf; Mark Dixon, *Public Education Finances: 2012* (Washington, DC: U.S. Census Bureau, 2014), 8 tbl. 8, http://www2.census.gov/school/12f33pub.pdf.

17. Ibid., 11.

18. See A. S. Wells, L. Fox, M. Warner, D. Ready, A. Wright, and A. Roda, "Studying the *Process* of Re-segregation in Public Education: The Role of Mixed-Methods Research and Reflexive Sociology" (unpublished manuscript, 2015).

19. The named district and school names are pseudonyms.

20. For a more detailed description of our mixed-methods design and data collection and analysis, see our methodological appendix in Amy Stuart Wells et al., *Divided We Fall. The Story of Separate and Unequal Suburban Schools 60 Years after* Brown v. Board of Education (New York: Center for Understanding Race and Education, Teachers College, Columbia University, 2014), http://www.tc.columbia.edu/cure/.

21. Annette Lareau, *Unequal Childhoods: Race, Class and Family Life* (Berkeley: University of California Press, 2003).

22. Gloria Ladson-Billings, "From the Achievement Gap to the Education Debt: Understanding Achievement in U.S. Schools," *Educational Researcher* 35, no. 7 (2006): 3–12.

23. James E. Ryan, *Five Miles Away, a World Apart: One City, Two Schools, and the Story of Educational Opportunity in Modern America* (New York: Oxford University Press, 2010), 161–164.

24. Wells et al., *Divided We Fall*.

25. Ibid.

26. Amy Stuart Wells et al., *Boundary Crossing for Diversity, Equity and Achievement: Interdistrict School Desegregation and Educational Opportunity* (Cambridge, MA: Charles Hamilton Houston Institute for Race and Justice, 2009), http://www.onenationindivisible.org/wp-content/uploads/2012/03/Wells_BoundaryCrossing.pdf.

27. See Wells et al., *Divided We Fall*; Amy Stuart Wells, "The Diverse Suburbs Movement Has Never Been So Relevant," *City Lab/The Atlantic*, October 3, 2014, http://www.citylab.com/politics/2014/10/the-diverse-suburbs-movement-has-never-been-more-relevant/381061/.

CHAPTER 6

1. San Antonio Independent School District v. Rodriguez, 411 U.S. 1, 11–15 (1973); Edgewood Independent School District v. Kirby, 777 S.W.2d 391 (Tex. 1989) (*Edgewood I*); Edgewood Independent School District v. Kirby, 917 S.W.2d 717 (Tex. 1995) (*Edgewood IV*); Neeley v. West Orange–Cove Independent School District, 176 S.W.3d 746 (Tex. 2005). See also Texas Taxpayer and Student Fairness Coalition (TTFSC) v. Williams, No. D-1-GN-11-003130 (Travis County Dist. Ct. Aug. 28, 2014) (currently on appeal to the Texas Supreme Court).

2. The extensive history of *Abbott v. Burke* and the twenty-one New Jersey Supreme Court rulings in the case can be found at www.edlawcenter.org and www.educationjustice.org.

3. N.J.S.A. § 18A:7F-43-63 (2008). See the full version of the New Jersey School Funding Reform Act of 2008 at http://www.njleg.state.nj.us/2006/bills/A0500/500_I2.pdf.

4. Bruce D. Baker, David G. Sciarra, and Danielle Farrie. *Is School Funding Fair? A National Report Card* (Newark: Education Law Center, 2010), 7, http://www.schoolfundingfairness.org/National_Report_Card_2010.pdf.

5. Ibid.

6. See, for example, W. S. Barnett, "Effectiveness of Early Educational Intervention," *Science* 333, no. 6045 (2011): 975–978, doi: 10.1126/science.1204534; Jennifer Sloan McCombs et al., *Making Summer Count: How Summer Programs Can Boost Children's Learning* (Santa Monica, CA: RAND, 2011), http://www.rand.org/pubs/monographs/MG1120.html; Margo Gardner, Jodie L. Roth, and Jeanne Brooks-Gunn, *Can After-School Programs Help Level the Academic Playing Field for Disadvantaged Youth?* (New York: Teachers College, Columbia University, 2009).

7. Richard Rothstein, *Class and Schools: Using Social, Economic, and Educational Reform to Close the Black-White Achievement Gap* (Washington, DC: Economic Policy Institute, 2004).

8. Bruce Baker, *Revisiting That Age-Old Question: Does Money Matter in Education?* (Washington, DC: Albert Shanker Institute, 2012), http://www.shankerinstitute.org/images/doesmoneymatter_final.pdf.

9. David Card and A. Abigail Payne, "School Finance Reform, the Distribution of School Spending, and the Distribution of Student Test Scores," *Journal of Public Economics* 83 (2002): 49–82.

10. C. Kirabo Jackson, Rucker Johnson, and Claudia Persico, "The Effect of School Finance Reforms on the Distribution of Spending, Academic Achievement, and Adult Outcomes" (working paper 20118, National Bureau of Economic Research, Washington, DC, 2014), http://www.nber.org/papers/w20118.

11. See, for example, Joydeep Roy, "Impact of School Finance Reform on Resource Equalization and Academic Performance: Evidence from Michigan," *Education Finance and Policy* 6, no. 2 (2011): 137–167; John Deke, "A Study of the Impact of Public School Spending on Postsecondary Educational Attainment Using Statewide School District Refinancing in Kansas," *Economics of Education Review* 22, no. 3 (2003): 275–284; Dana Ansel, Tom Downes, and Jeff Zabel, *Incomplete Grade: Massachusetts Education Reform at 15* (Boston: MassINC, 2009).

12. For a review, see Diane Whitmore Schanzenbach, *Does Class Size Matter?* (Boulder: National Education Policy Center, 2012), http://nepc.colorado.edu/files/pb_-_class _size.pdf.

13. Richard J. Murnane and Randall Olsen, "The Effects of Salaries and Opportunity Costs on Length of State in Teaching: Evidence from Michigan," *Review of Economics and Statistics* 71, no. 2 (1989): 347–352; David N. Figlio, "Teacher Salaries and Teacher Quality," *Economics Letters* 55 (1997): 267–271; Susanna Loeb and Marianne Page, "Examining the Link Between Teacher Wages and Student Outcomes: The Importance of Alternative Labor Market Opportunities and Non-Pecuniary Variation," *Review of Economics and Statistics* 82, no. 3 (2000): 393–408.

14. Bruce Baker, Danielle Farrie, and David Sciarra, *Mind the Gap: 20 Years of Progress and Retrenchment in School Funding and Achievement Gaps* (Princeton: Educational Testing Service, forthcoming).

15. *Digest of Education Statistics 2013* (Washington, DC: U.S. Department of Education, 2014), table 204.10, http://nces.ed.gov/programs/digest/d11/.

16. Ibid.

17. Susan Aud et al., *The Condition of Education 2014* (Washington, DC: U.S. Department of Education, 2014), 74.

18. See, for example, Richard D. Kahlenburg, *All Together Now: Creating Middle-Class Schools Through Public School Choice* (Washington, DC: Brookings Institution Press, 2001); Heather Schwartz, *Housing Policy Is School Policy* (New York: Century Foundation, 2010), http://tcf.org/assets/downloads/tcf-Schwartz.pdf.

19. Bruce D. Baker, David G. Sciarra, and Danielle Farrie, *Is School Funding Fair? A National Report Card,* 4th ed. (Newark: Education Law Center, 2015), http://www .schoolfundingfairness.org/National_Report_Card_2015.pdf.

20. Education Law Center, "The Right Way to Compare NJ Education Funding," http:// www.edlawcenter.org/research/school-funding-data.html#FWP.

21. Abbott v. Burke, 149 N.J. 145, 161 (1997) (*Abbott IV*).

22. Abbott v. Burke, 119 N.J. 287, 345–346 (1990) (*Abbott II*).

23. *Abbott IV,* 149 N.J. at 161.

24. Ibid. at 168.

25. Ibid. at 167–168. In 2005, the Kansas Supreme Court accepted state academic standards as the substantive definition of a constitutional education. See Montoy v. State,

102 P.3d 1160 (Kan. 2005). The New York court of appeals, however, declined to accept the state's Regents' standards to define the constitutional guarantee to New York schoolchildren. See Campaign for Fiscal Equity v. State, 100 N.Y.2d 893, 907 (2003).

26. *Abbott IV,* 149 N.J. at 168.

27. Ibid.

28. Ibid. at 169.

29. Ibid. at 176.

30. Ibid.

31. Ibid.

32. Abbott v. Burke, 153 N.J. 480, 562 (1998) (*Abbott V*); *Abbott IV,* 149 N.J. at 196. The court ruled that CIEFA's categorical aids for K–12 supplemental programs and preschool were also unconstitutional because the aid amounts were not based on any study of the actual needs of the students in those districts. Ibid. at 153. After extensive hearings, the court, a year later, ordered funding and implementation of a package of supplemental K–12 programs and high-quality preschool for three- and four-year-olds. *Abbott V,* 153 N.J. 480.

33. See Sherri C. Lauver, Gary W. Ritter, and Margaret E. Goertz, "Caught in the Middle: The Fate of the Non-Urban Districts in the Wake of New Jersey's School Finance Litigation," *Journal of Education Finance* 26 (Winter 2001): 281–296.

34. For a summary of the process of creating the school funding formula, see *Abbott VI,* 196 N.J. 552–555.

35. N.J.S.A. § 18A:7F-43-63 (2008). See the full version of the New Jersey School Funding Reform Act of 2008 at http://www.njleg.state.nj.us/2006/bills/A0500/500_I2.pdf.

36. The census-based methodology for funding special education and speech programs uses the statewide average classification rate to determine special education funding instead of each district's actual classification rates. The statewide classification rates for speech and special education are multiplied by each district's total enrollment and then by the excess cost of educating special education and speech students. Ellen Boylan and Shad White, *Formula for Success: Adding High-Quality Pre-K to State School Funding Formulas* (Washington, DC: Pew Center on the States, 2010), 15.

37. Abbott v. Burke, 199 N.J. 140, 172 (2009) (*Abbott XX*).

38. Ibid. at 172, quoting *Abbott V,* 153 N.J. at 528.

39. Ibid. at 169.

40. Ibid.

41. Abbott v. Burke, 206 N.J. 332, 359–360 (2011).

42. Education Law Center, "Governor's FY14 State Aid Proposal: The Underfunding of SFRA: FY10–FY14," http://www.edlawcenter.org/research/school-funding-data .html#FY14.

43. Margaret E. Goertz and Michael Weiss, *Assessing Success in School Finance Litigation: The Case of New Jersey, Education, Equity, and the Law* 1 (New York: Campaign for Educational Equity, Teachers College, 2009), http://www.equitycampaign.org/i/a /document/11775_edequitylawno1.pdf.

44. Alexandra M. Resch, "Three Essays on Resources in Education" (PhD diss., University of Michigan, 2008).

45. W. Steven Barnett et al., *Abbott Preschool Program Longitudinal Effects Study: Fifth Grade Follow-Up* (New Brunswick, NJ: National Institute for Early Education Research, 2013), http://nieer.org/sites/nieer/files/APPLES%205th%20Grade.pdf.

46. For an in-depth review of the substantial progress made by one of the special needs districts, Union City, see David Kirp, *Improbable Scholars: The Rebirth of a Great American School System and a Strategy for America's Schools* (Oxford: Oxford University Press, 2012).

47. *Abbott IV,* 149 N.J. at 169.

48. *Abbott XX,* 199 N.J. at 147.

49. Only a few other states utilized elements of state academic standards to determine education costs for their respective funding formulas. See Campbell City School District v. State, 907 P.2d 1238 (Wyo. 2001); Montoy v. State, 102 P.3d 1160 (Kan. 2005); Molly Hunter, *Maryland Enacts Modern, Standards-Based Education Finance System: Reforms Based on Adequacy Cost Studies* (New York: National Education Access Network, 2002), http://www.schoolfunding.info/resource_center/research /MDbrief.pdf.

50. Boylan and White, *Formula for Success.*

51. Between 1990 and 2007, many states undertook studies to analyze the cost of public education and, in some states, inform their funding formulas. However, in recent years, and as states face ongoing implementation of standards-based education, only a few states have commissioned studies that address the cost of those standards. See Allan Odden and Lawrence Picus, *School Finance: A Policy Perspective* (New York: McGraw Hill, 2014).

52. *Abbott IV,* 149 N.J. at 182.

53. U.S. Department of Education, "The Equity and Excellence Commission: Charter," www2.ed.gov/about/bdscomm/list/eec/eec-charter.doc.

54. The Equity and Excellence Commission, *For Each and Every Child—A Strategy for Education Equity and Excellence* (Washington, DC: U.S. Department of Education, 2013).

55. Ibid., 17.

56. Ibid., 19.

57. See, for example, Michael Foote and Marguerite Roza, "Measuring School Efficiency: Educational Return on Investment: A Case Study of An Urban District," *Journal of School Business Management* 20, no. 2 (2008): 20–33; W. Duncombe, J. Ruggiero, and J. Yinger, "Alternative Approaches to Measuring the Cost of Education," in *Holding Schools Accountable: Performance-Based Reform in Education*, ed. H. F. Ladd (Washington, DC: Brookings Institution Press, 1996).

58. Equity and Excellence Commission, *For Each and Every Child*, 17.

59. *Abbott XX,* 199 N.J. at 146.

60. *Abbott IV,* 149 N.J. at 192.

61. Ibid. at 193.

62. Equity and Excellence Commission, *For Each and Every Child*, 19.

63. See, for example, David G. Sciarra, Danielle Farrie, and Bruce Baker, "Filling Budget Holes: Evaluating the Impact of ARRA Fiscal Stabilization Funds on State Funding Formulas" (paper, Teachers College Equity Symposium, Columbia University, New York, February 8–9, 2010); Bruce D. Baker and Sean P. Corcoran, *The Stealth Inequities of School Funding: How State and Local School Finance Systems Perpetuate Inequitable Student Spending* (Washington, DC: Center for American Progress, 2012).

64. See, for example, David Sciarra, "Latest Race to the Top Grants Go to States at Bottom of School Funding Equity," *Huffington Post,* December 18, 2012, http://www .huffingtonpost.com/david-sciarra/race-to-the-top-funding_b_2317281.html.

65. Ibid.
66. 20 U.S.C. § 6301 et seq. (2001).
67. *Rodriguez*, 411 U.S. at 24.
68. Ibid. at 49.
69. *Abbott IV,* 149 N.J. at 167.
70. Ibid. at 167–168.
71. Ibid. at 201.

CHAPTER 7

1. Charles T. Clotfelter, Helen F. Ladd, and Jacob L. Vigdor, "Teacher-Student Matching and the Assessment of Teacher Effectiveness," *Journal of Human Resources* 41, no. 4 (2006): 778; Steven G. Rivkin, Eric A. Hanushek, and John F. Kain, "Teachers, Schools, and Academic Achievement," *Econometrica* 73, no. 2 (2005): 449; Jonah Rockoff, "The Impact of Individual Teachers on Student Achievement: Evidence from Panel Data," *American Economics Review* 94, no. 2 (2004): 247.

2. Julian R. Betts et al., *Equal Resources, Equal Outcomes? The Distribution of School Resources and Student Achievement in California* (San Francisco: Public Policy Institute of California, 2000), 87; Hamilton Lankford et al., "Teacher Sorting and the Plight of Urban Schools: A Descriptive Analysis," *Education Evaluation and Policy Analysis* 24, no. 1 (2002): 38.

3. Serrano v. Priest, 5 Cal.3d 584 (1971).

4. Serrano v. Priest, 18 Cal.3d 728, 776 (1976) (*Serrano II*).

5. Ibid. at 748.

6. Sean P. Corcoran et al., "Women, the Labor Market and the Declining Relative Quality of Teachers," *Journal Policy Analysis and Management* 23, no. 3 (2004): 449; Marigee P. Bacolod, "Do Alternative Opportunities Matter: The Role of Female Labor Markets in the Decline of Teacher Quality," *Review of Economics and Statistics* 89, no. 4 (2005): 737–751; Jennifer Y. Imazeki, "Teacher Salaries and Teacher Attrition," *Economics of Education Review* 24 (2005): 431; Eric Hanushek and Javier Luque, "Smaller Classes, Lower Salaries? The Effects of Class Size," in *Using What We Know: A Review of the Research on Implementing Class-Size Reduction Initiative for State and Local Policy Makers,* ed. Sabrina W. M. Laine and James G. Ward (Oak Brook, IL: North Central Regional Educational Laboratory, 2000), 35–57; Linda Darling-Hammond, "Access to Quality Teaching: An Analysis of Inequality in California's Public Schools," *Santa Clara Law Review* 43 (2003): 1124–1125; Steve Farkas, Juan Johnson, and Tony Foleno, *A Sense of Calling: Who Teaches and Why* (New York: Public Agenda, 2000); Susan M. Johnson and Sarah E. Birkeland, "The Schools That Teachers Choose," *Educational Leadership* 60, no. 8 (2003): 23; Glen I. Earthman, *The Effect of the Condition of School Facilities on Student Achievement* (expert report prepared for *Williams v. State of California* litigation, 2002), 10–11.

7. SRI International, *The Status of the Teaching Profession 2005* (Santa Cruz, CA: Center for the Future of Teaching and Learning, 2005), 73.

8. Ibid., 67.

9. "Quality Counts 2013," *Education Week,* January 10, 2013, 50; National Center for Education Statistics, *Digest of Education Statistics 2011* (Washington, DC: National Center for Education Statistics, 2012), 112, 113, 133.

10. Susanna Loeb et al., *Getting Down to Facts: School Finance and Governance in California* (Palo Alto: IREPP, 2007).

11. Governor's Committee on Education Excellence, *Students First: Renewing Hope for California's Future* (report, November 2007), 4.
12. Robles-Wong v. California, Case No. RG10515768 (Cal. Sup. Ct.); Campaign for Quality Education, Case No. RG10524770 (Cal. Sup. Ct.).
13. Full disclosure: I am counsel for the sixty-two plaintiff-children in the *Robles-Wong* matter.
14. 2013 Cal. Stat. Chapt. 47; 2013 Cal. Stat. Chapt. 70; 2013 Cal. Stat. Chapt. 357.
15. Williams v. California, No. 312236 (Cal. Sup. Ct.); Renee v. Duncan, 686 F.3d 1002 (2012).
16. First Amended Complaint at 6, Williams v. California, No. 312236 (Cal. Sup. Ct. Aug. 14, 2000).
17. Ibid. at 10–12.
18. Butt v. California, 4 Cal.4th 668, 685–687 (1992).
19. First Amended Complaint at 70, Williams v. California, No. 312236 (Cal. Sup. Ct. Aug. 14, 2000).
20. Ibid. at 58.
21. See Betts et al., *Equal Resources, Equal Outcomes?* xxiv, 209–210; Eric Hanushek, "The Trade-Off Between Child Quantity and Quality," *Journal of Political Economy* 100, no. 84 (1992); Ronald F. Ferguson and Helen Ladd, "How and Why Money Matters: An Analysis of Alabama Schools," in *Holding Schools Accountable: Performance-Based Reform in Education,* ed. Helen Ladd (Washington, DC: Brookings Institution Press, 1996), 265; Dan Goldhaber and Dominic Brewer, "Does Teacher Certification Matter: High School Certification Status and Student Achievement," *Educational Evaluation and Policy Analysis* 10, no. 42 (2000): 129–145; Darling-Hammond, "Teacher Quality and Student Achievement," 7–9.
22. Dan Goldhaber, "Teachers Matter, But Effective Teacher Quality Policies Are Elusive," in *Handbook of Research in Education Finance and Policy*, ed. H. F. Ladd and E. B. Fiske (New York: Routledge, 2008), 146–165.
23. 20 U.S.C. § 6311(b)(2)(F).
24. 20 U.S.C. § 6311(b)(3)(A); 20 U.S.C. §§ 7325, 6316(b)(5).
25. 20 U.S.C. § 6311(b)(2)(B).
26. Under NCLB, districts are charged with taking steps "to ensure that poor and minority children are not taught at higher rates than other children by inexperienced, unqualified or out-of-field teachers." 20 U.S.C. §§ 6311(b)(8)(C), 6312(c)(1)(L). Schools must notify parents if their child has been taught for four consecutive weeks by a teacher who is not "highly qualified." § 6311(h)(6)(B)(ii).
27. 20 U.S.C. § 7801(23)(A)(i).
28. 34 C.F.R. § 200.56(a)(2)(ii) (emphasis added).
29. Cal. Code Regs. tit. 5, §§ 6110(2), 6101(2).
30. Linda Darling-Hammond et al., "Does Teacher Preparation Matter? Evidence about Teacher Certification, Teach For America, and Teacher Effectiveness," *Education Policy Analysis Archives* 13, no. 42 (2005): 2–3; Charles T. Clotfelder et al., "Teacher Credentials and Student Achievement in High School: A Cross-Subject Analysis with Student Fixed Effects," *Journal of Human Resources* 45, no. 3 (2010): 655–681.
31. Thomas J. Kane et al., "Photo Finish: Certification Doesn't Guarantee a Winner," *Education Next* 7, no. 1 (2007): 64; Thomas J. Kane et al., "What Does Certification Tell Us About Teacher Effectiveness? Evidence from New York City," *Economics of Education Review* 27, no. 6 (2008): 615–661.

32. Goldhaber, "Teachers Matter," 146.

33. Renee v. Duncan, 623 F.3d 787, 796 (9th Cir. 2010) (*Renee II*).

34. Jason Song and Jason Felch, "Union Urges *Times* Boycott," *Los Angeles Times*, August 16, 2010.

35. Ibid.

36. "Los Angeles Teacher Ratings," *Los Angeles Times*, http://projects.latimes.com/value -added/. According to the *Times*, "A teacher's value-added rating is based on his or her students' progress on the California Standards Tests for English and Math. The difference between a student's expected growth and actual performance is the 'value' a teacher added or subtracted during the year. A school's value-added rating is based on the performance of all students tested there."

37. Verified Petition for Writ of Mandate, *Doe v. Deasy*, No. BS134604 (Cal. Sup. Ct. Nov. 18, 2011).

38. Cal. Educ. Code § 44662(b)(1) ("The governing board of each school district shall evaluate and assess certificated employee performance as it reasonably relates to . . . the progress of pupils toward [state adopted educational] standards").

39. Writ of Mandate at 24–25, *Doe v. Deasy*, No. BS134604 (Cal. Sup. Ct. Nov. 1, 2011).

40. John Fensterwald, "Do-or-Die Time for Teacher Evaluation Bill," *EdSource*, August 10, 2012, http://www.edsource.org/today/2012/do-or-die-time-for-teacher-evaluation-bill /18913#.Ue2UssPn-Hs.

41. John Fensterwald, "EdWatch 2013: Teacher Evaluation Law Will Be Taken on Again," *EdSource*, January 7, 2013.

42. Linda Darling-Hammond et al., *Creating a Comprehensive System for Evaluating and Supporting Effective Teaching* (Palo Alto: Stanford Center for Opportunity Policy in Education, 2012); Henry I. Braun, *Using Student Progress to Evaluate Teachers: A Primer on Value-Added Models* (Princeton: Educational Testing Service, 2005), 8, 10.

43. Complaint for Injunctive and Declaratory Relief, *Reed v. California*, No. BC434240 (Cal. Sup. Ct. Feb. 24, 2010).

44. First Amended Complaint for Declaratory and Injunctive Relief, *Vergara v. California*, No. BC484642 (Cal. Sup. Ct. Aug. 15, 2012).

45. Ibid. at 3.

46. Ibid.

47. Tentative Ruling, *Vergara v. California*, No. BC484642 (Cal. Sup. Ct. June 10, 2014).

48. Ibid. at 8.

49. Some might also believe that the case is merely a Trojan horse designed to attack public employee collective bargaining specifically or labor unions generally.

50. "Preparing World Class Teachers: Essential Reforms of Teacher Preparation and Credentialing in California," *EdSource*, October, 2014.

51. I am not suggesting that there will never be an instance in which statewide policies and statutes are best challenged at the state level. If it turns out that California's LIFO RIF statute has a pernicious effect in the vast majority of school districts, for instance, then litigation should be targeted at the state level. Removal of such obvious barriers to equity may be necessary. That said, I am suggesting that such broad-based litigation may be ill suited to the complex arena of teacher policy and the complex problems in ensuring the equitable distribution of teachers.

52. See Charles Sabel and William Simon, "Destabilization Rights: How Public Law Litigation Succeeds," *Harvard Law Review* 117, no. 4 (2004): 1016–1028; James

S. Liebman and Charles Sabel, "A Public Laboratory Dewey Barely Imagined: The Emerging Model of School Governance and Legal Reform," *New York University Review of Law and Social Change* 28 (2003): 183, 207.

53. David Tyack and Larry Cuban, *Tinkering Toward Utopia: A Century of Public School Reform* (Cambridge, MA: Harvard University Press, 1995).

CHAPTER 8

This chapter is condensed from Mildred Wigfall Robinson, "It Takes a Federalist Village: A Revitalized Property Tax as the Linchpin for Stable, Effective K-12 Public Education Funding," *Richmond Journal of Law and the Public Interest* 17 (2014): 549–590.

1. U.S. Census Bureau, *Profile America Facts for Features: Back to School, 2011–2012*, https://www.census.gov/newsroom/releases/archives/facts_for_features_special_editions /cb11-ff15.html; Mark Dixon, *Public Education Finances: 2011*, 1 table 1, http://www2 .census.gov/govs/school/11f33pub.pdf.

2. For fiscal year 2011, local sources provided slightly more than $259,490,000,000 to finance public elementary and secondary schools; this constituted 43.3 percent of all revenues. For fiscal year 2011, state sources provided $265,948,389,000 to finance public elementary and secondary schools; this constituted 44.4 percent of all revenues. For fiscal year 2011, the federal government provided $73,706,695,000 to finance public elementary and secondary schools; this constituted 12.3 percent of all revenues. Dixon, *Public Education Finances*, 1, table 1, 5, table 5.

3. 411 U.S. 1 (1973).

4. 411 U.S. 1, 59 (1973) (emphasis added).

5. U.S. Census Bureau, *Statistical Abstract of the United States 1973*, 94th ed. (Washington, DC: U.S. Department of Commerce, 1975), 108, table 162, https://www.census .gov/prod/www/statistical_abstract.html.

6. S. 1255 died in the Senate Committee for Government Operations. See "Search Bill Summary and Status," Library of Congress, http://thomas.loc.gov/home/Legislative-Data.php; *Property Tax Relief and Reform Act of 1973: Hearing on S. 1255 Before the Subcomm. on Intergovernmental Relations of the S. Comm. on Gov't Operations*, 93rd Cong. (1973).

7. These were the first and second elements in the explosive political mix that then existed in California. It was also the case that, though taxpayers complained with more and more stridency, the California legislature failed to address either situation.

8. See, for example, Steven Hayward, "The Tax Revolt Turns 20," *Policy Review* (July–August 1998): 9 ("Within two years [of the adoption of California's Proposition 13], 43 states implemented some kind of property-tax limitation or relief, 15 states lowered their income tax rates, and 10 states indexed their state income taxes for inflation"). Principal among these was Massachusetts' Proposition 2½, a 1980 ballot initiative that reduced property taxes in that state. A 1999 study concluded that by the 1990s, "people either regretted the severity of the Proposition's constraints or felt that its mission was accomplished"; of particular interest is the finding that voters in larger communities were particularly likely to support overrides. See David M. Cutler, Douglas W. Elmendorf, and Richard Zeckhauser, "Restraining the Leviathan: Property Tax Limitation in Massachusetts," *Journal of Public Economics* 71 (1999): 313. With regard to property tax limitations only, however, antitax activity has persisted. Alvin Sokolow reports that between 1970 and 1995, forty-two states adopted at least sixty-eight

measures, likely surpassing the number of such measures in any comparable quarter in U.S. history. See Alvin D. Sokolow, "The Changing Property Tax and State-Local Relations," *Publius: The Journal of Federalism* 28, no. 1 (1998): 170.

9. *Property Tax Relief and Reform Act of 1973: Hearing on S. 1255 Before the Subcomm. on Intergovernmental Relations of the S. Comm. on Gov't Operations*, 93rd Cong. 788 (1973).

10. Ibid.

11. Ibid., 743.

12. Ibid.

13. See, for example, Isaac William Martin, *The Permanent Tax Revolt: How the Property Tax Transformed American Politics* (Palo Alto: Stanford University Press, 2008).

14. The property tax is usually given in mills, with one mill equaling .10 of a cent. For example, a parcel of taxable property with an assessed value of $100,000 taxed by a governmental unit having a millage rate of 10 mills will have a property tax bill of $1,000 annually. Assessment limits restrict the extent to which the property tax base (the property's value) can be annually increased for property tax purposes. Proposition 13 quite famously limits the extent of annual increase to 2 percent. It is by no means the only such limitation extant today. Obviously, the extent of base erosion will be driven by the divergence between assessment cap and property appreciation. As the gap between these two values widens (lowering assessment rate and increasing value in property), the rate of erosion in the base will accelerate. See Terri A. Sexton, "Assessment Limits as Means of Limiting Homeowner Property Tax," in *Erosion of the Property Tax Base: Trends, Causes, and Consequences*, ed. Nancy Y. Augustine, Michael E. Bell, and David Brunori (Cambridge, MA: Lincoln Institute of Land Policy, 2009), 115–147; John H. Bowan, "Residential Property Tax Relief Measures," in ibid., 73–115.

15. Bing Yuaii et al., "Tax and Expenditure Limitations and Local Public Finances," in ibid., 148–195.

16. For an excellent general overview of TIFs, see Richard Briffault, "The Most Popular Tool: Tax Increment Financing and the Political Economy of Local Government," *University of Chicago Law Review* 77 (2010): 65.

17. Ibid., 70 n.63.

18. As originally designed, TIFs were intended to reverse blight, but at present the standard for establishment of a TIF has evolved to "something a lot more like 'underdevelopment.'" Ibid., 78.

19. Ibid.

20. Robert Bruno and Alison Dickson Quesada, "Tax Increment Financing and Chicago Public Schools: A New Approach to Comprehending a Complex Relationship" (white paper, Labor Education Program, University of Illinois, Urbana-Champaign, December 2011), 5, https://ler.illinois.edu/wp-content/uploads/2015/01/Bruno_Quesada_12152011.pdf.

21. See Robert W. Wassmer, "Property Tax Abatement as a Means of Promoting State and Local Economic Activity," in *Erosion of the Property Tax Base: Trends, Causes, and Consequences*, ed. Nancy Y. Augustine, Michael E. Bell, and David Brunori (Cambridge, MA: Lincoln Institute of Land Policy, 2009), 221–267.

22. Ibid., 224.

23. Ibid. Arguments against SAPTAPs include the questionable level of influence of taxes on location decisions; the effect of local pro-business expenditures; and the real

possibility that enactment of SAPTAPS is a zero-sum game as more and more states jump onto the bandwagon. Arguments supporting SAPTAPS focus on the positive effect on business location decisions. See also Kirk J. Stark and Daniel J. Wilson, "What Do We Know about the Interstate Economic Effects of State Tax Incentives?" *Georgetown Journal of Law & Public Policy* 4 (2005): 133, which invites Congress to "undertake a careful and thorough evaluation of the nationwide effects of state tax incentives."

24. Ohio taxpayers attempted to challenge tax benefits that included property tax breaks as well as research and development credits pursuant to an argument that these tax breaks diminished the funds available to the city and state and imposed a disproportionate burden on the plaintiffs. In *DaimlerChrysler Corp. v. Cuno*, 547 U.S. 332 (2006), the United Stated Supreme Court held that the plaintiffs lacked standing by virtue of their status as Ohio taxpayers to challenge the tax breaks.

25. See Noah Berger and Peter Fisher, "A Well-Educated Workforce Is Key to State Prosperity" (report, Economic Analysis and Research Network, Washington, DC, 2013), http://www.epi.org/publication/states-education-productivity-growth-foundations/.

26. See Nancy Y. Augustine et al., "The Property Tax Under Siege," in *Erosion of the Property Tax Base: Trends, Causes, and Consequences*, ed. Nancy Y. Augustine, Michael E. Bell, and David Brunori (Cambridge, MA: Lincoln Institute of Land Policy, 2009), 1–15. The following quote is instructive: "Although the property tax is the largest single source of state and local revenues, the extent of the decline of the property tax is clear. State and local governments raised $335.7 billion in property taxes in 2005, compared with $263 billion from the general sales tax and $240.9 billion from the personal income tax. Local property taxes accounted for 72.4 percent of local tax revenues in 2005 and 45.8 percent of total local general own-source revenues. Fifty years ago, local property taxes raised $14.4 billion in local revenues, which accounted for 87.2 percent of local tax revenues and 69.5 percent of total local own-source general revenues." Ibid., 2.

27. See Bing Yuaii et al., "Tax and Expenditure Limitations and Local Public Finances," in ibid., 162–167.

28. National Education Association, *Protecting Public Education from Tax Giveaways to Corporations: Property Tax Abatements, Tax Increment Financing, and Funding for Schools* (Washington, DC: National Education Association, 2002), 15, http://mea.org/tef/pdf/protecting_public_ed.pdf.

29. "[Thirty-five] states impose some type of TEL on their school district. However, most (26) of these states provide their local governments with some capacity to override the limitation, typically through a referendum held among voters in the school district." Garry Young et al., "Efforts to Override School District Property Tax Limitations," in *Erosion of the Property Tax Base: Trends, Causes, and Consequences*, ed. Nancy Y. Augustine, Michael E. Bell, and David Brunori (Cambridge, MA: Lincoln Institute of Land Policy, 2009), 197.

30. Ibid., 217 ("Overrides fail and they fail often").

31. The most recent census data reports that in 2010 55 percent of family households were childless. See U.S. Census Bureau, *Statistical Abstract of the United States, 2012*, 131st ed., (Washingon, DC: U.S. Department of Commerce, 2012), 56, table 64, http://www.census.gov/compendia/statab/2012edition.html.

32. National Education Association, *Protecting Public Education from Tax Giveaways to Corporations: Property Tax Abatements, Tax Increment Financing, and Funding for Schools* (Washington, DC: National Education Association, 2002), 17 n.85, http://mea.org/tef/pdf/protecting_public_ed.pdf.

33. Ibid.

34. Ibid., 18.

35. Ibid.

36. See, for example, Montana's legislative refinement and use of computer-assisted mass appraisal systems (CAMAs) in Karen E. Powell, "A Historical Perspective on Montana Property Tax: 25 Years of Statewide Appraisal and Appeal Practice," *Montana Law Review* 70 (2009): 21.

37. State expenditures for the same period averaged 23 percent of all spending. Ibid. Health-care spending for state and local governments increased to 31.5 percent as a share of revenue in 2012, consuming the largest share of state and local resources since 1987. Health-care spending remains a source of fiscal pressure and may double by 2060. See Pew Charitable Trusts, *State, Local Government Spending on Health Care Grew Faster Than National Rate in 2012* (Philadelphia: Pew Charitable Trusts, 2014), http://www.pewtrusts.org/en/research-and-analysis/reports/0001/01/01/state-local-government-spending-on-health-care-grew-faster-than-national-rate-in-2012.

38. Ibid.; National Association of State Budget Officers, *State Expenditure Report* (Washington, DC: National Association of State Budget Officers, 2014), 5, https://www.nasbo.org/publications-data/state-expenditure-report/state-expenditure-report-fiscal-2012-2014-data.

39. One exception to this is Virginia, which earmarks a percentage of revenues from its retail sales tax in order to finance public K–12 education. See "School Finance," Virginia Department of Education, http://www.doe.virginia.gov/school_finance/.

40. I use "gaming" in this context to include both lotteries and casino gambling.

41. Richard A. Leiter, ed., *National Survey of State Laws* (Farmington Hills, MI: Thomson Gale, 2005), 723, 781–790.

42. Ibid. This subset of states includes California, Florida, Georgia, Illinois, Nebraska, New Jersey, New Mexico, Ohio, South Carolina, Texas, Virginia, and West Virginia.

43. "'Games of chance,' in one variation or another, have been chosen by many state governments as their economic savior." Rodney E. Stanley and P. Edward French, "Can Students Truly Benefit from State Lotteries? A Look at Lottery Expenditures Towards Education in the American States," *Social Science Journal* 40 (2003): 327, 328.

44. This has led some commenters to characterize lotteries as a "fiscal hoax." The number of lottery players may be quite high in the early years of a lottery, but the lottery will receive less and less play as the newness wears off. States relying on gaming revenues may thus find actual revenues insufficient to cover expenses. Ibid., 329.

45. See, for example, Ross Rubenstein and Benjamin Scafidi, "Who Pays and Who Benefits? Examining the Distributional Consequences of the Georgia Lottery for Education," *National Tax Journal* 55, no. 2 (2002): 223, 236 ("The vast majority of research has found lotteries to be a regressive method of raising revenue"); and Thomas A. Garrett, "Earmarked Lottery Revenues for Education: A New Test of Fungibility," *Journal of Education Finance* 26 (2001): 219, 237 ("Lotteries are generally accepted as regressive").

46. Garrett, "Earmarked Lottery Revenues for Education," 237.

47. Stanley and French, "Can Students Truly Benefit from State Lotteries?" 329–330. The concept of fungibility explains this phenomenon. Lottery monies may replace rather than supplement nonlottery monies previously used to support education, leading one author to conclude that state lotteries are "robbing Peter to pay Paul." When lottery revenues fall short, legislatures may not redress the shortfall with nonlottery funds. Several studies have concluded that over time states which had adopted lotteries earmarking gaming revenues for support of public education actually decreased spending on education.

48. I.R.C. § 164 (2012).

49. See, for example, Wayne C. Riddle, "How Public Education Benefits from the Federal Income Tax Deduction for State and Local Taxes and Other Special Tax Provisions" (background paper, Center on Education Policy, Washington, DC, April 2011), 3, http://www.cep-dc.org/cfcontent_file.cfm?Attachment=Riddle_Paper_TaxExpenditures_41311.pdf.) The total deduction for property taxes levied against residential real property in 2009 was approximately $25 billion dollars.

50. See Benjamin H. Harris and Daniel Baneman, "Who Itemizes Deductions?" *Tax Notes* 130 (2011): 345, which notes that about 30 percent of taxpayers itemize.

51. For many of the reasons discussed earlier—lessening volatility and increasing stability, for example—Darien Shanske urges the federal government to provide an incentive to states to move to greater reliance on the property tax. Pursuant to his proposal, this would be accomplished by expanding the deduction for the property tax and limiting or eliminating the deduction for state income or sale taxes. Unlike what I propose here, he recommends an above-the-line deduction that could be taken by all taxpayers without itemizing. His proposal also goes to the deduction for property taxes generally rather than for that percentage allocated for support of public education. See Darien Shanske, "How Less Can Be More: Using the Federal Income Tax to Stabilize State and Local Finance," *Virginia Tax Review* 31 (2012): 413.

52. Perennial talk of tax reform always includes discussion of possible repeal of some or all of the presently available itemized deductions. The SALT deduction is continuously and prominently mentioned as a primary candidate for repeal. For a brief summary of the case for retention of the reduction, see Martin A. Sullivan, "Why the SALT Deduction Is Always Under Attack," *Tax Notes* 137 (2012): 1261–1264.

53. See Kirk J. Stark, "The Federal Role in State Tax Reform," *Virginia Law Review* 30 (2010): 407. Stark argues that the federal government has unwittingly stacked the deck in favor of state revenue volatility by permitting the deduction of some state taxes but not others. His suggestions include, short of repeal of the SALT deduction, using a flat-rate credit for some or all of the state and local taxes currently deductible. He characterizes the property tax as "a relatively stable source of revenue." Ibid., 438. The approach I advocate here stops short of providing a credit for *all* local property taxes paid. In this sense, it is less expansive than Stark's argument. My argument, however, aligns with Stark's view that the property tax is a more stable source of revenue, relatively speaking, than are state income or excise taxes. As such, I argue that making property taxes (but not state income or excise taxes) paid to support public education eligible for treatment as a credit for federal income tax purposes would signal a preference for as much stability as possible in funding education.

54. Thanks to my colleague Michael Doran for this suggestion.

55. The Internal Revenue Code § 170(c)(2)(B) (2012) defines a charitable contribution as one made for the use of an entity "organized and operated exclusively for religious, charitable, scientific, literary, or educational purposes, or to foster national or international amateur sports competition, or for the prevention of cruelty to children or animals."
56. Serrano v. Priest, 487 P.2d 1241, 1258–1259 (Cal. 1971).

CHAPTER 9

1. Parliament, *Chocolate City* (Casablanca Records NBLP 7014, June 1975).
2. Bradley v. Milliken, 338 F. Supp 582 (1971).
3. Milliken v. Bradley, 418 U.S. 717, 732–733 (1974) (quoting Pet. App. at 57a) (internal quotation marks omitted).
4. Robert Pratt, *The Color of Their Skin: Education and Race in Richmond, Virginia 1954–89* (Charlottesville: University of Virginia Press, 1992), 65–66.
5. Bradley v. School Board of Richmond, Virginia, 338 F. Supp. 67, 84 (E.D. Va. 1972).
6. Peter Irons, *Jim Crow's Children: The Broken Promise of the Brown Decision* (New York: Viking Press, 2002), 242.
7. Ibid.
8. Desegregation standards were outlined in *Green v. County School Board of New Kent County*, 391 U.S. 430 (1968). *Swann v. Charlotte-Mecklenburg Board of Education*, 402 U.S. 1 (1971), authorized the use of widespread transportation for the purposes of desegregation.
9. School Board of Richmond, Virginia v. State Board of Education of Virginia, 412 U.S. 92, 93 (1973).
10. Gary Orfield, *Must We Bus? Segregated Schools and National Policy* (Washington, DC: Brookings Institution Press, 1978), 18. Importantly, a recent line of research carefully documenting the historical evolution of school and housing decisions in different metropolitan communities may help bolster future cases. See, for example, Karen Benjamin, "Suburbanizing Jim Crow: The Impact of School Policy on Residential Segregation in Raleigh," *Journal of Urban History* 38, no. 2 (2012): 226–227; Ansley T. Erickson, "Building Inequality: The Spatial Organization of Schooling in Nashville, Tennessee after *Brown*," *Journal of Urban History* 38, no. 2 (2012): 253–258.
11. It may be argued that the 1973 *Keyes v. School District No. 1, Denver, Colorado*, 413 U.S. 189, 208–209 (1973), ruling represented a setback because the Court chose not to eliminate the de jure/de facto distinction. Though nearly all districts were guilty of the intentionally segregative actions outlined in *Keyes*, maintaining the distinction required that civil rights advocates gather the many resources needed to bring cases documenting intentional discrimination.
12. john powell, "A New Theory of Integrated Education," in *School Resegregation: Must the South Turn Back?*, ed. John Charles Boger and Gary Orfield (Chapel Hill: University of North Carolina Press, 2005), 298.
13. James Ryan, *Five Miles Away, a World Apart: One City, Two Schools, and the Story of Educational Opportunity in Modern America* (New York: Oxford University Press, 2010), 138–143; Derrick Bell, *Silent Covenants: Brown v. Board of Education and the Unfulfilled Hopes for Racial Reform* (New York: Oxford University Press, 2004), 161–162.
14. Susan Eaton, Joseph Feldman, and Edward Kirby, "Still Separate, Still Unequal: The Limits of *Milliken II*'s Monetary Compensation in Segregated Schools," in *Dismantling*

Desegregation: The Quiet Reversal of Brown v. Board of Education, ed. Gary Orfield and Susan Eaton (New York: New Press, 1996), 176–178; James Ryan, "Schools, Race and Money," *Yale Law Journal* 109 (1999): 289.

15. Evans v. Buchanan, 465 F. Supp. 445 (1979). NAACP lawyers strategically organized the Wilmington-area case around the proof required to show intentional discrimination on the part of multiple school districts that was outlined in *Milliken*. United States v. Board of School Commissioners of Indianapolis, Indiana, 573 F.2d 400, *aff'd*, 439 U.S. 824 (1978). Instead of merging school districts in the Indianapolis area, the Court ordered desegregation across multiple existing school districts.

16. Sheff v. O'Neill, 678 A.2d 1267, 1281 (Conn. 1996).

17. See generally Susan Eaton, *The Children in Room E4: American Education on Trial* (Chapel Hill: Algonquin Books, 2006). I use "metro area" or "metro" or "area" to describe the three sites under study: here the terms simply refer to the geographic area encompassed by the school district merger (or proposed merger, as was the case for the Richmond metro). This geographic unit is much smaller than a census-defined Metropolitan Statistical Area (MSA). But since the "metro" boundaries defined by this analysis encompass only areas directly affected by the school desegregation plan, they provide the most pertinent school and housing data.

18. Erica Frankenberg, "The Impact of School Segregation on Residential Housing Patterns: Mobile, Alabama and Charlotte, North Carolina," in *School Resegregation: Must the South Turn Back?*, ed. John Charles Boger and Gary Orfield (Chapel Hill: University of North Carolina Press, 2005), 168; Orfield, *Must We Bus?*, 77–78; Pearce, "Dynamics of Segregation," 85; Brief for Housing Scholars and Research and Advocacy Organizations as Amici Curae in Support of Respondents at 12–18, Parents Involved in Community Schools v. Seattle School District No. 1, et al., 551 U.S. 701 (2007) (Nos. 05–908, 05–915); U.S. Commission on Civil Rights, "Statement on Metropolitan School Desegregation" (Washington, DC: U.S. Department of Health, Education and Welfare and National Institute for Education, 1977), 1–126.

19. Frankenberg, "Impact of School Segregation," 208; Brief of Housing Scholars as Amici Curiae, *Parents Involved*, 551 U.S. 701 (2007) (Nos. 05–908, 05–915); Gary Orfield, "Metropolitan School Desegregation: Impacts on Metropolitan Society," in *In Pursuit of a Dream Deferred: Linking Housing and Education Policy*, ed. John A. Powell and Vina Kay (New York: Peter Lang, 2001), 122.

20. Frankenberg, "Impact of School Segregation," 176; Brief of Amici Curiae Housing Scholars, *Parents Involved*, 551 U.S. 701 (2007) (Nos. 05-908, 05-915).

21. Orfield, "Metropolitan School Desegregation," 147; Pearce, "Dynamics of Segregation," 85.

22. Roslyn Mickelson, "Exploring the School-Housing Nexus: A Synthesis of Social Science Evidence," in *Finding Common Ground: Coordinating Housing and Education Policy to Promote Integration,* ed. Phil Tegeler (Washington, DC: Poverty and Race Research Action Council, 2011).

23. Robert Linn and Kevin Welner, *Race-Conscious Policies for Assigning Students to Schools: Social Science Research and the Supreme Court Cases* (Washington, DC: National Academy of Education, 2007).

24. Jomils Braddock, "Looking Back: The Effects of Court-Ordered Desegregation," in *From the Courtroom to the Classroom: The Shifting Landscape of School Desegregation,* ed. Claire Smrekar and Ellen Goldring (Cambridge, MA: Harvard Education Press, 2009), 3–18;

Rucker Johnson and Robert Schoeni, "The Influence of Early-Life Events on Human Capital, Health Status and Labor Market Outcomes over the Life Course," *B.E. Journal of Economic Analysis and Policy Advances* 11, no. 3 (2011): 28–30; Roslyn Mickelson and Martha Bottia, "Integrated Education and Mathematics Outcomes: A Synthesis of Social Science Research," *North Carolina Law Review* 88 (2010): 1048–1051.

25. Annette Lareau and Kimberly Goyette, *Choosing Homes, Choosing Schools* (New York: Russell Sage Foundation, 2014).

26. Ryan, *Five Miles Away*, 81–89.

27. Gary Orfield and Erica Frankenberg, *Experiencing Integration in Louisville: How Parents and Students See the Gains and Challenges* (Los Angeles: The Civil Rights Project, University of California Los Angeles, 2011), 24.

28. Kristie Phillips et al., "Integrated Schools, Integrated Futures? A Case Study of School Desegregation in Jefferson County, Kentucky," in *From the Courtroom to the Classroom: The Shifting Landscape of School Desegregation*, ed. Claire Smrekar and Ellen Goldring (Cambridge, MA: Harvard Education Press, 2009), 242.

29. Davison Douglas, *Reading, Writing and Race: The Desegregation of the Charlotte Schools* (Chapel Hill: University of North Carolina Press, 2005), 50–85.

30. Stephen Smith, *Boom for Whom? Education, Desegregation and Development in Charlotte* (Albany: State University of New York Press, 2004), 57–62.

31. Ibid.

32. For a complete discussion of the study, see Genevieve Siegel-Hawley, "City Lines, County Lines, Color Lines: An Analysis of School and Housing Segregation in Four Southern Metropolitan Areas, 1990–2010," *Teachers College Record* 115, no. 6 (2013), http://www.tcrecord.org/content.asp?contentid=16988.

33. The Dissimilarity Index (*D*) indicates the proportion of persons in a particular racial/ethnic group that would have to change schools (in this case) in order to achieve an even spatial distribution of the races. It is one of the most common measures of segregation.

34. Genevieve Siegel-Hawley et al., *Miles to Go: A Report on School Segregation in Virginia, 1989–2010* (Los Angeles: The Civil Rights Project, University of California Los Angeles, 2013), 38–52. In 1989, the vast majority of segregation—about 72 percent—occurred between districts in the Richmond-Petersburg metro (between Richmond City and Henrico and Chesterfield Counties). More recently, however, segregation levels have been roughly the same within and between districts.

35. Ibid.

36. Genevieve Siegel-Hawley, "Educational Gerrymandering? Race and Attendance Boundaries in a Demographically Changing Suburb," *Harvard Educational Review* 83, no. 4 (2013): 31.

37. See, for example, Erica Frankenberg and Gary Orfield, eds., *The Resegregation of Suburban Schools: A Hidden Crisis in American Education* (Cambridge, MA: Harvard Education Press, 2012), 153–158; Jennifer Holme, Sarah Diem, and Anjale Welton, "Suburban School Districts and Demographic Change: The Technical, Normative and Political Dimensions of Response," *Educational Administration Quarterly* 50, no. 1 (2013): 15–28.

38. Holme, Diem, and Welton, "Suburban School Districts," 15–28.

39. *Parents Involved*, 551 U.S. 789 (Kennedy, J., concurring in part and concurring in the judgment).

40. U.S. Department of Education, Office for Civil Rights, U.S. Department of Justice, Civil Rights Division, Dear Colleague Letter on the Voluntary Use of Race to Achieve Diversity or Avoid Racial Isolation in Elementary and Secondary Schools (December 2, 2011), http://www2.ed.gov/about/offices/list/ocr/letters/colleague-201111.html.

41. *Keyes*, 413 U.S. at 240–241.

42. See Office of Sustainable Communities, "Sustainable Communities Initiative," U.S. Department of Housing and Urban Development, http://portal.hud.gov/hudportal /HUD?src=/hudprograms/sci.

43. David Rusk, *Inside Game, Outside Game: Winning Strategies for Saving Urban America* (Washington, DC: Brookings Institution Press, 1999), 291–295.

44. *Sheff*, 678 A.2d at 1281; Eaton, *The Children in Room E4*, 111.

45. Ryan, *Five Miles Away*, 177.

46. Suzanne Leland and Kurt Thumaier, eds., *Case Studies of City-County Consolidation: Reshaping the Local Government Landscape* (New York: M. E. Sharpe, 2004), 291–320.

47. Ibid.

48. At least one major report indicated that consolidation may not always save money. See Craig Howly, Jerry Johnson, and Jennifer Petrie, *Consolidation of Schools and Districts: What the Research Says and What It Means* (Washington, DC: National Education Policy Center, 2011), 11–12.

49. Michael Gormly, "Cuomo to Strapped NY Cities, Schools: Merge," *Yahoo News,* March 15, 2013, http://news.yahoo.com/cuomo-strapped-ny-cities-schools-182321047 .html.

50. Jennifer Jellison Holme, Sarah Diem, and Katherine Mansfield, "Regional Coalitions and Educational Policy: Lessons from the Nebraska Learning Community," in *Integrating Schools in a Changing Society: New Policies and Legal Options for a Multiracial Generation,* ed. Erica Frankenberg and Elizabeth DeBray (Chapel Hill: University of North Carolina Press, 2013), 151–164.

51. Robert Bifulco, Casey Cobb, and Courtney Bell, "Can Interdistrict Choice Boost Student Achievement? The Case of Connecticut's Interdistrict Magnet School Program," *Education Evaluation and Policy Analysis* 31, no. 4 (2009): 323.

52. Jennifer Jellison Holme and Amy Stuart Wells, "School Choice Beyond District Borders: Lessons for the Reauthorization of NCLB from Interdistrict Desegregation and Open Enrollment Plans," in *Improving on No Child Left Behind: Getting Education Reform Back on Track*, ed. Richard Kahlenberg (Washington, DC: Century Foundation, 2008), 197–206.

53. Meredith Richards, Kori Stroub, and Jennifer Jellison Holme, "Can NLCB Choice Work? Modeling the Effects of Interdistrict Choice on Student Access to Higher Performing Schools," in *The Future of School Integration: Socioeconomic Diversity as an Education Reform Strategy*, ed. Richard Kahlenberg (Washington, DC: Century Foundation, 2012), 223–256.

54. Ibid.

55. Myron Orfield and Thomas Luce, *Region: Planning the Future of the Twin Cities* (Minneapolis: University of Minnesota Press, 2010), 121–125; Deidre Pfeiffer, *The Opportunity Illusion: Subsidized Housing and Failing Schools in California* (Los Angeles: The Civil Rights Project, University of California Los Angeles, 2009), 7–8.

56. Rusk, *Inside Game*, 324.

57. John Engberg et al., "Evaluating Education Programs That Have Lotteried Admission and Selective Attrition," *Journal of Labor Economics* 32, no. 1 (2013): 4, 20.

58. Gary Orfield, *Toward a Strategy for Urban Integration: Lessons in School and Housing Policy from Twelve Cities* (New York: Ford Foundation, 1981), 20–24.

59. Ibid., 14–15; Phil Tegeler, ed., *Finding Common Ground: Coordinating Housing and Education Policy to Promote Integration* (Washington, DC: Poverty and Race Research Action Council, 2011), 51–66.

CHAPTER 10

This chapter is revised and condensed from Kimberly Jenkins Robinson, "Disrupting Education Federalism," *Washington University Law Review* 92 (2015): 959–1018.

1. San Antonio Independent School District v. Rodriguez, 411 U.S. 1, 4, 11–13 (1973); Equity and Excellence Commission, *For Each and Every Child: A Strategy for Education Equity and Excellence* (Washington, DC: ED Pubs, U.S. Department of Education, 2013), 14.

2. Council on Foreign Relations, "Remedial Education: Federal Education Policy" (New York: Council on Foreign Relations Press, 2013), 4.

3. See Campaign for Fiscal Equity, Inc. v. State, 655 N.E.2d 661, 667 (N.Y. 1995); James E. Ryan, *Five Miles Away, a World Apart: One City, Two Schools, and the Story of Educational Opportunity in Modern America* (New York: Oxford University Press, 2010), 127; Goodwin Liu, "Interstate Inequality in Educational Opportunity," *New York University Law Review* 81 (2006): 2068; Goodwin Liu, "Education, Equality, and National Citizenship," *Yale Law Journal* 116 (2006): 332–334; Bruce Baker, David Sciarra, and Danielle Farrie, *Is School Funding Fair? A National Report Card*, 4th ed. (Newark: Educational Law Center, 2015), 8–10, 37–40 tables C1 and C2.

4. Greg J. Duncan and Richard J. Murnane, *Restoring Opportunity: The Crisis of Inequality and the Challenge for American Education* (Cambridge, MA: Harvard Education Press, 2014), 2; Thomas Bailey, "Implications of Educational Inequality in a Global Economy," in *The Price We Pay: Economic and Social Consequences of Inadequate Education*, ed. Clive R. Belfield and Henry M. Levin (Washington, DC: Brookings Institution Press, 2007), 92–93.

5. Kimberly Jenkins Robinson, "The High Cost of Education Federalism," *Wake Forest Law Review* 48 (2013): 287, 290, 297–307, 309–314, 323–330. The Equity and Excellence Commission also noted that local control of education has hindered efforts to promote educational equity. Equity and Excellence Commission, *Each and Every Child*, 34.

6. *Rodriguez*, 411 U.S. at 33, 35, 44, 47–48, 54–55; Erwin Chemerinsky, "The Deconstitutionalization of Education," *Loyola University Chicago Law Journal* 36 (2004): 111.

7. Thomas Kleven, "Federalizing Public Education," *Villanova Law Review* 55 (2010): 369, 407.

8. Kimberly Jenkins Robinson, "The Case for a Collaborative Enforcement Model for a Federal Right to Education," *University of California Davis Law Review* 40 (2007): 1712.

9. Equity and Excellence Commission, *Each and Every Child*, 12.

10. Janice Petrovich, "The Shifting Terrain of Educational Policy: Why We Must Bring Equity Back," in *Bringing Equity Back: Research for a New Era in American Educational Policy*, ed. Janice Petrovich and Amy Stuart Wells (New York: Teachers College Press,

2005), 3, 12; Greg J. Duncan and Richard J. Murnane, "Introduction: The American Dream, Then and Now," in *Whiter Opportunity? Rising Inequality, Schools, and Children's Life Chances*, ed. Greg J. Duncan and Richard J. Murnane (New York: Russell Sage Foundation, 2011), 3, 15; Michael A. Rebell and Jessica R. Wolff, *Moving Every Child Ahead: From NCLB Hype to Meaningful Educational Opportunity* (New York: Teachers College Press, 2008), 30–33; Linda Darling-Hammond, *The Flat World and Education: How America's Commitment to Equity Will Determine Our Future* (New York: Teachers College Press, 2010), 73–74; Richard D. Kahlenberg, "Socioeconomic School Integration," in *The Future of School Integration: Socioeconomic Diversity as an Education Reform Strategy*, ed. Richard D. Kahlenberg (New York: Century Foundation Press, 2012), 1, 3; Kimberly Jenkins Robinson, "The Constitutional Future of Race-Neutral Efforts to Achieve Diversity and Avoid Racial Isolation in Elementary and Secondary Schools," *Boston College Law Review* 50 (2009): 327–336; Gary Orfield and Chungmei Lee, *Why Segregation Matters: Poverty and Educational Inequality* (Cambridge, MA: Harvard University, 2005), 7; Ryan, *Five Miles Away*, 278–280.

11. The American Recovery and Reinvestment Act of 2009, Pub. L. No. 111-5, 123 Stat. 115; President Barack Obama and Vice President Joe Biden, "Remarks at a Meeting with the Nation's Mayors," February 20, 2009, http://www.whitehouse.gov/the_press _office/Remarks-by-the-President-and-Vice-President-at-Meeting-with-Nations-Mayors /; Sam Dillon, "For Education Chief, Stimulus Means Power, Money and Risk," *New York Times*, February 17, 2009; U.S. Department of Education, "Duncan Hails Passage of President's Stimulus Package, Cites 'Historic Opportunity to Create Jobs and Advance Reform'" (press release, U.S. Department of Education, Washington, DC, February 18, 2009), http://www.ed.gov/news/press-releases/duncan-hails-passage -presidents-stimulus-package-cites-historic-opportunity-crea; Race to the Top Fund: Notice of Final Priorities, 74 Fed. Reg. 59,688 (Nov. 18, 2009); Grover Whitehurst, "A Discussion with Secretary of Education Arne Duncan" (panel remarks, Brookings Institution, Washington, DC, May 11, 2009), http://www.brookings.edu/~/media /events/2009/5/11-education-duncan/20090511_education_transcript_corrected.pdf; Patrick McGuinn, "Stimulating Reform: Race to the Top, Competitive Grants and the Obama Education Agenda," *Educational Policy* 26 (2012): 136, 143–147; Barry Friedman and Sara Solow, "The Federal Right to an Adequate Education," *George Washington Law Review* 81 (2013): 92, 146; Mike Johnston, "Regulation to Results: Shifting American Education from Inputs to Outcomes," *Yale Law and Policy Review* 30 (2011): 195, 206.

12. Pub. L. No. 107-110, 115 Stat. 1425 (codified as amended in scattered sections of 20 U.S.C.); 20 U.S.C. §§ 6311, 6319 (2012); Patrick J. McGuinn, *No Child Left Behind and the Transformation of Federal Education Policy, 1965–2005* (Lawrence: University Press of Kansas, 2006), 195. Although NCLB also established a new federal role in education, it did not provide an accompanying new understanding of education federalism to guide this role. Kamina A. Pinder, "Federal Demand and Local Choice: Safeguarding the Notion of Federalism in Education Law and Policy," *Journal of Law and Education* 39 (2010): 26–27.

13. David K. Cohen and Susan L. Moffitt, *The Ordeal of Equality: Did Federal Regulation Fix the Schools?* (Cambridge, MA: Harvard University Press, 2009), 10; Equity and Excellence Commission, *Each and Every Child*, 14, 34–35.

14. For instance, I have proposed a collaborative enforcement model for congressional legislation that would guarantee a federal right to education and that would require consistent federal oversight and support of state efforts to provide this right. Robinson, "Case for a Collaborative Enforcement Model," 1653, 1715–1722. An education law scholar and now a California Supreme Court justice, Goodwin Liu has argued that Congress should ensure "educational adequacy for equal citizenship." Liu, "Interstate Inequality," 2049. Michael Rebell and Jessica Wolff have proposed greater federal involvement in education that would require a joint federal-state effort to ensure that all children receive a meaningful educational opportunity and adequate funds for the education of all at-risk children. Rebell and Wolff, *Moving Every Child Ahead*, 152.

15. Heather K. Gerken, "Our Federalism(s)," *William and Mary Law Review* 53 (2012): 1549, 1552.

16. Carl F. Kaestle, "Federal Education Policy and the Changing National Polity for Education, 1957–2007," in *To Educate a Nation: Federal and National Strategies of School Reform,* ed. Carl F. Kaestle and Alyssa E. Lodewick (Lawrence: University Press of Kansas, 2007), 17; U.S. Const. amend. X; Rebell and Wolff, *Moving Every Child Ahead*, 43.

17. Brown v. Board of Education, 347 U.S. 483 (1954); Elementary and Secondary Education Act of 1965, Pub. L. No. 89-10, 79 Stat. 27 (codified as amended in scattered sections of 20 U.S.C.); Education for All Handicapped Children Act of 1975, Pub. L. No. 94-142, 89 Stat. 773 (codified as amended at 20 U.S.C. §§ 1400–1409 (2012)); Equal Educational Opportunities Act of 1974, Pub. L. No. 93-380, 88 Stat. 514 (codified at 20 U.S.C. §§ 1701–1758 (2012)); Civil Rights Act of 1964, Pub. L. No. 88-352, Title VII, 78 Stat. 241, 252 (codified at 42 U.S.C. § 2000 (2012)); Michael W. Kirst, "Turning Point: A History of American School Governance," in *Who's in Charge Here? The Tangled Web of School Governance and Policy*, ed. Noel Epstein (Washington, DC: Brookings Institution Press, 2004), 14, 22–23; Diane Stark Rentner, *A Brief History of the Federal Role in Education: Why It Began and Why It's Still Needed* (Washington, DC: Center on Education Policy, 1999), 8–9; 20 U.S.C. § 7861(a) (2012); No Child Left Behind Act of 2001, Pub. L. No. 107-110, 115 Stat. 1425 (codified as amended in scattered sections of 20 U.S.C.); Race to the Top Fund: Notice of Final Priorities, 74 Fed. Reg. 59,668, 59,688 (Nov. 18, 2009); McGuinn, *No Child Left Behind*, 180–181, 193–195; David J. Barron and Todd D. Rakoff, "In Defense of Big Waiver," *Columbia Law Review* 113 (2013): 279–281.

18. Derek Black, "Unlocking the Power of State Constitutions with Equal Protection: The First Step Toward Education as a Federally Protected Right," *William and Mary Law Review* 51 (2010): 1402–1403; Kirst, "Turning Point," 27.

19. Stephen Q. Cornman, *Revenues and Expenditures for Public Elementary and Secondary Education: School Year 2011–12 (Fiscal Year 2012)* (Washington, DC: National Center for Education Statistics, 2015), 2, 4, table 1, http://nces.ed.gov/pubs2014/2014301.pdf; Regina R. Umpstead, "The No Child Left Behind Act: Is It an Unfunded Mandate or a Promotion of Federal Educational Ideals?" *Journal of Law and Education* 37 (2008): 201–202; "Federal Programs for Education and Related Activities," in *Digest of Education Statistics: 2011* (Washington, DC: National Center for Education Statistics, 2012), table D, http://nces.ed.gov/programs/digest/d11/ch_4.asp.

20. Paul T. Hill, "Recovering from an Accident: Repairing Governance with Comparative Advantage," in *Who's in Charge Here? The Tangled Web of School Governance and Policy*,

ed. Noel Epstein (Washington, DC: Brookings Institution Press, 2004), 75, 77; Kirst, "Turning Point," 36–37.

21. James E. Ryan, "The Tenth Amendment and Other Paper Tigers: The Legal Boundaries of Education Governance," in *Who's in Charge Here? The Tangled Web of School Governance and Policy*, ed. Noel Epstein (Washington, DC: Brookings Institution Press, 2004), 42, 57, 60; Kirst, "Turning Point," 32; Hill, "Recovering from an Accident," 78.

22. Michael Heise, "The Political Economy of Education Federalism," *Emory Law Journal* 56 (2006): 131; Paul Manna, *Collision Course: Federal Education Policy Meets State and Local Realities* (Washington, DC: CQ Press, 2011), 12–14.

23. Gerald Frug, "The City as a Legal Concept," *Harvard Law Review* 93 (1980): 1068–1069; Aaron Saiger, "The School District Boundary Problem," *Urban Lawyer* 42 (2010): 518–519; Erika K. Wilson, "Leveling Localism and Racial Inequality in Education Through the No Child Left Behind Act Public Choice Provision," *University of Michigan Journal of Law Reform* 44 (2011): 632; Charles Tiebout, "A Pure Theory of Local Expenditures," *Journal of Political Economy* 64 (1956): 417.

24. Heise, "Political Economy of Education Federalism," 131; Kirst, "Turning Point," 38; Saiger, "School District Boundary Problem," 519–520.

25. Kaestle, "Federal Education Policy," 20; Heise, "Political Economy of Education Federalism," 131; Rebecca Jacobsen and Andrew Saultz, "The Polls—Trends: Who Should Control Education?" *Public Opinion Quarterly* 76 (2012): 388; Manna, *Collision Course*, 13.

26. Benjamin Michael Superfine, *The Courts and Standards-Based Education Reform* (New York: Oxford University Press, 2008), 123; Deborah A. Verstegen and Teresa S. Jordan, "A Fifty-State Survey of School Finance Policies and Prams: An Overview," *Journal of Education Finance* 34 (2009): 215 table 1; Ryan, *Five Miles Away*, 153–155, 171–172.

27. *Rodriguez*, 411 U.S. at 58.

28. Ryan, *Five Miles Away*, 127, 153–155; Kimberly Jenkins Robinson, "The Past, Present and Future of Equal Educational Opportunity: A Call for a New Theory of Education Federalism," *University of Chicago Law Review* 79 (2012): 437–438; Black, "Power of State Constitutions," 1371; Robinson, "High Cost of Education Federalism," 318–322; Marilyn Gittell, "The Politics of Equity in Urban School Reform," in *Bringing Equity Back: Research for a New Era in American Educational Policy*, ed. Janice Petrovich and Amy Stuart Wells (New York: Teachers College Press, 2005), 16, 26.

29. Baker, Sciarra, and Farrie, *Is School Funding Fair?* 8–9, figure 4; Ryan, *Five Miles Away*, 158; Equity and Excellence Commission, *Each and Every Child*, 17–18.

30. Darling-Hammond, *The Flat World and Education*, 23–26; Jane Waldfogel, Irwin Garfinkel, and Brendan Kelly, "Welfare and the Costs of Public Assistance," in *The Price We Pay: Economic and Social Consequences of Inadequate Education*, ed. Clive R. Belfield and Henry M. Levin (Washington, DC: Brookings Institution Press, 2007), 173; Celia Elena Rouse, "Consequence for the Labor Market," in ibid., 99, 101; Peter Muennig, "Consequences in Health Status and Costs," in ibid., 125, 137; Enrico Moretti, "Crime and Costs of Criminal Justice," in ibid., 142, 157.

31. Ryan, "Tenth Amendment and Other Paper Tigers," 60; Heise, "Political Economy of Education Federalism," 131; Kirst, "Turning Point," 38; Wilson, "Leveling Localism and Racial Inequality," 633–634.

32. Council of Chief State School Officers, *School Choice in the States: A Policy Landscape* (Washington, DC: Council of Chief State School Officers, 2013), 9–13; National League of Cities, *Educational Alignment for Young Children: Profiles of Local Innovation* (Washington, DC: National League of Cities, 2012), 1; Gerard Toussaint Robinson, "Can the Spirit of *Brown* Survive in the Era of School Choice? A Legal and Policy Perspective," *Howard Law Journal* 45 (2002): 295–307 (describing the growth of charter schools and voucher programs); Rebell and Wolff, *Moving Every Child Ahead*, 141–143; Erin Ryan, "Federalism and the Tug of War Within: Seeking Checks and Balances in the Interjurisdictional Gray Area," *Maryland Law Review* 66 (2007): 607, 613.

33. Robinson, "High Cost of Education Federalism," 287, 297–307, 309–314, 323–330.

34. Manna, *Collision Course*, 41; Robinson, "High Cost of Education Federalism," 325–329.

35. Michael J. Klarman, Brown v. Board of Education *and the Civil Rights Movement* (New York: Oxford University Press, 2007), 149–174; Benjamin Michael Superfine, *Equality in Education Law and Policy, 1954–2010* (New York: Cambridge University Press, 2013), 78–80, 125–126; Rebell and Wolff, *Moving Every Child Ahead*, 99–102.

36. Equity and Excellence Commission, *Each and Every Child*, 14–15, 17–18; Susan H. Fuhrman, "Less than Meets the Eye: Standards, Testing and Fear of Federal Control," in *Who's in Charge Here? The Tangled Web of School Governance and Policy*, ed. Noel Epstein (Washington, DC: Brookings Institution Press, 2004), 131, 150; Ryan, *Five Miles Away*, 153, 178.

37. Equity and Excellence Commission, *Each and Every Child*, 14.

38. Liu, "Education, Equality, and National Citizenship," 332–333.

39. Equity and Excellence Commission, *Each and Every Child*, 34–35.

40. Ryan, *Five Miles Away*, 127–129, 153, 178; Osamudia R. James, "Breaking Free of Chevron's Constraints: *Zuni Public School District No. 89 v. U.S. Department of Education*," *University of Kansas Law Review* 56 (2007): 149; Abbott v. Burke, 575 A.2d 359, 408 (N.J. 1990); Campaign for Fiscal Equity v. New York, 655 N.E.2d 661, 666 (N.Y. 1995); Black, "Power of State Constitutions," 1371; Robinson, "High Cost of Education Federalism," 318–321.

41. Equity and Excellence Commission, *Each and Every Child*, 15; Achieve, Inc., *Closing the Expectations Gap 2011: Sixth Annual 50-State Progress Report on the Alignment of High School Policies with the Demands of College and Careers* (Washington, DC: Achieve, 2011), 22, http://www.achieve.org/closingtheexpectationsgap2011; Rebell and Wolff, *Moving Every Child Ahead*, 163.

42. Council on Foreign Relations, *Remedial Education*, 1; Thomas Bailey, "Implications of Educational Inequality in a Global Economy," 74–75, 78–79; Dana Kelly et al., *Performance of U.S. 15-Year-Old Students in Mathematics, Science, and Reading Literacy in an International Context: First Look at PISA 2012* (Washington, DC: National Center for Education Statistics, 2013), 9–10.

43. Eric Hanushek, Paul Peterson, and Ludger Woessmann, *Endangering Prosperity: A Global View of the American School* (Washington, DC: Brookings Institution Press, 2013), vii.

44. Martin Carnoy and Richard Rothstein, *What Do International Tests Really Show About U.S. Student Performance?* (Washington, DC: Economic Policy Institute, 2013), 2; Richard A. Epstein and Jacob E. Gersen, "Understanding Education in the United States: Its Legal and Social Implications," *University of Chicago Law Review* 79 (2012): 467; Equity and Excellence Commission, *Each and Every Child*, 14–15.

45. Kaestle, "Federal Education Policy," 17; Ryan, *Five Miles Away*, 14; Education for All Handicapped Children Act of 1975, Pub. L. No. 94-142, 89 Stat. 773 (codified as amended at 20 U.S.C. §§ 1400–1409 (2012)); Margaret Winzer, *The History of Special Education: From Isolation to Integration* (Washington, DC: Gallaudet University Press, 1993), 381; Charles Barone and Elizabeth DeBray, "Education Policy in Congress: Perspectives from Inside and Out," in *Carrots, Sticks, and the Bully Pulpit: Lessons from a Half-Century of Federal Efforts to Improve America's Schools*, ed. Frederick M. Hess and Andrew P. Kelly (Cambridge, MA: Harvard Education Press, 2011), 61.

46. Brown v. Board of Education, 349 U.S. 294, 300 (1955); Brown v. Board of Education, 347 U.S. 483, 493–495 (1954); Kimberly Jenkins Robinson, "Resurrecting the Promise of *Brown*: Understanding and Remedying How the Supreme Court Reconstitutionalized Segregated Schools," *North Carolina Law Review* 88 (2010): 796–837; No Child Left Behind Act of 2001, Pub. L. No. 107-110, 115 Stat. 1425 (codified as amended in scattered sections of 20 U.S.C.).

47. Robinson, "Case for a Collaborative Enforcement Model," 1728–1734.

48. In arguing for a restructuring of education federalism, I join the call of other scholars who have recommended expanding the federal role in education and redefining the federal-state relationship to advance equal educational opportunity. See Rebell and Wolff, *Moving Every Child Ahead*, 69–76; Liu, "Interstate Inequality," 2049–2050.

49. Rebell and Wolff, *Moving Every Child Ahead*, 157–158, argues that NCLB should be revised to require that all children receive a "meaningful educational opportunity" and noting the "educational essentials" students should receive. See also Liu, "Interstate Inequality," 2103.

50. Manna, *Collision Course*, 160.

51. James E. Ryan, "The Perverse Incentives of the No Child Left Behind Act," *New York University Law Review* 79 (2004): 989; Paul T. Hill, "The Federal Role in Education," in *Brookings Papers on Education Policy 2000* (Washington, DC: Brookings Institution Press, 2000), 11, 34; Manna, *Collision Course*, 160.

52. Robinson, "Case for a Collaborative Enforcement Model," 1715–1722.

53. "Congress is duty-bound to secure equal national citizenship by serving as the ultimate guarantor of educational opportunity." Liu, "Interstate Inequality," 2049.

54. Manna, *Collision Course*, 159–161.

55. President Barack Obama, transcript of speech to the U.S. Hispanic Chamber of Commerce, March 10, 2009, http://www.washingtonpost.com/wp-srv/politics/documents /Obama_Hispanic_Chamber_Commerce.html.

56. Cohen and Moffitt, *The Ordeal of Equality*, 9.

57. Hanushek, Peterson, and Woessmann, *Endangering Prosperity*, vii.

58. Paul T. Hill, "Getting It Right the Eighth Time: Reinventing the Federal Role," in *New Directions: Federal Education Policy in the Twenty-First Century*, ed. Marci Kanstoroom and Chester E. Finn, Jr. (Washington, DC: Thomas B. Fordham Foundation, 1999), 163; Manna, *Collision Course*, 159–160; Chester E. Finn, Jr., "Agenda-Setters and Duds: A Bully Pulpit, Indeed," in *Carrots, Sticks, and the Bully Pulpit: Lessons from a Half-Century of Federal Efforts to Improve America's Schools*, ed. Frederick M. Hess and Andrew P. Kelly (Cambridge, MA: Harvard Education Press, 2011), 217, 226–227; Michael Mintrom and Sandra Vergari, "Education Reform and Accountability Issues in an Intergovernmental Context," *Publius* 27 (1997): 152; Elementary and Secondary Education Act of 1965, Pub. L. No. 89-10, 79 Stat. 27 (codified as amended

in scattered sections of 20 U.S.C.); Economic Opportunity Act of 1964, Pub. L. No. 88-452, 78 Stat. 508 (repealed 1981).

59. Rebell and Wolff, *Moving Every Child Ahead*, 69–74; Elaine McArdle, "What Happened to the Common Core?" *Harvard Ed. Magazine*, September 2014, 23; "Frequently Asked Questions," Common Core State Standards Initiative, http://www.corestandards.org/about-the-standards/frequently-asked-questions/Notes.docx; "Standards in Your State," Common Core State Standards Initiative, http://www.corestandards.org/standards-in-your-state/.

60. Darling-Hammond, *The Flat World and Education*, 74.

61. Ibid., 73–74; McGuinn, *No Child Left Behind*, 96, table 5.1, 109; Goals 2000: Educate America Act, Pub. L. No. 103-227, § 3(a)(7), 108 Stat. 125 (1994) (codified as amended in scattered sections of 20 U.S.C.); Improving America's Schools Act of 1994, Pub. L. No. 103-382, 108 Stat. 3518 § 1111(b)(8), 108 Stat. 3518 (codified as amended in scattered sections of 20 U.S.C.); Rebell and Wolff, *Moving Every Child Ahead*, 52–53, 68. Under Goals 2000, the National Education Standards and Improvement Council was created to develop voluntary OTL standards. In addition, states were permitted to develop their own OTL standards.

62. Equity and Excellence Commission, *Each and Every Child*, 18; Rebell and Wolff, *Moving Every Child Ahead*, 157–164; Lawyer's Committee for Civil Rights Under Law et al., *Framework for Providing All Students an Opportunity to Learn Through Reauthorization of the Elementary and Secondary Education Act* (Cambridge, MA: National Opportunity to Learn, 2010), 3; National Opportunity to Learn Campaign, *Federal Recommendations* (Cambridge, MA: National Opportunity to Learn, 2009), 8–10.

63. McGuinn, *No Child Left Behind*, 86; Javier C. Hernandez, "Responding to Critics, New York State Plans to Scale Back Standardized Tests," *New York Times*, October 25, 2013; Valerie Strauss, "Slow Down Reforms, Say School Chiefs in Maryland," *Washington Post*, January 31, 2014; Rose v. Council for Better Educ., Inc., 790 S.W.2d 186, 212 (Ky. 1989); Rebell and Wolff, *Moving Every Child Ahead*, 68.

64. Cohen and Moffitt, *The Ordeal of Equality*, 14; Manna, *Collision Course*, 49–52; Nancy Kober, Jack Jennings, and Jody Peltason, "Better Federal Policies Leading to Better Schools" (report, Center on Education Policy, Washington, DC, 2010), 8, http://www.cep-dc.org/displayDocument.cfm?DocumentID=181; Fuhrman, "Less than Meets the Eye," 151.

65. Education Sciences Reform Act of 2002, Pub. L. No. 107-279, 116 Stat. 1940 (codified as amended in scattered sections of 20 U.S.C.); Benjamin Michael Superfine, "New Directions in School Funding and Governance: Moving from Politics to Evidence," *Kentucky Law Journal* 98 (2009–2010): 686–689.

66. Marshall S. Smith, "Rethinking ESEA: A Zero-Base Reauthorization," in *Carrots, Sticks, and the Bully Pulpit: Lessons from a Half-Century of Federal Efforts to Improve America's Schools*, ed. Frederick M. Hess and Andrew P. Kelly (Cambridge, MA: Harvard Education Press, 2011), 233; Fuhrman, "Less than Meets the Eye," 151; Manna, *Collision Course*, 160; Jonathan H. Adler, "Cooperation, Commandeering, or Crowding Out? Federal Intervention and State Choices in Health Care Policy," *Kansas Journal of Law and Public Policy* 20 (2011): 216, 218.

67. Manna, *Collision Course*, 49.

68. Adler, "Cooperation, Commandeering, or Crowding Out?" 205–206.

69. Friedman and Solow, "The Federal Right to an Adequate Education," 146; McGuinn, "Stimulating Reform," 143–147; Paul Manna and Laura L. Ryan, "Competitive Grants and Educational Federalism: President Obama's Race to the Top Program in Theory and Practice," *Publius* 41 (2011): 542; Cohen and Moffitt, *The Ordeal of Equality*, 111; Manna, *Collision Course*, 95.

70. Liu, "Interstate Inequality," 2114; Gittell, "Politics of Equity," 39; Manna, *Collision Course*, 160; Ryan, "Perverse Incentives," 989; Kober, Jennings, and Peltason, "Better Federal Policies," 5; Jack Jennings, *Reflections on a Half-Century of School Reform: Why Have We Fallen Short and Where Do We Go from Here?* (Washington, DC: Center on Education Policy, 2012), 3; Mun Tsang and Henry M. Levin, "The Impact of Intergovernmental Grants on Educational Expenditure," *Review of Educational Research* 53 (1983): 334–335.

71. Eric A. Hanushek, "Why the Federal Government Should Be Involved in School Accountability," *Journal of Policy Analysis and Management* 24 (2005): 171.

72. Robinson, "Case for a Collaborative Enforcement Model," 1715–1722.

73. Paul Manna, *School's In: Federalism and the National Education Agenda* (Washington, DC: Georgetown University Press, 2006), 111; Manna, *Collision Course*, 66.

74. David T. Conley, *Who Governs Our Schools? Changing Roles and Responsibilities* (New York: Teachers College Press, 2003), 32; Erik W. Robelen, "The Evolving Federal Role," in *Lessons of a Century: A Nation's Schools Come of Age* (Bethesda, MD: Education Week Press, 2000), 240; Frederick M. Hess and Andrew P. Kelly, "Reflections on the Federal Role: A Half-Century of Hard-Won Lessons," in *Carrots, Sticks, and the Bully Pulpit: Lessons from a Half-Century of Federal Efforts to Improve America's Schools*, ed. Frederick M. Hess and Andrew P. Kelly (Cambridge, MA: Harvard Education Press, 2011), 273, 275–276; Petrovich, "Shifting Terrain of Educational Policy," 3–4.

75. Rebell and Wolff, *Moving Every Child Ahead*, 69–74; Liu, "Interstate Inequality," 2049.

76. Gittell, "Politics of Equity," 39; Kirst, "Turning Point," 15–16; Elementary and Secondary Education Act of 1965, Pub. L. No. 89-10, 79 Stat. 27 (codified as amended in scattered sections of 20 U.S.C.); Title IX of the Education Amendments of 1972, Pub. L. No. 92-318, 86 Stat. 373 (codified as amended at 20 U.S.C. §§ 1681–1688 (2012)); Education for All Handicapped Children Act of 1975, Pub. L. No. 94-142, 89 Stat. 773 (codified as amended at 20 U.S.C. §§ 1400–1409 (2012)); Robinson, "Past, Present and Future of Equal Educational Opportunity," 457.

77. Joseph F. Zimmerman, "National-State Relations: Cooperative Federalism in the Twentieth Century," *Publius* 31 (2001): 15, 19; McGuinn, *No Child Left Behind*, 1.

78. Maurice R. Dyson, "Are We Really Racing to the Top or Leaving Behind the Bottom? Challenging Conventional Wisdom and Dismantling Institutional Repression," *Washington University Journal of Law and Policy* 40 (2012): 238–243; Monica Texeira de Sousa, "A Race to the Bottom? President Obama's Incomplete and Conservative Strategy for Reforming Education in Struggling Schools or the Perils of Ignoring Poverty," *Stetson Law Review* 39 (2010): 630–631; Ryan, *Five Miles Away*, 244–245; Finn, "Agenda-Setters and Duds," 219–226.

79. Hess and Kelly, "A Half-Century of Hard-Won Lessons," 275–276; Jennings, *Reflections on a Half-Century*, 2–3; Barone and DeBray, "Education Policy in Congress," 63.

80. Michael C. Dorf and Charles F. Sabel, "A Constitution of Democratic Experimentalism," *Columbia Law Review* 98 (1998): 434; Manna, *School's In*, 111–112; Cornman,

Revenues and Expenditures, 2, 4, table 1; Heise, "Political Economy of Education Feder-alism," 141; Robinson, "Past, Present and Future of Equal Educational Opportunity," 462–464.

81. 132 S. Ct. 2566, 2606–2607 (2012) (plurality opinion) holds that the Medicaid expan-sion that required the states to insure anyone under age sixty-five with an income of less than 133 percent of the federal poverty line was unconstitutionally coercive in vio-lation of the Spending Clause. Ibid. at 2664–2667 (Scalia, Kennedy, Thomas, & Alito, JJ., dissenting). For a full analysis of why my chapter's theory would not violate the Spending Clause, see Robinson, "Disrupting Education Federalism," 1006–1012.

82. Samuel R. Bagenstos, "The Anti-Leveraging Principle and the Spending Clause af-ter NFIB," *Georgetown Law Journal* 101 (2013): 871; Eloise Pasachoff, "Conditional Spending after *NFIB v. Sebelius*: The Example of Federal Education Law," *American University Law Review* 62 (2013): 594.

83. Ryan, "The Tenth Amendment and Other Paper Tigers," 57–59; Hill, "Recovering from an Accident," 78.

84. Manna, *Collision Course*, 49–52; Liu, "Interstate Inequality," 2047; David J. Barron, "A Localist Critique of the New Federalism," *Duke Law Journal* 51 (2001): 389.

85. Ryan, "Federalism and the Tug of War Within," 607.

86. Adler, "Cooperation, Commandeering, or Crowding Out?" 204.

87. Wendy Kopp, *A Chance to Make History: What Works and What Doesn't In Providing an Excellent Education for All* (New York: Public Affairs, 2012), 207–208; Theresa Perry et al., eds., *Quality Education as a Constitutional Right: Creating a Grassroots Movement to Transform Public Schools* (Boston: Beacon Press, 2010); Southern Education Founda-tion, *No Time to Lose: Why America Needs an Education Amendment to the United States Constitution to Improve Public Education* (Atlanta: Southern Education Foundation, 2010); Equity and Excellence Commission, *Each and Every Child*, 34–35; Kaestle, "Federal Education Policy," 17.

CHAPTER 11

1. San Antonio Independent School District v. Rodriguez, 411 U.S. 1 (1973).

2. Education Trust, *Funding Gaps 2006* (Washington, DC: Education Trust, 2006), 7, table 3, http://www.edtrust.org/sites/edtrust.org/files/publications/files /FundingGap2006.pdf.

3. Bruce D. Baker, David G. Sciarra, and Danielle Farrie, *Is School Funding Fair? A National Report Card* (Newark: Education Law Center, 2010), 16, table 3, http:// www.schoolfundingfairness.org/National_Report_Card_2010.pdf.

4. Jeannie Oakes, Adam Gamoran, and Reba N. Page, "Curriculum Differentiation: Opportunities, Outcomes, and Meanings," in *Handbook of Research on Curriculum: A Project of the American Educational Research Association*, ed. Philip W. Jackson (New York: Macmillan, 1992), 570–608; Charles T. Clotfelter, Helen F. Ladd, and Jacob Vigdor, "Who Teaches Whom? Race and the Distribution of Novice Teachers," *Eco-nomics of Education Review* 24, no. 4 (2005): 377–392; Susan Moore Johnson, Jill Harrison Berg, and Morgaen L. Donaldson, *Who Stays in Teaching and Why: A Re-view of the Literature on Teacher Retention* (Cambridge, MA: Harvard Graduate School of Education, 2005), 6; Education Trust, *Their Fair Share: How Texas-Sized Gaps in Teacher Quality Shortchange Low-Income and Minority Students* (Washington, DC: Education Trust, 2008), 5–6, http://files.eric.ed.gov/fulltext/ED500011.pdf.

5. Jane L. David, "Teacher Recruitment Incentives," *Poverty and Learning* 65, no. 7 (2008): 84; Wendy Parker, "Desegregating Teachers," *Washington University Law Review* 86 (2008): 34–35; Benjamin Scafidi, David L. Sjoquist, and Todd Stinebrickner, "Race, Poverty, and Teacher Mobility" (working paper, Andrew Young School of Policy Studies Research Paper Series, Atlanta, August 2005), 11.

6. See Richard D. Kahlenberg, *All Together Now: Creating Middle-Class Schools Through Public School Choice* (Washington, DC: Brookings Institution Press, 2001), 49–50; James S. Coleman et al., *Equality of Educational Opportunity* (Washington, DC: U.S. Department of Health, Education, and Welfare, 1966): 302–310.

7. Pub. L. No. 91-230, sec. 105(a)(3), § 109, 84 Stat. 121, 124 (1970).

8. 45 C.F.R. § 116.26 (1972) (requiring comparability at a 5 percent variance between Title I and non–Title I schools); 45 C.F.R. § 116 (1978) (making no reference to numerical comparability).

9. McClure, "The History of Educational Comparability in Title I," 21.

10. National Center for Education Statistics, *Numbers and Types of Public Elementary and Secondary Schools from the Common Core of Data: School Year 2006–07* (Washington, DC: U.S. Department of Education, 2009), 6–7, table 2, http://nces.ed.gov/pubs2009 /2009304.pdf (indicating that 58,021 of the nation's total 98,793 schools are Title I schools).

11. 34 C.F.R. § 200.71 (2008).

12. See 20 U.S.C. §§ 6333, 6337 (2006) (indicating that fair funding for low-income schools requires a 40 percent funding increase adjustment); National Center for Education Statistics, *Inequalities in Public School District Revenues* (Washington, DC: U.S. Department of Education, 1998), 62 (identifying 40 percent as the appropriate adjustment for low-income students); Ross Wiener and Eli Pristoop, "How States Shortchange the Districts That Need the Most Help," in Education Trust, *Funding Gaps 2006* (Washington, DC: Education Trust, 2006), 6, http://www.edtrust.org/sites /edtrust/org/files/publications/files/FundingGap2006.pdf (stating that authors Wiener and Pristoop use a 40 percent adjustment).

13. Education Trust, *Funding Gaps 2006*, 3, table 1, 4, table 2.

14. Goodwin Liu, "Improving Title I Funding Equity Across States, Districts and Schools," *Iowa Law Review* 93 (2008): 1010, citing Stephanie Stullich, Brenda Donly, and Simeon Stolzberg, *Targeting Schools: Study of Title I Allocations Within School Districts* (Washington, DC: U.S. Department of Education, 1999), 14.

15. See Coleman et al., *Equality of Educational Opportunity*, 20–23; Kahlenberg, *All Together Now*, 39–40.

16. 20 U.S.C. §§ 6335(c)(1)(b), 6337(d)(1)(A); §§ 6335(c)(1)(b), 6337(d)(1)(A).

17. Kahlenberg, *All Together Now*, 39–40.

18. U.S. GAO, "Title I Funding: Poor Children Benefit Though Funding per Poor Child Differs" (report to congressional addressees, January 2002), 33–34, http://www.gao .gov/assets/240/233331.pdf.

19. Ibid.

20. Goodwin Liu, "How the Federal Government Makes Rich States Richer," in Education Trust, *Funding Gaps 2006* (Washington, DC: Education Trust, 2006), 2.

21. 20 U.S.C. § 6337 (2006); 34 C.F.R. § 222.162 (2008).

22. Compare 20 U.S.C. § 6335(c)(2)(C) with § 6335(c)(1)(C) (giving roughly the same weight in the funding formula to district sizes of approximately 94,000 students and to districts with 30 percent poverty).

23. Liu, "Improving Title I Funding Equity," 1003.
24. 20 U.S.C. §§ 6333(d), 6334(b), 6335(e), 6337(b)(1)(B).
25. Education Trust, *Funding Gaps 2006*, 3, table 1.
26. Ibid.
27. David G. Sciarra, "Critiquing Existing Reform Efforts that Advance Equal Education Opportunity," from Rodriguez *at 40: Exploring New Paths to Educational Opportunity* (video presentation, University of Richmond School of Law, Richmond, VA, March 8, 2010), 84:23, http://lawmedia.richmond.edu/vid/jwwrap.php?fac=library&file=VTS_01_1rg.flv&width=640&height=480.
28. See, for example, David G. Sciarra, "Request to Require New Jersey to Restore FY10 Primary Formula Aid to Approved SFSF Program Level" (letter to secretary of education, Education Law Center, Newark, NJ, February 21, 2010); Amy Schur et al., "Request to Require Revisions to California's SFSF Phase 2 Application & to Reject Phase 2 Funding and California's Race to the Top Application Pending Revisions" (letter to secretary of education from Parents and Students for Great Schools, February 8, 2010).
29. 20 U.S.C. §§ 6321(a), 7901.
30. "Disadvantaged Students: Fiscal Oversight of Title I Could Be Improved" (report, U.S. GAO, Washington, DC, February 2003), 19–20, 24–26, http://www.gao.gov/assets/240/237499.pdf.
31. Ross Wiener, "Strengthening Comparability: Advancing Equity in Public Education," in *Ensuring Equal Opportunity in Public Education: How Local School District Funding Practices Hurt Disadvantaged Students and What Federal Policy Can Do About It* (Washington, DC: Center for American Progress, 2008), 40, http://www.americanprogress.org/issues/2008/06/pdf/comparability.pdf.
32. 20 U.S.C. § 6576 (2006).
33. 20 U.S.C. § 6321(c).
34. 20 U.S.C. § 6321(c)(2)(B).
35. 20 U.S.C. § 6321(c)(2)(A).
36. See Erica Frankenberg, "The Segregation of American Teachers," *Education Policy Analysis Archives* 17, no. 1 (2008): 24–29, http://epaa.asu.edu/ojs/article/view/3; Parker, "Desegregating Teachers," 35–37 (evaluating research showing that white teachers tend to leave high-minority schools).
37. Marguerite Roza, "How Districts Shortchange Low-Income and Minority Students," in Education Trust, *Funding Gaps 2006* (Washington, DC: Education Trust, 2006), 9–11, http://www.edtrust.org/sites/edtrust.org/files/publications/files/FundingGap2006.pdf.
38. U.S. Department of Education, "ESEA Flexibility" (Washington, DC: U.S. Department of Education, 2015), http://www2.ed.gov/policy/elsec/esea-flexibility/index.html.
39. North Carolina Department of Public Instruction, Financial and Business Services, *2010–2011 Allotment Policy Manual* (2011), 26–27, http://www.ncpublicschools.org/docs/fbs/allotments/general/2010-11policymanual.pdf (based on HB 1473, Section 7.8 (a)). The provision stated that "in determining whether to approve an [Local Education Agency's] plan for the expenditure of funds allocated to it for disadvantaged student supplemental funding, the State Board of Education shall take into consideration the extent to which the LEA's policies or expenditures have contributed to or is contributing to increased segregation of schools on the basis of race or socioeconomic status."

40. Yuna Shin, "Resegregating Schools in Wake County and New Hanover County," *Huffington Post*, January 21, 2011, http://www.huffingtonpost.com/yuna-shin/resegrating -schools-in-no_b_811977.html.

CHAPTER 12

1. 347 U.S. 483 (1954).
2. I develop this more fully in *The Case Against the Supreme Court*. Erwin Chemerinksy, *The Case Against the Supreme Court* (New York: Viking, 2014). See also Gary Orfield and Erica Frankenberg, *Brown at 60: Great Progress, a Long Retreat and an Uncertain Future* (Los Angeles: The Civil Rights Project, University of California Los Angeles, 2014), 2, 36.
3. "Today, education is perhaps the most important function of state and local governments. Compulsory school attendance laws and the great expenditures for education both demonstrate our recognition of the importance of education to our democratic society. It is required in the performance of our most basic public responsibilities, even service in the armed forces. It is the very foundation of good citizenship. Today it is a principal instrument in awakening the child to cultural values, in preparing him for later professional training, and in helping him to adjust normally to his environment. In these days, it is doubtful that any child may reasonably be expected to succeed in life if he is denied the opportunity of an education." 347 U.S. at 493.
4. See Milliken v. Bradley, 418 U.S. 717 (1974) (holding that merging metropolitan school districts requires proof of interdistrict constitutional violations); San Antonio Independent School District v. Rodriguez, 411 U.S. 1 (1973).
5. See text accompanying notes 13–15.
6. 551 U.S. 701 (2007).
7. Gary Orfield, *Schools More Separate: Consequences of a Decade of Resegregation* 2 (2001).
8. Ibid., 29.
9. Ibid.
10. Ibid., 31.
11. See Kimberly Jenkins Robinson, "The High Cost of Education Federalism," *Wake Forest Law Review* 48 (2013): 287, 304–305 ("Despite growing diversity in the public school population, school segregation has been increasing in recent decades and has led to increasingly racially isolated schools"). See also, "New National Study Finds Increasing School Segregation," Harvard Graduate School of Education (June 1999), http:// www.gse.harvard.edu/news/new-national-study-finds-increasing-school-segregation ("After greatly increasing desegregation of public schools a generation ago, the United States public education system is now steadily consolidating a trend toward racial resegregation that began in the late 1980s").
12. Kimberly Jenkins Robinson, "Resurrecting the Promise of Brown: Understanding and Remedying How the Supreme Court Reconstitutionalized Segregated Schools," *North Carolina Law Review* 88 (2010): 811–833.
13. 498 U.S. 237 (1991).
14. 503 U.S. 467 (1992).
15. 515 U.S. 70 (1995). Earlier, in Missouri v. Jenkins, 495 U.S. 33 (1990), the Supreme Court ruled that a federal district court could order that a local taxing body increase taxes to pay for compliance with a desegregation order, although the federal court should not itself order an increase in the taxes.

16. Belk v. Charlotte-Mecklenburg Board of Education, 269 F.3d 305 (4th Cir. 2001) (en banc).
17. Manning v. School Board of Hillsborough County, Florida, 244 F.3d 927 (11th Cir. 2001).
18. Marilyn Brown, "Beyond Black and White," *Tampa Tribune,* February 10, 2000, A1.
19. Tresa Baldas, "Saying Goodbye to Desegregation Plans," *National Law Journal,* June 16, 2003, 4.
20. U.S. General Accounting Office, *School Finance: Per-Pupil Spending Differences between Selected Inner City and Suburban Schools Varied By Metropolitan Area* (Washington, DC: GAO, 2002), 17. The GAO report describes how the difference in spending between city and suburban schools varies across the country.
21. Ibid., 9.
22. Bruce D. Baker, David Sciarra, and Danielle Farrie, *Is School Funding Fair: A National Report Card*, 4th ed. (Newark, NJ: Education Law Center, 2015), 6–18., http://www.schoolfundingfairness.org/National_Report_Card_2015.pdf.
23. National Center for Education Statistics, *Characteristics of the 100 Largest Public Elementary and Secondary Schools in the United States, 2008–09* (Washington, DC: National Center for Education Statistics, 2011), table A-9, http://nces.ed.gov/pubs2011/2011301.pdf.
24. Preston C. Green III, Bruce D. Baker, and Joseph O. Oluwole, "Achieving Racial Equal Educational Opportunity Through School Finance Litigation," *Stanford Journal of Civil Rights and Civil Liberties* 4 (2008): 283, 298.
25. U.S. Department of Education, National Center of Education Statistics, Digest of Education Statistics 2013 (Washington, DC: National Center of Education Statistics, 2015), table 205.40, http://nces.ed.gov/programs/digest/d13/tables/dt13_205.40.asp.
26. Thomas F. Pettigrew, "A Sociological View of the Post-*Milliken* Era," in Milliken v. Bradley—*The Implications for Metropolitan Desegregation: Conference Before the United States Commission on Civil Rights* (Washington, DC: Government Printing Office, 1974), 69–70.
27. Ziemba, "School Desegregation Called Key to City," *Chicago Tribune*, February 8, 1983.
28. T. A. Smedley, "Developments in the Law of School Desegregation," *Vanderbilt Law Review* 26 (1973): 405, 412.
29. 418 U.S. 717 (1974).
30. Ibid. at 744–745.
31. Ibid. at 745.
32. See Kimberly Jenkins Robinson, "Resurrecting the Promise of Brown: Understanding and Remedying How the Supreme Court Reconstitutionalized Segregated Schools," *North Carolina Law Review* 88 (2010): 787, 812–819; Erwin Chemerinsky, "Lost Opportunity: The Burger Court and the Failure to Achieve Equal Educational Opportunity," *Mercer Law Review* 45 (1994): 999, 1001–1003.
33. See, for example, United States v. Board of School Commissioners, 456 F.Supp. 183 (S.D. Ind. 1978); Evans v. Buchanan, 416 F.Supp. 328 (D. Del. 1976) United States v. Board of School Commissioners, 637 F.2d 1101 (7th Cir. 1980) (approving interdistrict remedies), *cert. denied*, 449 U.S. 838 (1980). See also Hills v. Gatreaux, 425 U.S. 284 (1976) (approving an interdistrict remedy for housing discrimination).
34. Christopher Jencks et al., *Inequality: A Reassessment of the Effect of Family and Schooling in America* (New York: Basic Books, 1972), 28.

35. Jonathan Kozol, *Savage Inequalities: Children in America's Schools* (New York: Harper-Collins, 1991), 236, table 1.

36. Ibid., 236, table 2.

37. Roberta L. Steele, "All Things Not Being Equal: The Case for Race Separate Schools," *Case Western Reserve Law Review* 43 (1993): 591, 620 n.173. Similarly, Camden was predominantly minority and Princeton was overwhelmingly white. Ibid.

38. 411 U.S. 1 (1973).

39. Ibid. at 12–13.

40. Ibid. at 28–29.

41. Ibid. at 35.

42. Ibid. at 37.

43. Ibid. at 39.

44. See James T. Patterson, *Brown v. Board of Education: A Civil Rights Milestone and its Troubled Legacy* (New York: Oxford University Press, 2001, xx). For further information on funding disparities, please see Baker, Sciarra, and Farrie, *Is School Funding Fair?*.

45. 268 U.S. 510 (1925).

46. 494 U.S. 872 (1990).

47. 406 U.S. 205 (1972).

CONCLUSION

1. Michael Klarman, *Unfinished Business: Racial Equality in American History* (New York: Oxford University Press, 2007), 181–182; United States v. Carolene Products Co., 304 U.S. 144, 152 n.4 (1938); Equity and Excellence Commission, *For Each and Every Child: A Strategy for Educational Equity and Excellence* (Washington, DC: ED Pubs Education Publications Center, 2013), 14; James E. Ryan, *Five Miles Away, a World Apart: One City, Two Schools, and the Story of Educational Opportunity in Modern America* (New York: Oxford University Press, 2010), 121.

2. Ryan, *Five Miles Away*, 153.

3. Jane Waldfogel, Irwin Garfinkel, and Brendan Kelly, "Welfare and the Costs of Public Assistance," in *The Price We Pay: Economic and Social Consequences of Inadequate Education*, ed. Clive R. Belfield and Henry M. Levin (Washington, DC: Brookings Institution Press, 2007), 173; Cecilia Elena Rouse, "Consequence for the Labor Market," in ibid., 99, 101; Peter Muennig, "Consequences in Health Status and Costs," in ibid., 125, 137; Enrico Moretti, "Crime and the Costs of Criminal Justice," in ibid., 142, 157; Thomas Bailey, "Implications of Educational Inequality in a Global Economy," in ibid., 74, 78–79.

4. Siegel-Hawley and Wells, Fox and Miles also note the far-reaching impacts of the *Milliken v. Bradley* decision, in which the Supreme Court severely limited the ability of courts to order interdistrict desegregation by requiring plaintiffs to show intentional interdistrict segregation before an interdistrict remedy could be ordered. Milliken v. Bradley, 418 U.S. 717, 744–745 (1974).

5. Ryan, *Five Miles Away*, 157, 278–280.

6. See also Kimberly Jenkins Robinson, "The High Cost of the Nation's Current Framework for Education Federalism," *Wake Forest Law Review* 48 (2013): 297–307, 309–314, 323–330.

7. San Antonio Independent School District v. Rodriguez, 411 U.S. 1, 42–43 (1973).

8. DeRolph v. State, 677 N.E.2d 733, 746 (Ohio 1997).

9. See, for example, Abbott v. Burke, 575 A.2d 359, 403 (N.J. 1990) (*Abbott II*); Horton v. Meskill, 376 A.2d 359, 374 (Conn. 1977); McDuffy v. Secretary, 615 N.E.2d 516, 545, 552 (Mass. 1993).

10. For these studies, see chapter 6, this volume, notes 9–14.

11. For these studies, see chapter 4, this volume, notes 19–29.

12. Bruce D. Baker, *Revisiting That Age-Old Question: Does Money Matter in Education?* (Washington, DC: Albert Shanker Institute, 2012), iv–v.

13. Abbott v. Burke, 693 A.2d 417, 429, 442–443 (N.J. 1997) (*Abbott IV*).

14. Eric A. Hanushek, "Financing Schools," in *International Guide to Student Achievement*, ed. John Hattie and Eric M. Anderman (New York: Routledge, 2013), 136 ("It is not possible to expect higher achievement of students from simply providing extra resources to schools. Some specific thought must be given to how any resources affect the incentives of people in the schools").

15. W. Norton Grubb, *The Money Myth: School Resources, Outcomes, and Equity* (New York: Russell Sage Foundation, 2009), 275 ("A new emphasis on 'what works,' even though it is politically embattled, at least points in the direction of effective resources. The concern for making money matter acknowledges that money alone is usually not sufficient to improve outcomes. In this transformation, the role of the improved school finance is to provide a new narrative with a broader conception of resources, including the compound, complex, and abstract resources that must be constructed rather than bought and that are, if anything, *more* unequally distributed than are money and simple resources").

16. The Texas Taxpayer and Student Fairness Coalition v. Williams, No. D-1-GN-11-003130, 2014 WL 4254969, at *9 (D. Tex. Aug. 28, 2014).

17. See, for example *Abbott IV*, 693 A.2d at 429, 442–443; *Abbott II*, 575 A.2d at 394–400.

18. Equity and Excellence Commission, *For Each and Every Child*, 17.

19. Ryan, *Five Miles Away*, 242–244.

20. Ibid., 151–153.

21. Bruce D. Baker, David G. Sciarra, and Danielle Farrie, *Is Funding Fair? A National Report Card* (Newark: Education Law Center, 2015), http://www.schoolfundingfairness.org/National_Report_Card_2015.pdf.

22. See, for example, Nicole Baker Fulgham, *Educating All God's Children: What Christians Can—and Should—Do to Improve Public Education for Low-Income Kids* (Grand Rapids, MI: Brazos Press, 2013), 22; Southern Education Foundation, *No Time to Lose: Why America Needs an Education Amendment to the United States Constitution to Improve Public Education* (Atlanta: Southern Education Foundation, 2009); Wendy Kopp, *One Day, All Children . . .: The Unlikely Triumph of Teach for America and What I Learned Along the Way* (New York: Public Affairs, 2001).

23. Waldfogel, Garfinkel, and Kelly, "Welfare and the Costs of Public Assistance," 173; Rouse, "Consequence for the Labor Market," 99, 101; Muennig, "Consequences in Health Status and Costs," 125, 137; Moretti, "Crime and the Costs of Criminal Justice," 142, 157; Bailey, "Implications of Educational Inequality in a Global Economy," 74, 78–79.

ACKNOWLEDGMENTS

CHARLES J. OGLETREE, JR.

Writing this book with Kimberly Robinson has been a wonderful experience. I wish to thank all who were involved in making this book a reality.

I especially thank my wife, Pamela Ogletree, for forty years of companionship and for helping me express things in a positive way as I moved forward.

Many thanks as well to my son, Charles Ogletree III; daughter-in-law, Rachelle Ogletree; granddaughters Marquelle, Nia Mae, and Jamila Ogletree; daughter, Rashida Ogletree George; son-in-law, Jeremy George; and granddaughters Salema and Makayla George.

I also am grateful for the careful editing and cite checking of Harvard Law students Sabrina El-Amin, Michael Athy, Justin Dews, John Geise, Anisha Queen, and Chelsea Rogers. David Harris, Susan Eaton, and Johanna Wald provided critical perspectives and assistance on this book. Darrick Northington has provided valuable assistance and guidance on this project.

I am truly blessed.

KIMBERLY JENKINS ROBINSON

It has been an honor and a privilege to work on this book with Charles J. Ogletree, Jr. I also am grateful to Dean Wendy Perdue at the University of Richmond School of Law for the funding and support she provided to host a conference on *Rodriguez* in March 2013 (*Rodriguez* at 40: Exploring New Paths to Equal Educational Opportunity, videos at http://law.richmond.edu /events/rodriguez.html). David Harris and Susan Eaton of the Charles Hamilton Houston Institute for Race and Justice provided valuable assistance with the book and in planning the conference. In addition, Associate Dean Kristine Henderson and my assistant, Michelle Carpenter, contributed their time, energy, and talents to making the conference a success, as did many members of the *Richmond Journal of Law and the Public Interest*. Amy Braun, Nick Dantonio, Adam Pratt, Joseph Szesko, and Kathleen Travis at the University of Richmond School of Law provided exceptional and thorough research assistance for the book. Joyce Janto also provided helpful editorial suggestions and library assistance for the book.

My work on issues of equal educational opportunity is driven by the conviction that the United States denies too many schoolchildren equal access to the high-quality education that all children should receive. Each day the United States has an opportunity to choose to chart a new path that leads to greater equality of educational opportunity and excellent schools for all children. It is my hope that this book will help nudge the nation in that direction.

I am grateful for my husband, Gerard Robinson, and for his enduring and sacrificial support of my scholarship, intellectual pursuits, and professional success. Thank you for your continuous encouragement, enduring faith in me and my abilities, and your inspiring work on behalf of children.

I also thank our daughters, Sienna, Naomi, and Kamaria, because they inspire me to work for an excellent education for all children. I also greatly appreciated the prayers of my dear friends Carol N. Brown, Erica Burnette, and Nicole Baker Fulgham throughout the writing process.

My parents, Wilbur H. Jenkins, Jr., and the late Doris Sroufe Jenkins, instilled in me at a young age a firm belief in the importance of education. They moved our family to the suburbs of Richmond, Virginia, when I was nine to pursue better educational opportunities for my brother and me. They also emphasized the importance of fighting against injustice and inequality in its many forms. I seek to continue this family legacy through my work on issues of equal educational opportunity. Thank you both for leading me by example throughout your lives.

Finally, I thank God for the opportunity and privilege to write about and work on these challenging and important issues.

ABOUT THE EDITORS

CHARLES J. OGLETREE, JR., the Harvard Law School Jesse Climenko Professor of Law and founding and executive director of the Charles Hamilton Houston Institute for Race and Justice, is a prominent legal theorist who has made an international reputation by taking a hard look at complex issues of law and by working to secure the rights guaranteed by the Constitution for everyone equally under the law. Ogletree opened the offices of the Charles Hamilton Houston Institute for Race and Justice (http://www.charleshamiltonhouston.org) in September 2005 as a tribute to the legendary lawyer, mentor, and teacher of such great civil rights lawyers as Thurgood Marshall and Oliver Hill. The Institute has engaged in a wide range of important educational, legal, and policy issues over the last ten years.

Ogletree is the author of several important books on race and justice, with his most recent publication (coedited with Austin Sarat) being *Life Without Parole: America's New Death Penalty?* (New York University Press, 2012). His other publications include *The Presumption of Guilt: The Arrest of Henry Louis Gates, Jr. and Race, Class, and Crime in America* (Palgrave Macmillan, 2010), *The Road to Abolition: The Future of Capital Punishment in the United States* (coedited with Austin Sarat, New York University Press, 2009), and his historical memoir *All Deliberate Speed: Reflections on the First Half-Century of Brown v. Board of Education* (W. W. Norton, 2004).

He has received numerous awards. In 2009 he was awarded the prestigious American Bar Association Spirit of Excellence Award in recognition of his many contributions to the legal profession, and in 2008 the *National Law Journal* named Ogletree one of the 50 Most Influential Minority Lawyers in America. In 2006 he also received the first Rosa Parks Civil Rights Award, given by the City of Boston; the Hugo A. Bedau Award given by the Massachusetts Anti-Death Penalty Coalition; and Morehouse College's Gandhi,

King, Ikeda Community Builders Prize. He also received honorary degrees from Morehouse College in 2011 and from Amherst College in 2002.

KIMBERLY JENKINS ROBINSON is a professor at the University of Richmond School of Law and a researcher at the Charles Hamilton Houston Institute at Harvard Law School. A national expert on the federal role in education, civil rights, and educational equity, she has published her work in a variety of scholarly journals and books, including the *Chicago Law Review*, *North Carolina Law Review*, *Wake Forest Law Review*, *Washington University Law Review*, and *William & Mary Law Review*. Robinson joined the University of Richmond School of Law faculty in 2010, and she currently teaches education law and policy, legislation and regulation, pretrial drafting, and a seminar on law and educational equity. She previously served on the faculty at Emory University School of Law from 2004 to 2010. Prior to becoming a law professor, she served at the U.S. Department of Education's Office of General Counsel for five years, where she helped draft federal policy regarding race, national origin, sex, and disability discrimination. Her professional experience also includes clerking for the U.S. Court of Appeals for the Ninth Circuit and representing school districts in funding and race discrimination cases while at Hogan & Hartson LLP (now Hogan Lovells). Robinson graduated with honors in 1996 from Harvard Law School, where she served as an articles editor for the *Harvard Law Review*.

ABOUT THE CONTRIBUTORS

FOREWORD AUTHOR

JAMES E. RYAN is the eleventh dean of the Harvard Graduate School of Education and the Charles William Eliott Professor of Education. A leading expert on law and education, Ryan has written extensively about the ways in which law structures educational opportunity. His articles and essays address such topics as school desegregation, school finance, school choice, standards and testing, pre-K, and the intersection of special education and neuroscience. Ryan is also the co-author (with Mark G. Yudof, Betsy Levin, Rachel F. Moran, and Kristi L. Bowman) of the textbook *Educational Policy and the Law* (Wadsworth Cengage Learning, 2012) and the author of *Five Miles Away, a World Apart* (Oxford University Press, 2010). In addition, he has authored articles on constitutional law and theory and has argued before the U.S. Supreme Court.

CHAPTER AUTHORS

DEREK W. BLACK is a professor of law at the University of South Carolina School of Law. Prior to becoming a professor, Black served as a staff attorney for the Education Project for the Lawyers' Committee for Civil Rights under Law, where he litigated issues relating to school desegregation, diversity, finance equity, discipline, and special education. He began his career in teaching at Howard University School of Law, where he founded and directed the Education Rights Center, which studies the causes and extent of educational inequalities in public schools, provides advocacy resources to parents, and shapes national and local education policy. Black is the author *of Education Law: Equality, Fairness, and Reform* (Wolters Kluwer, 2013).

ERWIN CHEMERINSKY has served as dean of the University of California at Irvine School of Law since he founded the school in 2008. Prior to becoming a dean, he served as a professor at Duke Law School and the University of Southern California School of Law. His areas of expertise are constitutional law, federal practice, civil rights and civil liberties, and appellate litigation. He frequently argues cases before the nation's highest courts and also serves as a commentator on legal issues for national and local media. Chemerisky is the author of seven books, most recently *The Conservative Assault on the Constitution* (Simon & Schuster, 2010), and nearly two hundred articles that have appeared in top law reviews.

DANIELLE FARRIE is the research director for the Education Law Center (ELC) in Newark, New Jersey, where she maintains an extensive education database and conducts analyses to support litigation and public policy for ELC and partner organizations. She is the coauthor (with Bruce Baker and David Sciarra) of "Is School Funding Fair? A National Report Card," an award-wining report that regularly documents the inequity in many of the nation's state education finance systems. Before joining ELC, Farrie conducted research in the field of urban education on such topics as school choice, racial and economic segregation, and reactions to racial integration and coauthored peer-reviewed articles on parental involvement among low-income families.

LAUREN FOX is an advanced doctoral student in sociology and education at Teachers College, Columbia University. A native of North Carolina, she earned her bachelor's degree from the University of North Carolina at Asheville. Fox is currently a research associate at the Center for Understanding Race and Education and has previously worked as a consultant to the Department of Justice and the Ford Foundation. Her research interests include school choice, racial attitudes, and school desegregation.

DAVID G. HINOJOSA is the national director of policy for the Intercultural Development Research Association and the former southwest regional counsel for the Mexican American Legal Defense and Educational Fund (MALDEF). While at MALDEF from 2003 until April 2015, he was a leading litigator and advocate in the area of civil rights, with a focus on educational civil rights impact litigation on behalf of Latinos. He has litigated in nearly every major area of educational civil rights, including school finance, school desegregation, language rights, affirmative action in higher education, and higher education access and tuition. Among his more recent cases, Hinojosa served as MALDEF's lead counsel for low-income and English language learner children, challenging the constitutionality of the school finance systems of Colorado, Texas, and New Mexico. A graduate of Edgewood High School in San Antonio, Hinojosa also coauthored (with Karolina Walters) "How Adequacy Litigation Fails to Fulfill the Promise of *Brown,* but How It Can Get Us Closer," published in *The Pursuit of Racial and Ethnic Equality in American Public Schools: Mendez, Brown and Beyond* (ed. Kristi Bowman, Michigan State University Press, 2015).

WILLIAM S. KOSKI is the Eric and Nancy Wright Professor of Clinical Education, a professor of law, and a professor of education (by courtesy) at Stanford University. He teaches educational law and policy, directs a legal clinic that advocates for equality of educational opportunity for disadvantaged children, and serves as plaintiffs' counsel in path-breaking school finance litigation in California. Koski has published articles on educational equity and adequacy, the politics of judicial decision making, and teacher assignment policies.

ALANA MILES is a third-year law student at Rutgers School of Law–Newark. Seeing firsthand the inequalities in education, Miles has always been interested in education-related issues. She received her bachelor's degree from Syracuse University, where she majored in African American studies, sociology, and psychology, and her master's from Teachers College, Columbia University, where she was a research assistant in the Center for Understanding Race and Education. Miles hopes to use her legal degree to influence education reform.

MICHAEL A. REBELL is a professor of law and education practice and the executive director of the Campaign for Educational Equity at Teachers College, Columbia University, and an adjunct professor at the Columbia Law School. Previously, Rebell cofounded and served as the executive director of and counsel for the Campaign for Fiscal Equity, which won a major education adequacy ruling on behalf of New York City's public school students.

He lectures at universities throughout the country and consults widely with advocacy groups, litigants, state education departments, and legislatures on education policy and education adequacy issues. Rebell has written or cowritten five books, among them *Courts and Kids: Pursuing Educational Equity Through the State Courts* (University of Chicago Press, 2009), and many articles on a wide range of education issues, including educational equity, education finance, testing, and the rights of students with disabilities.

MILDRED WIGFALL ROBINSON is the Henry L. and Grace Doherty Charitable Foundation Professor of Law at the University of Virginia School of Law, where she teaches in the area of taxation. Robinson has written extensively on tax and finance issues, access to education, and, most recently, the impact of the recent recession across race and gender. She is the coeditor (with Richard J. Bonnie) of *Law Touched Our Hearts: A Generation Remembers* Brown v. Board of Education (Vanderbilt University Press, 2009).

DAVID G. SCIARRA is the executive director of the Education Law Center in Newark, New Jersey. A practicing civil rights lawyer since 1978, Sciarra has served as lead counsel for the urban schoolchildren in New Jersey's landmark *Abbott v. Burke* litigation. The *Abbott* rulings on adequate school funding, universal preschool, and other equity issues are considered among the most important since *Brown v. Board of Education.* He is also an adjunct professor at the University of Virginia School of Law and recently served on the U.S. Department of Education's Commission on Education Equity and Excellence. He is the coauthor (with Bruce Baker and Danielle Farrie) of "Is School Funding Fair? A National Report Card" and has published numerous articles on education finance, early education, and education law and policy.

GENEVIEVE SIEGEL-HAWLEY is an assistant professor in the Department of Educational Leadership at Virginia Commonwealth University and a research associate at the Civil Rights Project. Her research focuses on segregation, inequality, and opportunity in U.S. schools, along with policy options to promote an inclusive, integrated society. She has published numerous articles on these topics in such journals as the *Harvard Educational Review, Urban Review,* and *Teachers College Record.* She is also the author of *When the Fences Come Down: Twenty-First-Century Lessons from Metropolitan School Desegregation* (University of North Carolina Press, forthcoming).

CAMILLE WALSH is an assistant professor at the University of Washington at Bothell. Her research is centered on the interdisciplinary intersections of law, inequality, race, and class and the implications of particular historical processes on social justice movements. She is currently completing a book on the historical legacy of unequal and racialized taxation in education funding and politics. Even more significantly, Walsh has a strong belief in quality education as a potentially transformative experience that should be accessible to all and strives to bring that commitment to her classrooms.

AMY STUART WELLS is a professor of sociology and education and the coordinator of Policy Studies at Teachers College, Columbia University. Her research and writing have focused broadly on issues of race and education and, more specifically, on educational policies such as school desegregation, school choice, charter schools, and tracking and how they shape and constrain opportunities for students of color. Wells is the recipient of several honors and awards, including a 2001–2002 fellowship from the Carnegie Corporation's Scholars Program; the 2000 Julius & Rosa Sachs Lecturer, Teachers College, Columbia University; and the 2000 American Educational Research Association Early Career Award for Programmatic Research.

INDEX

Abbott v. Burke, 13, 42, 119–120, 268–269
Abbott II, 126
Abbott IV, 125, 127–129, 132, 136
Abbott V, 132
Abbott XX, 131–132
academic identity, 109–111
academic standards, 44
accountability, 210, 216, 223–224
achievement gaps, 14, 39, 108, 132, 205, 212, 220, 228–229, 234, 263, 271
adequacy claims, 12, 33–34, 36, 38–39, 76–79
admissions officers, 102–103
ad valorem tax, 28, 34, 36
affluent families/students, 100–103, 109–111, 260
affluent school districts, 97–103, 109–111
affordable housing, 197
African American students, 5, 31, 35–36, 47, 251, 252–253, 256–257. *See also* minority students
Alabama, 123
Alamo Heights district, 47–48
alcoholic beverages taxes, 175, 181
Alexander v. Sandoval, 11
Alvarado ISD plaintiffs, 26, 31
Amar, Akhil Reed, 82–83
American Civil Liberties Union (ACLU), 52
American Dream, 2
American Recovery and Reinvestment Act, 179, 206
anticommunism, 53–59, 264
AP courses, 110
appellate process, 52–53

Belvedere Public Schools, 97–103, 108–111, 113–114
Bender, Michael, 43
bilingual education, 31, 33, 48
Bitensky, Susan, 75
Blackmun, Harry, 50
Board of Education of Oklahoma City v. Dowell, 252
Brandeis, Louis, 72, 208
Brennan, William, 9, 50, 54
Brown v. Board of Education, 1, 7, 50, 54, 55, 61, 67, 183, 230, 249, 251, 261
Burger, Warren, 50, 76
Burger Court, 60
Bush, George W., 216
business cycle, 179
Butt v. California, 149

Calhoun County ISD, 36, 37, 40
California, 13, 69
  Governor's Local Control Funding Formula, 147
  property tax opposition in, 170
  school finance in, 41–42, 144–148
  Serrano v. Priest decision in, 41–42, 48, 144–146, 168, 170
  tax and expenditure limitations in, 170–171
  teacher quality gap in, 143–165
California Supreme Court, 41–42, 68
California Teachers Association, 160
Campaign for a Quality Education v. California (CQE), 146–147
Campaign for Fiscal Equity v. State (CFE), 13

Campaign for Fiscal Equity v. State (CFE), 78–80
Canales, Yolanda, 38
capitalism, 53, 58–59
Carey, Sarah, 48
CEIFA. *See* Comprehensive Educational Improvement and Financing Act (CEIFA)
Challenged Statutes, 161
charitable contributions, 178–179
Charlotte-Mecklenburg, North Carolina, 188–193, 198–199, 253
Charter School Association, 37, 39
charter schools, 37, 39
children, of illegal immigrants, 10
Christie, Chris, 131–132
citizenship skills, 78–80
civil rights
  court decisions and, 1–2
  support for, 55
Civil Rights Act of 1964, 230, 243
  Title VI of, 2, 11, 230, 243
Civil Rights Cases, 82
Clark, Harley, 26
class discrimination, 46–53, 63–64, 265
class sizes, 33, 35, 36, 38–39, 121, 266, 267
Clear Creek ISD, 38
Clearview school district, 112
Cold War discourse, 46, 53–59, 264
Coleman, James, 57
collaborative enforcement model, 220–221
collective bargaining agreements, 155, 156–157, 164
college admissions, 101–103
college-readiness standards, 39
Colorado school funding, 42–43
Colorado Supreme Court, 42–43
colorblind constitutionalism, 52
Commission on Equity and Excellence. *See* Equity and Excellence Commission
Common Core State Standards, 84, 108, 206, 216–217
common opportunity-to-learn (OTL) standards, 216–218
common school movement, 69
communism, 53–59, 264

community partnerships, 106
comparability standard, 230–231, 240
Comprehensive Educational Improvement and Financing Act (CEIFA), 126–128, 133
compulsory education, 260
concentrated poverty, 121–122, 233–234, 242–243, 265–266
Congress
  property taxes and, 170
  right to education and, 75, 83–84
  role of, 81, 138, 139, 140
  Title I and, 19–20, 228–233, 238, 243, 246–247
  unitary system of education and, 258–259
Connecticut, 186, 195
corruption, 113
Cortez, Nabor, 38
courts, role of, 42
curriculum
  differentiated, 107–111
  state mandates on, 108–109

Daly, Richard M., 171
decentralized governance, 121–122, 208
de facto segregation, 134, 195
DeGrasse, Leland, 78–80
de jure segregation, 134, 183–184, 186, 255–256
Delaware, 123, 186
Dennis v. U.S., 54
Department of Education, 58–59, 82, 194, 221, 231, 239, 243, 244
DeRolph v. State, 266
desegregation, 54–55, 183–199, 230, 250–256, 261. *See also* school desegregation; segregation
Detroit, 183–184
Dietz, John K., 37, 40
differentiated curriculum, 107–111
disparate impact regulations, 11
dissenting opinions, 7–9, 25, 51–52, 66
Douglas, William O., 49, 50
dual federalism, 211
Dudziak, Mary, 54–55
Duncan, Arne, 156, 206

early decision applications, 103
earmarking, of funds, 175–176, 180–181
economic inequality, 61
Economic Opportunity Act, 216
economic revitalization, 171
economy, 213
Edgewood District Concerned Parents
    Association, 3
Edgewood High School, 23–24
Edgewood I, 25–27, 41
Edgewood II, 27–29
Edgewood III, 29–32
Edgewood Independent School District,
    24–27, 30, 31, 38, 47–48
Edgewood IV, 32–34, 37–38
Edgewood V, 34–35
Edgewood VI, 34–39
education
    adequacy, 68–72, 76–79
    bilingual, 31, 33, 48
    compulsory, 260
    equal access to, 205–206, 215–216,
        221–223
    federal role in, 75, 82–84, 138–139,
        206, 214–225, 270–271
    First Amendment rights and, 66, 77
    as fundamental interest, 66–67
    importance of, 180
    local control over, 6, 8, 88, 89, 134–135,
        139, 174, 208–211, 223–224
    money and, 70–72. *see also* school finance
    research on, 218–219
    as right, 1, 5–8, 10, 24, 26, 46, 59, 61,
        75–78, 80–85, 257, 258, 264
    standards-based reform, 70, 75, 141–142,
        228
    state control over, 207
    unitary system of, 250, 255–261
educational opportunities
    equal. *see* equal educational opportunity
    unequal, 38, 203–204, 212–214,
        249–261, 264–266
Education Amendments of 1972, 243
education federalism, 19, 203–225,
    265–266, 270
    benefits of reconstructing, 223–224
    current structure of, 207–209

inconsistencies in benefits of,
    209–211
inequality and, 212–214
reasons for reexamining, 209–214
research on, 214
as roadblock to equal educational
    opportunity, 211–212
theory for disrupting, 214–223
Education for All Handicapped Children
    Act, 214
Education Sciences Reform Act (ESRA),
    219
Elementary and Secondary Education
    Act (ESEA), 19–20, 196–197, 207,
    227–247
Employment Division v. Smith, 259
end-of-course (EOC) exams, 35, 40
English language learners (ELLs), 31, 33,
    35, 129, 146
Equal Educational Opportunities Act,
    243
equal educational opportunity, 2, 10, 19,
    20, 44, 47–48, 204–206, 211–212,
    221–223
    boundary lines and, 183–199
    causes of lack of, 264–266
    fiscal equity and, 68–72
    pathways to, 263–273
    unitary system of education and,
        249–261
equal protection analysis, 46, 59–63,
    148–150, 154
Equal Protection Clause, 7–10, 61, 88,
    139–140, 144–145, 168, 204
equal protection rights, 4
Equity and Excellence Commission, 14,
    135–139, 206–207, 210, 212
equity litigation, 12, 29, 36, 37
equity standards, 243–244
excise taxes, 175–176, 181

facilities
    disparities in, 32–33
    funding for, 35
fair housing, 197
Fair Housing Act, 197
federal budget, 179

federal financial assistance, 220
federal funds, 4, 5, 19–20, 176–181,
    206–208, 227–247
federalism
    dual, 211
    education, 203–225, 265–266, 270
    fiscal, 169
federal litigation, 10–11. *See also specific
    cases*
federal policies
    on educational equality, 214–223
    on federalism, 214
    on funding equity, 138–139
    on regionalism, 194–195
federal research, 218–219
Fifteenth Amendment, 83, 84
First Amendment rights, 66, 77,
    258–259
fiscal equity, 67–72
fiscal federalism, 169
fiscal neutrality, 4
Fort Worth, Texas, 254
Fourteenth Amendment, 3, 4, 10, 81, 82,
    83, 84, 88, 168, 258
free enterprise, 53, 58
Freeman v. Pitts, 252
funding cuts, in Texas, 35
funding disparities, 3–4, 119, 120–125,
    168, 266–268
    entrenched, 15
    federal funds and, 227–247
    impact of, 107–111
    interstate, 203–204
    in New York, 91–92, 96–97
    in Pennsylvania, 11
    persistence of, 120–125, 203–204,
        212–214, 227, 253–254
    reduction in, 14
    root causes of, 204
    segregated schools and, 254–257
    teacher quality gap and, 144–148
    in Texas, 3–4, 24–40, 119, 254
funding formulas, 241–243

gaming taxes, 175–176, 181
gentrification, 90
Gerken, Heather, 207

Goals 2000: Educate America Act, 217
Gochman, Arthur, 3, 46–47
Gotanda, Neil, 52, 61
Governor's Local Control Funding
    Formula, 147
Grantsville district, 103–107, 112–115
Guinier, Lani, 46, 52, 53

Hammond, Larry, 62
Hanushek, Eric, 70–71
Head Start, 216
health-care costs, 174
*Helena Elementary School District No. 1 v.
    State*, 41
Henrico County, Virginia, 193–194
highly qualified teachers, 149–151. *See
    also* teacher quality
high-poverty districts, 20, 103–107,
    120–121, 137, 210, 233–234,
    239–243, 246
    funding in, 123–125
    lack of political accountability in,
        112–115
high school graduation rate, 210
high-stakes testing, 35, 40
Hillsborough County, Florida, 253
Hoar bill, 81–82
hold-harmless provisions, 32
home schooling, 258, 260
home-school nexus, 100–101, 105–106
housing segregation, 19, 188, 190,
    192–193, 198–199

illegal immigrants, children of, 10
Illinois, 12
Improving America's Schools Act (IASA),
    217
income taxes, 169, 176–179, 181
Indiana, 186
Indiana Supreme Court, 12
Individuals with Disabilities Education
    Act (IDEA), 75, 181, 243
innovation, 223–224
integration, 244–246, 251, 265
international competitiveness, 213–214,
    268
interstate disparities, 203–204

Jenner-Butler bill, 54

Kansas City schools, 252–253
Kennedy High School, 23
Keyes v. School District No. 1, 59–60
Koski, William, 13
Kozol, Jonathan, 73

Lakewood district, 108–109, 114
La Raza, 52
last-in, first-out (LIFO) layoff processes, 157, 159–160, 163
Latino students, 31, 35–36, 47–48
Lawyers' Committee for Civil Rights, 48
Leesburg district, 114
Liu, Goodwin, 80–82
Lobato v. Colorado, 42–43
local control, 6, 8, 88, 89, 134–135, 139, 174, 208–211, 223–224
Long Island school districts, 91–92, 95–96, 111–115. *See also* Naussau County
Los Angeles Unified School District (LAUSD), 153–155, 158
Louisville-Jefferson County, Kentucky, 188–193, 199
Low Income Housing Tax Credit, 197
low-income students, 33, 35–36, 103–107, 112, 121–122, 210, 230, 233–234

magnet schools, 196
majority opinion, 4–7, 25, 50–51, 65–68, 77–78, 168, 257
Marbury v. Madison, 42
Marshall, Thurgood
    dissenting opinion by, 7–8, 25, 51–52, 66
    on education as right, 82
Maryland brief, 57–58
McCarthyism, 53, 54
McDonald v. Board of Election Commissioners, 60
McKinney-Vento Homeless Assistance Act, 243
McLaurin v. Oklahoma State Regents of Higher Education, 7
medical care, 250
Merhige, Robert, 184

metropolitan desegregation, 183–199
metropolitan migrations, 89–97
Mexican American Legal Defense and Educational Fund (MALDEF), 26, 32
Mexican Americans, 5, 48–49
middle-income schools, 240
migration patterns, 16, 89–97
Milliken v. Bradley, 16, 87–116, 184–186, 211, 255–256
    decision in, 87–88
    impact of, 88–89, 257–258
minority students, 5, 11, 31, 35–36, 39, 46–47, 112, 203, 265
Missouri v. Jenkins, 211, 252–253
Montoy v. State of Kansas, 71
Moving to Opportunity programs, 197

Nader, Ralph, 170
Nassau County
    concentrated poverty in, 103–107
    context for, 90–93
    demographics in, 90–91
    differentiated curriculum in, 107–111
    funding disparities in, 92, 93–94
    interplay of public and private resources in, 97–107
    migration patterns in, 16
    per-pupil funding in, 91–92
    politics in, 111–115
    research on, 89, 93–97
National Assessment for Educational Progress (NAEP), 33, 132
National Center for Education Statistics (NCES), 120
National Commission on Equity and Excellence in Education, 73–75, 85
National Federation of Independent Business v. Sevelius (NFIB), 223
National Opportunity to Learn Campaign, 218
New Deal, 53
New Jersey
    court decisions in, 125–128
    funding disparities in, 125
    progressive funding in, 123

New Jersey, *continued*
   school finance in, 42
   School Funding Reform Act, 129–139
   school funding reform in, 119–142
New Jersey Supreme Court, 13, 14, 42,
   126–128, 131, 137, 141, 142, 267
New York, 14, 70. *See also* Nassau County
   consolidation efforts in, 196
   per-pupil funding in, 91–92, 96–97
New York City Public Schools, 13
Nineteenth Amendment, 84
Ninth Amendment, 82, 83
Nixon, Richard, 170, 183
No Child Left Behind (NCLB), 19, 70, 75,
   83–84, 108, 138, 150–151, 204, 206,
   211, 216, 219, 222, 228, 229
North Carolina, 189, 245

Obama, Barack, 156, 195, 206
Obledo, Mario, 64
OCR. *See* Office for Civil Rights (OCR)
Office for Civil Rights (OCR), 11
Oklahoma, 12, 252
opportunity gap, 205–207, 220, 264–266,
   270–271
opportunity-to-learn (OTL) standards,
   216–218
Ortega v. Colorado, 42–43

Papasan v. Allain, 76
parents
   affluent, 100–103, 109–111
   expectations of, 109–111
   low-income, 105–106, 112–115
   socioeconomic status of, 100
*Parents Involved in Community Schools v.
   Seattle School District No. 1*, 250
parochial schools, 250, 258, 259
Pasadena ISD, 38
payment in lieu of taxes (PILOT), 173
Pennsylvania school finance system, 11
per-pupil funding, 12, 91–97, 234–236,
   246, 267
Perry, Rick, 35
personnel funding, 121
Pierce v. Society of Sisters, 259
Plessy v. Ferguson, 183

Plyler v. Doe, 10, 63, 67
political boundaries, 183–199
politics
   anticommunism, 53–59
   of education federalism, 214
   of school rezoning, 194–196
   state, 173–174
   of unequal school districts, 111–115
poll taxes, 60
poverty, 52, 140, 257
   concentrated, 121–122, 233–234,
   242–243, 265–266
   as suspect class, 46, 59–61, 66,
   140, 257
Powell, Lewis, 183
   on communism, 55–57, 264
   equal protection analysis by, 62–63
   majority opinion by, 4–7, 50–51,
   77–78, 168, 257
   on race and class, 49–50
   on school finance reform, 11–12
Powell v. Ridge, 11
pre-K programs, 39, 104, 132
private resources, 97–107
   impact of unequal, 107–111
   interplay of public resources and,
   97–107
private right of action, 243–244
private schools, 250, 254–255, 258, 260
proficiency, 108
progressive school funding, 17, 122–125,
   235–236, 237, 242–243
property-poor districts
   school funding and, 23–40
   tax rates in, 37–38
property taxes, 4, 5, 7–9, 12, 15, 18, 98,
   125, 140, 180, 257
   abatement of, 171–172
   base for, 169
   caps on, 34
   deduction for, 176–179, 181
   finance reform and, 167–181
   reliance on, 174, 213
   taxpayer opposition to, 169–170
property values, 169, 173, 180
public resources, interplay of private
   resources and, 97–107

public schools, 266
   funding of. *see* school finance
   migration patterns and, 89–97
   requirement to attend, 250, 258–261

qualitative data, 94–95
quantitative analysis, 94

race, 46–53, 265
Race to the Top (RTTT), 19, 75, 156, 206,
   220, 222
racial discrimination, 11, 46–53, 56,
   63–64
racial isolation, 18, 186, 187, 189, 197,
   205, 265. *See also* segregation
racial liberalism, 46, 53
rational basis test, 60
Ratliff, Bill, 34
Rebell, Michael, 13
reduction-in-force (RIF) layoffs, 157–162,
   163
Reed v. California, 157–159
regionalism, 194–195
regressive school funding, 122–125
Rehnquist, William, 50, 183, 253
religious education, 259–260
Renee v. Duncan, 148, 151–153
Renee v. Spellings, 151
Report Card, 120–123, 125
resegregation, 192, 228, 245, 250–253
residential segregation, 19, 188, 190,
   192–193, 198–199
retail sales taxes, 169
Rhee, Michelle, 156
Richmond, Virginia, 183, 184, 188–193,
   199
Ridge, Thomas, 11
Robinson v. Cahill, 42
Robles-Wong v. California, 146–147
Rodriguez, Demetrio, 3, 9, 24, 44, 46
Rodriguez, Patricia, 9
Rodriguez case. *See San Antonio Indepen-
   dent School District v. Rodriguez*
Rosenberg, Gerald, 55
Rose v. Council for Better Education, 41
Roth, Stephen, 183–184
Ryan, James, 14–15

sales taxes, 169
SALT deduction, 176–177
*San Antonio Independent School District v.
   Rodriguez*
   aims of, 204
   anticommunism discourse and, 53–59
   case overview, 3, 203
   decision in, 1, 119, 139–140, 204–205,
      257
   dissenting opinions in, 7–9, 25, 51–52,
      66
   district court decision in, 3–4
   equal protection analysis and, 59–63
   events leading to, 24–25
   historical context of, 45–64
   impact of, 1–2, 41, 88–89, 140–142,
      168, 257–258, 263
   legacy of, 2, 10–15, 24, 44, 64, 264–266,
      272–273
   majority opinion in, 4–7, 25, 50–51,
      65–68, 77–78, 168, 257
   race and class issues in, 46–53
   reconsideration of, 72–80
   as wrongly decided, 65–68
school assigment policies, 187–188,
   194–198
school boards, accountability of, 112–115,
   210
school choice, 196, 198
school desegregation, 1–2, 7, 16, 18–19,
   54, 183–199
   metro desegregation, 187–199
   Milliken decision on, 87–116
school districts
   affluent, 97–103, 109–111
   boundary lines, 183–199
   consolidation efforts, 195–196
   cooperation between, 196–197
   differentiated curriculum in, 107–111
   equity standards for, 243–244
   fragmentation of, 91, 93
   grants based on size of, 236–237
   high-poverty, 103–107, 112–115,
      120–121, 123–125, 137, 210,
      233–234, 239–243, 246
   interplay of public and private resources
      in, 97–107

school districts, *continued*
  metro desegregation, 187–199
  overcoming fences within, 193–194
  political fallout of unequal, 111–115
  within-district diversity strategies,
    197–198
school finance, 2
  as broken system, 73–74
  in California, 144–148
  desegregation and, 186
  disparities in. *see* funding disparities
  federal funds for, 4, 5, 19–20, 176–180,
    181, 206, 207–208, 227–247
  interplay of public and private resources
    in, 97–107
  linking to standards, 133–139
  local-state funding environment,
    169–174
  per-pupil funding, 12, 91–97, 234–236,
    246, 267
  progressive school funding, 17, 122–125,
    235–237, 242–244
  regressive school funding, 122–125
  sources of, 167, 169, 174–176, 180–181,
    257
  state funds for, 4, 5, 207–208, 238–241
  state litigation, 268–270
  student achievement and, 266–267
  teacher quality and, 144–148
  Title I funds, 227–247
  wealth-equalization formulas for, 12,
    41
school finance reform, 267–268
  federal litigation on, *see also specific
    cases*, 10–11
  importance of, 270–272
  in New Jersey, 119–142
  progress in, 14, 44, 88
  property taxes and, 167–181
  recommendations for, 74–75
  setbacks in, 14–15, 209–210, 212–213
  state litigation on, 11–15, 25–44, 68–73,
    76, 77, 209–210, 212–213
School Funding Reform Act (SFRA), 126,
  129–139, 142
school spirit, 99
Scott, Robert, 35, 38

segregated schools, 18–20, 47–48, 87–88,
  228, 251–255, 265. *See also* school
  desegregation
  boundary lines and, 183–199
  funding disparities and, 254–257
  migration patterns and, 89–97
  penalizations for, 244–246
  in South, 186–199, 251, 253
segregation, 61, 64, 134. *See also*
  desegregation
  housing, 19, 188, 190, 192–193,
    198–199
  resegregation, 192, 228, 245, 250–253
  school. *see* segregated schools
Senate Bill (SB) 351, 28
Senate Bill (SB) I, 27
Serrano v. Priest, 41–42, 48, 144–146,
  168, 170
SFRA. *See* School Funding Reform Act
  (SFRA)
Shapiro v. Thompson, 66
Sheff v. O'Neil, 186, 195
sinking fund taxes, 35
Slaughterhouse Cases, 82
Smith Act, 54
Snid, Alberta, 24
socioeconomic status, 100, 265
South, segregated schools in, 186–199,
  251, 253
Spending Clause, 223
stand-alone property tax abatement programs (SAPTAPs), 171–172, 173
standardized testing, 206, 216
standards-based reform, 70, 75, 119–142,
  228
state budgets, 174
state constitutions, 69, 195
State Fiscal Stabilization Funds, 179
state funds, 4, 5, 207–208, 238–241
state litigation, *see also specific cases*, 11–15,
  25–44, 68–73, 76, 77, 209–210,
  212–213, 268–270
state mandates, 108–109
State of Texas Assessment for Academic
  Readiness (STAAR), 35
state policies, on regionalism, 194–195
state politics, 173–174